HUMAN RIGHTS AND THEIR LIMITS

Human Rights and Their Limits shows that the concept of human rights has developed in waves: each call for rights serves the purpose of social groups that try to stop further proliferation of rights after their own goals are reached.

Although defending the universality of human rights as norms of behavior, Wiktor Osiatyński admits that the philosophy on human rights does not need to be universal. He calls for a "soft universalism" that will not impose rights on others but will share the experience of freedom and help the victims of human rights violations. He also suggests that the enjoyment of social rights should be contingent on the recipient's contribution to society.

Although a state of unlimited democracy threatens rights, excessive rights can limit resources indispensable for democracy. This book argues that although rights are a prerequisite of freedom, they should be balanced with other values that are indispensable for social harmony and personal happiness.

Wiktor Osiatyński is a professor at the Central European University in Budapest, where he teaches at the CEU Legal Program. He is a former codirector of the Chicago Law School's Center for the Study of Constitutionalism in Eastern Europe and an advisor to a number of constitutional committees in Poland's Parliament. The author of more than twenty books, Osiatyński is on the boards of the Open Society Institute (OSI), the OSI Justice Initiative, and the Human Rights and Governance Grant Program. In 2007, he cofounded the Women's Party in Poland.

Human Rights and Their Limits

WIKTOR OSIATYŃSKI

Central European University, Budapest

CAMBRIDGE
UNIVERSITY PRESS

CAMBRIDGE UNIVERSITY PRESS
Cambridge, New York, Melbourne, Madrid, Cape Town, Singapore,
São Paulo, Delhi, Dubai, Tokyo

Cambridge University Press
32 Avenue of the Americas, New York, NY 10013-2473, USA

www.cambridge.org
Information on this title: www.cambridge.org/9780521125239

First published 2009

Printed in the United States of America

A catalog record for this publication is available from the British Library.

Library of Congress Cataloging in Publication data

Osiatyński, Wiktor, 1945–
Human rights and their limits / Wiktor Osiatyński.
    p.   cm.
Includes bibliographical references and index.
ISBN 978-0-521-11027-3 (hardback) – ISBN 978-0-521-12523-9 (pbk.)
1. Human rights.   I. Title.
K3240.082   2009
341.4'8 – dc22   2009011792

ISBN   978-0-521-11027-3 Hardback
ISBN   978-0-521-12523-9 Paperback

To my daughter Natalia,

with hope that your generation will possess human rights
and not cease to sustain them

Contents

Preface

The ideas that form this book are my most significant learning, gathered from more than 20 years of research and teaching on human rights. My interest in rights extends beyond the past 20 years, however, as I have witnessed firsthand the world around me slowly wake up to the concept of human rights. For that reason, my interest in rights has always had a practical focus, more immediate than theory itself. For me, this book represents a personal culmination of a lifetime's involvement with rights and other values.

My boyhood was spent in the communist Poland of the 1950s, among many schoolmates orphaned by the war and in the ruins of a city burned by the Nazis after the 1943 ghetto and 1944 Warsaw uprisings. Countless former activists were in jail, sentenced for the slightest – or purported – unwillingness to cooperate with the oppressive postwar system. After Stalin's death and the ensuing political thaw, this system became less brutal, but it was still a regime that thwarted freedom at every turn. Most unbearable for intellectuals was the lack of freedom of speech. The state's monopoly over the media, along with the strictest kind of censorship, made it difficult for ordinary citizens to learn the truth, both about "the rest of the world" and about Poland's own history. Communication between people came in whispers, cloaked in fear of being manipulated or overheard by secret police informants. In the evenings, we would tune in to the Voice of America and Radio Free Europe, making sure to keep the volume on the shortwave low enough to avoid being caught.

Every few years, the people of Poland rebelled. Workers would go on strike, sometimes initiating demonstrations that would ultimately be silenced by force. The intelligentsia would write letters and sign resolutions demanding freedom. In March 1968, I was among the university students who rallied in defense of the freedom of expression. These led to reprisals in which a wave of anti-Semitism was unleashed by the communist government. The protesting students were labeled outlaws; our intellectual leaders were pronounced Zionist enemies of the state. In search of justification for our protest, we turned to the Communist Constitution.

Although we knew that the Communist Constitution had been a useless document since its adoption in 1952, we nonetheless were able to construct on it our argument that the authorities were not living up to their own standards. As one would expect, however, our voices were never heard.

Eight years later, as a new wave of protest swept over Poland, the justification for the rebellion changed dramatically. Now, with the adoption of UN Human Rights Covenants and the signing of the Helsinki Agreement in 1975, international human rights standards could serve to legitimize protests and demands for freedom. In 1980–1981, human rights became an important element of the Solidarity movement. After its forceful suppression, rights provided arguments for those who did not succumb to power. By invoking human rights, the dissents were legitimately able to claim the support of the free world in their struggle. Such was also the case with Charter 77 in Czechoslovakia and with human rights groups in the Soviet Union.

It was around that time that I focused my research on human rights. I was interested primarily in defining the social and political conditions in which the idea of rights and freedoms could flourish. In 1989, as communism in Poland disintegrated, these ideas became practical. I attempted to put them to use as advisor to several constitution-making bodies in Poland, as well as in other transition countries. In 1992, I coauthored the draft of the Bill of Rights submitted by President Lech Wałęsa to the Polish Parliament, and, subsequently, I wrote a number of the provisions to Poland's new Constitution, which was formally adopted in 1997. I continued my research as codirector of the Center for the Study of Constitutionalism in Eastern Europe at the University of Chicago Law School, where I taught one quarter of every year, between 1990 and 2001. In the mid-1990s, I also became involved in various activities of the Open Society Institute and the network of Open Society Foundations: first, in the post-Communist world and, later, in Africa, Asia, and Latin America. In this capacity, I have been involved in a number of projects that aimed to make human rights both respected and enforceable. During that time, I watched as an important evolution in the thinking about human rights took place in several transition countries: a two-stage shift from mere education about rights to the advocacy of those rights based on the hope that governments would respect them, and – finally – to strategic litigation aimed at forcing governments to respect rights.

Thus, practical involvement has influenced my research. In fact, throughout my entire life, my academic curiosity has been guided by real-life experiences. Situations that I encountered repeatedly led me to new theoretical questions that I wanted to clarify. Before I delve into the theory and practice that make up the chapters of this book, I will share some of these formative experiences.

My first experience related to the idea of freedom in general: Under communism, with its censorship-based notion of "truth," our most cherished value was the freedom of expression. We enjoyed being dissidents and we respected ourselves for it. Not only did we disagree with the party line, we also disagreed among ourselves as much as we could. We had a saying: "Wherever you have two Poles, you have at least three opinions." Such was the idea of freedom among those who did not have it.

To us, freedom was in the United States. Because I was not able to travel to America, I did my best to let America come to me; as a university student I became a tour guide for American visitors to Poland. I clearly remember waiting for that first bus to arrive on the Czechoslovak/Polish border in the summer of 1963. For the first time, I was about to meet free people from a free country. How would this freedom express itself in a face-to-face encounter, I wondered.

For days, I got to talk with and listen to people from America, and I remember being overwhelmed not by any sense of freedom but by the conformity I was witnessing. The tourists were members and relatives of the U.S. military and support personnel stationed in West Germany. The majority were nearing the end of their term of service and wanted to see "the demon behind the iron curtain" before the trip back to the States. I was shocked to encounter sixty people who had identical opinions on almost everything. Unimaginably to me, these opinions were also nearly identical to the official line of the U.S. State Department. And thus, the first important question arose for me: Why do we cherish freedom so much when we don't have it and neglect it when it is a given? Both the dynamics of the post-Communist transition to democracy and the recent events surrounding the "war on terror" in the United States have only reconfirmed the importance of this question.

The idea of rights that appealed to us in the 1970s and 1980s was a relatively simple one. It consisted of personal liberty, which translated into freedom from being jailed by the state, the freedoms of speech and expression, a free press, the freedom of association and other civil liberties, and political rights. These were the rights and freedoms we did not have, and they defined our demands and aspirations.

In 1974, I visited Laos as a journalist. The country was still suffering from the consequences of bombings by the U.S. Air Force during the Vietnam war, and politically, it was torn between a conservative pro-Western government headed by Prince Souvanphouma in Luangpragang and the pro-communist Consultative Council led by the "red prince" Souphanavong in Vientiane. I had a young guide named Phouang who reminded me a lot of myself, 11 years earlier. One day, Phouang asked me if there was freedom in Poland. I replied that the freedom we had was limited. He asked if there was censorship. Yes, I said, but we try to manipulate it by writing between the lines. My answer did not satisfy Phouang. I would not like to live in such a country, he informed me.

Phouang had attended the American school in Luang Prabang. There, he had learned that censorship was bad. At the time, there was no such thing as censorship in Laos, simply because there was just one major newspaper, probably printed by the military itself. A few days later, Phouang and I talked about education. "How difficult is it to get a university degree in Poland?" he asked. "You have to pass an entrance exam and then you have to pass exams in all your courses," I replied. How does one afford it? No problem – it is free. I also mentioned that the government had introduced a type of affirmative action in the 1970s, and the children of workers and peasants from small towns and villages were given additional points on their entrance exams to compensate for any unequal opportunities. Phouang liked the sound of this. When I told him that we had foreign students from many Third World countries, he decided he too wanted to come and study medicine in Poland. I asked him if he would not mind censorship. No, he said, he wouldn't.

This took place just as the first international campaigns for human rights were being launched. Westerners saw other nations as trading freedom for equality and assumed that their role was to promote freedom. But to me, it did not appear that the choice facing Phouang was one of freedom versus equality. No one in his family had ever known either of the two; they had no freedom to trade for equality. What Phouang wanted was the opportunity to be able to afford freedom – and he believed that education would grant him both. I recall wondering if there existed an order of rights and freedoms. Do they reflect the hierarchy of human needs? Is it so that we do not have to starve before we can think of freedom? Then why did such a strong desire for freedom exist among those starving in death camps? Years later, my understanding of the connection between bread and freedom that began with my talks with Phouang would shape my proposals for a way of constitutionalizing social and economic rights in Poland.

Under communism, the people in Poland were oppressed by the state. So were the people of Chile under Pinochet, as well as the citizens of many other authoritarian countries. We needed human rights to protect ourselves from oppression by police and prosecutors, servile courts, and sadistic prison staff. Documenting the details of these forms of oppression was what human rights monitoring was about.

In 1985, I had the good fortune of being invited to teach at Antioch University in Los Angeles. During this time, Antioch had a program at the Frontera prison for women. Every Wednesday, I taught American history and human rights to the inmates of an American prison. This was, of course, a riveting experience for a person coming from a communist country under martial law. At the beginning of the course, I asked my new students to write a paper describing the specific situations in which their rights had been violated. I was expecting documentations of abuses committed by the stereotypical violators, such as police officers and prison guards.

To my surprise, only one of the thirty inmates mentioned police. For all the others, the violators were not state officials at all but fathers, husbands, and lovers. These were the people who shattered these women's lives: most often by abusing them and, sometimes, by using their coercive power to make the women accessories to their crimes. At the time, such "private" abuse was not covered by what was understood as human rights. It was believed that these were matters for civil and criminal law rather than human rights. But in the cases I read about in these women's personal accounts, appropriate laws were nonexistent or unenforced. Does it matter, for one's sense of violation, who administers the suffering? Should the victims of private violations be left alone? What is the role of the state in relation to the violations of rights by private perpetrators? Thus began my research into the so-called horizontal application of human rights.

At one time, human rights and democracy were synonymous. We were ruled by "them," and "they" were the source of evil. We believed that if we could only have "our" government, our rights would be safe.

One of the first bold moves in Poland's transition to democracy consisted of decentralization: meaning, more power to local self-governments. One such democratically elected local government, in an affluent suburb of Warsaw, soon issued a local law banning HIV-positive people from the community. This ordinance had the clear support of the majority of voters. Suddenly, Poles everywhere were proving James Madison's thesis from two centuries ago: namely, that a majority can be insensitive to the interests and rights of minorities and, therefore, minorities need protection – even in democracies. But in 1990, Poland did not yet have an enforceable Bill of Rights. Decisions of local councils could only be made void by the president of Poland, provided he deemed them illegal. As it happened, the first postcommunist head of state was former communist leader General Jaruzelski, whose appointment was part of the compromise allowing for the transition in Poland. He did, in fact, waive the ordinance and, thus, paradoxically, the same man who had introduced martial law in 1981 became the first defender of minority rights in the young democracy a scant decade later.

Tensions between democracy and human rights have been resonating throughout the entire period of transition. Today, we realize that democracy and human rights are interdependent, but it is clear that the excesses of democracy threaten human rights. At the same time, excessive constitutional rights can impoverish democracy. The need for a balance is one of the themes I address in this book.

The vision of rights we sought in order to protect ourselves against the communist state led us to overlook many problems, including those of social equality and inclusion. After all, we all suffered equally by the hand of our oppressors. We fought for the rights of the nation, not for the rights of particular groups. We were afraid that special claims would dilute our struggle and rob us of our resources. It turned out that it was easier to demand that the state stop oppression than to reconcile our own behavior and beliefs with respect for human rights. Most difficult, perhaps, was acknowledging and addressing gender inequality.

In the mid-1990s, I visited a foundation in the Balkans, accompanied by others from the United States and East Central Europe, all supporters of democratic transition and human rights. At the beginning of our meeting, it was announced that the wife of one of the hosts had just delivered a baby. Someone asked, "Boy or girl?" I remember observing that everyone was stunned into silence. "Boy," came the answer. The congratulations that ensued carried a distinct flavor of relief, as if news of a baby girl would have been a curse. I wondered how many times I had not noticed anything awry in similar situations in the past, and I wondered how the women in the room were feeling. That was the first time I clearly understood the venom of prevailing gender stereotype.

In 2001, I accompanied two colleagues to Peru on behalf of the Open Society Institute, seeking to assist in the transition to democracy, launched after the collapse of the Fujimori-Montesinos regime. We met with the new president and the political elite. We discussed the reform of the criminal justice system with the minister of justice and the needs for assistance to political parties with their leaders. Toward the end of our trip, we left Lima and went on to Cuzco, where we met with a number of activists for the local nongovernmental organizations. We asked them what their problems were and what they thought needed to be done. Only two problems were raised: one was that wives were being beaten and raped by their husbands. The second was the plight of young girls from villages, who were being given away to work as domestic servants in the cities and towns. Essentially a form of slavery, it was a practice that helped the poorest citizens escape poverty and starvation, but the price was high: deprived by their masters of any personal liberty, these young women had no protection from abuse. It was clear that no other problems were as destructive to the communities in and around Cuzco as these – yet none of the politicians in Lima had even mentioned either of these issues. I wondered how many of these men of state had young village girls for servants. I remember thinking that if they did, they probably thought that they were doing them and their families a favor.

I have already mentioned that human rights have always been, for us, an American idea. This perception was reinforced in 1977, during President Jimmy Carter's visit to Poland. The communist government badly needed American subsidies. Carter asked that the press conference at the end of his visit be aired live on Polish television. The government agreed, knowing that they could screen the journalists and provide them with appropriate questions. But just before the end of the conference, Carter announced that the U.S. embassy in Poland had passed along a question from the editors of an underground newspaper who had not been allowed to attend the conference. He took a piece of paper from his pocket and read aloud a question about the prospects for human rights in Poland. He then answered it, saying that the U.S. government would do its best to promote human rights around the world in accordance with the 1975 Helsinki Agreement.

It was what we expected. To us Poles, the American roots of the idea of individual rights were obvious – from the Declaration of Independence to FDR's Four Freedoms, the Atlantic Charter, and U.S. leadership in the defense of the free world during the Cold War. In fact, in the 1980s, I wrote a paper about the influence of the U.S. idea of rights on Poland's history.

In 1990, I was invited by the University of Chicago to teach human rights. The dean of the law school was a recognized constitutional scholar. One day, after he and I had become friends, he asked me to tell him what exactly I was teaching in my human rights course. I told him some general things about rights and their role in the world, but he was not satisfied with my answer. He wanted to know the specific subject matter of the individual sessions. When I progressed from general theory to the details of the freedoms of speech, expression, and association, he exclaimed that what I was teaching was, in essence, the very same thing he was teaching in Constitutional Law I and II. I then realized that, for Americans, human rights was an export product. They thought that they had no need for them at home, precisely because they had their Constitution and constitutional law. I understood why the United States had ratified so few international human rights treaties, covenants, and declarations. This experience awakened me to a reinterpretation of the history of human rights. A reader may find many surprising ideas in the historical chapter of this book.

The last experience I want to mention occurred in November 2001 at a conference on the universality of human rights at Columbia University. Many of the speakers challenged the universal validity of human rights. Some even invoked the notion of "human rights imperialism" and spoke out against the forceful imposition of the idea of human rights by the West. The discussion, although heated, was highly theoretical. Philosophical and moral arguments for and against the universality of rights were flung with considerable force. I will never forget when the dark-skinned man sitting in the back of the auditorium stood up and spoke.

"My name is Koi," he said. "I am from Kenya. I was imprisoned for seventeen years. I was tortured. There is probably not a single bone in my body that has not been broken. Eventually, the regime changed, I was released on amnesty, and, finally, I was allowed to emigrate. I live in New York and I am a writer. I attend conferences like this one. I want to share two things. The first is that while I was in prison, my oppressors talked to me. They wanted me to collaborate with them and give up my comrades. They alternately threatened me and promised me things. I understood everything they were saying. But, here, as I listen to you basically discuss my life,

I understand very little. Perhaps, this is too sophisticated for me. But I understand enough to make my second point. I hear some of you say that human rights are not universal. You give arguments that sound complicated. But I want to say that while I was in jail being threatened and tortured, it never occurred to me, even for a second, that there might exist some reason that would justify one human being administering such pain to another."

Koi ended his brief speech with that simple statement and, to this day, he may not be aware that by standing up to speak when he did, he provided me with the strongest argument for the universality of human rights that I have ever known.

Thank you, Koi.

Acknowledgments

This book is the result of both years of research and countless real-world experiences that have challenged my prior knowledge and questioned conventional wisdom. I hope that my readers will be stimulated not only to seek knowledge but also to reflect on their own experiences. I believe that it is from within that real understanding and wisdom emerge.

Many people and institutions helped me with the research that is the basis of this book. The beginnings of my research on human rights took place in the 1980s at the Center for the Study of Human Rights at Columbia University under the most precious guidance of Louis Henkin and Paul Martin. In 1985–1987, I taught human rights at Antioch University Los Angeles, a position I owed to Alvin Toffler, who was on the Antioch Board and Bill Birenbaum, who was the president of the university. In the early 1990s, I received a grant from the Ford Foundation to write a book on constitution making in Poland. Only now, however, having completed this work, can I say that I have fulfilled the intentions of that long-forgotten grant. In 1992, I was a research scholar at the University of Bremen; in 1994, I was in residence at the Maison des Sciences des Homme in Paris; and in 1994–1995, I spent a year at the Wissenschaftskolleg in Berlin, a venture made possible through a grant from the Mellon Foundation. In 1996, I was a Fellow at the Hoover Institute in Palo Alto. On several occasions, I visited the Institute for the Study of Man in Vienna. In 2000, I was a Marsha Lilien Gladstein visiting professor in human rights at the University of Connecticut; it was then that I began to write this book. My most recent research projects were at the Human Rights Center of the University of Connecticut, completed in collaboration with Richard Ashby Wilson; at the University of Siena with Marcello Flores; and at the Central European University with Andras Sajo and other scholars from all over the world. Many of the ideas presented in this book were first formulated as lectures to the Polish and international participants of the School of Human Rights, organized annually since 1990 by the Helsinki Foundation for Human Rights in Warsaw. I am grateful to all my sponsors, colleagues, and hosts.

Because this book is the result of many years of research, some parts of this book are based on my past published writings. Chapter 2 ("A Short History of Human Rights") includes sections of the article "On the Universality of the Universal Declaration of Human Rights," which was published in *Human Rights with Modesty: The Problem of Universalism*. Chapter 4 is an extended combination of two previous articles: "Social and Economic Rights in a New Constitution for Poland," which is in *Western Rights, Eastern Applications*, and "Needs-Based Approach to Social and Economic Rights," which is in *Economic Rights: Conceptual, Measurement, and Policy Issues*. Chapter 6 is based on one previous article, "Beyond Rights," which is in *Abuse: The Dark Side of Fundamental Rights*. I extend my thanks to the publishers of these articles.

Many thanks to all the people who helped me shape the ideas developed in this book. Years ago, I received many important comments on the first version from the late Marek Nowicki and from Zaza Namoradze. The penultimate draft was improved thanks to comments by Joanna Weschler, David P. Forsythe, Jerzy Celichowski, and Richard Ashby Wilson. Andrzej Rapaczynski provided me with such an abundance of detailed comments and suggestions that I decided to rewrite the entire book and change its original structure. I owe a lot to discussions with scholars at the University of Chicago Law School, Columbia University, Stanford University, CEU, and the University of Connecticut, as well as my colleagues at the Open Society Institute. I am particularly grateful to the members of boards and staff of the Open Society Justice Initiative in New York and the Human Rights and Governance Grants Program in Budapest. Our formal meetings and informal conversations have created fertile soil in which my understanding of human rights could grow. I hope that as you read this book you will be able to appreciate just how much you have contributed to it.

I owe as much to the students of the universities of Chicago, Connecticut, and Siena, and, most importantly, of the Central European University, whose truly multicultural student body allowed me to test my ideas about the relevance of human rights and their universality.

My most affectionate thanks go to my wife, Ewa Woydyłło-Osiatyńska, who has supported me throughout years of my immersion in research and tolerated my ensuing absence from our daily life. We have often discussed my ideas and, by challenging many of them, Ewa has helped me to clarify and develop my thoughts. I also thank Ewa for her insightful first readings of the subsequent versions of each chapter.

Finally, this book would not exist if it were not for my daughter, Natalia, who refined my crude English version of this book into the readable text before you. Although formally trained as a linguist, Natalia faultlessly edited every flaw in substance along the way. If she missed anything, I must have misled her and it is I who should be held responsible.

1

A Short History of Human Rights

The idea of human rights is of moral rather than legal nature. Although a growing number of human rights have legal protection, human rights primarily reflect people's aspirations. They proclaim widely accepted standards for freedom, for limitations on state power, and for services that can be expected from a society as represented by the state in accordance to an underlying set of moral values.[1] Although some of these standards may be enforced by law, new ones appear and are claimed as moral postulates. Human rights are, therefore, universal moral rights of fundamental character.[2] They belong to every person in his or her relations with the state and with any other authority in a position to use coercive power against the individual. Although some moral rights can be acquired (inherited, earned, bought, received, or exchanged for something else), human rights are inherent and belong to the human being *as such*. It is believed that every person comes to existence endowed with these rights.

Let us accept this working description of the nature of human rights for now and leave the more detailed discussion for the rest of this book. The concept of human rights, as described here, consists of at least six fundamental ideas:

1. The power of a ruler (a monarch or the state) is not unlimited.
2. Subjects have a sphere of autonomy that no power can invade and certain rights and freedoms that must to be respected by a ruler.[3]

---

[1] "Human rights are those liberties, immunities, and benefits which, by accepted contemporary values, all human beings should be able to claim 'as of right' of the society in which they live" (Rudolph (ed.) 1985, 268).

[2] The moral character of human rights is emphasized by Feinberg (1973, 85): "Human rights are generically moral rights of a fundamentally important kind held equally by all human beings, unconditionally and unalterably."

[3] This is not the same as the preceding point. The power of a ruler can be limited, for example, by God's commandments – with the subjects still having no rights.

3. There exist procedural mechanisms to limit the arbitrariness of a ruler and protect the rights and freedoms of the ruled (points 1 and 2, above, have already transformed "subjects" into the "ruled") who can make valid claims on the state for such protection.

4. The ruled have rights that enable them to participate in the decision making (with this concept, the "ruled" are transformed into the "citizens").

5. The authority has not only powers but also certain obligations that may be claimed by the citizens.

6. All these rights and freedoms are granted equally to all persons. (This transforms individual rights/privileges into human rights).

The ideas on this list have been emerging, disappearing, reemerging and evolving throughout history, reflecting changing social conditions and serving various needs.[4] Before the concept of human rights could be formulated and adopted, a number of specific customs, legal provisions, institutions, and ideas had to emerge.

This chapter focuses on two distinct ideas: notions of individual rights that emerged by the eighteenth century and human rights, which are essentially a twentieth-century concept. Continuities and differences between these two ideas are relevant today, influencing the very understanding of the nature, the meaning, and methods for the implementation of human rights.

INDIVIDUAL RIGHTS

The Origins

Individual rights evolved over a long period of time,[5] beginning with the assertion of freedoms that characterized the "old constitutionalism" that became widespread

---

[4] This list can be also used as a yardstick to help gauge precisely where a given culture (or a state or nation) stands in relation to rights.

[5] The origin of rights is the subject of much debate. Some authors claim that rights are a modern idea, beginning with the industrial era (e.g., Kenneth Minogue and H. L. A. Hart, quoted by Tierney 1989, 617). Others see these origins in antiquity (e.g., Ishay 2004, 16–69; Lauren 1998, 4–36; for a critique of this view, see Afshari 2007, 4–9) despite the limited continuity between ancient times and the emergence of rights in Europe. The most common view locates the beginning of human rights in the Enlightenment and the eighteenth-century revolutions (e.g., Hunt 2007 and Flores 2008, who points, however, to roots of human rights in previous epochs). Villey (1969) and Golding (1978) claims that the first theory of rights was formulated by William Ockham in the fourteenth century. According to Tierney (1989, 625), the concept of rights "first grew into existence in the works of medieval Decretists." (See also Helmholz 2001, 2). In sum, we can talk about *antecedents* of rights in ancient cultures and about *roots* of human rights in medieval Europe.

in medieval Europe.[6] Over time, society has gradually acknowledged both individual freedoms and the scope of limitations placed on the power of rulers and governments.[7] Simultaneously, instruments of due process of law that limit the arbitrariness of governments have also grown.[8] With the emergence of kings' councils, church councils, and early parliaments, the notions of participation and representation slowly gained acknowledgment. Finally, Christian communities accepted their responsibility for the basic survival needs of all their members.[9] Such responsibility was later assumed by absolute monarchs, becoming, in fact, one of the justifications for the absolute power held by the "enlightened" monarch. Later, some of these obligations were transformed into social rights or, more precisely, into the expectation of social benefits.

Medieval rights differed substantially from today's concept of rights. Indeed, the idea of the separateness of individual identity and the notion of individualism first appeared in the medieval West,[10] but rights, as a rule, were granted to groups and not individuals.[11] Although they contained the rudiments of relief and welfare, medieval rights and immunities were not equal; they were bestowed by kings on individuals, estates, or corporate bodies. They resembled privileges rather than rights, in the

---

6 See McIlwain 1947. Early constitutionalism was primarily the reaffirmation of ancient properties and the contract between the king and the nobility: privileges in return for loyalty, for serving the king with arms, or for money, as in the case of the Magna Carta in England. (See Orend 2002, 102.) A king's power was not challenged and ancient constitutions did not deal with the organization of power.

7 Of crucial importance was the departure from "cesaropapism," which accompanied the dissolution of the Western Empire and the separation of sacrum from publicum, expressed in the "theory of two swords" formulated by pope Gelasius as early as 493 AD. "The West's separation of the sacred and the secular, the ideological and political spheres, was uniquely fruitful, and without it the future 'freedoms,' the theoretical emancipation of 'society,' the future nation-states, the Renaissance and the Reformation alike could never have ensued" (writes Szucs 1981, 300).

8 Due process and the ban on arbitrary deprivation of property were essential for the Magna Carta and similar charters of privileges for the nobles. They were also recognized by canon law and the *ius commune*. These rights were based on "the feudal principle that the vassal could, by the judgment of his fellow vassals, obtain justice even against his own overlord and in the latter's court" (Caenegem 1995, 17).

9 In extreme cases, such responsibilities created claims on the part of the needy. A person whose life was endangered by poverty and hunger could take what was needed for basic survival from the superfluous wealth of a rich man. The institution of *denunciatio evangelica* helped to enforce this right. (See Tierney 1989 and Helmholz 2001.)

10 "The concern with individual intention, individual consent, individual will that characterized twelfth-century culture spilled over into many areas of canon law," writes Tierney (1989, 637). This individualism was further reinforced during the Renaissance.

11 "Medieval political thinkers perceived such rights largely, if not exclusively, in a corporatist context that afforded little positive recognition to members of the political community as individuals. Nor was there any clear expression at the time of the contemporary notion of personal rights" (Monahan 1994, 295).

contemporary sense. It was only after the principle of equality gained acceptance that these privileges for the few could become rights for everyone.[12]

During the Enlightenment, numerous medieval ideas converged to form a coherent philosophical concept of the rights of man. This idea was directed against the absolutism of monarchs and emphasized individual freedoms and limited government. John Locke, the best known theoretical opponent of absolutism, suggested that people transfer to the state only limited prerogatives – to protect them, to administer justice, and to punish wrongdoers – while retaining all other powers as inalienable rights.[13] These inalienable rights form the basis for limited government. This means that the state cannot claim that it has powers in those spheres where individuals have retained their inalienable rights.[14] The contract could be dissolved by the people at any time if the ruler did not fulfill his or her obligation or otherwise violated the people's rights.[15] This idea provided justification for American colonists' claim for independence and became the foundation of American statehood. In England, where the absolutist king had to surrender to the revolution, the triumphant Parliament itself became absolutist. Its power, however, was limited by the Bill of Rights and other documents, by common law and an independent judiciary, by the free press, and by other institutions of a strong, independent society. In France, the idea of the rights of man and citizen provided justification for the Great Revolution of

[12] Sen has noticed the uneven growth of two basic elements of the modern concept of human rights – freedom/tolerance and equality (Sen 1997, 31).

[13] There are two aspects of Locke's notion of inalienability. One, suggested by Taylor (1999, 127), emphasizes the necessity to prevent individuals from waiving their human rights. Taylor's argument finds support in Locke's assertion that "nobody can transfer to another more power that he has in himself, and nobody has an absolute arbitrary power over himself, or over any other, to destroy his own life, or take away the life or property of another" (see Locke 1980, 70 of paragraph 135). Another interpretation focuses on Locke's theory of contract. For Locke, individuals enter the contract endowed with the full range of rights and, in the contract, they transfer some limited rights to the state authority, which they have just appointed. In other words, they alienate such rights from themselves, undertaking the obligation that they will refrain from enforcing these rights because they trust that the authority will use its powers to protect them. All other rights remain with the individuals. They are inalienable in the sense that rights cannot be given away by individuals in a contract with the state.

[14] The *Virginia Declaration of Rights* of 1776, (drafted by George Mason and amended by Thomas Ludwell Lee), justified inalienable rights in a similar way: "That all men are by nature equally free and independent, and have certain inherent rights, of which, when they enter into a state of society, they cannot, by any compact, deprive or divest their posterity; namely, the enjoyment of life, and liberty, with the means of acquiring and possessing property, and pursuing and obtaining happiness and safety" (*Virginia Declaration of Rights*, section 1, quoted in Henkin et al. 1999, 126). Thomas Jefferson added one more argument to Locke's reasoning: even if people could transfer their own rights to life, liberty, and property to the government, the present generation cannot give away such rights of future generations.

[15] Locke's theory was revolutionary but not new. All of its major elements had been discussed by medieval political theorists. For example, French Huguenot Philippe du Plesis Mornay (1544–1633) developed an elaborate theory of two subsequent social contracts with the right of resistance built into them (*Vindiciae contra tyrannos*, 1579).

1789. Although the revolution transferred power from the king and aristocracy to the bourgeoisie – as well as to the bureaucracy and the army – it did not change the absolutist character of the state. From the seventeenth century onward, the French state was in control of society and of the rights of its citizens. We can trace the consequences of absolutism's victory in continental Europe (with the exception of Holland) and the victory of civil society in the United States, Holland, and, to some degree, England – all the way to modernity.

In antiabsolutist states, people have antecedent rights that limit the government. Instead of living as mere subjects, they are on an equal footing with state officials. Independent courts protect the rights of citizens and work to ensure that the government acts within the limited powers assigned to it by the constitution. Whether written or not, it is this constitution – and not the will of a ruler – that constitutes the supreme law. In post-absolutist states, however, the government has power and the people have duties. The government is usually highly centralized and has a monopoly on most social activities, including charity. This limits potential for social innovation and change.

Two Traditions of Rights

The difference between triumphant and defeated absolutism is reflected in the two traditions of rights in the West. One emphasizes the inherent rights of the individual and the rights of the such "natural" social groups as family or church that may be claimed against a state's authorities. This tradition, best elaborated by Locke, dominated in seventeenth century England and, particularly, in the eighteenth-century American colonies that struggled against the British state. Although England has been making incremental departures from it since the eighteenth century, this tradition is still referred to as Anglo-American.

On the European continent, another tradition of rights prevailed. Andrzej Rapaczyński concludes his study of the influence of the U.S. Constitution abroad by stating that

> The American idea of a weak, divided government, restrained by judicially enforceable individual rights had only limited attractiveness in those countries, including most European democracies and the majority of countries of the developing world, in which the state has been viewed as a guardian of the common good and a provider of individual benefits, and not as a necessary evil always threatening the interests of the citizens.[16]

---

[16] Rapaczyński (1990, 461). For a more detailed analysis of the American and European understanding of constitutionalism and rights, see Rapaczyński (1996). "The idea of 'unlimited sovereignty' was clearly rejected by the American founding fathers in the name of a government of limited powers, subject to constitutional restraints" (ibid., 11).

Outside the United States, rights were perceived as a sort of grant given by an enlightened state to fulfill its obligations to society.[17] Among these obligations was a ruler's duty to protect the citizens and take care of them in times of need or deprivation. Understood in this way, rights existed not to protect individuals *from* government but, instead, to be realized *through* the government of an active rather than passive state. This vision of rights was embodied in the French revolutionary constitution of 1790, as well as in the second Declaration of the Rights of Man and Citizen of 1793.[18] It was also present in the General Code of Prussia of 1794, the constitution of Norway of 1815, and in the social legislation that spread throughout Europe, this time including England, in the late nineteenth century.

Louis Henkin defines the two traditions in the following way. According to the first, "individual rights protect autonomy and freedom, limit government, and provide immunity from undue, unreasonable exercise of authority. . . . But in the nineteenth century there began to grow another sense of rights, rooted not in individual autonomy but in community, adding to liberty and equality the implications of fraternity." This suggests "a broader view of the obligations of society and the purposes of government – not only to maintain security and protect life, liberty and property, but also to guarantee and if necessary provide basic human needs."[19]

Mary Ann Glendon distinguishes between the "individualistic" Anglo-American tradition of rights that has emphasized individual liberty without much attention to constraints and responsibilities and the "dignitarian" tradition prevailing on the European continent.[20]

The Second Generation of Rights

Despite these differences, the English Bill of Rights (1689), the U.S. Declaration of Independence (1776), and the French Declaration of Rights of Man and Citizen (1789) have forever remained crucial milestones in the history of freedom.

---

[17] In a comprehensive study of the influence of American Declaration of Independence in Germany, Horst Dippel (1977, 163–7) demonstrated that the concept of binding inalienable rights preceding the government was simply incomprehensible for a majority of European elites in the late eighteenth century. Particularly in Germany, "the way in which the bourgeoisie dealt with the declaration of human rights in the American Revolution is another example of their incapacity to grasp the problem" (ibid., 164). Also in the context of Germany, Steinberger (1990, 202) suggests that "rights were not conceived of as 'inalienable,' deriving from natural law. (. . .) They were 'grants' by the prince, who might revoke them; they were rights of 'subjects' – not of people." For factors of resistance to the idea of individual rights in Poland, see Osiatyński (1990, 296–7).

[18] The 1789 Declaration, however, belonged to Anglo-American rather than to continental tradition; this may explain why it was muted a year later and replaced in 1793.

[19] Henkin et al. (1999, 280).

[20] See Glendon (2001, 226–8).

The eighteenth-century concept of rights, however, was limited. Although some philosophers of the time used the term human rights and insisted on their universal application,[21] the Enlightenment idea of rights was limited to a handful of property owners, excluding women,[22] children, those who did not own property, and the entire non-White population of the world.[23] In the United States, the idea of rights did not prevent the extermination of native people and the continued enslavement of Black Americans.[24]

In contrast to their medieval predecessors, eighteenth-century rights were individual, in that it was an individual person rather than a group that was the locus of these rights. As they were limited to only some individuals, however, these rights were not yet "human."[25]

The nineteenth century did not provide fertile soil for the idea of rights. New concepts took over whose authors were eager to sacrifice the individual for the benefit of groups, including nations, societies, unlimited majorities, and social classes.[26] In Europe, where the social problem was growing ever more acute, the eighteenth-century idea of civil liberties and political rights was too limited. The second generation of rights emerged with the aim of offering protection of basic social and economic needs for members of an industrial society.[27] This new concept included positive obligations of the state to regulate labor relations and markets to protect workers vis-à-vis the predominant power of owners and prevent excessive

---

[21] See Hunt (2007, 22–34). The most comprehensive argument for universal rights was presented by Thomas Paine in *The Rights of Man* (1791–1792).

[22] This limitation prompted protests. In France, Olimpie de Gouges published *The Declaration of the Rights of Women* (1791) for which she was executed during the Revolution. In England, Mary Wollstonecraft wrote A *Vindication of the Rights of Women* (1792).

[23] Hunt suggests that, in the case of women, the deprivation of rights was much more severe: "Children, servants, the propertyless, and perhaps even slaves might one day became autonomous, by growing up, by leaving service, by buying property, or by buying their freedom. Women alone seemed not to have any of these options; they were defined as inherently dependent on their fathers or husbands," writes Hunt (2007, 28).

[24] It is worth noting that John Locke himself justified slavery (see paragraph 85 of the *Second Treatise of Government*, 1980 edition, 44).

[25] The limited character of eighteenth century rights was noted by the Executive Committee of the American Anthropological Association in its statement on human rights: "The problem of drawing up a Declaration of Human Rights was relatively simple in the eighteenth century, because it was not a matter of *human* rights, but of the rights of men within the sanctions laid by a single society. Even as noble a document as the American Declaration of Independence, or the American Bill of Rights, could be written by men who themselves were slave-owners, in a country where chattel slavery was a part of the recognized social order. The revolutionary character of the slogan 'Liberty, Equality, Fraternity' was never more apparent than in the struggles to implement it by extending it to the French slave-owning colonies" (quoted in Winston 1989, 119).

[26] Henkin (1978, 14–18) discusses these ideas under the heading "The nineteenth-century antithesis."

[27] See Flores (2008, 118–27).

exploitation. Thus, the concept of "freedom from government" was extended to include "freedom through government." Social legislation was adopted in Bismarck's Prussia and in England, where it was accompanied by the gradual lifting of property requirements for voting and by growing franchise.

This development accelerated in the interwar period with the formation of the International Labor Organization and the adoption of social policies by the United States government during the New Deal. In the Four Freedoms speech of 1941, President F. D. Roosevelt spoke of freedom – including the freedom from want – "everywhere in the world," thus embracing the continental concept of rights.[28]

Few people, however, thought in terms of human rights at the peak of colonization in a time of rife nationalism, imperial states, and class struggle. Despite the condemnation of slavery in the Paris Peace Treaty of 1814,[29] the colonization by Whites of non-White people continued and could not be reconciled with the idea of human rights.[30] In fact, colonization actually increased the popular appeal of social Darwinism and racism. Among White people, demands for better life were not justified in terms of human rights but in categories of a nation's well-being and history, the notion of the greater good for the greater number of people, social justice or humanitarian assistance. At last, with the mid-nineteenth-century abolitionist movement in the United States and international opposition to the atrocities committed by Belgian troops and entrepreneurs in the Congo, international humanitarian movements were formed.[31]

Humanitarian considerations led to the formation, in 1863, of the International Committee of the Red Cross and to the adoption of a number of international

---

[28] See Sunstein (2004, 9 and 80–4). The New Deal was a radical departure from the late-nineteenth century practice of the U.S. Supreme Court consequently invalidating social legislation as a violation of the constitutional right to property and freedom of contracts.

[29] "Part of the reason why racism flourished so mightily in this period is that it had no really effective opposition where one might have expected it, since it also flourished among the liberals," writes Gosset (1963, 174). John Stuart Mill in his treaty *On Liberty* wrote: "It is, perhaps, hardly necessary to say that this doctrine is meant to apply only to human beings in the maturity of their faculties (. . .) Those who are still in a state to require being taken care of by others, must be protected against their own actions as well as against external injury. For the same reason, we may leave out of consideration those backward states of society in which the race itself may be considered as in its nonage" (quoted in Kabasakal Arat 2006, 420). Although American liberals accepted racist theories chiefly because of their fear of immigration; in Europe, colonialism was what encouraged people to believe in the White man's superiority.

[30] In England, slave trade was banned in 1807; slavery in the British colonies was abolished in 1833. The 1884–1885 Berlin Conference, which decided Africa's division among the colonial powers, also passed a ban on the slave trade. Slavery itself was abolished in 1926 by the League of Nations Convention to Suppress the Slave Trade and Slavery (amended in 1953 and supplemented in 1956). Despite this, slavery still flourishes in a number of countries, particularly in Mauritania.

[31] See Hochschild (1998) and Hochschild (2005). See also Afshari (2007, 9–34), who claims that the abolitionists and other "single-cause" movements of the nineteenth century (e.g., women's rights, anti-imperialist, and labor movements) cannot be considered human rights movements.

conventions limiting the arbitrary application of force during armed conflicts.[32] The crisis of nineteenth-century empires led to growing concerns about the plight of minorities. Some of the great powers invoked a right to humanitarian intervention "to prevent the Ottoman Empire from persecuting minorities in the Middle East and the Balkans."[33] Minority rights were of great concern after World War I, when the multicultural Russian and Austro-Hungarian empires disintegrated into numerous new states with substantial minorities. At the Paris Peace Conference, the recognition of independent Poland, Czechoslovakia, and other states in Central Europe was made contingent on the guarantees of certain collective rights to the minorities.[34] The mechanism of protection through general constitutional provisions, peace treaties, and bilateral minority treaties[35] designed in Paris proved unsuccessful and gave way to the growth of nationalism and racism in authoritarian Germany, Italy, and a number of other countries in Central Europe.

Nevertheless, minority clauses in a number of peace treaties with Austria, Bulgaria, Hungary, and Turkey, as well as bilateral minority treaties, included provisions that concerned other groups as well. They assured protection of life and liberty to all inhabitants of the countries in question, as well as equal civil and political rights for all minority nationals in such countries. In 1922, when the states concerned protested that their sovereignty was being violated as other states were not subject to such limitations, the Assembly of the League of Nations adopted a resolution recommending that all other states voluntarily adopt similar standards with respect to their minorities. Even though no further steps were taken on the intergovernmental level, the provisions in minority clauses became the basis for proposals to codify human rights in international law.

HUMAN RIGHTS

First Proposals

Mass displacement of people after World War I and minority problems were exacerbated by the *pogroms* in Russia and the aftermath of the Bolshevik revolution. The national upheavals resulted in members of the White middle class and upper classes who had hitherto enjoyed privileges joining the traditional victims of

[32] This process had begun with the 1856 Paris Declaration, which set the rules of maritime warfare. Captured enemy soldiers and civilian populations were protected by a number of Geneva Conventions, signed in 1864, 1906, 1929, and 1949.

[33] Davidson (1993, 8).

[34] See Mazower (2004, 382).

[35] The first treaty to establish such protections was the treaty signed in Versailles on June 29, 1919 between the Principal Allied and Associated Powers and Poland.

abuse – the poor, the enslaved, and the excluded: "The fact that citizens, all citizens, had to be protected from the abusive instruments of the modern state would become increasingly clear between two wars, the period that helped to shape the vision of human rights in its current form."[36]

One such victim was Russian jurist Andre Mandelstam, head of the legal office of the Russian ministry of foreign affairs in 1917. After the Bolsheviks claimed power, Mandelstam escaped to Paris, where he taught international law. After 1926, he joined Antoine Frangulis, who had founded the International Diplomatic Academy.[37] In November 1928, the Academy adopted a resolution prepared by Mandelstam and Frangulis that generalized obligations contained in minority clauses in the form of a declaration of rights.[38] A year later, the International Law Institute in New York adopted a Declaration of the International Rights of Man drafted by Mandelstam, who admitted that the need for the recognition of human rights became manifest after "the horrors perpetrated under the government of the Soviet Union."[39] The Declaration was widely publicized in the 1930s by a number of non-governmental organizations and academic institutions that called for the adoption of standards that would limit coercive powers of states and protect fundamental rights.[40] Protestant churches also called for the establishment of a peaceful global order centered around human rights.[41]

The awareness of the need for rights was hastened by the developments in Germany after Hitler's ascent to power in January 1933. The Nazis rejected the concept of the rule of law (the *Rechtstaat*) and sought to build a new legal order based on German traditions (*Volksseele*).[42] It was introduced in a sweeping wave of emergency decrees, based on powers given to Hitler by president Paul von Hindenburg and

[36] Afshari (2007, 39).

[37] In 1920–1922, Frangulis represented his native Greece at the League of Nations. He left Greece when the army under general Venizelos abolished monarchy. In the 1930s, Frangulis represented Haiti in the League of Nations. See Burgers (1992, 450–9).

[38] For other efforts by the individuals and nonstate institutions to generalize the protection of minorities in declarations of rights, see Simpson (2001, 151–6) and Clapham (2007, 26–9).

[39] Quoted in Burgess (2002, 24), who comments: "The use of forced labour and religious persecution were decisive for the emergence of this new *droit humain*, and a dramatic growth in support for the notion of 'universal human rights' while reinforcing the belief that state sovereignty was not absolute when it came to the respect of human rights" (ibid., 24).

[40] In the 1920s and 1930s, a number of NGOs were concerned with human rights. They included, among others, the Women's International League for Peace and Freedom, The Institute de Droit International, the Federation Internationale des Droits de l'Homme, the Ligue Pour la Defense des Droits de l'Homme, and the International Institute of Public Law.

[41] See Nurser (2003).

[42] The theory behind Nazi law was exemplified by the speeches of Hans Frank, who later became the governor of occupied Poland. Frank wanted law to "recognize the concept of 'racial comrade' (*Volksgenosse*)" (quoted in Schleunes 2002, 85). According to Schleunes, Frank rejected Roman law "because it elevated the individual person, the *civis Romanus*, to its center. In Roman law, he noted, the individual finds legitimization 'not as being part of a larger whole but in being the possessor of certain objectively assigned rights'" (ibid., 85).

justified by the Reichstag fire on February 27, 1933.[43] As a result of the March 5 general election, the Nationalsozialistische Deutsche Arbeiterpartei (NSDAP) became the largest party but one still dependent on its coalition partner, the German National People's Party, for a majority in Parliament. This obstacle toward absolute rule was overcome on March 23, when the Reichstag adopted the Enabling Act that authorized the cabinet – for 4 years – to enact legislation, including laws deviating from or altering the constitution, without the consent of the Reichstag.[44] Thus, a dictatorship was legally established. A new wave of laws followed, primarily stripping Jews of any citizen's rights.[45] These laws influenced society and, beginning with the German Swimming Association's April 1933 decision to exercise "purification," Jews were expelled from all civic associations in Germany. The Nuremburg Laws (promulgated at the annual NSDAP rally in Nuremburg in September 1935) sealed this process and opened the doors for a subsequent extermination of Jews.

Almost immediately, the new German laws were tested against the minority protection mechanism of the League of Nations. On May 12, 1933, Franz Bernheim (1899–1990), a German citizen who sought refuge in Prague from German Upper Silesia, filed a petition to the League claiming that his April 1933 termination of employment by the Deutches Familien-Kaufhaus, Gleiwitz branch – on the grounds of his Jewish origins – violated the minorities protection provisions of Part III of the 1922 German-Polish Convention on Upper-Silesia.[46] Bernheim enumerated a number of provisions in various laws inconsistent with the Convention[47] and

---

43 On February 4, Hitler issued the "Decree for the Protection of German People." In the Reichstag Fire Decree of February 28, Hitler nullified *habeas corpus* rights as well as the freedom of speech and publication, the rights of assembly and association, the privacy of communication, and the inviolability of home and private property.

44 The Enabling Act was considered by the Nazis as a basis for the legitimacy of their regime. Because it included powers to depart from the Weimar Constitution, the act itself was considered a constitutional amendment and thus its adoption required a two-thirds majority, with at least two-thirds of deputies attending the session. The act was passed in an atmosphere of terror and intimidation. After the Reichstag Fire the government had already arrested all Communist and twenty-six social democrat deputies who would vote against the Enabling Act. When remaining social democrats planned to boycott Reichstag session, so that it does not have a quorum, its president, Hermann Göring, changed procedural rules, declaring that any deputy "absent without excuse" will be considered present. On the day of voting SA troops surrounded the meeting; some were present in the chamber. However, the votes needed for the supermajority were voluntarily delivered by the Centre Party "in exchange for the protection of Catholics' civil and religious liberties, religious schools and the retention of civil servants affiliated with the Centre Party" and, perhaps, for the promise of the Reichskonkordat with the Holy See (quoted from the entry "Enabling Act of 1933" in Wikipedia). See also Schleunes (2002, 88).

45 The so called "Aryan paragraph" defined as a Jew anyone who had one Jewish grandparent.

46 For the details of Bernheim case, see Burgess (2002) and Burgers (1992, 455–7).

47 April 7, 1933: law "for the organization of civil service" (it provided for compulsory retirement or dismissal of non-Aryan officials); April 10, 1933: law "on admission to legal profession" (it expelled Jews from legal professions); April 1, 1933: decree of Reich Commissioner for Prussia regarding the exercise of the calling of notary (it called on Jewish notaries to refrain from exercising their calling); April 25,

asked that these laws be rendered null and void, the situation guaranteed by the convention be restored and the affected Jews be reinstated in their rights and granted compensation. The Council of the League of Nations acted speedily on the petition, considering it between May 22 and June 6, 1933. The Council was satisfied by the German delegate August von Keller's explanation that "German internal legislation could in no case affect the fulfillment of Germany's international obligations and that any measures taken by subordinate authorities that might be incompatible with the 1922 Convention would be corrected."[48] The Council referred the case for redress to the Mixed Commission. It decided that Bernheim had been dismissed "because of bad quality of work and his communist tendencies, and not because of instructions from any official agency."[49] As a result of a compromise, Bernheim was paid 1600 marks as compensation.[50]

Such an outcome was disappointing for Bernheim, who justified his petition in terms of a general threat to non-Aryans in Germany and sought the means to nullify discriminatory laws and prevent the deterioration of the situation beyond the point of no return.[51] His case proved that bilateral treaties and the minority protection mechanism of the League of Nations were unable to stop a state from discrimination and oppression within a territory of its own sovereignty. This experience reinforced attempts to protect all people, including minorities, by some general mechanism based on individual rights.[52]

1933: law "against the alienization of the German schools and high schools (it introduced a *numerus clausus* of 1.5 percent of non-Aryan pupils) and the decree of the Minister of Labor "on admission of doctors to the panels of health insurance funds" that forbade doctors of non-Aryan descent to practice medicine. For the whole text of the Bernheim petition, see Bernhiem 1933.

[48] Burgers (1992, 456).

[49] Burgess (2002, 17). In fact, Nazi authorities complied with the Convention and discriminatory laws were not applied in Upper Silesia until July 15, 1937, when the Convention expired; after that date the Nuremberg Laws and policy of discrimination and extinction of Jews were introduced on a full scale in the region.

[50] The Mixed Commission dealt with 47 complaints by Jewish employees, doctors, and lawyers under the minority clauses of the Upper Silesia Convention. Eight cases were dismissed, 16 plaintiffs were reinstated to work, and 23 were resolved by a compromise (ibid., 17–18).

[51] In the closing paragraph of his petition, Bernheim (1933) wrote: "The reason for this request is that, as the above-quoted laws and decrees demonstrate, the application of the principle of inequality to German nationals of non-Aryan and Jewish descent is being systematically pursued in all spheres of private and public life so that already an enormous number of Jewish lives have been ruined, and if the tendencies at present prevailing in Germany continue to hold sway, in a very short time every Jew in Germany will have suffered permanent injury so that any restoration or reparation will become impossible, and thousands and tens of thousands will have completely lost their livelihood."

[52] More and more people "believed that the rise of Germany and the persecution of the German Jews showed that such rights could only be defended internationally" (Mazower 2004, 385). The events in Germany in the 1930s and in occupied Europe after 1939 proved that – in the absence of a Jewish state – bilateral agreements between states could not effectively protect the rights of Jewish minorities within other states. "By 1945 many Jews, if they had not turned to Zionism, felt that being singled out

General principles involved in the Bernheim case were discussed in the Assembly of the League of Nations from September 25 to October 11, 1933. At this session, Poland submitted a draft resolution that would generalize the protection of minorities. Other delegates had similar suggestions. Antoine Frangulis, now as a delegate for Haiti, opposed such plans, arguing that the proper approach would be the "generalization of the human rights pertaining to *all* people, whether belonging to a minority or a majority."[53] Frangulis submitted a draft resolution with a catalog of rights identical to the one prepared by the International Diplomatic Academy in 1928 and called for a worldwide convention that would ensure the protection of rights enumerated in the resolution. His proposal was largely ignored, although the delegates from Greece and Ireland advocated the adoption of a universal convention to protect human rights. The Assembly concluded its deliberation with a weak resolution reaffirming principles adopted in 1922. Three days later, Germany withdrew from the League of Nations and from the Disarmament Conference. The threat of an introduction of the Nazi order outside Germany by military means became real.

In October 1933, at the 5th Conference for the Unification of Penal Law in Madrid, Raphael Lemkin, a prosecutor and lecturer at the Free University of Poland, proposed a multilateral convention that would define and punish a new international crime – similarly to slavery, trafficking of women and children, or piracy – that had been universally recognized as "offences against the law of nations." Lemkin included in his list such acts of extermination directed against the ethnic, religious or social collectives whatever the motive (political, religious, etc.) as massacres, pogroms, actions undertaken to ruin the economic existence of the members of collectivity, etc. Also belonging in this category are all sorts of brutalities which attack the dignity of the individual in cases where these acts of humiliation have their source in a campaign of discrimination directed against the collectivity in which the victim is a member.[54]

Although Lemkin sought a universal application for new law and consequently did not in his report refer to Germany by name, he viewed the rise of Nazism in Germany as the immediate threat that necessitated such a new convention.[55]

But, attempts to codify human rights during the interwar period were isolated. Undoubtedly, there were threats to human dignity, violations of rights, and the specter of war and genocide by the totalitarian regimes of Nazism and Communism.

as a minority was itself inviting trouble; better to stand – as they had done in the nineteenth century – on their rights as individuals than as a group," writes Mazower (ibid., 388).

53 Burgers (2002, 458).

54 See Lemkin (1933, 5). In 1933, Lemkin called such crimes "acts of barbarity"; in 1943 – already in England – Lemkin coined for them a new word: *genocide*. On the development of the concept of genocide and the 1948 Convention on the Prevention and Punishment of the Crime of Genocide, see Flores (2008, 206–13).

55 In 1943, Lemkin referred to the 1933 report as "a proposal for international repression of Nazi activities."

The need for a response in terms of universal rights, however, was seen only by a few.[56] Even if it was more widespread, however, the political will to address emerging threats in terms of human rights was missing. This changed during and after World War II, when the idea of rights experienced its renaissance.[57]

The Formulation

At the very beginning of the war, English writer Herbert George Wells published a letter in *The Times* containing a draft "Declaration of Rights" that could be adopted as a goal of the war.[58] Subsequently, he launched a worldwide movement and even reached F. D. Roosevelt with his Declaration.[59] Between 1941 and 1944, a number of books and draft charters of international human rights were prepared by individuals, academic institutions, and nongovernmental organizations (NGOs).[60] This time, however, human rights proposals resonated at the highest levels of power. The genocide committed in Europe by Germany brought back ideas of limited government, liberal democracy, and fundamental freedoms.

In the Atlantic Charter, an eight-point declaration issued on August 14, 1941, U.S. president F. D. Roosevelt and British Prime Minister Winston Churchill reasserted the basic ideas of democracy and individual freedom as a shared goal among the Allies.[61] In the Declaration of the United Nations (UN) of January 1, 1942, twenty-six nations allied in the war against the Axis jointly supported the conviction that "complete victory over their enemies is essential to defend life, liberty, independence and religious freedom, and to preserve human rights and justice in their own lands as well as in other lands." Thus, universal human rights and justice were declared common aims of war. The Declaration was directed to potential members of a worldwide coalition that was to join the Allies in war efforts.[62] The use of the term *human rights* could be perceived as a promise made by the West to extend the

---

[56] Burgers (1992, 460–4), who analyzed most of prodemocratic and antitotalitarian works of the 1930s, was surprised by the almost total absence of the very term *human rights* or *rights of man* in this literature.

[57] For a detailed analysis of the development of human rights during and after World War II, see Morsink (1999), Lauren (1998), Simpson (2001), and Glendon (2001).

[58] See Wells (1940).

[59] See Burgers (1992, 464–8).

[60] An impressive number of titles is listed by Burgers (ibid., 472–6).

[61] The two leaders declared, among other things, respect "for the right of all people to choose the form of government under which they will live" (point 3); the "desire to bring about the fullest collaboration between all nations in the economic field with the object of securing, for all, improved labor standards, economic advancement and social security" (point 5); and the dedication to peace "which will afford assurance that all the men in all the lands may live out their lives in freedom from fear and want" (point 6).

[62] The Declaration was eventually signed by 46 states.

benefits of what had thus far been "Western" liberty to include the non-Western allies as well.

The idea of human rights was upheld in the Charter of the United Nations signed on June 26, 1945, in San Francisco. Along with the convention on genocide, human rights were to codify natural law, which had been used, with some reluctance, in the Nuremburg trials of Nazi leaders. Although most of the post–WWII constitutions provided for institutional arrangements that could refine and balance the passions of a majority, human rights could limit the risk that formally legitimate governments might commit crimes and cruelties in the name of majority or "a nation," as was the case with Germany under Hitler. The work of the Economic and Social Council focused on enshrining within human rights documents at least some of the progressive labor legislation that had been developed by welfare state reformers and accepted by the International Labour Organization (ILO) between the wars.

Undoubtedly, all these rights had Western origins, but now they were to be treated as truly human – that is, extended to all the people of the world. In some sense, human rights could be seen as a self-limitation of dominant powers, just as a constitution can be perceived as the self-limitation of those who wield the power within a state.[63] A closer look at the origins of human rights, however, reveals a more complex picture. Although the idea of human rights was attractive to Western intellectuals and most NGOs, preparatory work on human rights did not have strong support from Western governments, particularly the great powers.[64] Each of them had a record that was not compatible with the standards proclaimed: Russia had domestic terror and the Gulag; England and France had colonies; and the United States racism and legal segregation.[65] The great powers also wanted to protect their supremacy in the post–WWII world and used the concepts of domestic jurisdiction and state sovereignty

---

[63] Ignatieff has suggested that the drafters of the UDHR wanted to protect the rest of the world from committing atrocities similar to those that had recently been committed by the Europeans. He writes that "a consciousness of European savagery is built into the very language of the Declaration's preamble" and that "human rights norms are not so much a declaration of the superiority of European civilization as a warning by Europeans that the rest of the world should not reproduce their mistakes" (2001, 107).

[64] See Lauren (1998, 165–71), Glendon (2001, 4–20), and Freeman (2002, 32–40).

[65] The position of the United States was more ambivalent than was the case with Great Britain or the Soviet Union. President Roosevelt was committed to his Four Freedoms policy. On December 10, 1942, the State Department completed the first draft of an international bill of rights. Five days later, in a radio address on the 150th anniversary of the Bill of Rights, President Roosevelt called for a worldwide defense of the principles embodied in that document. Simultaneously, the nongovernmental Commission to Study the Organization of Peace (CSOP) prepared a number of subsequent drafts that influenced the State Department and the President (see Mitoma 2008, 616). It seems that Roosevelt's enthusiasm for the international bill of rights significantly waned after his meeting with Churchill and Stalin in Tehran from November 28 to December 1, 1943. Since then, Secretary of State Cordell Hull "effectively ended participation by outside groups in...the development of specific human rights policy" (ibid., 621).

to exclude possible interventions in their affairs by less powerful nations. Therefore, to these powerful states, "the human rights project was peripheral, launched as a concession to small countries and in response to demands of numerous religious and humanitarian associations that the Allies live up to their war rhetoric."[66]

In Dumbarton Oaks, in the summer of 1944, the great powers made plans for a future international organization that would serve peace, security, and international cooperation and "agreed to their opposition to any meaningful provisions concerning international human rights."[67] Although the United States wanted to include human rights among the general principles of the Charter of the United Nations, the Soviets claimed that such provisions are "not germane to the main tasks of an international security organization."[68] China emphasized the need for the international organization "to be able to enforce justice in the world" and agreed "to cede as much of its sovereign power as may be required."[69] Wellington Koo, a Chinese representative, also raised the issue of the right of all people to equality and nondiscrimination, as well as the need to secure social welfare in the future world order. The Soviet Union and Great Britain rejected the Chinese proposals and all three powers "shared a deep concern over 'the equality of races question' specifically and the larger issue of human rights in general."[70] The United States still insisted on a general statement about human rights but agreed that it be included in the context of social and economic cooperation. The Chinese proposal about racial equality was completely deleted from the Dumbarton Oaks final statement; the document ended up written in the language of state powers and not the rights of individuals.

In April 1945, at the start of the San Francisco conference of the United Nations, it was obvious that the great powers would not foster the idea of human rights.[71] During the conference, however, they realized that:

> Crusades once unleashed are not easily reined in or halted. Expectations had been raised, promises made, and proposals issued during the "people's war" that were not about to be denied. Countless men and women, including those among minority groups, smaller nations, and colonial peoples, had been led to believe that their personal sacrifices in war and their witness to genocide would bring certain results to the world.[72]

[66] Glendon (ibid., XV).
[67] Lauren (1998, 166).
[68] Ibid., 169.
[69] Ibid., 166.
[70] Ibid., 167.
[71] See Glendon (2001, 10).
[72] Lauren (1998, 171). Similarly, Mazower (2004, 392) notes that the British and the Russians "had failed to foresee the force of public opinion within the United States, as well as the storm of criticism from governments across the world – from India and New Zealand to South America – which greeted the Dumbarton Oaks attempt to backtrack on the many wartime declarations promising human rights in the future."

Such sentiments were voiced by representatives of the smaller nations that had managed to subvert the plans of the great powers. The organizers of the San Francisco conference invited all those states that had declared war on Germany and Japan by March 1, 1945.[73] The largest group of participants was made up of the independent states of Latin America. The non-Western countries represented were China, the Commonwealth of the Philippines, India, Iraq, Iran, Syria, Lebanon, Saudi Arabia, Turkey, Egypt, Ethiopia, Liberia, and South Africa. Most of these countries found a spokesman in the person of Carlos Romulo of the Philippines, a journalist who had received the Pulitzer Prize for a series of articles about the coming end of colonialism. Romulo succeeded in inserting the formulation on the "self-determination of peoples" as one of the purposes of the United Nations in the Charter's Preamble. He also pressed for antidiscrimination provisions, for which he gained support from representatives from Brazil, Egypt, India, Panama, Uruguay, Mexico, the Dominican Republic, Cuba, and Venezuela.

The human rights cause was endorsed by over forty NGOs, mostly from the United States, invited to San Francisco as consultants and observers.[74] In early May, representatives of several NGOs met with U.S. Secretary of State Edward Stettinius, who agreed to press for the formation of the Human Rights Commission.[75] On the insistence of the coalition of NGOs and smaller countries, the Charter of the United Nations included a reference to human rights among the UN's purposes in the Preamble and in an additional six articles.[76] Article 68 assigned to the Economic and Social Council the task of establishing a commission for the promotion of human rights. This commission was created in February 1946.[77]

The commission's work was dominated by a small number of leading participants, including Chinese philosopher, playwright, and diplomat Peng-chun Chang; French Nobel Peace Prize laureate René Cassin, who had lost twenty-nine close relatives in Nazi death camps during the Holocaust; existentialist philosopher Charles Malik, student of Alfred North Whitehead and Martin Heidegger who turned diplomat and main spokesman for the Arab League after his homeland, Lebanon, had received independence; and Eleanor Roosevelt, who brought to the entire effort the commitment of her late husband and her own dedication to humanitarian causes. Other active participants included Canadian director of the United Nations Human

---

73 As well as Argentina, who declared war in March.

74 See Mitoma (2008, 621–9), who claims that the "prominence of human rights in the UN Charter represents more than the triumph of the US diplomacy; it represents the ascendant influence of civil society in global affairs" (ibid., 619).

75 This was the single exception from the firm opposition to naming any special commission in the UN Charter agreed upon by the great powers. Glendon claims that this meeting "marked a crucial turning point" (2001, 17).

76 Articles 1, 13, 55, 62, 68, and 76.

77 The first item on the Commission's agenda was the discussion of a draft international bill of rights prepared in 1943 by British jurist Hersch Lauterpacht (1945, 69–74).

Rights Division John P. Humphrey, who prepared the Declaration's preliminary draft; Carlos Romulo; Hansa Mehta of India, who helped to bring the issue of women's rights into the Declaration; and Chilean leftist Hernan Santa Cruz, who brought to the work a Latin American dedication to social and economic rights.

From among the official representatives of the participating states, Latin American governments were the most dedicated advocates of the adoption of the Declaration. Toward the end of 1948, as the final draft was under discussion by the so-called Third Committee, the Latin Americans were joined by representatives from a number of Islamic and Buddhist states, as well as from some independent African countries. It was this coalition of states and individuals that pressed for the adoption of the Universal Declaration of Human Rights (UDHR) and influenced its content. The character of this coalition suggests that, at the time, "the mightiest nations on earth bowed to the demands of smaller countries for recognition of common standards by which the rights and wrongs of every nation's behavior could be measured."[78]

The document was adopted by the UN General Assembly on December 10, 1948, with not a single vote against and eight abstentions. The Soviet Union and their satellites justified their abstaining vote by pointing out insufficient emphasis on social and economic rights in the Declaration.[79] Despite the inaccuracy of this claim, it nevertheless influenced the formation of "the myth of Western opposition" to such rights.[80] South Africa's abstention resulted from the incompatibility between the principles of human rights and the system of apartheid introduced legally in April 1948. Saudi Arabia justified its abstention on the grounds of conflict with its religious and cultural values.

Many colonial nations of Asia, and particularly of sub-Saharan Africa, were not represented in the United Nations in 1948. Subsequently, the newly independent states signed and ratified the Declaration, confirming their dedication to the idea of human rights and signing the human rights covenants after these were adopted in 1966.[81] Before this, at a conference of nonaligned states held in April 1955, in Bandung, Indonesia, six independent African states and all independent Asian states declared their "full support of the fundamental principles of human rights."[82] One hundred seventy-one states sent their delegates to the 1993 Vienna conference on human rights. The UDHR served as a model for some ninety constitutions; in

---

[78] Glendon (2001, xv).

[79] See Donnelly (2007, 41).

[80] See Whelan and Donnelly (2007).

[81] As of May 15, 2000, 144 states signed the Covenant on Civil and Political Rights (CCPR) and 142 signed the Covenant on Economic, Social, and Cultural Rights (CESCR).

[82] Quoted in Burke (2006, 956). In Egypt's closing address, president Nasser endorsed the conference as a success because of the "deep concern and full support which all the Asiatic and African countries have shown with regards to the question of human rights" (ibid., 952).

nineteen constitutions of new postcolonial states, mainly in Africa, specific references to the Declaration were made.[83]

However, the support of Universal Declaration of Human Rights by the Third World did not automatically translate into the dedication to the entire body of human rights-related values or to individual freedoms. Since the nineteenth century, progressive philosophers and political leaders in colonial countries were convinced that the concept of freedom applied to nations rather than to individuals and that such freedom should be perceived in the context of nationalism and progress. Such progress should be achieved through a strong state.[84] After World War I in Central Europe[85] and after World War II in the Third World, rights and freedoms of individuals were subordinated to the right to self-determination and, later, to the nation-building process.[86] Self-determination and the promise of national independence were the elements of drafting process within the UN that attracted the elites of colonial or postcolonial nations.[87] "Their minds engaged the rhetoric of rights as the most potent weapon in their anti-colonial arsenal."[88] Their human rights demands were directed against the imperial West and were not concerned with their own future states. At home, human rights were subordinated to self-determination, nation-building, statism, and progress via unlimited state. In the course of this process, many rights of indigenous populations were violated, both during national liberation struggles and later, when local communities were forcibly subordinated to centralized independent states.[89]

---

[83] For a full list, see Glendon (2001, 228); it is the source of all data in this paragraph.

[84] Afshari (2007, 36–9) demonstrated this for Sun-Yat-sen in China, Ataturk, and the Young Turks and Reza Shah of Iran.

[85] Asfhari (ibid., 42) draws the following lesson from Easter European self-determination efforts: "Human rights (indivisible and interdependent) suffer wherever political discourse creates an intense passion around one particular cause, correctly or mistakenly defined as human right. The fervor .created around the 'right to self-determination' blinded the nationalists to the legitimacy of the same 'right' for their own minorities or for the neighbors in conflict with them over the territories." For an analysis of the understanding of freedom primarily as "national freedom" in nineteenth- and twentieth-century Poland, see Osiatynski 1990.

[86] Afshari argues that anticolonial struggles "heroic as they were, remained in essence a single-issue struggle, lacking the necessary human rights conscience" (ibid., 44).

[87] It should be noted that while the UDHR provided arguments in favor of self-determination and for claims by newly independent states for international aid, human rights were not a driving force of the decolonization itself. More important were nationalist sentiments of the elites of colonized people as well as economic and military assistance provided by the Soviet Union (and, later, by China). National liberation movements were perceived by Communist powers as an important arena of the Cold War. Combined with the re-creation of colonial power structure by postcolonial elites – these were important factors in the rapid emergence of oppressive regimes and dictatorships in postcolonial states.

[88] Ibid., 44.

[89] "Human rights, properly understood as such, became the victims of success of the right to self-determination..." and "national independence became an albatross hanging around the necks of the citizens of the new nations... Anticolonialism had became a consequential ideology, not much

Afshari claims that indications of an instrumental attitude to human rights were already visible at the 1955 Bandung Conference. The primary goal of the conference was to consolidate the nonaligned movement around the developmental needs of African and Asian states, as well as around a common struggle against racism, colonialism, and neoimperialism.[90] The second summit of the nonaligned states in Belgrade in 1961 adopted twenty-seven demands and postulates, primarily addressed to the West, without even mentioning the obligation of the states to protect the rights of citizens internally. By then, most postcolonial leaders had become dictators and were violating human rights and basic principles of rule of law.[91] "National liberation movements of the post-Declaration entrapped the individuals it liberated into vicious circles of authoritarian rules, military coups, and blatant disregard for the equal dignity of all citizens."[92]

The commitment to human rights of the independent countries of Latin America seemed deeper and more genuine, although their main interest was in social and economic rights. Active champions of human rights were also intellectuals and leaders of relatively new – or reinstated – democracies in Europe and Asia, with a particularly important role played by India. This confirms a theory according to which human rights are advocated primarily by the governments of the new and still unstable democracies who want to "lock-in" democratic changes and secure them against potential setbacks in the future. Authoritarian governments may be pressed by circumstances, by great powers, or by economic needs to pay lip service to human rights declarations but will resist the implementation of human rights instruments at home. Paradoxically, the attitude displayed by a majority of well-established democracies is similar; they do not see the need to limit sovereignty for additional protection of what they believe exists in their internal legal system anyway.[93] Like the

different than communism, in the sense that as it liberated nations it also paralyzed the human rights discourse and left the individual citizen unprotected in the hands of the indigenous elites," writes Afshari (ibid., 49–50).

[90] See ibid., 55–8. Afshari demonstrated his thesis by the future evolution of the attitudes of the Third World elites toward human rights on the examples of Charles Malik of Lebanon and Carlos Romulo of the Philippines, both of whom raised the issue of human rights in Bandung. With time, Malik became a right-wing Phalangist, deaf to the needs of non-Christians and Palestinians, while Romulo became a defender of the Ferdinand Marcos authoritarian regime in the Philippines.

[91] "... it is curious to see how much postcolonial despots often resemble their old colonial masters," writes Buruma (2005).

[92] Afshari (2007, 66).

[93] Moravcsik (2000) demonstrated this thesis on the analysis of support for the European Convention of Human Rights in the early 1950s. The champions of the convention were new democracies while established ones, led by Great Britain, strongly opposed two measures that limit sovereignty, i.e., compulsory jurisdiction and individual petitions. Similarly, during the negotiation of the UN Covenant on Civil and Political Rights "the most stable among modern democracies, including the United States and the United Kingdom, allied with authoritarian and totalitarian states like Soviet Union, China, South Africa, and Iran, in opposition to the inclusion of compulsory, enforceable commitments. The

authoritarians, they exhibit skepticism and active opposition to enforceable instruments. Many nondemocratic states supported the Universal Declaration of Human Rights, seeing in it a mechanism for global redistribution or an instrument in their anti-imperialist struggle while at the same time remaining certain that it may never be enforced. Western powers had the same hopes. In fact, they had good reason to accept an unenforceable international mechanism.

One surprising element of the post–World War II mechanism is the total absence of minority rights, both in the UN Charter and in the UDHR,[94] surprising in view of the role this issue played in the League of Nations, as well as of the minority-related violations and conflicts in the interwar period and after World War II. Buergenthal speaks about "relatively little interest" of the international community "in the establishment of international system for the protection of minority rights" during the formative years of the United Nations.[95] However, Mazower sees the absence of minority provisions as the logical consequence – and a central piece – of the entire system of international protection of rights after World War II.[96]

After the collapse of the minority protection offered within the League of Nations and particularly in view of the German atrocities during World War II, East European states clearly rejected any prospect of granting collective rights to German – or any other – minority. Czechoslovak and Polish leaders announced that they would not accept new minority treaties and sought the solution of the problem in expulsion of Germans from their territory. The three great powers made it clear that they would not oppose the implementation of this plan.[97]

This solution was convenient for the great powers. It was obvious that the Soviet Union would not allow international oversight of the treatment of minorities in its empire. England and France had been as reluctant to offer minority protection within theirs as they were after World War I.[98] The United States worried about its segregated racial minority. "It is scarcely surprising that none of the Big Three showed

alliance in favor of such commitments . . . included recently established democracies in continental Europe, Latin America, and Asia" (ibid., 244). One more example of the opposition of an established democracy to the limitation of its sovereignty for the sake of international commitments is the United States attitude to international justice: the rejection of the International Criminal Court with general jurisdiction and simultaneous support for the *ad hoc* tribunals for Rwanda, former Yugoslavia, and Cambodia.

94 The UN Charter contains a broad nondiscrimination clause; the UDHR has an equal protection clause in Article 7 in addition to a nondiscrimination clause in Article 2.

95 Buergenthal (1997, 720).

96 Mazower (2004).

97 See ibid., 387. Exiled Czechoslovak president Eduard Benes stated that Czechs and Germans will not be able to live together and argued for the transfer of population in as early as 1942. As to general mechanism for the protection of minority, Benes pointed to general human rights rather than specific national rights. See Benes (1942).

98 In 1919, the powers were against any general minority convention that would bind them; bilateral minority treaties concerned just some selected countries of East Central Europe.

the slightest desire for making [minority rights] the centerpiece of the new rights discourse. Behind the smokescreen of the rights of the individual, in other words, the corpse of the League's minority policies could be safely buried."[99] Minorities were no longer under special protection of the international community. They were to be protected as individuals by the emerging human rights regime.[100]

The new regime, however, offered rather limited protection.[101] Although the Covenant of the League of Nations had included a domestic jurisdiction clause, the UDHR did not. Even the UN Charter did not provide for domestic jurisdiction in courts. The League provided for the right to petition by individuals; the new regime did not. In fact, immediately after its formation in December 1946 (i.e., before the adoption of the UDHR), the Commission on Human Rights received many individual petitions concerning violations of rights. Soon afterward "the Commission was instructed in no uncertain terms to announce publicly that it had no power to take any action in response to charges by individuals about alleged human rights violations by governments."[102] Individual petitions that seemed a crucial element of rights were removed from international human rights.[103]

As we can see, there was nothing inevitable in the emergence of a human rights regime during and after World War II. The motivations of the major actors were complex, ambiguous, and, at times, contradictory. The only exception was the activity of nongovernmental organizations and civic movements that exerted pressure on governments for the adoption of an international bill of rights. Despite the toothless

---

[99] Mazower (2004, 389). Mazower says that the UN system may be perceived by cynics "not an advance on the League but in fact a step backward" (ibid., 396).

[100] It should be noted, however, that the International Covenant on Civil and Political Rights made an explicit reference to minorities ("In those states in which ethnic, religious or linguistic minorities exist, persons belonging to such minorities shall not be denied the rights, in community with other members of their group, to enjoy their own culture, to profess and practice their own religion, or to use their own language." Article 27.) With time, the mechanisms for the protection of minorities were further developed.

[101] "The higher human rights moved up the agenda, the greater the pressure for a further limitation on the new organization's ability to intervene in the domestic affairs of member states," notes Mazower (ibid., 393).

[102] Ibid., 395. See also Lauren (1998, 218) and Afshari (2007, 52). Mazower (2004, 395) suggests that a triggering incident for the U.S. position on this issue was the petition submitted to the United Nations in October 1947 by W. E. B. du Bois on behalf of the National Association for the Advancement of Colored People about racial discrimination in the United States.

[103] One of the most vocal critics of this limitation was a British jurist, Hersch Lauterpacht. When his book "The International Bill of the Rights of Man," written in 1943, went to print, the Dumbarton Oaks proposals for future international order were made public. The author added a note in which he warned that in the great powers' proposal the General Assembly of the United Nations that was supposed to be responsible for protecting human rights does not have power of enforcement (Lauterpacht 1945, 213–14). In a subsequent book, published in 1950 Lauterpacht declared "the natural right to petition" as a corollary of human rights (see Lauterpacht 1968, 221–51) and criticized the UN system for the lack of it (ibid., 286–92, 337, 375–7).

character of the Universal Declaration of Human Rights, and limited enforceability of the Covenants, human rights movements did not spare efforts to make use of these documents. Then, and only then, was the potential for such use significant. One reason for this was the multitude of values and ideas included in the UDHR – a result of a number of compromises.

A Compromise

The Declaration was both a compromise among and a synthesis of various traditions, values, and needs, many of which had never been articulated before in the language of rights. Most of these traditions were rooted in European social and philosophical thought, but these roots were diverse and the Declaration combined the two Western traditions of rights discussed above.[104] Although the very concept of civil and political rights, as well as their inalienability (mentioned in the Preamble), come from the liberal Anglo-American tradition, the crucial notion of dignity was brought in from Christian thought, particularly the philosophy of personalism represented by Jacques Maritain. This was also the philosophical source of the notion of free or full development of personality that runs through the Declaration.[105]

Although the "free development of human potential" could be understood as a type of the "pursuit of happiness" mentioned in the Declaration of Independence, it was probably much closer to the hearts of Marxists, for whom the full development of everyone's potential had been an essential element of Marx's concept of freedom.[106]

European conservatives could join both Christian philosophers and Marxists in supporting the importance of one's duties to the community, as emphasized in Article 29.1.[107] The inclusion of duties into the Declaration was also welcomed by Asians, for whom duties rather than rights had been an essential element of dignity. It also satisfied the representatives from Latin America, who had adopted, in May

---

[104] Glendon claims that the Declaration embodies the essence of the continental tradition, which was compatible with the traditions and aspirations of non-Western countries. "In the spirit of the latter vision, the Declaration's 'Everyone' is an individual who is constituted, in important ways, by and through relationships with others. 'Everyone' is envisioned as uniquely valuable in himself (there are three separate references to the free development of one's personality), but 'Everyone' is expected to act toward others 'in a spirit of brotherhood.' 'Everyone' is depicted as situated in a variety of specifically named, real-life relationships of mutual dependency: families, communities, religious groups, workplaces, associations, societies, cultures, nations and an emerging international order. Though its main body is devoted to basic individual freedoms, the Declaration begins with an exhortation to act in 'a spirit of brotherhood' and ends with community, order, and society," writes Glendon (2001, 227).

[105] See Articles 22; 26.2; and 29.

[106] See Walicki (1983).

[107] "Everyone has duties to the community in which the free and full development of his personality is entirely possible."

1948, the American Declaration of Rights and Duties that set forth individual duties in ten articles.[108]

Although they welcomed duties, Marxists – as well as liberals – were more reluctant to accept a number of provisions campaigned for by the conservative-Christian coalition, that is, that the family is "the natural and fundamental group unit of society and is entitled to protection by society and the State," that "parents have a prior right to chose the kind of education that shall be given to their children," or that "special care and assistance" should be offered to support motherhood and childhood.[109] In Article 17, which granted everyone "the right to own property," Marxists and socialists were satisfied by adding the words "alone as well as in association with others."

Finally, there was a broad coalition of Christians, Marxists, socialists, and social democrats who liked the idea of "social progress and better standards of living in greater freedom" mentioned in the Preamble. They were supported by the American New Dealers, who remembered the freedom from fear and freedom from want declared by President Roosevelt in 1941, as well as the emphasis on social security and economic justice present in both the Atlantic Charter and the Declaration of the United Nations.[110] The same coalition was supportive of the social and economic rights described in detail in Articles 22–26. These provisions had the unanimous support of representatives from the developing countries. According to Eleanor Roosevelt, the social and economic provisions had become, for them "a symbol of aspirations and needs of these countries. They did not understand or attach the same importance to civil and political rights as does the United States or some of the more developed countries (. . .) they look to [economic, social and cultural rights] as a lever which may help to raise them out of their present depressed conditions."[111]

The intelligentsia and intellectuals were pleased with the right to participate in culture and science. Those who believed in a classical individualistic concept of

---

[108] Latin American delegates to the Third Committee working on the draft Declaration insisted that the Universal Declaration of Human Rights should also enumerate the duties of individuals. But the majority of delegates rejected this proposal, agreeing on general statements of duties in Article 29. They decided that "while human beings undoubtedly owe duties to their societies, any effort to write such duties into international law on the basis of equality with human rights would provide governments with excuses to limit those rights. As a result, they decided not to list private duties at all" (Knox 2008, 3). An example of this danger may be seen in the African Charter of Human and Peoples' Rights (1961), which contains duties; some of them are "an invitation to the imposition of unlimited restrictions on the enjoyment of rights," writes Henkin et al. (1999, 348). Moreover, the final formulation avoided any reference to the duties of citizens vs. state authorities, thus rendering the community rather than the state the locus of human duties.

[109] Articles 17; 26.3; and 25.2, respectively.

[110] See Sunstein (2004, 61–950), Donnelly (2007), and Whelan and Donnelly (2007). See also discussion in chapter 3.

[111] Quoted in Whelan and Donnelly (2007, 930–1).

rights welcomed the provision on protection of the intellectual property of authors in Article 27.2.[112] At the same time, no single participant challenged the civil and political rights that were at the core of the liberal concept. The entire project was led in the spirit of cooperation and mutual enrichment. Glendon has noted that "there was remarkably little disagreement regarding its basic substance, despite intense wrangling over some specifics. At every stage, even the communist bloc and Saudi Arabia voted in favor of most of the articles when they were taken up one by one. The 'traditional' political and civil rights – the ones now most often labeled 'Western' – were the least controversial of all."[113]

All of the Declaration's provisions (except the right to free marriage in Article 16 and the right to change one's religion in Article 18, both challenged by Saudi Arabia) had strong support from a great majority of non-Western participants who hoped to take from various European traditions such principles and values as seemed important for their own people. Therefore, we can see the Declaration not merely as a compromise but as a unique synthesis of the various concepts of rights that had been hitherto formulated and advocated.

In view of future developments, it warrants repeating that an important element of this synthesis was the combination of freedom with economic security. Civil liberties and political rights on the one hand and social, economic, and cultural rights on the other seemed equally important from the point of view of the main goal of the Declaration – the preservation of world peace. The Declaration extended them beyond mere aspirations by creating moral grounds to claim rights.[114] It even went a step further by setting grounds for civic and political action toward changing the social and international order to be congruent with rights.[115] Its primary goal, however, was educational. The framers of the Declaration emphasized its cultural significance. They did not deal with the enforcement mechanisms, with criminal courts for the perpetrators of abuses, or with military interventions to stop such abuses – not only because such mechanisms were left to other agencies, notably the Security Council, but also because they believed that "culture is prior to law."[116]

[112] The most far-reaching departure from the liberal concept of rights was a right to "periodic holidays with pay" (Article 24) that later prompted Cranston to reject the entire concept of social and economic rights as "lofty ideas." See Cranston (1973, 65–71).

[113] Glendon (2001, 226).

[114] "Everyone is entitled to all the rights and freedoms set forth in this Declaration." (Article 2)

[115] Everyone is entitled to social and international order in which the rights and freedoms set forth in this Declaration can be fully realized (Article 28).

[116] Glendon (238–9) quotes some framers on this subject: Rene Cassin has said that "respect for human rights depends on the mentalities of individuals and social groups"; Charles Malik has suggested that before the aspirations are implemented, "men, cultures, and nations must first mature inwardly"; and P. C. Chang considered as the UDHR's main goal "to build up better human beings, and not merely to punish those who violate human rights."

This spirit of the framers in 1948 was best encapsulated in Article 26.2 of the Declaration.[117]

Human rights and the underlying theory were to become the subject of an educational effort that, in the minds of the framers, would bring the world closer to the standards and aspirations declared in the document.

Individual and Human Rights

There are significant differences between the eighteenth- and twentieth-century concepts of rights. The first concept can be summarized by the term *individual rights*, for rights were understood as located in the individual. However, they were not yet human because rights were reserved for just some individuals: namely, white male property owners. There are many other differences between individual and human rights. Below is a discussion of some of them.[118]

Although the primarily theoretical eighteenth-century concept of individual rights was created by philosophers, the twentieth-century idea of human rights was formulated by politicians and involved citizens. Lacking underlying theory, it was focused on political practice, even though it included some philosophical content in the guise of dignity. The theoretical basis for individual rights consisted of theories of natural law, natural rights, and the notion of the social contract, with right originating in a contract or – in a continental mutation – being granted by a benevolent ruler. Human rights spring from dignity – and from natural law in the Christian theory of rights – instead of originating in contract. Therefore, no granting of rights is needed and, consequently, they are considered inherent rather than inalienable. The contractual basis for individual rights is replaced by the notion of popular sovereignty underlying human rights. The goal of individual rights – to protect freedom and prevent tyranny – was expanded in human rights: they are to protect not only freedom but also peace and justice and they are to foster friendly relations between individuals and states. They aim to prevent not only tyranny but rebellion as well.

The main value protected by the twentieth-century theory of rights is human dignity rather than individual autonomy, as was the case in the eighteenth century. Although individual rights were closely linked to the economic principles of the new market economy, twentieth-century rights included the needs of industrial workers; moreover, many specific rights and institutions make little sense outside of

---

[117] "Education shall be directed to the full development of the human personality and to the strengthening of respect for human rights and fundamental freedoms. It shall promote understanding, tolerance and friendship among all nations, racial and religious groups, and shall further the activities of the United Nations for the maintenance of peace."

[118] The following comparison expands the ideas first presented by Henkin (in Henkin et al. 1999, 280–4.)

the industrial setting.[119] Individual rights were a political principle that had vertical application between individual citizens and the state. Human rights are not only a political principle but also a moral one, whose implementation depends primarily on the education of citizens and state elites alike. But the application of human rights goes beyond the relations between citizens and the state; rights are also applicable nonvertically to relations between individuals and private parties. This horizontal aspect of human rights goes beyond mere claim rights, including duties that every individual may have toward others and toward society as a whole.

Human rights are universal. In this sense, they belong to every human being. They are also more broadly defined than individual rights, the latter being limited to civil liberties and political rights with a strong emphasis on property. Human rights also include social and economic benefits, as well as other solidarity rights – and they give much weaker protection to property. In the International Covenant on Civil and Political Rights, there exists no provision on the right to property; the formulation adopted in the UDHR includes collective property. We can say that eighteenth-century rights were necessary in a middle-class civil society that wanted protection from absolutist intrusion and to gain access to power. Twentieth-century rights, by contrast, were more needed for (and demanded by) the weak, the poor, and the marginalized.

The twentieth-century concept of rights opens the door for the so-called third-generation rights (such as the right to peace, to development or to clean environment), which do include some group rights. The protection and implementation of these positive rights, however, implies a new role for the state. Consequently, although the eighteeth-century concept focused primarily on freedoms from the state and assumed a passive, or protective, state, the idea of human rights implies a much more active state, one that has many obligations toward its citizens.

Individual rights were domestic. Ideally, they were enshrined in enforceable constitutions or bills of rights. They were to be protected by a number of internal measures, beginning with petitions and court cases, all the way to the right to resist as a last resort. In the case of a continued violation of rights, resistance was justified; this was the element of Lockean theory that Thomas Jefferson and his collaborators had used to justify the American claim to independence. In contrast, the twentieth-century concept of human rights did not grant such a right, for it would not have been reconcilable with the principle of state sovereignty dominant in the arrangements following World War II.[120] Rather, the twentieth-century notion accepted the principle of state sovereignty over its citizens and made human rights international.

---

[119] Examples include the right to work in conditions of unemployment or holidays with pay, in Article 24.

[120] The Preamble to the UDHR talks about "rebellion against tyranny and oppression" as the recourse of "last resort" to which people may be compelled. This is based, however, on the premise that if

Human rights began to form a code of conduct for states, simultaneously implying that when a given state violates this code other states will exert pressure to bring the perpetrator to order.[121]

One can talk about eighteenth-century rights in terms of judicial enforcement (or rebellion). In the case of twentieth-century rights, however, the more proper term would be *implementation*. In some cases, this would include legislation and enforcement. But for a number of aspirational rights and standards that cannot be enforced in a justiciable way, implementation remains possible. Often gradual, it takes place through the enactment of applicable state policies or as a result of actions by the international community, such as foreign aid.

This difference between the eighteenth- and twentieth-century concepts of rights is reflected in the different mechanisms introduced by international human rights law within the framework of the United Nations and the European system of the protection of rights that includes the European Convention for the protection of Human Rights and Fundamental Freedoms (adopted in 1950 by the Council of Europe) and the Charter of Fundamental Rights of the European Union ("solemnly proclaimed" by the European Parliament, the Council of the European Union and European Commission in December 2000[122]). Although the UN system embodies the concept of human rights, the European Convention enforces individual rights, extending them beyond the boundaries of national states to citizens of all member states of the Council of Europe.[123] Every citizen of a country that is member of the Council of Europe – after exhausting all available legal remedies in one's own state – has

---

human rights are protected by the rule of law, people will not need to rebel. There exists no explicit or implicit right to resist in the catalog of human rights.

[121] Human rights only reluctantly weakened the principle of state sovereignty by granting an extremely limited and ineffective right to individual complaint in the First Optional Protocol to ICCPR. At their inception, human rights were formulated as moral standards and aspirations; therefore, framers did not pay much attention to the way in which such international pressure would take place. Military intervention or criminal responsibility for heads of state were not even discussed during the preparation of the UDHR.

[122] An adapted version of the Charter was proclaimed on December 12, 2007, in Strasbourg, before the signing of the Treaty of Lisbon, according to which after the ratification of the Treaty the Charter will be legally binding in all member states of the EU (except Poland and the United Kingdom that restricted the enforcement of the Charter on their territories). The need for a separate charter emerged in 1996, after the European Court of Justice decided that the European Union does not have a power to become a party to the European Convention of Human Rights. Thus, EU institutions would not be bound by the European Convention. The final EU Charter differed from the European Convention including a number of social and solidarity rights that were not included in the ECHR. (The Charter has six chapters dealing with dignity, freedoms, equality, solidarity, citizens' rights, and justice.)

[123] Moravcsik (2000, 234) notes that advocates of the European system saw it "not simply as a continuation of the UN system, but also as a pragmatic *reaction* to it. The UN system was widely viewed as too broad to be effective; the ECHR system was designed to be potentially enforceable, which required that the scope of rights be narrowed considerably."

the individual right to appeal to the European Court of Human Rights[124] Thus, the European Convention can be seen as an extension of domestic protection on a larger, multinational scale. An individual is still a claimant, calling her state to accountability before a court whose jurisdiction the state has accepted. The court makes a ruling in which a given action of the state may be held to contradict the European Convention (which in practice is almost like rendering it unconstitutional or illegal in the internal legal order) and may award compensation for harm and suffering.[125]

In the system of the United Nations, by contrast, a victim of violations has limited standing. The case is brought against his or her state not by him or her but by other states. The protection of human rights ceases to be a matter between the offending state and an individual and it becomes a matter between two or more states. Thus, international human rights by definition belong to the realm of international relations. This makes them prone to abuse and double standards.

THE RIGHTS REVOLUTION

International Human Rights

It took 20 years to adopt two enforceable human rights covenants within the UN framework. Kenneth Roth and Joanna Weschler suggest that the purpose of the exclusive focus of the UN Commission on Human Rights on drafting human rights treaties and standards was "to avoid even the discussion of human rights violations in specific countries."[126] Although the drafting was almost complete by 1953, the covenants were shelved for more than 10 years because of ideological rivalry and the Cold War. In the Soviet bloc, Stalin's terror reigned and the very mention of human rights could land one in prison. China had fallen into Communism. Indeed,

---

[124] The justiciability of human rights was the reason why a number of rights present in the Universal Declaration were missing from the European Convention. In addition to social and economic rights, the European Convention does not include the right to recognition as a person before the law (provided in Article 6 of the UDHR), freedom of movement (13), the right to asylum (14), the right to nationality (15), or the right to take part in government and periodic elections (21). According to Alexandre Berenstain, to be included in the European Convention, "any right must be fundamental and enjoy general recognition, and be capable of sufficiently precise definition to lay legal obligations on a State, rather than simply constitute a general rule" (quoted in Whelan and Donnelly 2007, 942).

[125] In the 1990s, former Soviet republics in Caucasus were admitted to the Council of Europe – despite their poor standing on human rights and democratic institutions. Subsequently, the European Court faced a dilemma: whether to use different standards for old and new members or to lower all standards. In addition, the European Court was overloaded to the point of inefficiency with cases from these new member states. To amend the situation, the Court has been sending back many of the cases to national jurisdictions – claims about the slow judicial procedures of the member states in particular.

[126] Roth and Weschler (1998, 1).

Western European states had assured human rights for their citizens in the European Convention of 1950, but they were suddenly even further away from universal human rights than during World War II. European colonial powers sought to stop national liberation movements unleashed before 1948. France went to war to perpetuate its colonial rule in Indochina and Algeria; Great Britain used force to suppress the Mau Mau uprising in Kenya. Western representatives in the United Nations' Third Committee argued for a special clause that would exempt their colonies from the application of human rights covenants. René Cassin, one of the main drafters of the UDHR, now argued in favor of relativism, asserting that "human rights might 'endanger public order' among backward colonial populations, and 'subject different people to uniform obligations.'"[127]

The United States emphasized its sovereignty rather than international human rights. It had a well-developed system of constitutional and statutory rights that were enforceable in domestic courts. Equally enforceable domestically were international treaties ratified by the United States. This prompted the U.S. government's caution about ratifying aspirational human rights declarations and covenants. For that reason Secretary of State John Foster Dulles announced that the United States "would not become party to any human rights treaty approved by the United Nations."[128] U.S. citizens had enjoyed better protection than could be offered by international instruments, but this was limited only to those rights that were accepted by the U.S. legal system. It did not include the rights of Black Americans or other vulnerable groups not covered by the U.S. system of rights. In the atmosphere of the Cold War, the U.S. government did not support individual human rights.[129]

At that time, the notion of human rights was rarely used or mentioned by political leaders – or by those who opposed them. Human rights were not invoked during the Berlin uprising of 1953 or the Hungarian uprising 3 years later. True, some Western intellectuals criticized violations of civil liberties and political rights taking place in the East and West, but their governments were basically indifferent to human rights abuses. Communist governments stressed social promises and progress. In the 1950s, only the leaders of Third World countries seemed interested in human rights. As noted, leaders from Asia and Africa reasserted their commitment to human

---

[127] Quoted in Burke (2006, 962). Burke summarizes the arguments of a Belgian representative as follows: "Human rights were for advanced, civilized people, not those in African and Asian colonies" (ibid.).

[128] Quoted in Ignatieff (1999, 59).

[129] The human rights scene in the United States at this time was vividly described by Ignatieff: "McCarthy was persecuting the liberal internationalists of the previous era; Republican Senator John Bricker fulminated against UN human rights documents as 'completely foreign to American law and tradition'. One of John Foster Dulles's first acts as the incoming secretary of state was to pull Mrs. Roosevelt off the Commission on Human Rights at the UN ... America effectively withdrew all efforts to turn the Declaration into a binding covenant. Successive secretaries of state, from Dulles to Kissinger, regarded human rights as a tedious obstacle to the pursuit of great power politics" (ibid.).

rights at the 1955 Bandung Conference. But that commitment was motivated by decolonization, national self-determination, and the redistribution of resources on a global scale and had very little to do with domestic protection of rights.

During the thaw that followed Stalin's death and the twentieth Congress of the Communist Party of the Soviet Union, the international situation improved enough for the adoption of human rights covenants by the UN General Assembly in 1966. The International Covenant on Civil and Political Rights obliged state parties to respect the rights listed within the document and provided for international mechanisms of control in optional protocols. The International Covenant on Economic, Social and Cultural Rights listed the ideals state parties were to aim for and encouraged them to include a number of selected rights into domestic law (although not necessarily into constitutions). The division of human rights into two documents – originally proposed by India – was not a result of the Cold War conflict, reflecting instead the consciousness of the different means for implementation of the two categories of rights[130] rather than a perception of their importance or hierarchy. "The covenants simply recognized that most states in the 1950s and 1960s had considerable capability to create subjective civil and political rights (Hohfeldian claim rights[131]) in national law for all individuals, whereas most states lacked the combination of will and resources needed to provide comparable legal guarantees for most economic and social rights," write Wheelan and Donelly.[132]

It took another 10 years for the covenants to be ratified and enter into force. By then, however, the first steps toward the international enforcement of human rights had been taken. The UDHR did not provide for monitoring or reporting on the implementation of human rights standards. As noted, by 1947, the Commission decided that it had no power to take any action related to individual complaints.[133] This situation changed when numerous African states in the UN attempted to put an

---

[130] The United States did not ratify the ICESCR primarily because it could make many aspirational rights enforceable in U.S. courts. The skepticism toward ICESCR was also a result of the so-called "market revival" and general departure from New Deal ideas. In the 1970s, the U.S. Supreme Court moved further away from the recognition of social rights: "Nixon appointees stopped an unmistakable trend in the direction of recognizing social and economic rights," writes Sunstein (2004, 168–9).

[131] Wesley Hohfeld introduced, in 1913, the distinction between claim right and other rights. He suggested that the word "claim" is the best synonym for "right" in its proper meaning. The essence of rights consists in someone else's duty to grant what one has a right to. In this sense, claim-rights differ from freedoms, which include liberties, immunities, and powers. Liberties suggest the freedom of choice; immunities define the spheres in which we are protected from other people; and powers give us permission to do something to others. It is worth noting that for Hohfeld *liberties* originate in privilege, which can be considered an exemption from a duty that others have (see Hohfeld 1923, 42–3). *Immunity*, in turn, amounts to the exemption from being subject to a power that others need to obey (see ibid., 60–1).

[132] 2007, 933.

[133] See Roth and Weschler (1998, 1), and Mazower (2004, 395). The Commission did not investigate the observance of human rights on its own initiative.

end to apartheid in South Africa. From 1963 onward, the Security Council passed a number of resolutions that made reference to the Universal Declaration of Human Rights and called on the government of South Africa to take specific measures dealing with detentions, fair trial, amnesty for political prisoners, suspension of death penalties, return of exiles, and other human rights issues.[134] As part of the UN antiapartheid policy, the Economic and Social Council adopted, in June 1967, Resolution 1235 authorizing the Commission on Human Rights "to make a thorough study of situations which reveal a consistent pattern of violations of human rights." In 1970, the ECOSOC Resolution 1503 created a procedure toward this end by authorizing the UN Sub-Commission on the Prevention of Discrimination and Protection of Minorities "to develop a mechanism for dealing with communications from individuals and groups revealing 'a consistent pattern of gross and reliably attested violations of human rights.'"[135] Being originally meant for South Africa, these measures were supported both by the Soviet bloc and by Western states. Their potential, however, was universal. Initially, complaints were accepted from state governments only. With time, the Commission on Human Rights developed a set of so-called special procedures that included working groups, special rapporteurs, independent experts, and special representatives that could monitor a given human rights situation in a particular country or specific types of violations globally.[136] In March 1976, the First Optional Protocol to the International Covenant on Civil and Political Rights entered into force. It introduced a mechanism for complaints about violations of rights under the Covenant to be submitted by individuals and groups after having exhausted domestic remedies. The UN Human Rights Committee was empowered to consider such complaints, to bring it to the attention of the relevant party, and to forward its conclusions to the complainant and to the state involved.[137]

---

[134] This was a departure from Security Council's principle of strict separation between peace and security (that belonged to the Council competencies) on the one hand and human rights (which – as the Security Council maintained – were beyond its mandate and interests) on the other. (See Weschler 2004, 55.)

[135] Buergenthal (1997, 710).

[136] Parallel to the admission of individual communications (complaints) is the fact that prosecutors at the UN International Tribunals (ICTY, ICTR, and ICC) are investigating cases of individual responsibility of perpetrators of international crimes rather than deal with the responsibility of states. This may turn out to be a more effective deterrent against mass violations than sanctions imposed on states. Buergenthal (1997, 717) writes that the growth of terrorism, organized crime on an international scale, and private armies of war lords "are increasingly forcing the international community to explore the ways not only to hold the state responsible but also to act directly against individuals whom the state is too weak or unwilling to punish."

[137] By the end of 2008, 111 states became parties to the First Optional Protocol. Similar mechanisms were introduced by optional protocols to the UN Convention on the Elimination of All Forms of Discrimination against Women (in 2000) and to the UN Convention on the Rights of Persons with Disabilities (in 2008).

This development of instruments for the international protection of human rights would not be possible without the revolutionary change in the attitude toward rights by governments and societies that took place in the 1960s and 1970. It was then that human rights began to play an important role in international politics.

The Restoration of Rights

The politicization of human rights was a relatively late event in the Cold War. Earlier on, in the late 1940s and early 1950s, the Cold War had been fought not with ideas but with the increasing militarization of Europe by American and Soviet troops. The main instruments of this war were NATO and the Warsaw Pact, nuclear tests, the American money helping to rebuild Western Europe under the Marshall Plan, and U.S. military aircraft carrying food to Berlin during the Soviet blockade of 1948–1949.

The weapons of the communists consisted of money, arms, and ideology. Slogans of equality, social justice, and the end of neocolonial exploitation constituted a great-sounding justification for a worldwide communist mission, accompanied of course by criticism of Western colonialism and American racism, as well as by reports of the apparent economic successes of communist countries. In 1957, such a success story materialized in the form of the Soviet satellite Sputnik.

By the mid-1960s, however, the picture of the Soviet empire was no longer so idyllic. In fact, by 1956, at the twentieth congress of the Communist Party of the Soviet Union, Soviet leader Nikita Khrushchev had already revealed the horrendous crimes committed under Stalinism. This secret speech soon leaked its way out into the world. After a short thaw period, during which some victims were rehabilitated,[138] the repressions against critics of the regime and dissents increased again.[139] Controlled by politburos and armies, the economies of communist countries were unable to adapt to the demands of the intensive phase of industrialization. They fell into stagnation instead. Attempts at reform from within ended in 1968,

---

[138] Interestingly, the party was much more interested in the persecuted communists (who comprised a minor fraction of all victims) than in the plight of "ordinary Soviet citizens"; only a handful of the latter were rehabilitated. (See Chalidze 1974, 51.) This is one of a number of reasons why the Khrushchev's policies can be best understood as "the bill of rights for the party apparatchiks."

[139] A secret report of December 29, 1975, addressed by Yuri Andropov, the Chairman of the Committee for State Security to the USSR Council of Ministers, says that about 1,583 persons sentenced between 1967 and 1975 for anti-Soviet agitation and propaganda (Article 70 of the Criminal Code of the USSR) and for dissemination of allegations were known to be untrue, which defame the Soviet regime (Article 190.I). In addition, between 1971 and 1974, 63,108 persons were subjected to "prophylactic work to prevent crimes against the state." Andropov claimed that "prophylactic work" disrupted in the "formative stage" the activity of 1,839 anti-Soviet groups. "Such measures as stripping certain persons of their Soviet citizenship and exiling them abroad (Solzhenytsin, Chalidze, Maksimov, Krasin, Yesenin-Volpin, and others) have proven to be effective as well," claimed Andropov (1975, 4).

with purges of revisionists from the communist party in Poland and the invasion of a reforming Czechoslovakia by Warsaw Pact troops. Dissidents and oppositionists began to appear in Soviet bloc countries, seeking legitimacy for their calls for freedom and expressing their reliance on Western support. As it happened, they found both in the idea of human rights.

In the other camp of the Cold War, developments took a different course. The Western European states – however reluctantly and not without bloodshed – had let go of their colonies. In the United States, the Supreme Court initiated the rights revolution, directed against racism and discrimination. Black and White Americans participated hand in hand to form the civil rights movement, which initially gained support from the Supreme Court and eventually also from presidents Kennedy and Johnson. The latter persuaded Congress to adopt civil rights legislation that made legal equality one of the principles of American domestic policy. The American Civil Liberties Union solidified human rights legislation and – through deliberate strategic litigation – dismantled the legacy of Senator McCarthy.[140]

With their newly clean hands, Western leaders discovered in human rights a new weapon in their battle with communism. After the forced resignation of president Nixon that followed the Watergate affair, sensitivity to rights heightened in the United States. In 1974, Nixon's successor, president Gerald Ford, created the post of Undersecretary for Human Rights at the State Department. Consequently, human rights were added on as a "third basket," augmenting the agreements on cooperation and security in Europe.[141] In 1977, president Jimmy Carter and his national security adviser Zbigniew Brzezinski adopted human rights as a major principle of American foreign policy.

After the August 1, 1975, signing of the Final Act of the Helsinki Conference on Security and Cooperation in Europe, human rights became an accepted standard of international conduct. The signatory states could monitor the observance of human rights and appeal for ending violations of rights by other governments that were party to the Agreement.[142]

---

[140] See Neier (2003, 1–145). In an interview given to this author in June 2002, Neier explained that, under his leadership as executive director (1965–1970), the ACLU acted in defense of five broad categories of rights: freedom of inquiry and expression; due process of law (fairness); equal protection of laws (anti-discrimination); prohibition on cruel and unusual punishment; and the right to privacy. The ACLU made efforts "to defend rights of women to obtain abortions, opposed the compulsory commitment of drug addicts and supported their rights to obtain methadone maintenance – a novelty at the time – and launched efforts to protect the rights of classes of people who were not previously the object of civil liberty advocacy, such as primary and secondary school students, soldiers, juveniles in detention, prisoners, and mental patients. At the time, much of this was revolutionary," writes Neier (2003, 7).

[141] See Korey (1998, 229–48).

[142] The CSCE was institutionalized, first by establishing follow-up meetings in Belgrade (1977–1978), Madrid (1980–1983), Vienna (1986–1989), Copenhagen (1990), Helsinki (1992), Budapest (1994),

The Covenant on Civil and Political Rights and the Helsinki Agreement provided international recognition and support for the human rights groups emerging in the Soviet bloc. They found legal basis in the right "to know one's rights" inserted into the Helsinki Agreement.[143] In May 1976, a group of Soviet dissidents founded the Moscow Helsinki Group, the first human rights organization to attempt to work openly in the communist world.[144] Similar organizations and movements were soon formed in Poland and Czechoslovakia. In June 1976, with dissenting intellectuals in Poland rushing to defend the rights of workers, human rights became an effective instrument for mobilizing mass support for the opposition.[145] These developments gave new impetus to the emerging international human rights movement.

The movement was a reaction to a number of often unrelated events in many countries.[146] Perhaps the first was the public exposure of the atrocities committed by General Augusto Pinochet after the 1973 coup d'état in Chile.[147] Almost immediately after the coup, the Archbishop of Santiago took steps to defend the foreign advisors to president Salvador Allende whose lives had been threatened by the Pinochet junta. This effort evolved into the formation of the Vicaría de la Solidaridad and, soon afterward, a number of Christian democrats created the Chilean Commission on Human Rights. In India, massive reprisals against the opposition following the

---

Vienna and Lisbon (1996), and Vienna and Istanbul (1999). In 1995, it was turned into the Organization for Security and Co-operation in Europe. Despite initial setbacks (the 1977–1978 meeting in Belgrade did not produce consensus), with time the CSCE made progress in upgrading standards and seeking precision in the original formulations of the Helsinki Document. The conference in Vienna, held in 1986–1989, was very successful. Korey (1991) demonstrates that a turning point was the adoption by the U.S. delegation of a policy to link Western concessions in the field of security (demanded by Moscow) with increased respect for human rights in the Soviet bloc. Another important factor was Mikhail Gorbachev's cooperation during the 1986–1989 meetings in Vienna.

[143] In Chapter VII of the Helsinki Agreement, titled "Respect for Human Rights and Fundamental Freedoms," the signatory states agreed to monitoring the observance of human rights and confirmed "the right of the individual to know and act upon his rights and duties in this field."

[144] Human rights organizations existed in the Soviet Union before 1976. The first one was the Committee on Human Rights founded in 1966 by Valery Chalidze. An unprecedented fact was that the Moscow Helsinki Group publicly announced its formation, as well as the names and addresses of its founders.

[145] It is important to note that during the 1968 intellectual and student protests in Poland claims for more freedom were justified on the grounds of the 1952 Communist Constitution and not in terms of human rights. Similarly, in the USSR, intellectuals taking part in the first human rights demonstration on December 5, 1965 – protesting against the arrest of Andrey Sinyavsky and Juli Daniel – shouted slogans: "Respect the Constitution, the Basic Law of the USSR." "Defenders of human rights in the USSR are still calling for observance of the constitutional guarantees of rights and for the admission of the public to political trials," wrote Chalidze before the Helsinki Agreement (1974, 53).

[146] For more on the events in the late 1970s that prompted the growth of human rights movements, see Neier (2003, 149–52).

[147] There had been many violent coups d'état before Pinochet. But his was the first in the television age. TV reporters were able to bring immediate footage from the scene to audiences all over the world.

introduction of military rule by Indira Gandhi in 1975 led to the relaunch of the India Civil Liberties Union. The human rights movement was further fuelled by support for victims of dictatorships in Latin America and elsewhere, as well as by anti-apartheid campaigns. The 1976 Soweto Riots and the murder of Steve Biko brought about worldwide awareness of gross violations of human rights in South Africa. The Nobel Peace Prize awarded in 1977 to Amnesty International (established in 1961 in connection with an international campaign to pardon prisoners of conscience in Portugal) was a sign of recognition and a boost of confidence for human rights activists worldwide. In 1978, a number of other human rights organizations were created, including Human Rights Watch (renamed from Helsinki Watch), the Lawyers Committee for Human Rights, and the International Human Rights Law Group.[148] Human rights had become, at last, a truly powerful idea.

However, the concept of human rights that became popular in the 1970s was different from the one that had been formulated in the UDHR some 30 years earlier. The Soviets and the Pinochets of the world were violating civil liberties and political rights – not social ones. In fact, the Soviets took great (and otherwise false) pride in their protection of social and economic rights. The West, in turn, accused the Soviets (quite correctly) of violations of civil liberties and political rights. Meanwhile, United States foreign policy could not promote, or even condone, social and economic rights that the United States itself did not recognize. Thus, civil and political rights became what Western governments concentrated their attentions on. Similarly, the emerging nongovernmental human rights movement was forming itself around monitoring and protesting the violations of civil liberties and political rights taking place in Chile, India, South Africa, and the Soviet Union. Social and economic rights dropped out of the picture and would long remain neglected by Amnesty International, Human Rights Watch, and other international human rights organizations and by private and governmental international donors.

One aspect of this process was the "juridification" of the concept of human rights. The ability to claim rights in courts, known as "justiciability," was elevated to a constitutive element; if something was not justiciable it could not be considered belonging to human rights.[149] Although justiciability is an indispensable element of civil rights, in 1948 human rights were defined much more broadly, including also aspirations that were to be achieved gradually through political process. The positive obligations of states, constitutional directives, state tasks, and other instruments were to serve human rights as well. The narrowing of rights to what is merely justiciable weakened these political aspects of rights, as well as the moral dimension of human rights as a kind of yardstick for the assessment of existing laws (or a sort of higher

---

[148] See Korey (1998) and Weschler (1998).
[149] A textbook example of this reasoning is provided by Cranston (1973).

law). Justiciability is not the only measure of a given institution's moral value – nor is it even the highest.[150]

Rights and Duties in the Socialist and Catholic Concepts of Rights

This change in the content of human rights raised questions outside the West. Communist authorities and scholars retaliated with what was then called the "socialist concept of human rights."[151] In essence, the idea followed Karl Marx's claim that the liberal concept of freedom petrifies an unjust social structure, guaranteeing equal freedom to the rich, who can exercise it for their own benefit, and to the homeless or poor, who cannot translate formal freedoms or legal rights into anything useful to them.[152] Accordingly, the socialist concept emphasized the priority of social and economic rights over civil liberties and political rights.

In theory, the socialist concept limited the discussion of rights to positive law only and rejected the roots of rights in natural law or in a sense of justice. Following the continental European tradition, it perceived rights as a grant from the state rather than inherent and inalienable attributes of human nature. It emphasized the primacy of public interests, as represented by the state, over interests or rights of individuals. It substituted legal and procedural safeguards of rights with so-called "material guarantees." For example, freedom of expression was guaranteed by "public" ownership (in practice, state ownership) of the media (press, radio, television, publishing houses, etc.), rather than by any ability to claim the violation of such freedom in a court.[153] There existed no legal remedies from arbitrary administrative decisions, nor were there any independent courts that could make use of the formal rights included in constitutions.

The socialist conception of rights introduced – and perverted – the correlation of rights and duties. Every enforceable right implies a corresponding legal duty. If X has

---

[150] "The assumption that justiciability is evidence of higher value, however, is ludicrous. Access to courts is a poor, even perverse, measure of social [recognition of] value. For example, national defense is a paramount obligation of the state but no country permits the individual to take the government to court if it fails to meet these obligations. Although judicial remedies do usually enhance the value of a right to a right-holder, justiciability does not exhaust the essential functions of rights, and justiciable rights are not the only kind of rights. Even legal rights are not always justiciable" (Whelan and Donnelly 2007, 934).

[151] For a description of the socialist concept of rights and its evolution, see Wieruszewski (1988).

[152] See Marx (1843). On Marx's concept of freedom and his critique of rights, see Haughey (1982), Walicki (1983), and Nordahl (1992).

[153] For example, Article 50 of the 1977 Soviet Constitution provided for the freedom of speech, freedom of the press and freedoms of assembly, meeting, street processions, and demonstrations. Guarantee of these rights was formulated as follows: "Exercise of these political freedoms is ensured by putting public buildings, streets and squares at the disposal of the working people and their organizations, by broad dissemination of information, and by the opportunity to use the press, television, and radio."

a right, someone has a duty. "If the choice which is provided by full liberty seems to be one ingredient in our ordinary concept of rights, another such ingredient seems to be the imposition of some constraints on others."[154] Similarly, mere declarations of intentions, even if they assume the form of constitutional provisions, cannot be considered rights when they lack the acknowledgment of the state's duty to enforce them. Although human rights imply corresponding duties, such duties fall on the state and should not be confused with the duties of citizens.[155]

The correlation between rights and duties has been emphasized in the social teachings of the Catholic Church.[156] Pope John XXIII discussed this issue in his *Pacem in Terris* encyclical of 1963. Both rights and duties originate in natural law, which "in conferring the one imposes the other."[157] This correlation of rights and duties takes two forms. First, a person who has rights needs to fulfill duties. These duties, however, are strictly related to each right, binding the very person who claims the right. In some sense, such duties can be interpreted as a requirement for self-discipline: "Thus, for example, the right to live involves the duty to preserve one's life; the right to a decent standard of living, the duty to live in a becoming fashion; the right to be free to seek out the truth, the duty to devote oneself to an ever deeper and wider search for it." Second, there exists a reciprocity of rights and duties between persons: if one has a right, others have a duty to respect it.[158]

This theory of rights and duties was elaborated on in *The Church and Human Rights*, the official document on human rights issued on December 10, 1974, the twenty-sixth anniversary of the Universal Declaration by the Papal Commission Iustitia et Pax.[159] It is important to note that Catholic social teachings do not postulate

---

[154] Precisely because of the lack of corresponding duties, Sumner (1987, 35) challenges Thomas Hobbes's concept of natural rights, allegedly enjoyed by everyone in the state of nature: "a mere half-liberty by itself, without any supporting duties of assistance or noninterference imposed on others, does not constitute a right."

[155] Citizens' duties were not listed in the Declaration of Independence, the United States Constitution, the Bill of Rights, or the 1789 French Declaration; they first appeared in the 1795 Constitution of France.

[156] During preparatory work on the Universal Declaration of Human Rights, Jacques Maritain insisted that the Declaration also includes human duties, as well as rights of the family. (See Mazurek 2001, 129.)

[157] Pope John XXIII, section 28.

[158] "It follows that in human society one man's natural right gives rise to a corresponding duty in other men; the duty, that is, of recognizing and respecting that right. Every basic human right draws its authoritative force from the natural law, which confers it and attaches to it its respective duty. Hence, to claim one's rights and ignore one's duties, or only half fulfill them, is like building a house with one hand and tearing it down with the other" (Pope John XXIII, section 30).

[159] According to Kądziela (1977, 56) the correlation between rights and duties suggested in this document means that rights necessitate "the assumption by individuals of duties which derive from identical rights of other people" and of such additional duties "which result from the responsibility for social life. (. . .) The acceptance of such duties results in the limitations imposed on individual and collective freedoms and, above all, in the rejection of the individualist vision of absolute freedom." This interpretation reinforces the similarity of duties to the Christian concept of self-discipline.

state enforcement of social obligations. But that was precisely what the Communists did. Socialist constitutionalism developed a theory that the enjoyment of rights of the individual can be contingent on the performance of his duties toward the state and society.[160] In the late 1970s, Communist authorities in Poland unsuccessfully attempted to put such a provision into the amendment to the Constitution. In the Soviet Union, the lexical concept "social parasites" came to denote people who did not fulfill their duties and consequently could be deprived of rights.[161] In 1981, with the introduction of martial law in Poland, the authorities imposed a "right to work" for all males between the ages of 18 and 45; failure to comply formed grounds for deprivation of rights and possible imprisonment. Such a position is impossible to defend on the basis of human rights, chiefly because it results in using the concept of duties to arbitrarily limit the rights of individuals – hence its usefulness in suppressing political opposition.

An important aspect of the socialist concept of rights was its emphasis on economic and social equality and the conviction that there can be "no freedom without bread."

This claim was challenged by the very evolution of socialist economy and society. One of the basic tenets of the 1980–1981 Solidarity movement in Poland was, in fact, that there can be "no bread without freedom."[162] One of the shortfalls of centrally planned economies was that they did not provide for market feedback on the results of economic decisions. Consequently, such feedback could be provided only by independent unions and other associations or by free media coupled with freedom of expression. In the absence of a market and the necessary freedoms, there was no way to have a functioning economy. With the growing inefficiency of the economic system and a deepening social crisis, the very same philosophers and legal theoreticians who had created the socialist concept of rights began to change their minds. Now they called for the acknowledgment of individual interests, stronger protection of civil liberties and political rights, and the introduction of procedural guarantees of rights, as well as for the establishment of such institutions as administrative courts, the ombudsman for citizens' rights and constitutional courts.[163]

As we shall see, some elements of the socialist concept endured socialism itself, adopted by new critics of human rights representing non-Western governments or speaking in the name of non-European cultures. In the non-Western world, social and economic rights were emphasized for many reasons, while civil and political rights were often criticized as an instrument of Western domination or, in more

[160] A precedent in Article 7.1 of the 1935 Constitution of Poland provided that political rights were to be awarded according to one's efforts and merits in the service (performance of duties) to the state.

[161] Among such duties was a duty to work. A number of Soviet dissidents, including Andrey Siniyavski and the late Nobel laureate Josip Brodsky, were first fired from work and banned from any job in the state-controlled economy – and subsequently tried as "social parasites" and sentenced to exile in labor camps in Siberia.

[162] See Osiatyński (1990, 297–8; 1991, 832–7; 2000, 36–8).

[163] See Wieruszewski (1988).

recent terminology, a tool of globalization. The final declaration of the 1993 Vienna World Conference on Human Rights held that "all human rights are universal, indivisible and interdependent, and interrelated. The international community must treat human rights globally in a fair and equal manner, on the same footing and with the same emphasis."[164] Even today, debates about the meaning of human rights still concern setting priorities between the different categories of rights or understanding what the notions of interconnectedness and indivisibility of human rights really entail.

NEW CHALLENGES

Over time, human rights have become a recognized code of conduct, making their way into a majority of contemporary constitutions and providing a standard for relations between the state and the citizen. Although they were not fully respected and often were violated, human rights were what provided the moral legitimacy for the demands of dissidents and others who fought against authoritarian regimes and tyrannies in every part of the world. In the 1980s, human rights motivated the students who called for a boycott of South Africa, aiding the internal struggle that led to the abolition of apartheid. Human rights also played a crucial role in the battle against communism, accelerating its moral bankruptcy and final collapse.

In the 1990s, human rights were advancing to the center of international relations. Paragraph 4 of the 1993 Vienna Declaration on Human Rights stated that "the promotion and protection of *all* human rights is a legitimate concern of the international community." Thus, one obstacle to the implementation and protection of rights was rejected: namely, "the artificial distinction between domestic and international human rights concerns."[165] Also refuted were the most radial arguments against human rights based on cultural relativism. Paragraph 5 announced that "all human rights are universal, indivisible and interdependent and interrelated." Considered similarly "interdependent and mutually reinforcing" were democracy, development, and respect for human rights and fundamental freedoms. The Vienna Declaration also increased the catalog of human rights by adding rights that had turned out to be inadequately protected, such as the rights of refugees and internally displaced persons, the rights of minorities and indigenous people, the rights of women and of children, the rights of the disabled, and rights emphasizing humanitarian law issues.

In the 1990s, in the context of immense minority problems accompanying the dissolution of the Soviet empire and the brutal wars that included ethnic cleansing in former Yugoslavia, the international community undertook new efforts to protect

---

[164] Quoted in Brems (2001, 67).
[165] Buergenthal (1997, 713).

minorities. The Organization on Security and Cooperation in Europe (OSCE) was first to address minority issues in the 1990 Copenhagen Concluding Document; it later developed a number of instruments, including creating in 1992 a special office of the OSCE High Commissioner for National Minorities. In the same year, the UN General Assembly adopted the Declaration on the Rights of Persons Belonging to National or Ethnic, Religious and Linguistic Minorities. Subsequently, a Working Group on Minorities was established to review the promotion and practical realization of the Declaration. In 1994, the Council of Europe adopted the Framework Convention for the Protection of National Minorities. That same year, the Central European Initiative (CEI) adopted an Instrument for the protection of minority rights.[166]

Around the same time, the UN system of special procedures within the UN came to fruition. "With just a few such mechanisms in the early 1980s, some thirty had been authorized by mid-1990s to address problems such as extrajudicial executions, disappearances, torture, arbitrary detention, racism, violations of freedom of expression, religious intolerance, and human rights violations in more than a dozen countries."[167] An important factor has been that these special procedures have opened the doors for human rights NGOs to present the UN system, often with better monitoring reports and more advanced policy documents than official representatives of member states. At times, it is the NGOs themselves that set the human rights agenda of the United Nations.

The UN Security Council also became involved in human rights. With rare exceptions, the Council had for a long time narrowly understood its mandate to mean protection of international peace and security as distinct from human rights and humanitarian considerations.[168] After 1997, a new UN Secretary General, Kofi Annan, "particularly during his first years, emphasized that human rights were integral to all UN activities, including security and development."[169]

Simultaneously, the principle of responsibility for perpetrators of international crimes and human rights violations began to outweigh the importance of state sovereignty and impunity of top officials.[170] Moreover, responsibility was moved from the states to individual perpetrators and leaders who condoned crimes and

---

[166] See Buergenthal (1997, 721) and Vijapur (2006).

[167] Roth and Weschler (1998, 2).

[168] The Council accepted human rights as its legitimate concern in Resolution 688 on Iraq issued in 1991, in which it explicitly stated that "repressions led to threats against international peace and security." Later, however, this resolution was not quoted as the basis for subsequent ones as is usual practice within the United Nations. See Weschler (2004, 57).

[169] See Weschler (2004, 64) for specific examples of Annan's commitment to human rights.

[170] "Potential violators will obviously not be deterred from engaging in massive human rights abuses . . . if they know that they will enjoy domestic impunity and that, at most, only the state will be held internationally responsible for their acts," writes Buergenthal (1997, 717).

abuses.[171] In the General Pinochet case of 1998, the British "Law Lords" declared that the duties of a head of state do not include ordering or accepting torture or sanctioning killings and treacherous political assassinations; therefore, such acts by a head of state should not be protected by immunity. At the same time, human rights – along with humanitarian law and the laws of war – provided standards for the International Criminal Court and for *ad hoc* tribunals. Despite the opposition by the United States, the Charter of the International Criminal Court was ratified by a sufficient number of states for the Court to operate, even though so far it had not accomplished much.[172] Although the Tribunal for Yugoslavia gained widespread respect,[173] Tribunals for Rwanda and Cambodia began operations with long delays and amid accusations of corruption. With time, the Rwanda Tribunal delivered a number of sentences, but only one perpetrator of genocide in Cambodia has been put on trial by June 2009.[174] Nevertheless, international criminal justice enlarged the instruments of human rights enforcement and changed the balance between the principle of sovereignty and the principle of individual responsibility for crimes. It is expected that bringing tyrants to justice can stop ongoing violations and deter others.[175]

---

[171] For details of the enforcement of international human rights by international criminal tribunals, see Meron (2008c). In conclusion, he writes: "By criminalizing (. . .) human rights norms, the Tribunals have also enhanced the bite of human rights law. Although victims of human rights violations were once confined to seeking redress from States through civil remedies, by importing human rights norms into the courtroom, the tribunals are providing additional enforcement mechanisms for human rights against individual actions" (ibid., 36).

[172] By March 2008, 105 states had become parties to the ICC statute (see ibid., 12). In 2005, the UN Security Council referred the situation in Darfur to the ICC (Resolution 1593). The ICC proceeded to indict two individuals in connection with this investigation, neither of whom remained in ICC custody. On March 4, 2009, the ICC issued an arrest warrant against the Sudanese president Omar Al-Bashir in connection with crimes committed in Darfur. Overall, by February 2008, the ICC has indicted nine individuals of whom only two suspects (from the Democratic Republic of Congo) were in the Court's custody by late 2008. On January 26, 2006, the ICC began its first trial of former Congolese warlord Thomas Lubanga (see www.lubangatrial.org).

[173] Despite numerous shortcomings "the ICTY has been widely praised and rightly so for providing fair trials under formidably challenging conditions," concludes her analysis of the ICTY Orentlicher (2008, 87).

[174] On March 26, 2009, the Extraordinary Chambers in the Courts of Cambodia started the trial of Kaing Guek Eav (aka Dutch) who ran the Tour Sleng torture center in Phnom Penh during the Khmer Rouge rule.

[175] The first step toward criminal responsibility for war crimes was the Nuremberg trial at which the leaders of Nazi Germany were held responsible. Their trial exposed the magnitude of the crimes – in a way consistent with the principles of the rule of law. (It is worth noting that Winston Churchill opposed the trials and opted for summary executions of captured Nazi leaders. See Goldstone 2005, 178.) However, while in Nuremberg, Nazi criminals were tried on the basis of natural law; today, there exist recognized international standards for bringing them to justice, as well as an availability of institutions through which said justice can be administered. Since 1994, the United Nations has created or participated in the establishment of international courts to deal with crimes committed in Rwanda, Sierra Leone, East Timor, Kosovo, Cambodia, and Lebanon.

In the 1990s, with the collapse of communism, the end of the Cold War, the end of apartheid, and the democratization of many authoritarian states in Latin America and Asia, it seemed that human rights should prevail all over the world. Francis Fukuyama wrote about "the end of history" and the coming triumph of liberal ideas and institutions. But his hope, shared by many intellectuals, constitution-makers, and political leaders, did not materialize. New problems have emerged and the very idea of rights has once again been challenged. These new challenges are of a practical rather than ideological nature. Paradoxically, they pose more serious threats to human rights than any ideology ever has or could. Below is a discussion of some of them.

Some threats are related to globalization. This process is driven by private companies rather than by states. Private entrepreneurs are acting on a global scale, benefiting from unequal labor costs and other factors of production. Technological innovations permit the transfer of capital in a fraction of a second to anywhere on Earth. The essential problem of globalization is the disproportion between the economy and the political principle of the sovereignty of national states. No international political mechanism exists capable of regulating the global economy and imposing rules of conduct on multinational corporations outside their home countries. Often, those of their activities that violate human rights wind up escaping the coercive power of any given state. As a result, traditional mechanisms for the protection of rights from abuse by private actors via instruments of national laws are inadequate.[176]

International NGOs are trying to alleviate what they deem the most visible abuses of rights. Nevertheless, any effective protection requires the creation of a mechanism that will act beyond borders for the implementation of international human rights. It seems that human rights law could play a more active role in such cases.[177] Such a mechanism should compel states to protect individuals from abuse by supranational companies – especially given that claims based on rights are always directed against the state.[178] Recently, the United Nations have been trying to address this

---

[176] "The root cause of the business and human rights predicament today lies in the governence gaps created by globalization – between the scope and impact of economic forces and actors, and the capacity of societies to manage their adverse consequences. These governance gaps provide the permissive environment for wrongful acts by companies of all kinds without adequate sanctioning or reparation. How to narrow and ultimately bridge the gaps in relation to human rights is our fundamental challenge," reports Ruggie (2008, 3).

[177] "In particular, human rights law should elaborate the duties of the governments with respect to corporations subject to their jurisdiction when those corporations violate human rights within the territory of governments unable or unwilling to regulate them adequately. Specification of those duties would address legitimate concerns about the conduct of multinational corporations in developing countries without threatening the current structure of human rights," writes Knox (2008, 47).

[178] Frynas and Pegg (2003) demonstrate that it is almost impossible to regulate transnational corporations so that they respect human rights without the determined support of state powers.

issue. In July 2005, the Secretary-General appointed John Ruggie as a special representative on the issue of human rights and transnational corporations and other business enterprises. His final report to the UN Human Rights Council presented a conceptual and policy framework to deal with the issue of human rights in business. It comprises three core principles: "the State duty to protect against human rights abuses by third parties, including business; the corporate responsibility to respect human rights; and the need for more effective access to remedies."[179]

Human rights are also threatened by a number of developments in international and national politics. The supremacy of trade interests over human rights concerns was, perhaps, the first element that eroded human rights principles as part of international politics. Established democracies were inconsistent in their relations with dictatorial and atrocious regimes, often giving priority to business and profit over principles. Some U.S. diplomats have, in turn, insisted that free trade is one of the basic human rights. Such practices have eroded the appeal of human rights among many people in developing countries for whom free trade was equivalent to the economic supremacy of the West.

Double standards have also been applied for political reasons.[180] During the Cold War, the great powers expressed criticism of the violations of rights by their enemies while turning a blind eye on the abuses by friendly regimes, as with Panama, Guatemala, Nicaragua, and other U.S. allies, as well as a number of African regimes befriended by France. (This was paralleled by Soviet criticism of neocolonialism and racism, coupled with the USSR's simultaneous support for the Castro regime in Cuba and oppressive regimes in Africa and Asia.[181]) Soon after the end of the Cold War, double standards reappeared with the introduction of the war on terror.

In the United States, the war on terror has dominated the internal political agenda, pushing away civil liberties and being used to justify undue increase of unaccountable presidential power. In Western Europe, the need to deal with growing

---

[179] Ruggie (2008, 1). As a part of the duty to protect "governments need actively to encourage a corporate culture that is respectful of human rights at home and abroad," said Ruggie introducing his report to the Human Rights Council on June 3, 2008. (See http://www.business-humanrights.org/Documents/Ruggie-Human-Rights-Council-3-Jun-2008.pdf.)

[180] The potential for double standards was implied in the very concept of international human rights. When human rights are the subject of international politics, they have to compete with other values – such as national security, peace, international stability, trade, and other national interests – that also must be considered in international relations. Although for nongovernmental human rights organizations human rights can be the sole priority, in international relations they are just one of many concerns and need to be balanced accordingly with other considerations. Often, however, they have to be compromised. Certainly, the international community can intervene without much cost or risk in East Timor, but it would be much more difficult – and irresponsible – to send armies to stop human rights violations in Chechnya and risk nuclear war with Russia.

[181] In the Soviet case, however, it is difficult to talk about double standards because the USSR never really accepted or promoted human rights standards in the first place.

immigration and the fear of Muslim minorities has taken priority over the protection of human rights. In postcommunist countries, many former human rights defenders who today hold positions of power are preoccupied with economic problems, the frustrated expectations of the masses, and the deterioration of law and order. Fear of crime breeds repressive attitudes rather than sensitivity to human rights. At times, leaders of transition countries have discounted their former human rights activities in exchange for popularity and votes. They have come to believe that a strong, centralized government would be more suitable for dealing with problems of transition. Some of them end up turning to traditional conservative and right-wing ideas that are skeptical, if not hostile, to human rights, separation of powers, and checks and balances. In many post-Soviet countries, former elites have tried to find new sources of legitimacy. Often, it has been nationalism that has posed the greatest threats to minorities. In multiethnic Yugoslavia, nationalism led to the disruption of a state, to war, and to mass atrocities. In Central Asia, Belarus, and, recently, Russia, postcommunist regimes have become clearly authoritarian, oppressive, and opposed to human rights.

In the face of populism, nationalism, and various fundamentalisms, human rights must be defended as strongly as ever. The difference is that both the role played by defenders of rights and the public attitude toward them have recently changed. Under an oppressive regime, when any person can become a victim, the human rights movement tends to speak for all of society. When regimes collapse, however, this changes and human rights movements begin to defend specific vulnerable groups, which are perceived as interest groups by "all of society." In such an environment, defenders of rights count on support from foreign foundations far more than on their own governmental institutions or civil society. Despite the great wave of democratization that swept through the "third world" in the 1990s, modern-day elections held in Asia, Africa, and South America do not offer the citizens any real choice, leading to what Fareed Zakaria has called "illiberal democracies."[182]

An informal coalition of such "illiberal democracies" and authoritarian countries have been acting to slow down the process of inclusion of human rights into the main purposes of the Organization of the United Nations.[183] As a result, the UN Security Council, which during the late 1990s and early 2000s had come to accept and appreciate the importance of including human rights in all levels of its activity, has recently been retreating from such a proactive position. After the 2006 replacement of the Commission on Human Rights with the newly established Human Rights Council, some governments have argued that all human rights issues should be considered by the new body and that by even considering such issues the Security

---

[182] Zakaria (2003, 89–118); more on this issue in Chapter 2.
[183] For the strategies adopted in that purpose, see Roth and Weschler (1998).

Council would be encroaching on the competencies of the Human Rights Council. Other international organizations have been similarly guided by the dominance of security considerations over human rights. With the reversal from democratization and liberalization in the former Soviet Union, the OSCE and its Office for Demo-cratic Institutions and Human Rights has become less effective than it used to be. In the new international atmosphere, the United States and Russia speak against attaching much weight to human rights in ODIHR activities. And the OSCE itself has become an overly centralized bureaucratic organization.[184]

Even in established liberal democracies, human rights appear to be in a state of retreat. One example is the changing attitude toward personal liberty, perhaps the most fundamental of all rights and freedoms, increasingly violated as an ever-greater number of people are kept in jails and prisons before receiving a legitimate court sentence. Globally, on a randomly chosen single day, three million people are held in pretrial detention; in the course of a year that number is of course much higher.[185] Pretrial detainees constitute 48 percent of all persons incarcerated in Asia, 35 percent of all those incarcerated in Africa, and 20 percent of those in Europe. But when we examine the ratio of pretrial detainees to the total population, in 2006, only North America (137 jailed per 100 000) and Europe (46,2) were above the world average (43, 6).[186] What this shows is that Western countries are the least committed to principles of personal liberty and the presumption of innocence. With rare exceptions, politicians, journalists, and the public in general seem to be insensitive to this huge abuse of pretrial detention. Security, law and order, and simple fear seem to trump human rights.

In the new realities, attention moves away from human rights and to the responsibilities and duties that people owe both to each other and to society.[187] Recently, a number of proposals suggested to incorporate duties into human rights law.[188] Although morally justified, these proposals in fact potentially threaten human rights. Undoubtedly, human rights impose some duties on individuals and leave the

---

[184] Human rights NGOs with whom ODIHR used to cooperate complain that the latter has become increasingly self-sustaining and less cooperative than before. Moreover, the short tenures and fast rotation of international officials makes cooperation based on durable personal links difficult.

[185] "If the world's three million pre-trial detainees were to stand in a straight line with arms outstretched and touching, they could form a continuous line stretching from London to New York City, with enough people to spare to continue to reach Washington, D.C." (Schönteich 2008, 4). The actual number may be much higher, for nobody knows the true number of detainees in China.

[186] All figures from ibid.

[187] See Knox (2008).

[188] In 1997, the Inter Action Council proposed a Universal Declaration of Human Responsibilities. In 2003, two drafts were submitted to the UN Commission on Human Rights: the Declaration on Human Social Responsibilities and the Norms on the Responsibilities of Transnational Corporations and Other Business Enterprises with Regard to Human Rights.

enforcement of such duties to governments.[189] Such duties, however, are specific and well defined and thus differ from general duties owed by an individual to society. Unspecific duties, by contrast, may be used by governments to limit rights arbitrarily. Although acceptable as a moral standard guiding human behavior, such a norm could serve as a pretext to limit rights if governments wield the power to enforce it.[190]

New emphasis on duties, priority of community over individuals, and issues such as social cohesion have been growing in popularity. U.S. neoconservatives and right-wing parties in Europe have long blamed human rights for an excessive sense of entitlement, neglect of "normal" people, rampant permissiveness, and the break-down of law and order. Such were the criticisms voiced by George W. Bush and his neoconservative advisors during the 2000 presidential campaign. After September 11, 2001, President Bush's administration was able to implement these ideas within the framework of the "war on terror."[191] Their decisions have since led to an unprece-dented increase of the power of the executive branch, a high level of abuse, and the creation of additional threats to human rights.

Human Rights and the "War on Terror"

Undoubtedly, terrorism poses a serious threat to human rights and people's basic security. Individuals are unable to defend themselves from these types of threats and their prevention via "normal" means of law enforcement is difficult. Before proper mechanisms can be activated, victims are long dead. It is reasonable that the response to the threat of terrorism has to warrant the limitation of some rights, such as unrestricted freedom of movement or the privacy of electronic communication. It is the duty of every state to prevent terrorist acts and to protect citizens from the conse-quences of these acts, should they occur. Individual freedoms and moral principles, including human rights, need to be balanced with the needs of security.[192] Very few people object to relatively unobtrusive limitations on freedom, such as the necessity to show ID cards and permit one's luggage to be X-rayed before boarding a plane. Such limitations, however, should not increase beyond what is necessary to fight

---

[189] Examples are the duty not to discriminate on grounds of race and the duty not to commit genocide. Such duties are enforced by the International Criminal Court and special tribunals.

[190] For example, Article 12 of the draft Declaration on Human Social Responsibilities (patterned on Article 27.2 of the African Charter) imposes on each person a duty "to exercise his or her recognized rights and freedoms, with due consideration and respect for (. . .) the security of his or her society and the morality prevailing in it."

[191] For analysis of the "war on terror" from the perspective of various ideologies, see Holmes (2007, 131–213). Holmes refers to the war in Iraq as "the conservative intifada" (ibid., 197).

[192] Tesón believes that "restrictions on liberty are justified, if they are, *only* by the need to preserve liberty itself, not by other values such as order or security" (2005, 58).

terrorism. They must not lead to excessive concentration of executive power, to the arbitrary use of coercive powers by the state, or to unnecessary restrictions on individual liberties. To avoid the abuse of power and violations of rights, it is important to establish standards for determining what rights, in what situation, to what degree, and by what kind of a procedure can be suspended.[193] It is equally important to use a principle of proportionality in the application of such standards.[194]

Ignatieff proposed "a lesser evil position," according to which the "war on terror" may require the suspension of some rights, but such measures should not be arbitrary.[195] They "must be strictly targeted, applied to the smallest possible number of people, used as a last resort, and kept under adversarial scrutiny of an open democracy." Due process should be upheld: "no one should be held indefinitely, without charge, without access to counsel or judicial review."[196] Blanket detentions are inadmissible because they violate the principle of individualized guilt. Despite supporting a number of extraordinary measures adopted by the U.S. government, including the unilateral use of military power, Ignatieff concludes that "by these standards, the United States failed the test in its detention of nearly five thousand aliens, mostly single males of Muslim or Arab origin, after September 11."[197] Many authors are much more critical of the U.S. antiterror measures than Ignatieff.

The Patriot Act of 2001 drastically curtailed the rights of U.S. citizens and paved the way for further limitations by the executive branch of government. It also limited the rights of resident aliens in the United States. The habeas corpus rights of suspects accused of terrorism were drastically limited, as best demonstrated by the conditions in Guantanamo, where detainees have been kept indeterminately, as well as by the "extraordinary rendition" program for transporting terrorism suspects to secret prisons outside the United States. Special military commissions have been created to try suspects without access to counsel or the right of appeal. Torture and cruel treatment of prisoners were used in the Abu Ghraib prison in Iraq and other places.[198]

---

[193] An example of such standards is the International Commission of Jurists Declaration on Upholding Human Rights and the Rule of Law in Combating Terrorism adopted in 2004 (the Berlin Declaration).

[194] The principle of proportionality has guided a number of decisions of the Supreme Court of Israel in cases linked with terrorism and antiterrorist measures. According to former Israeli Supreme Judge Aharon Barak, proportionality requires that "the governmental agency must maintain a reasonable balancing between the needs of the collective and the harm to the individual." For Barak, proportionality suggests that a torturer should always be convicted of a crime; no security-related benefit from information obtained by torture could exonerate the guilty, though it could be taken into consideration in alleviating a sentence (see Barak 2007, 8).

[195] "Rights may have to bow to security in some instances, but there had better be good reasons, and there had better be clear limitations; otherwise rights will soon lose all their value," writes Ignatieff (2004, 9).

[196] Ibid., 8.

[197] Ibid., 9–10.

[198] For a list of inconsistencies between the measures adopted within the "war on terror" and the principles of the rule of law, see Goldstone (2005, 163). For inconsistencies with international law, see Duffy (2005, 443–50 passim for summary).

Seriously affected by this "war on terror" are the rights to free speech and privacy – both violated by surveillance – and the right to information, violated by the excessive use of secrecy in the U.S. government.[199]

Some measures adopted in the war on terror were declared unconstitutional by the U.S. Supreme Court. In *Rasul v. Bush* (2004), American law was extended to Guantanamo detainees. In the *Padilla* and *Hamdi* cases (2004), the Court granted the right to judicial review for all persons held by the U.S. military. In the *Hamdi* decision, the Court stated that a "state of war is not a blank check for the President when it comes to the rights of citizens."[200] In *Hamdan v. Rumsfeld* (2006), military commissions were forced to comply with the Geneva Convention and with the Uniform Code of Military Justice. In *Boumedienne v. Bush* (2008), Guantanamo detainees were granted the right to challenge their continued detention at U.S. federal court. In the *Khouzam* case (2008), a federal court in Pennsylvania blocked the Bush administration's attempt to deport an Egyptian man to Egypt.[201]

In September 2007, the U.S. Senate voted in favor of an amendment that would restore the right to *habeas corpus* eliminated by the Military Commissions Act. On February 13, 2008, the Senate passed legislation barring the CIA and other intelligence officials from using mock drowning (waterboarding) and other cruel interrogation techniques. As was expected president Barack Obama and the new legislature in the United States closed the camp in Guantanamo and eliminated other extreme acts of the Bush administration. Nevertheless, undoing the damage done by that "war on terror" to the rule of law and civil rights in the United States will be both extremely difficult and very slow.[202]

One result of the war on terror has been a new antiterrorist international alliance. With the military actions in Afghanistan and Iraq, a number of autocratic regimes in the region have become allies with the United States. The violations of rights

---

[199] There has been a growing body of books, articles, and research studies dealing with violations of rights in the "war on terror." For a short review of such violations, see Mertus and Sajjad (2008). For review of violations of International Humanitarian Law, see Forsythe (2008). For summary arguments, see Wilson (ed., 2005), Duffy (2005), and Holmes (2007).

[200] Quoted in Duffy (2005, 442).

[201] Similar decisions nullifying excessive antiterrorist legislation have been issued by courts in Canada and the United Kingdom, as well as by the European Court of Human Rights. (Including the ECHR decision of April 24, 2008, in *Ismailov v. Russia* in which the Court prohibited Russia from extraditing a group of Uzbek refugees to Uzbekistan, where the refugees feared they would be tortured on return.) In most of such cases, an important role was played by human rights NGOs – particularly Amnesty International and Human Rights Watch – that brought cases, offered assistance to plaintiffs, produced briefs, and documented abuses. NGOs also influenced decisions by the administration. For example, in a response to advocacy by the Human Rights Watch, the Bush administration issued waivers in February and April 2007 to allow individuals falsely labeled as terrorists to be admitted to the United States.

[202] In November 2008, Human Rights Watch issued a publication *Fighting Terrorism Fairly and Effectively: Recommendations for President-Elect Barack Obama* in which ten measures necessary to restore the respect for the rule of law are described in detail.

perpetrated by these "friendly" regimes have been overlooked and left unchallenged. Thus, double standards and the practice of selective enforcement, both proven major obstacles to the implementation of international human rights, have in fact become more widespread and less objectionable. Moreover, the leaders of several new U.S. allies have recently intensified coercive measures against their domestic opposition, calling all opponents terrorists. Under the pretext of fighting terrorists, Uzbekistan, Tajikistan, Kyrgyzstan, and other states in Central Asia are persecuting ethnic and religious minorities without criticism from the West.

In Russia, an October 2002 terrorist attack on the Nord Ost theatre in Moscow was used as justification for renewed military action against Chechnya and a broad array of legislative measures restricting freedom of the media and other civil rights. In February 2005, President Putin used the threat of terrorism as an excuse to cancel direct elections for governor in 89 regions of Russia, even though there was no proof of linkage between elections and terrorism. In many other countries, human rights defenders are being equated with terrorists and new exceptional laws that violate human rights are being enacted en masse.[203] The threat of terror and the response to it has also resulted in a radical change of attitude toward immigrants in the Western world. There is proof of increased racial profiling by police in many countries, including the United States, Russia, France, Spain, and Bulgaria.[204]

The "war on terror" and the war against Iraq have weakened the idea of human rights. After failing to demonstrate that Saddam Hussein was developing weapons of mass destruction, U.S. leaders have shifted emphasis to the struggle against tyranny and the protection of the rights of Iraqi people.[205] Human rights have been treated instrumentally, as justification for invasion when the first justification did not work.[206] The wave of anti-Americanism that has swept the globe as a result of the unilateral invasion of Iraq has further compromised the idea of human rights in

---

[203] The Atlanta Declaration, issued in 2003 by human rights defenders from 43 countries, stated that both terrorism and the war on terror "pose new challenges for the promotion of human rights." See Hicks (2005, 209).

[204] See Open Society Justice Initiative 2007 and 2009 reports.

[205] On September 21, 2003, in a lecture at the New School for Social Research, Paul Wolfowitz, then Deputy Secretary of Defense, justified the military intervention in Iraq as a defense of the human rights of the Iraqi people. For human rights-based arguments justifying the war in Iraq, see Cushman (2005).

[206] International law does not permit intervention years after a genocide has taken place. In Iraq, the most destructive use of poison gas against civilians occurred in March 1988 in Halabja. When the war in Iraq was launched, there was no gross slaughter going on in the country. There was "no compelling case to be made for humanitarian intervention in Iraq. The Baghdad regime is brutally repressive and morally repugnant, certainly, but it is not engaged in mass murder or ethnic cleansing; there are governments as bad (well, almost as bad) all over the world," wrote Michael Walzer in September 2002 (quoted in Walzer 2005, 149). Nor was Iraq a failed state, torn apart by private armies. Therefore, the invasion did not meet the criteria of humanitarian intervention. (See Roth 2005, 155.)

the world. And because human rights have almost always have been identified (even if erroneously[207]) with the United States, anti-Americanism appears to call for the rejection of human rights. Conversely, human rights activists in developing countries have been desperately trying to dissociate human rights from the United States. In short, the "war on terror" has further deprived the United States of credibility in the field of human rights.[208] In fact, the "war on terror" has confirmed a more general rule: namely, that for the United States sovereignty has always taken precedence over international jurisdiction, and international human rights have always been an export rather then a self-limitation.[209]

Responsibility to Protect

The invasion of Iraq was a consequence of the unilateralism that has replaced the balance of power as a guiding principle of American foreign policy following the Cold War. The U.S. intervention in Iraq has proved that military measures do not promote democracy and freedom. It is a painful example of the difficulties with unilateral military intervention. Although it is easier to launch such an intervention than to go through the painstaking process of collective decision making by the Security Council, unilateral measures lack legitimacy, harm even the most noble causes, and can easily be abused to cover up motives other than the protection of peace and human rights.

The multilateral protection of the international order and promotion of human rights also pose numerous difficulties. The deficiencies of the United Nations' mechanisms of enforcement are well known. UN member states may take action

[207] The role of the United States as human rights champion has always been problematic. The United States did not ratify a great number of international human rights instruments, including the Optional Protocols to ICCPR; the Covenant on Social, Economic and Cultural Rights; and the Convention on the Rights of the Child. The United States also opposed the ratification of a treaty on the International Criminal Court and used economic and political instruments to prevent other states from ratification. (See Johansen 2006.) According to Forsythe (2000, XXV) "the U.S. that sees itself as a shining city on a hill and a beacon to others regarding human rights and democracy has many problems at home that certainly could benefit from review within the framework of international human rights." For such a review of human rights situation in the United States before the Bush administration, see Amnesty International Report, 1998.

[208] "In a deeply polarized global political environment, where many US policies are controversial, human rights defenders with any perceived or actual association with the United States now face added threats and pressures." In the Middle East and the broader Muslim world, "US support for human rights and democracy has tended to reflect negatively on local activists who are ostensibly pursuing some of the same objectives," writes Hicks (2005, 219).

[209] "There is no question that international human rights remain a foreign concept today in many – perhaps most – communities around the United States," write Alan Jenkins and Larry Cox, (2005, quoted in Afshari 2007, 64.) However, "no one has ever purported to present a book on universal human rights and American society," writes Forsythe (2000, XIV). For a general study of human rights in the consciousness of the Americans see *Human Rights in the United States* 2007.

only when no permanent member of the Security Council perceives the proposed measures as a threat to its own vital interests. The superpowers have also vetoed "any proposed intervention against one of its allies or clients."[210] By neglecting human right issues, the Security Council has been unable to stop violations before they reach genocidal proportions. Moreover, even in cases of genocide, the UN has proven incapable of action, its forces neither preventing nor stopping the mass murders in Somalia (1993), Rwanda (1994), and Bosnia (1995). In these and other cases, either the UN did not act at all or its actions were ineffective if not counterproductive.[211] At present, the international community is helpless in the face of atrocities being committed in Darfur and the Democratic Republic of Congo, among other places.[212]

During the Cold War, interventions were rare and usually unilateral. Such was the case with India putting an end to the massive killings and rapes in East Pakistan (now Bangladesh) in 1971, Vietnam conquering the murderous Pol Pot regime in Cambodia in 1979, and Tanzania putting an end to the cruel and cannibalistic rule of Idi Amin in Uganda, also in 1979.[213] In the 1990s, interventions have become more common – and increasingly multilateral – as the balance between the principle of sovereignty (which implies nonintervention) and humanitarian intervention began to change in favor of intervention. Buergenthal wrote about "the increasing willingness of the international community to confront mass violations of human rights with force, if necessary."[214] According to Donnelly, international human rights norms and values "have produced an environment where the previously unchallengeable legal norm of non-intervention is beginning to give way."[215] With time, arguments and criteria justifying humanitarian intervention have been elaborated in more detail.[216]

---

[210] Sandholtz (2002, 203).

[211] UN special rapporteur for Bosnia Tadeusz Mazowiecki visited Srebrenica a few days after the massacre and "in an almost unprecedented move – by UN standards – resigned from his post upon his return, explaining that he no longer could be associated with the UN after it failed so horribly the people it was supposed to protect" (Weschler 2004, 59). She implies partial responsibility of the Security Council for the massacres in Rwanda and in Srebrenica.

[212] See Flores (2008, 280–6).

[213] "Interventions of this sort are probably best carried out by neighbors, as in these cases, since neighbors will have some understanding of local culture," writes Walzer (2005, 69).

[214] Buergenthal (1997, 722).

[215] Donnelly (2002, 93). Tesón presents the following argument in favor of intervention: "a major purpose of states and governments is to protect and secure human rights. (. . .) Governments and others in power who seriously violate those rights undermine the one reason that justifies their political power, and thus should not be protected by international law. A corollary of the argument is that, to the extent that state sovereignty is a value, it is an instrumental, not intrinsic, value. Sovereignty serves valuable human ends, and those who grossly assault them should not be allowed to shield themselves behind the sovereignty principle. Tyranny and anarchy cause the moral collapse of sovereignty" (2003, 93).

[216] For a review of the debate about humanitarian intervention, see Holzgrefe (2003).

A crucial condition for humanitarian intervention is that basic security-related rights are being violated. This means that the violation of the rights to life, to bodily integrity, and to liberty, as through murder, physical harm, or expulsion, can justify intervention – but the abuse of political or socioeconomic rights cannot.[217] A second condition is that the violations be massive and systematic. Additionally, an intervention must be an option of last resort after all other means have been tried unsuccessfully. "Humanitarian intervention is morally necessary whenever cruelty and suffering are extreme and no local forces seem capable of putting an end to them," writes Walzer.[218] An intervention ought to be undertaken with a humanitarian purpose, which means that it should aim at restoring security and increasing the welfare of the victims of abuse.

A review of interventions from the 1990s clearly demonstrates that "the international community is reluctant to provide explicit assent for interventions against functioning governments."[219] Most of the analyzed interventions took place in the so-called "failed states," where government does not control the territory and the population is prey to warlords fighting one another for natural resources.[220] Liberia and Sierra Leone, Sudan and Somalia, and the Democratic Republic of Congo and Uganda are examples of such states in Africa alone, although international "intervention" has taken place in only some of them.

It seems difficult, if not impossible, to make interventions mandatory. "When faced with massive suffering, intervening and not intervening seem both demanded and prohibited."[221] International norms have been evolving, however, toward accepting humanitarian intervention. This issue was raised on September 20, 1999, by UN Secretary General Kofi Annan in his address to the General Assembly. Annan introduced the concept of individual sovereignty and described it in terms of human rights and fundamental freedoms.[222] Such sovereignty could limit state sovereignty

---

[217] There were two exceptions: the 1992 intervention in Somalia, caused by inability to provide aid to victims of famine, and the 1992 intervention in Haiti to restore democratically elected president Aristide to power.

[218] Walzer (2005, 69).

[219] Sandholtz (2002, 221). For a review of the U.S. reluctance to intervene in Rwanda and Bosnia and the motives behind the intervention in Haiti, see Shattuck (2003).

[220] Ignatieff describes these as "war economies." "War becomes a business to maintain and reproduce the profits of the various combatants and their supporters. Civil war endures there for three basic reasons: because a resource base permits it; because the two sides are so evenly balanced that neither can prevail; and, finally, because it is in neither side's economic interest to bring the combat to an end" (2003, 303).

[221] Donnelly (2002, 93). Walzer (2002, 32) suggests that "intervention is more than a right and more than an imperfect duty" and that "nonintervention in the face of mass murder or ethnic cleansing is not the same as neutrality in the time of war."

[222] See Weschler (2004, 65).

when the former were abused. Annan called for the attempts to forge "international unity behind the principle that massive and systematic violations of human rights should not be allowed."[223] Such violations could justify international humanitarian intervention.

This issue was considered by the International Commission on Intervention and State Sovereignty (established by the government of Canada) in a 2001 report entitled "Responsibility to Protect," which included a set of principles guiding humanitarian interventions, particularly through military means. Central to the report was the idea that all governments have a "responsibility to protect" their own citizens and those within their jurisdiction from genocide, mass killing, war crimes, crimes against humanity, and sustained human rights violations. The report further suggested that the international community has a responsibility to act when governments fail to protect the most vulnerable groups.

The report also stated that the "right of humanitarian intervention" should override the principles of state sovereignty and nonintervention when a state commits such acts of violation of international law as genocide, ethnic cleansing, or systemic rape, among others. Soon after the publication, Commission co-chairs and authors of the report Gareth Evans and Mohamed Sahnoun wrote: "It is only a matter of time before reports emerge again from somewhere of massacres, mass starvation, rape, and ethnic cleansing. And then the question will arise again in the Security Council, in political capitals, and in the media: What do we do?"[224] The authors believed that the steps suggested in the report would provide the answer. At the 2005 World Summit, world leaders endorsed an extremely narrow interpretation of these recommendations, but even this was widely criticized by many leaders of states and established international organizations. Neither the report nor the World Summit's endorsement could prevent continuing massacres, starvation, rapes, and other atrocities in Darfur and the Democratic Republic of Congo. The question posed in the "Responsibility to Protect" document and central to the 2005 Summit – "What do we do?" – remains unanswered.

Another unanswered question is who should conduct such intervention. "Anyone who can help should help," suggests Walzer, drawing a parallel between humanitarian intervention and such cases of basic good will as helping to put out a house on fire or responding on hearing a victim of abuse scream for help.[225] Walzer believes, however, that creating a reliable international military force would be more effective. The difficulty lies in establishing how such a force is to react legitimately but swiftly

---

[223] Ibid.
[224] Evans and Sahnoun (2002; quoted from the Web site http://www.foreignaffairs.org/20021101faessay9995/gareth-evans-mohamed-sahnoun).
[225] See Walzer (2002, 31).

and decisively in a world of conflicting state interests. When this problem is solved, even the most committed pacifists would probably agree that the use of force would be justified in extreme situations.[226]

Rights and Resources

Military means of enforcement should be an exception. Although it seems that even a unilateral intervention would be justified to stop an ongoing genocide, political pressures and economic sanctions could be used in less drastic situations, even though the effectiveness of sanctions is controversial.[227] One thing is certain: to be effective, sanctions require universal solidarity – and such is difficult to attain with economic powers competing for resources and markets.[228]

Another method consists of replacing formal sanctions against perpetrators with rewards for those governments that are willing to respect democracy and human rights. One such example is the Global Fund connected with the Millennium Development Goals, a set of development targets agreed on by the international community, which center on cutting poverty by half and improving the welfare of the world's poorest populations by the year 2015. The goals, set in September 2000 at the UN Millennium Summit, aim at the use of developmental aid to promote good

---

[226] One example can be His Holiness the Dalai Lama, who admits the existence of the regional security forces that eventually would be replaced by a worldwide police. "The main purpose of this force would be to safeguard justice, communal security and human rights worldwide. Its specific duties would be various, however. Protecting against the appropriation of power by violent means would be one of them. As to its operation, I imagine that it could be called in by communities which came under threats – from neighbours or from a minority of its own members, such as violently extreme political faction – or it would be deployed by the international community itself when violence seemed the likely outcome of conflict," writes the Dalai Lama (1999, 199).

[227] There is a debate about the effectiveness of economic sanctions in recent decades. In the case of South Africa, sanctions, combined with the boycott of sporting events, seemed to work well. In the early 1980s, sanctions imposed by President Reagan against the military government in Poland initially seemed not to work because, in the words of the Polish government spokesperson of the time, "the government was capable of feeding itself." By the end of the 1980s, however, these sanctions multiplied the effect of the economic crisis, helping to bring about peaceful transition. In the 1990s, economic sanctions against Iraq seemed to have a limited influence on Saddam Hussein's behavior and actually further harmed the victims of his dictatorship. Economic sanctions against Cuba and Burma were also ineffective. On the other hand, sanctions seemed to positively influence the behavior of Libya. For a review of the effectiveness of economic sanctions, see Neier (2000), who suggests that in each case they should be narrowly and deliberately targeted to bring about the intended result.

[228] For example, in the late 1990s member states of the European Union decided not to support even a mild resolution that did not imply sanctions but simply pointed to the violations of human rights in China. Such a resolution has been proposed – and defeated – every year following the 1989 Tiananmen Square massacre. In late 1990s, France and Germany stopped supporting the resolution for commercial reasons and soon all EU countries followed. (At some point, Poland was a lone warrior sponsoring the resolution and Chinese diplomats accused their U.S. counterparts in Geneva of hiding behind Poland.)

governance by setting conditions for foreign aid and international trade with developing countries. Similarly, a number of governments and intergovernmental and nongovernmental organizations have been working to persuade private business to enhance the accountability of governments.[229] In 2000, the United Nations Global Compact was established as a corporate and citizenship initiatative to encourage businesses worldwide to adopt sustainable and socially responsible policies. The Global Compact adopted "ten universally accepted principles" in the areas of human rights, labor, environment, and anticorruption.[230] The first two principles call for businesses "to support and respect the protection of internationally proclaimed human rights" and to "make sure that they are not complicit in human rights abuses."[231]

Because a great number of corrupt dictatorships are providers of natural resources, the idea of creating a common front of buyers has been suggested. A number of NGOs (including Extractive Industries Transparency International or Resource Transparency) and initiatives (e.g., the *Publish What You Pay* campaign) aim at making Western companies that do business with autocratic countries publish what they pay for resources to increase the accountability of governments.[232] For legitimacy reasons, a number of governments from among the developing countries have joined the campaign. Others were about to join when a significant change took place on world markets.

Until recently, almost all natural resources produced outside the West were purchased by companies with headquarters in Western democratic countries and Japan. In the past decade, however, a new aggressive buyer has emerged – namely, China, with vast savings, unprecedented economic growth, and almost unlimited human resources. Low wages permit China to produce cheap goods for export. To be able to do this, China needs energy and natural resources. For these, it is looking primarily to Africa. With no history of respect for human rights, China is not eager to join the efforts to increase transparency, accountability, and governance in the resource-producing countries. In fact, China can economically sustain friendly dictatorships in Africa and other places.

Because China's economic growth is fueled to a large degree by Western buyers, the boycott of Chinese goods could seem an appropriate response to both China's massive internal violation of rights and China's support for oppressive regimes. As

---

[229] In 2000, International Labour Organization adopted the Tripartite Declaration of Principles Concerning Enterprises and Social Policy and the OECD issued Guidelines for Multinational Enterprises.

[230] The purpose of the Global Compact is "to catalyze actions in support of broader UN goals, such as the Millenium Development Goals" and to "mainstream the ten principles in business activities around the world."

[231] In 2006, a group of the world's largest institutional investors adopted Ten Principles as the Principles of Responsible Investment. As noted, the corporate responsibility to respect human rights was the second principle in the framework for business and human rights debate suggested in Ruggie's report.

[232] See Soros (2006, 178–82) for details on launching these initiatives.

noted, boycotts played a major role in abolishing the apartheid regime in South Africa.[233] It was also boycotts that prevented Nike, Reebok, and other companies from condoning child labor and other violations by their subsidiaries.[234] In the case of China, however, an effective boycott seems unrealistic as demonstrated by the failure of calls for the boycott of the 2008 Olympic games. The reasons for this lie outside China and are as relevant to the future of human rights as the politics of China itself.

Sanctions worked in the 1980s, when a significant number of Americans and Western Europeans resolved not to buy products from companies that did business with South Africa. The owners and chief executives of such companies could be shamed in public and held responsible for supporting an inhuman system. Consumers had alternative sources of similar products, available more or less for the same price. Likewise, students that boycotted Nike or Reebok could get their tennis shoes and tracksuits from another sportswear manufacturer.[235] In both cases, the targeted companies were losing money. Moreover, the buyers did not have to act

---

[233] In the past years, similar efforts have been undertaken in relation to the genocide in Darfur. In 2004, the Genocide Intervention Network (GI-Net) was founded by two students at Swarthmore College. Operating within the framework of the 2001 *Responsibility to Protect* report, GI-Net soon focused its attention on Darfur, calling on companies to divest from corporations that do business with Sudan government. In 2006, GI-Net formed Sudan Divestment Task Force to coordinate Sudan divestment movement. The calls for divestment were endorsed by hundreds of companies and twenty-seven states of the United States. In 2007, the federal Sudan Accountability and Divestment Act was adopted in the United States. The focus of the Investors Against Genocide, an NGO founded in 2006 in Massachusetts, is to convince mutual fund and other investment firms to avoid or divest holdings in the four major oil companies (PetroChina and Sinopec from China, ONGC from India, and Petronas from Malaysia) that are partners with the government of Sudan and thus are helping to fund genocide in Darfur.

[234] Human rights movements have recently extended their interpretation of human rights violations, turning not only against abusive governments but also against private corporations. One of the chief prerequisites for such a change has been the increased awareness of human rights among consumers in Western countries. According to Deborah Spar (1998, 10), "firms adhere to the higher standards because public attention forces them to do so."

[235] These campaigns were related to child labor in India and Pakistan. The subsidiaries of Reebok in these countries contracted out portions of manual production to local enterprises that were using child labor. When human rights activists in the West challenged Reebok, executives initially rejected responsibility, pointing to the lack of jurisdiction over foreign contractors. As a rule, perpetrators of violations committed in a foreign country are not the multinational corporations per se but their local contractors. In Reebok's case, human rights groups in the West reacted by boycotting the company's products – a measure particularly popular among students. To avert the devastating results of the boycott, Reebok renounced its policy, banning further contracts with companies that employ children. "No child or slave labor used on this product" was stamped across all new inventory and the company even funded a special "Reebok Human Rights Award." Similar abuses by Disney, Levi-Strauss, Macy's, Liz Claiborne, and other corporations and their sub-subsidiaries abroad were also revealed. When threatened with boycotts and other measures, a group of companies formulated the Social Accountability 8000 act to promote standards required of multinational corporations, as well as the instruments for monitoring adherence to such standards. See Spar (1998).

against their own interest, because there was no reason for them to be vested in buying the "tainted" products.[236]

All this has recently changed. The difference in cost is so large that few producers can compete with China. Wholesale buyers of Chinese products and Western investors in China are also different from the corporate owners of the past. Today, the majority of business is done by faceless money management funds. Money managers have one ultimate goal: the maximization of profits for which they are accountable to thousands of investors – investing their money either directly or through pension funds – who can hardly be held responsible for the actions of fund managers. Buyers of cheap Chinese products profit twice: paying less today and expecting higher pensions in the future. Thus, the vital choice is located in the wealthy north, and it is the choice between our own prosperity and a secure future on one hand and our own standards of human rights and justice on the other. Very few people choose to pay the price for justice and the rights of others.[237]

The rise of China as the new great economic power is paralleled by Russia's recovery as a major exporter of natural gas. In fact, a new coalition of rich authoritarian regimes is emerging. It includes Russia, China, Iran, and Venezuela. This coalition expresses openly its reservations toward human rights, as well as its weariness of nongovernmental organizations that sustain and protect rights. In this new international order, the ability of the West to influence other states has been steadily declining.[238] The West cannot impose its standards unilaterally on the others, even if it were to decide to use force. The only potential instrument for influencing China or Russia is the UN, because both countries have veto power in the Security Council. That veto, however, sets the limits to potential influence; Russia and China can always veto international measures that threaten their and their clients' interests.[239]

---

[236] In 1995, 75 percent of American consumers said that they would prefer to buy in textile shops that do not exploit their workers; 84 percent would pay one extra dollar for a product worth 20 dollars if had been produced without exploitation. Spar (1998, 10).

[237] An analysis of the attitudes held by Americans about human rights gives some hope, though. "The majority of Americans *do* weigh human rights concerns when reminded of their relevance. Although the majority appear unwilling to risk American troops to defend others' human rights, they are willing to take less costly actions such as withholding trade" (McFarland and Mathews 2005, 317). Research shows that influencing public opinion is of importance. This, in turn, suggests that public campaigns of the "Do you know whom you support by buying this cheap product?" variety may be useful.

[238] "In the 1990s, the EU enjoyed up to 72% support on human rights issues in the UN General Assembly. In the last two Assembly sessions, the comparable percentages have been 48 and 55%. This decline is overshadowed by a leap in support for Chinese positions in the same votes from under 50% in the later 1990s to 74% in 2007–2008" (Gowan and Brantner 2008, 2). Russia's support was 76%, while the support of the U.S. position dropped from 77% in the 1977–1978 session to 30% in 2007–2008 (ibid., 4).

[239] China and Russia are leading the "axis of sovereignty" in the UN. A Chinese–Russian veto blocked the U.S.–UK resolution on Burma in 2007 and a resolution on Zimbabwe in 2008. The failure to condemn Zimbabwe by the UN Security Council was hailed by Russia's ambassador to UN as "a victory of traditional sovereignty" (ibid., 6).

Perhaps the more effective way to influence China would be by pressure from regions other than the West, preferably those countries where China buys its resources. More generally, there continues to be a growing role for the global South in the protection of rights worldwide. India is still committed to democracy and human rights. And although the governments of Brazil and the Republic of South Africa do not care much about human rights, in both countries there exist vital human rights NGOs that could pressure their governments to take a stronger stand globally.

Unlike those in the 1970s, the internal developments in authoritarian countries occurring today foster no awareness of or desire for human rights. Fear of crime, fear of terror, or simply the desire for material well-being are more important considerations for contemporary populations. It seems that in the near future human rights campaigns will probably be less effective than ones centered around the rule of law, procedural rights, and remedies that limit arbitrariness and promote fairness in public administration – all of which are important preconditions for market economy. In fact, it may be consumer rights that offer some prospects for bringing the idea of rights closer to the experience of the common men and women who do not themselves experience abuse and violations on a daily basis. Victims and international human rights organizations may also be turning to tort law as more effective remedy than political actions or economic sanctions. Such actions can be particularly useful against transnational companies that do business with oppressive regimes.[240]

The concept of human rights has also lost its ability to shape domestic policies in the West. The economic crisis that followed the 2008 collapse of the banking system has increased competition rather than solidarity with the weak. It has also diminished resources needed for the protection of rights. In times of crisis as well as in electronic democracies in general, people do not respond too well to logical and legal arguments. They do respond to suffering, though. Victims of abuse attract more attention and shape attitudes more effectively than their advocates. Instead of appealing to abstract legal standards and a sense of fairness, the human rights campaign could

---

[240] Recently, a number of organizations representing victims have been using the Alien Tort Claims Act of 1789, originally issued to facilitate fighting piracy, to sue companies guilty of complicity in violation of rights. The Act allows suits to be filed in the U.S. courts against companies and persons that are not U.S. citizens. Cases were brought in the U.S. courts against UNOCAL for the violations in 1997 in Burma; against Yahoo for releasing the information that allowed the Chinese government to identify and arrest an Internet user Wang in 2002; and against Royal Dutch Shell for supplying arms to the Nigerian security forces knowing that it will be used agains farmers who protested against the building of a pipeline. Texaco was sued for destroying the natural environment in Equador, Coca-Cola for using paramilitary forces to fight unions in Colombia, and ExxonMobil for allowing gross abuses of rights in Indonesian Aceh. Most of the cases are settled with plaintiffs being granted compensation for losses and suffering. Betton (2008, 18) argues that the emergence of cases involving Alien Tort Claims Act is "the key development with regard to corporate social responsibility."

begin to address feelings and entice compassion. Basically, human rights advocates may need to begin using instruments that have so far belonged to humanitarian actions.

HUMAN RIGHTS AND HUMANITARIANISM

Humanitarianism contains legal, moral, religious, and interpersonal components. In a broad sense it implies help to the needy and vulnerable. In the strictly legal sense, it deals primarily with the laws of war. For a long time, international humanitarian law referred predominantly to the Hague Conventions and the Geneva Conventions and to the protections offered to victims of war, such as civilians, prisoners of war, and wounded soldiers (and property). Special humanitarian care was offered to children, women, and the elderly. Law of war was applied between states and was based on the principle of collective responsibility: sanctions assumed the form of reprisals during wars and reparations after a war. The state was held responsible for the perpetrators, and it was the state, rather than the victims, that was awarded compensation.

Humanitarian law of war has always been based on customary laws, the "principles of humanity" and the "dictates of public conscience."[241] Nevertheless, it has drastically changed under the influence of human rights.[242] The first step toward this direction was Common Article 3 of the 1949 Geneva Convention in which the applicability of the international humanitarian law was enlarged to include also internal conflicts. The same article conferred on individuals (rather than states) some rights that cannot be waived even during the war.[243] The next step was the recognition by the international humanitarian law that individual rights affected by war can be enforced not only through reprisals between states but also by means of individual criminal responsibility of perpetrators.[244]

Protections offered by international humanitarian law of war were limited to victims of international wars and not to victims of internal conflicts – despite the fact that, in theory, the latter should be able to rely on human rights treaties. But such treaties were easily waived during emergencies. And with intranational

[241] These formulations appear in the Martens Clause, proposed in 1899 by Russian delegate to the Hague Peace Conference, F. F. Martens. The clause was included in the Preamble to the Hague Conventions of the Laws and Customs of War on Land. (See Meron 2006, 16–29.)

[242] "The humanization of the law of war received its greatest impetus from the post-UN Charter international human rights instruments and the creation of international process of accountability," writes Meron (ibid., 5). For details about the ways in which human rights have influenced humanitarian law, see Meron (2008b).

[243] The Vichy government of France under German occupation waived the right of French citizens not to be deported and very soon French Jews were transported to concentration camps abroad.

[244] See Meron (2008b; 2008c).

hostility and the number of civil wars on the rise, the separation of humanitarian and human rights laws has left a growing number of people without protection. Theodore Meron claims that these two systems have been reintegrated by statutes and the jurisprudence of international criminal tribunals. Such decisions have "made a tremendous contribution to expanding the applicability of protective norms to national conflicts and strife."[245] This is just one example of the evidence for the growing convergence between human rights and humanitarian law.[246]

Indeed, humanitarianism – from now on understood more broadly than as simple referring to the humanitarian laws of war[247] – and human rights have a common goal: to limit human suffering. Both find it important to share resources, provide help to the needy and offer protection to the weak. The main difference is that humanitarians often do not publicize violations because their main goal is to obtain access to victims. To achieve this end they are prepared to make deals with regimes.[248] Despite this, there exists a visible – and often deliberate and agreed on – division of labor between humanitarians and human rights activists. Each activity has its advantages and shortcomings.[249]

One difference between humanitarianism and human rights is related to the object of the intervention: humanitarian action implies a passive victim who needs to be protected and assisted; a crucial word here is *need* rather than *right*. Human rights, in turn, assume an active right-holder who can claim a legitimate right. Humanitarian action – even when it is a relief to victims of natural disaster – is a sort of gift. Human rights, in turn, are based on preexisting rights, not on gifts. Human rights are intended to empower an individual to acknowledge his or her own status as equal to that of the authorities.

---

[245] Meron (2008a, 13).

[246] Many differences will remain, however. "International humanitarian law permits certain deprivation of freedom without judicial process; it allows warring powers to intern people in camps, to limit their appeal rights, and to put broad restrictions on the rights to freedom of speech and assembly. Yet human rights law strictly forbids, except for lawful derogations, all of these actions," writes Meron (2008b, 23).

[247] Proximity of names often leads to confusing humanitarian aid with the international humanitarian law. The latter implies rights that are enforceable in courts. They are increasingly codified and fine-tuned by the international courts. They are enforceable through both compensatory liability of a state and criminal responsibility of a perpetrator. None of these characteristics apply to humanitarian action. (For these reasons, perhaps it would be better to talk simply about the "international law of war" rather than humanitarian laws of war.)

[248] Rieff claims that, if needed, "a humanitarian relief worker has to make deals with gunmen. Otherwise, you don't get your supplies through." A human rights activist, by contrast, "has to be absolutist." (See David Rieff's interview by Harry Kreisler on the Web site http://globetrotter.berkeley.edu/people3/Rieff/.)

[249] Some groups that claim to promote human rights are acting to foster their own interest or "promote one or another side in civil conflict" Neier (1989). The author points out that, during the civil war in Nicaragua, the "human rights issue has been a weapon to use against the enemy." He suggests a number of criteria to distinguish partisan efforts from genuine efforts to promote human rights. (Ibid.)

Human rights imply a reciprocal relation between rights and duties. If one has a right, others have a duty not to trespass on this right and to provide that which is one's right. Humanitarianism is not reciprocal. There exists no duty on the part of the giver. The care is one-sided and cannot be legally claimed by a beneficiary. The giver acts on a moral impulse rather than on a legal obligation.

The motives for actions may also differ. Humanitarianism is closer to religion than it is to either law or the philosophy of rights. Inhuman behavior is considered evil and, as such, it is condemned on moral grounds. For humanitarian narratives, the innocence of victims (be they children, women, the handicapped, or otherwise powerless people) is of crucial importance. No one feels obligated to render humanitarian assistance to evil people. By contrast, even an "evil" person (say, an apprehended murderer) has rights that deserve to be respected and protected.

This difference is visible in human rights reports that usually stay within the human rights paradigm. These tend to be objective and impartial and based on legal reasoning. They focus on violations of specific human rights norms. Their appeal is to reason. Humanitarian narratives, by contrast, focus on suffering.[250] They appeal to emotions. At times, they are even sentimental, with emotions used to influence people and create the impulse to give or to help. When we are exposed to a tragedy, see suffering, or hear a person cry, we feel. Film, television, and the World Press Photo competition are the most powerful instruments of humanitarianism. Their role in fostering human rights, however, is rather limited.

Human rights are not based on the narratives of suffering. Neither the general theory of rights nor particular rights are about suffering. To be claimed rights do not need suffering. There was an exception to this rule: suffering mattered in the case of the original formulation of welfare rights.

In nineteenth century England, the Parliament called a number of special investigative commissions to study the conditions of miners and workers in general. The subsequent reports emphasized exploitation and suffering.[251] They were used to influence public opinion by swaying legislators to adopt regulatory measures for industry and grant workers welfare benefits.[252] Novels and investigative reporting played a similar role in industrial Europe and the United States.

---

[250] See Dudai (2008).

[251] "Like novels and medical case histories, the parliamentary inquiry is characterized by rich layers of detail and by more or less explicit commitment to expose the naturalistic origins of suffering. (. . .) Inquiry is specifically tied to sympathy for the plight of strangers. The 'interests of humanity demand consideration,' said the first parliamentary select committee to investigate mine disasters in its technically sophisticated 1835 report," writes Thomas W. Laqueur (1989, 190–1) in a comprehensive review of the role of humanitarian narratives in changing public attitudes toward workers in England.

[252] The most significant humanitarian bills passed in the British Parliament following the Industrial Revolution were the Factory Acts of 1833 and 1844.

So the welfare policies and social rights of the nineteenth century originated from humanitarian impulses rather than from the concept of rights. This is consistent with another historical observation, namely that the very idea of social rights, as distinct from civil liberties and political rights, had its source in the obligations of the society – the obligations of a ruler and eventually obligations of the state. For the emergence of social rights, humanitarian and moral traditions were more relevant than the concept of individual freedom.

These observations suggest a strict sequence in the historical development of humanitarianism and rights.

By the eighteenth century, the concept of individual rights slowly emerged. Individual rights were to limit the application of state power toward those who had some stake in a society, such as the nobility (as in the Magna Carta) or the civil society and the bourgeoisie (as in the seventeenth- and eighteenth-century declarations and bills of rights). The Enlightenment revolutions ensured liberties and granted political rights to new elites. Individual rights were not justified in terms of suffering but in the terms of power, tradition, and pre-existing privileges or immunities.

As noted, the eighteenth-century concept of individual rights was limited to adult White male property owners. It was created by the West and for Westerners, who did not care about the rights of non-Whites or females, children, or the poor – even when members of these groups suffered. Rights did not prevent exploitation or inequality.

Industrialization increased the misery of workers uprooted from traditional security nets. Slavery, colonialism, and racism brought about incredible suffering and unleashed cruelty toward non-White people. Individual rights did not prevent these atrocities because they were never extended to those who became the victims.

The sufferings of the nineteenth century provoked the humanitarian response of an imperative to care about victims, lessen hardship, and help those who suffered, whether as a result of natural disasters, wars, or exploitation. Humanitarian campaigns rescued slaves in the British Empire and later in the United States, cared for workers in England, and helped African victims in King Leopold's Congo.

In short, humanitarianism was a Western idea toward others – specifically toward all those, both in the West and outside of the West, who had not been granted rights. It was a matter of policy and paternalism.[253] It was a gift rather than a grant of rights. Neither could the sufferers themselves claim rights, nor could their defenders. So the defenders would create narratives of suffering to persuade people to give gifts of charity.

This began to change after World War I and the Bolshevik Revolution. As noted, these events produced a new kind of victim: not enslaved, exploited, or otherwise

---

[253] Analyzing David Hume's theory of moral response to pain, Laqueur emphasizes that "'humanitarians' do implicitly claim a proprietary interest in those whom they aid. They speak more authoritatively for the sufferings of the wronged than those who suffer can speak themselves" (1989, 180).

powerless. "Now for the first time and on a significant scale, the modern states, which [had] already borne the stigmas of colonial oppression and class exploitations, brought forth new victims that belonged to none of the previously familiar and still existing categories of the enslaved and exploited. They included a more or less privileged citizenry of centralized states."[254] They preferred to talk about their rights rather then ask for humanitarian assistance. The concept of individual rights reemerged in the form of human rights and proposals for an international bill of rights were drafted. In the post–WWII formulation, the traditions of humanitarianism and individual rights were, to a degree, combined. The new concept backed a moral response to suffering with legal force. Some aspects of this new twentieth-century theory of rights relate directly to historical difference between individual rights and humanitarian action.

One is the very architecture of the protection of rights. The UN system of human rights resembles humanitarian intervention in that rights are a matter between independent states while the victims of abuse are merely objects of human rights politics. By contrast, the European Convention, which is embedded in the individual rights tradition, empowers an individual victim to stand up against an oppressive state.

As a result, today we have two regimes for the protection of victims. One is a political regime, based on general principles of humanitarianism. The other is a legal system, based on human rights (and on humanitarian law of war). A common core theme in both systems is the notion of responsibility. In the case of rights, this is the legal responsibility (duty) to respect rights and provide that which can be claimed. In humanitarianism, it is the moral responsibility (obligation) to provide help or intervene.

Thus, the concept of the "responsibility to protect" can be perceived as a synthesis of both regimes. It begins with humanitarian preconditions for intervention, expecting those in need to be "apolitical, immobile, helpless and suffering," but it ends with empowering the international community to use force to protect victims of massive abuses of rights.[255] The new concept is not limited to conditions for intervention. In fact, intervention, defined as "the responsibility to react," is only

---

[254] Afshari (2007, 39).

[255] The international humanitarian order and the concept of "the responsibility to protect" is strongly criticized by Mamdani who sees in it the re-creation of colonial practices and dependency. "The language of humanitarian intervention has cut its ties with the language of citizen rights. To the extent the global humanitarian order claims to stand for rights, theses are residual rights of the human and not the full range of rights of the citizen. If the rights of the citizen are pointedly political, the rights of the human pertain to sheer survival; they are summed up in one word: protection. The new language refers to its subjects not as bearers of rights – and thus active agents in their emancipation – but as passive beneficiaries of an external 'responsibility to protect.' Rather than rights-bearing citizens, beneficiaries of the humanitarian order are akin to recipients of charity. Humanitarianism does not claim to reinforce agency, only to sustain bare life. If anything, its tendency is to promote dependence. Humanitarianism heralds a system of trusteeship," writes Mamdani (2008, 18–19).

one element of the responsibility to protect. It is preceded by the "responsibility to prevent" and followed by "the responsibility to rebuild."[256] Experience indicates that, without the means and efforts to rebuild society and its infrastructure, even the most successful intervention leaves a country at the prey of warlords and profiteers.[257]

The differences between humanitarianism and human rights also reveal an emerging gap between the international human rights regime and the international human rights movement. Objective, factual, and unemotional human rights reports addressed to governments, international organizations, and sometimes to courts belong to the international human rights regime. Nongovernmental human rights movements, particularly those that attempt to raise consciousness and attract new followers, have been departing from objective reporting and increasingly relying on narratives of suffering. One important reason is that the consumers of modern media respond better to suffering than to legal reasoning. This may explain why the language of the human rights community has recently been shifting to humanitarian concerns or why poverty has been included into the human rights agenda. It seems that there will be more convergence between human right movements and humanitarianism in the future.[258]

CONCLUSIONS

The history of human rights is the story of often unfulfilled promises and their unintended consequences. In the eighteenth century, the ideas of freedom, equality, and fraternity mobilized people to abolish the feudal order. In 1942, human rights were promised by the leaders of the United Stated and United Kingdom to all

---

[256] Similarly Shattuck (2003) suggests redefinition of the concept of international security and intervention. The response to human rights crises should be preventive measures. Direct intervention and the use of military force would be called for when gross violations continue despite peaceful efforts.

[257] "Where chaos and state collapse is the challenge, the test of a successful intervention is no longer whether it defeats an enemy or stops a human rights abuse, but whether it sets in train the nation-building process that will prevent the area from becoming a security threat once again," claims Ignatieff (2003, 306). Walzer's ideas about a proper end to intervention have evolved. In *Just and Unjust Wars* (1997, Chapter 6), Walzer suggested that it should take place immediately after the killings stop ("quickly in and out" principle). With a growing number of "failed states" and experience of the interventions in the 1990s, Walzer came to believe that the time to withdraw is when local authorities "who are capable of governing the country and who command sufficient popular support so that their government won't be massively coercive" are established (2002, 35).

[258] For an opposite view, see Rieff (2002; 2003). "Many NGOs, particularly those influenced by the British and American aid traditions, assume that relief groups could play a useful role if they could only increase their human rights-enforcing and peace-building capacities. Dissenting figures, notably in French humanitarian circles, argue that humanitarianism needs to remain a world apart, no matter how worthy the larger goals of advancing human rights, resolving conflict, and fostering development," writes Rieff 2002 (quoted from the Web site http://www.foreignaffairs.org/20021101faessay9996/david-rieff/humanitarianism-in-crisis.html).

those who would join them in the struggle against the Axis. In 1948, the Universal Declaration of Human Rights promised freedom, democracy, and security to all people in the world. In the Helsinki Agreement of 1975, Soviet leaders agreed to promise freedoms to people under their rule; in 1989, that promise was repeated by the leaders ascending to power in post-Communist states.

Most of these promises remained unfulfilled because they were not meant to be. They usually served other needs that did not imply freedom for all. During the Enlightenment, the idea of rights primarily served the needs of the middle class in England and France. In the British colonies in North America, it served as the justification of a claim to national independence. In 1942, human rights were subordinated to the war needs of the great powers. In 1948, they served the leaders of national independence movements who needed arguments for their struggles. And in 1975, they primarily served the needs of the West in the Cold War.

The idea of rights has seldom served the poor, destitute, dispossessed, and oppressed. Such people usually do not claim rights. Instead, they ask for mercy, expect charity, and seek benefits from benevolent masters. Although a great number of altruistic and well-meaning individuals opposed slavery, serfdom, exploitation, and abuse and called for humanitarianism toward vulnerable groups and weaker members of society – rights have usually been claimed by those strong enough to demand them. Powerful barons in the year 1215, the advancing bourgeoisie of the eighteenth century, and the new political elites in 1948 and 1989 all adopted the idea of rights at a time when it could foster their interests. Once they had assured access to power for themselves, they often abandoned the idea of rights. Such was the case with those Third World leaders who after having became heads of independent states turned into dictators. Similar change experienced a number of former dissents in the Soviet bloc who discarded the cause of human rights after their own ascent to power. One reason was that once they could enjoy power or privileges they no longer had a need for the rhetoric of rights. Another reason was the lack of available resources necessary if equal rights were to be assured for everyone. Both the revolutionaries in the eighteenth-century and the twentieth-century leaders of postcolonial states were satisfied when they got what they wanted and created new walls between themselves and those who had supported their struggles – the city-based proletarians in the eighteenth century and the common people of the postcolonial states.

Regardless of the real, often humane and benevolent, motives of eighteenth-century revolutionaries, poor people in the nineteenth century could well have thought that the bourgeoisie had demanded freedom for all people specifically so that their labor ("freed" from the bonds of servitude) could now be exploited in factories. Likewise, at the time of the Dumbarton Oaks Conference, the leaders of non-Western countries could have thought that Roosevelt and Churchill had announced the Atlantic Charter and the UN Declaration merely because they wanted the whole world to join "their" war. Imprisoned members of the opposition in postcolonial states could think that their oppressors had endorsed the Universal Declaration of Human Rights to get freedom to torture them behind the veil of state sovereignty. In the 1970s, victims of authoritarian regimes in Latin America could well feel that they were abandoned by the human rights offensive of the West. Often, the expectations of the weak, raised during a revolutionary wave of change, have wound up suppressed afterward by dictators and force. This explains why rights have developed in waves: each upsurge of freedom has been followed by a period of regress or oppression and a sense of betrayal among those who were left behind. All these groups ever could do was wait for the next wave of change.[259]

But the promises made and standards announced in waves past would take on lives of their own and, eventually, wind up encouraging people to take a stand. Thus, the unfulfilled promise of the French Revolution encouraged workers to fight for their rights in the nineteenth century. A vision offered by the Atlantic Charter provided the necessary energy for Third World leaders to not allow the great powers to forget their promise. The Universal Declaration of Human Rights provided arguments to justify claims to national independence by the leaders of colonized people. The Helsinki Agreement assured a moral force for the dissidents living under Communist dictatorships. As these emerging groups got strong enough to claim their rights, the new waves would begin.[260]

Whatever the reasons and motivations of the main actors, concepts of rights brought about change and increased the scope of freedom. The content of rights has also been evolving with every new wave of change. The eighteenth-century idea of rights was defined by the needs of an emerging market economy and consequently was limited to civil liberties and political rights. In the nineteenth century, a changed concept of rights included social and economic rights, thus beginning to reflect the needs of the industrial society. Since the twentieth century, sovereignty over land and resources has been becoming a crucial part of the concept of rights. We can expect further evolution with the next wave.

Historical evidence suggests the following sequence of the waves of rights. First, rights are claimed by a powerful social or political group because the idea serves their interests. (Examples are the bourgeoisie before eighteenth-century revolutions, United States and Great Britain at the time of the Atlantic Declaration, the developing states in the UN when they fought apartheid, and the West in the 1970s, when it used human rights in Cold War confrontation with Russia.) We can call this the "ascending" phase of the rights dynamic. In this phase, other nations, states, groups, and organizations join the original impulse because they believe that human rights will serve their own needs and interest. When the original actors realize these interests, including their own access to power, their enthusiasm toward rights wanes.

[259] For the idea to perceive the development in waves, I am indebted to Alvin Toffler (1980).
[260] Interestingly, as each former elite that had abused its power and privileges was swept away, its members would often start to complain that their rights had been violated.

From now on, they think about limiting the calls for rights by their followers and allies in the ascending phase. At that point the original powers ignore the needs of the followers or hide human rights under the carpet (as three powers tried at Dumbarton Oaks) or turn against them (as was the case with Cromwell killing off the diggers, with the postrevolutionary terrors, and with national independence leaders turned into dictators). Now, the followers need to act on the original impulse and continue it. In fact, the emergence of independent social and political movements in favor of rights in the "ascending" phase has been crucial to the depth and durability of a change. The better organized the movement, the broader and more durable the possible change (as with the coalition of well-meaning intellectuals, NGOs, and some small states that assured the adoption of the Universal Declaration of Human Rights in 1948; with the social and legal organizations that led the "revolution of rights" in the United States in the 1960s and worldwide in the 1970s; and with the organized "civil society" opposing Communism). Thus it has been social movement, human rights NGOs, and organizations using law in the public interest that have helped to consolidate the achievements of each wave[261] – often bringing about consequences not intended by the original actors that had launched the wave.[262]

The most recent wave of rights dates back to the Cold War. The usefulness of human rights in the offensive of the "free world" against Communism made human rights an attractive political tool at the time. But when the Communists lost power, their successors became less sensitive to rights. So did the Western governments who had supported them when they were still fighting communism. Less than one decade later, only NGOs, a handful of international agencies, and few state governments were still committed to the human rights cause. At the turn of the century, things changed even further. The Cold War was replaced with the "war on terror" being fought against "the axis of evil." But in that war, human rights were an obstacle rather than a tool.[263] Many other factors discussed above have converged to endanger the very idea of human rights today.

[261] Evidence shows that the durability of human rights movements may primarily depend on the existence and sustainability of non-governmental human rights NGOs: of monitoring, watchdogs, and strategic litigation types. Charles Epp (1998) demonstrated that the persistent action of NGOS was the crucial factor in achieving durable effects of human rights campaigns in the U.S., while the lack of such NGOs resulted in the lack of long-term effects of human rights in India after 1975.

[262] For example, in 1948, the UDHR was not intended to erode the sovereignty of states; in the late 1960s, the decision of the Commission on Human Rights to allow individual communiqués was intended to fight apartheid in South Africa and not to empower individuals vis-à-vis the very same states that advocated the adoption of special procedures. Similarly, the human rights process within the Helsinki Conference began with a modest aim of re-uniting families and was not intended as a means to legitimize human rights movements in the Soviet bloc and, eventually, to subvert Communism.

[263] It seems that the metaphor of war in general is antithetical to human rights. This can be seen with other "war-based" campaigns, such as the "war on crime" or the "war on drugs," both of which lead to immense abuses of human rights.

The present crisis of the idea of rights seems primarily related to the fact that there exists no strong power that could foster its own political interests under the banner of human rights. However, the international human rights movement and human rights organizations within state boundaries have become a power unto themselves. This movement may achieve small victories in daily struggles for rights, defend rights when threatened, and will probably keep the case for human rights alive until a new ascending phase is triggered. That new wave, however, is neither automatic nor inevitable.

Experience proves that ideas flourish in favorable conditions. When these conditions change or an idea fulfills its role it becomes obsolete. In fact, historical records are full of ideas that once mobilized people but eventually ended up buried at the cemetery of social thought. People once thought in terms of contracts and immutable laws ruling the physical and social universe. Then, ideas of change, evolution, and progress took over, only to find a shameful end in social Darwinism and racism. It is difficult to imagine today how popular and "self-evident" and powerful some of these ideas had once been.

Is the idea of human rights bound to follow this trajectory – and share this fate? We cannot rule out that teachers will one day describe human rights as a concept by which a majority of people justified their desires for better life and for a more just world order in the last quarter of the twentieth century. But that need not happen if the idea of human rights proves flexible enough to be adapted to changes in today's society.

Revitalizing the idea of human rights necessitates that we distinguish between what human rights are and what they are not. It is important to realize that human rights are not some magic key that opens all doors leading to justice and happiness. They are just one of many principles and instruments that need to coexist in a democratic state ruled by law. Human rights have to be guarded against further inflation. They should not be confused with other values, nor should they grow at the expense of any other values. Rights must always be reconciled with the needs of democracy, social security, identity, and human dignity.

The search for the balance between human rights and other values will be the subject of this book's remaining chapters.

2

Rights and Democracy

Despite the proliferation of declarations, covenants, and other international agreements in the majority of countries in today's world, human rights still are an ideal rather than the norm. Likewise, the presence of human rights in constitutions does not translate into actual respect for all human rights. In truth, the protection of rights requires more than ratified conventions, constitutions, or even independent judiciary. It depends primarily on the character of a political system and on the social conditions and beliefs about the political system that prevail among the elites and common citizens.[1]

Historical experience and a review of the violations in today's world suggest that human rights are better protected in political systems based on the principle of separation of powers and with checks and balances that prevent excessive concentration of political power. Ever since the writings of Baron de Montesquieu and James Madison, it has been well known that without separation of power the rights of individuals and minorities cannot be effectively protected.[2]

One such check consists of independent courts to which citizens can bring complaints about violations. The courts, however, often are subordinated to the executive. Almost everywhere courts depend on executive power for the enforcement of their decisions. The implementation of constitutional decisions, in turn, is up to the legislature. Hence, the mechanisms that make legislatures respect the decisions of constitutional courts and replace unconstitutional laws with new statutes are indispensable for the protection of rights.

---

[1] "Maintaining limits on the state requires that political leaders find it in their interests to abide by them. . . . Citizen attitudes, values, and behavior are thus central to democratic stability," writes Weingast (1997, 254).

[2] For the eighteenth-century authors, rights were to protect against tyranny rather than to serve the efficiency of the government. (See Montesquieu 1748 part 2, book 11, chapter 6, and Madison 1788.) Accordingly, the 1789 French Declaration stated that "any society in which the guarantee of rights is not assured or the separation of powers not settled has no constitution" (Article 16).

Various mechanisms of checks and balances serve mutual control and oversight between legislative and executive powers. The presidential veto and the power to send laws to courts for judicial review checks the legislature. The executive, in turn, is controlled by the legislative arm with the vote of confidence, questions submitted to the government, and oversight by parliamentary commissions. For the protection of human rights of particular relevance, there is civilian control over the military and security services.

The separation of power is not limited to institutional differentiation between branches of government; it may also have a territorial dimension. Such is the case of federal states where the powers of central authorities are limited and cannot intrude on the competencies of the units of a federation. However, states or lands cannot issue laws or make decisions that violate the federal constitution. Federal judiciary serves as an additional safeguard for the separation of power and for the rights of individuals and minorities.[3]

Human rights are also enhanced by the independence of the media and freedom of speech. Right to information prevents concentration and abuse of power under the veil of secrecy. The exercise of freedom and protection of rights is proportional to the strength and institutional organization of civil society. It should be independent from the state and capable of the protection of rights via various political and judicial mechanisms. Rights and freedoms seem to be enhanced in a social system with a substantial number of independent producers, relatively widespread distribution of wealth, and the absence of dominant economic or social elites.[4]

Human rights can exist and be respected in all political systems that recognize limitation of power.[5] Limited government and a system of checks and balances enabled the protection of rights of individuals and minorities long before the concept of universal human rights was formulated. Limited government and guarantees of individual freedom were introduced in England after 1688[6] and in the United States of America by 1791. As discussed, such freedoms were first granted to small minority of White male property owners. With time, the rights were extended to all males

---

3 This was the main reason why Western powers and all major internal political forces insisted on the federal character of Western Germany after World War II. See Merkl (1982, 28–34), Steiner (1991, 166), and Currie (1994, 10).

4 It is noteworthy that the concentration of dictators' powers coincides with the abundance of such natural resources like oil or gas that can be relatively easily controlled by a tiny political and economic elite. The absence of one dominant resource was considered as one of main reasons for the relative strength of civil society and benign form of government in Kyrgyzstan, particularly when compared with other countries of Central Asia.

5 Conversely, where power is not limited even the best-meaning constitutions and ratified international treaties do not guarantee rights.

6 Such guarantees often resulted from motives other than the protection of rights. North and Weingast demonstrate that the creation of an independent judiciary and legislature by the king of England in 1688 "was an attempt to produce self-enforcing limits on his own actions in order to commit himself credibly to the market reforms he desired" (1998, 13).

and eventually to everyone. Since the end of World War II, human rights have been considered an indispensable element of democracy. Conventional opinion holds that human rights cannot exist in the absence of democracy and democracy cannot exist without human rights. In reality, however, the relation between democracy and human rights is more complex.

DEMOCRACY AND HUMAN RIGHTS

Democracy assures participation, whereas rights protect dignity. However, dignity can hardly exist without participation – and true democracy is not possible without the recognition and protection of individual dignity. Democracy and human rights are interdependent.

In the most basic sense, rights are the foundation of modern democracy. There can be no democracy without such political rights as the right to take part in the conduct of public affairs or the rights to vote and be elected, among others.[7] Similarly, democracy requires freedom of association and the right to assembly, freedom of expression, freedom of movement, and other traditional civil liberties. The right to information is another prerequisite for democracy. Some political philosophers claim that the right to education and other "inclusion rights," such as that to basic social security, are also necessary in a democracy.[8]

Although calls for the recognition of rights are often heard in the absence of democracy – it is only in the democratic state that human rights can flourish. By definition, human rights are equal for everyone regardless of distinctions of sex, race, wealth, hierarchy, and so on. Democracy entrenches such equality because the democratic system of government provides a mechanism for control over those who exercise power. The very fact that each ruling group can be dismissed in a subsequent election – or that a government can lose support of a minority coalition partner – already limits their power. Without the separation of powers that usually accompanies democracy, any protection of rights is only illusory, with the state presiding as judge in its own case. Because the individual is in a weaker position than the state body or the official who violates her rights, she should be able to seek the state's help (in the guise of the courts, police, and prosecutors, etc.) against abuses by state officials. The protection of rights requires a strong, effective state,[9] but state powers need to be divided and the "protective powers" of the state have to be made accessible to individuals and minorities.

---

[7] Rosas (1990, 17–57).

[8] Claus Offe (Elster, Offe, and Preuss 1998, 27) extends the traditional formulae of "life, property and liberty" to include "other material life chances" as an equivalent to property.

[9] Stephen Holmes (1997) demonstrated how a weak state is unable to protect individual rights. Subsequently, Holmes and Sunstein (1999, 48–58) proved that rights without access to the state are meaningless.

Although democracy and human rights are synergetic, there is also potential for tension between them. It is known that democracy may pose a threat to the rights of individuals and minorities, such as when the majority in power is tempted to manipulate political rights to increase its chances for reelection. A majority might suspend the rule of law to protect its interest or under the influence of a momentary passion. A majority may set aside the rights of an ethnic or religious minority, acting on such "standing passion" as religious fanaticism or ethnic hatred.[10] Ever since the trial of Socrates, it has been known that a majority can be self-righteous and insensitive toward dissents. Since the Holocaust, we have known that a majority can also become genocidal.

Even though individual rights originally emerged as protection against the tyranny of absolutist governments, they are as necessary in a democracy as under autocracy. Human rights are to protect the individual from a majority, whether as a dissident or as a member of a minority. Therefore, some decisions should never be promulgated as valid laws nor carried out by the government, even when this government is acting with the support of a majority.

Moreover, individual rights protect a person against the will of a majority not only when this majority pursues evil goals or persecutes dissidents or minorities. Human rights also protect the individual when the majority, in pursuing goals beneficial for the whole of society, trespasses on the rights of individuals. In other words – rights protect an individual when the majority wants to pursue its happiness at the expense of this individual. Therefore, human rights cannot be sacrificed in the interest of the majority nor limited by other utilitarian arguments. Rights are a luxury of a sort, protecting individuals and minorities when their legitimate interests clash with the interest of the majority.[11] Ronald Dworkin has said that a right is a claim that "is wrong for the government to deny an individual even though it would be in the general interest to do so."[12] Rights are trumps taking precedence over the principles of democracy and the public good.

CONSTITUTIONAL DEMOCRACY

Human rights can be protected from threats posed by democracy itself thanks to a number of countermajoritarian devices, such as special protection for constitutions against easy amendments, judicial review, separation of power, and checks and balances. Such mechanisms are the institutional ingredients of modern

[10] Elster (1993, 175–216).
[11] "Rights are one thing; interests are another; and when they collide rights are trumps," writes J. Roland Pennock (Pennock and Chapman 1981, 5).
[12] Dworkin (1977, 269). Dworkin argues that rights are justified as limitations on the will of the majority because they serve two values which are even higher than majority will itself, namely political equality and human dignity (see ibid., 198–9).

constitutionalism and they serve the limitation of the will of the majority, as well as the protection of constitutional democracy. In particular, constitutions protect such minority and individual rights that can be threatened by a majority under interest or passion.[13] Such constitutional rights differ from statutory rights and benefits because they cannot be curtailed by democratic legislators.

Although statutes protect individuals and minorities against executive power, they leave them helpless vis-à-vis legislature that can change a statute at will. In countries where the separation of powers and constitutional courts do not exist, a temporary majority can take certain rights away. As noted, the "Enabling Act" of March 23, 1933, which gave the veil of legitimacy to Nazi rule and to the subsequent Nurnberg laws directed against Jews was adopted by a majority of votes in the German *Reichstag*. Communist legislatures in the Soviet Union also passed many laws that curtailed or violated citizens' rights. Even though in both cases, the bodies called "parliaments" were intimidated and subordinated to executive powers, Hitler and Stalin presented themselves as the executors of the will of the people as revealed in statutes. In many less drastic cases, seemingly democratic legislatures are often tempted to enact laws that disregard rights of minorities.

Constitutions offer protection of rights against legislatures.[14] Legislators may adopt any bill except for such that may be in conflict with the constitution. Therefore, a statute cannot violate the rights of national minorities or the rights of believers or nonbelievers, to name two examples, even if the majority is in favor of such a law. The constitution itself cannot be changed by the same rules as the statutes that are being adopted.[15]

Although democratic procedures define the way in which social decisions are made, human rights set the limits to the content of such decisions.[16] However, even fundamental rights cannot be absolute. Rather, they can be put aside when they clash with other important values. Imprisonment contradicts personal freedom. The ban on racist propaganda or on calls to rebellion limits freedom of expression. Some actions undertaken by police and courts violate privacy. It is essential that such intrusions into the realm of individual rights not be arbitrary, that they be limited to

[13] "The first objective of constitutional self-limitation is to increase resistance against the dictates of the actual moment," writes Sajo (1999, 8). For the discussion of constitutionalism as limitations on democracy see ibid., 49–68.

[14] Significantly, the United States Bill of Rights begins with a prohibition on legislature: "Congress shall make no law...."

[15] Most constitutions require special procedure for constitutional change. Some constitutions exclude altogether the possibility of abridging rights through amendments. Others require a more difficult procedure for changing sections on constitutional rights. (For example, in Poland any change in the chapter on rights in the Constitution may be submitted to national referendum. Article 235, sections 5 and 6 of the 1997 Constitution.)

[16] According to Sajo (1999, 60) "... the extrication of certain issues from majority decision making goes to the heart of constitutionalism."

situations that are defined before a given case of intrusion occurs, and that these intrusions do not violate the due process of law.

In a constitutional state, the conditions under which human rights can be limited or suspended are spelled out in the constitution. Statutory limitations of rights are allowed only to protect such values as national security, public safety, public health, and, sometimes, public morality. A constitution also says which rights can be limited by the legislature. In fact, restricting the power of the legislature to limit constitutional rights is one of the most important steps on the road from parliamentary supremacy to a constitutional system of government, in which democratic decisions are subordinated to pre-established constraints.[17]

Even during emergencies, constitutional rights cannot be left to the arbitrary will of the authorities. Constitutions usually define the situations in which an emergency can be invoked and the authority and procedure by which this emergency can be declared. Constitutions also specify the limitation of constitutional rights allowed during an emergency. In fact, not all rights can be suspended or limited in emergency. Some constitutions specify the rights that cannot be limited while others specify the rights that can be suspended, implying that all other rights cannot be derogated or limited even in emergency.[18] Rights that are upheld during an emergency and cannot be abridged within the process of constitutional change can be considered "supraconstitutional."

[17] It took time and effort for the framers of postcommunist constitutions even to understand the need for restriction on the will of the majority to limit constitutional rights. For example, when the draft constitution was prepared by the Polish Senate in 1990, some members of the Senate's Constitutional Commission discussed with professors Herman Schwartz from the American University in Washington and Herbert Hausmaninger from the University of Vienna the provision that "constitutional rights could be limited only by the statute." For Polish drafters, this was an enormous step forward from a situation in which constitutional rights could be changed by executive order or altogether neglected by an administrative decision. For Western critics, however, this provision took away the very rights the constitution allegedly offered.

[18] Article 8, section 4, of the 1949 Hungarian Constitution (as amended in 1989) enumerates rights and freedoms that cannot be derogated even during emergency. (The right to life and human dignity; a ban on torture and cruel punishment; freedom and security of one's person; a ban on arbitrary detention and arrest; the right to recognition as a person before law; the presumption of innocence; the right to defence in case of penal offenses; the right to due process of law and a ban on retroactivity of the law; freedom of thought, conscience, and religion; gender equality; the rights of children; the protection of women; the rights of ethnic and national minorities; a ban on the deprivation of Hungarian nationality; a ban on expulsion; the right to return to Hungary; protection by the Hungarian state during a citizen's stay abroad; and the right to social security.) Poland's 1983 Act on State of War and States of Emergency Act, in contrast, enumerated rights that could be limited (personal inviolability; sanctity of the home; secrecy of correspondence; the right to associate; freedom of assembly, demonstration, marches, and manifestations), thus implying that all other constitutional rights and freedoms could not be suspended during emergency. The 1997 Constitution of Poland combines both approaches, enumerating those rights that cannot be limited during a state of war or emergency (Article 233, sections 1 and 2), as well as those that can be limited in case of natural disaster (Article 233, section 3).

Constitutional provisions that limit the power of the majority can be understood as exceptional limitations imposed by the framers on political process. This process is a prescribed way in which decision-making bodies debate, argue, bargain, make compromises, and reach decisions about the fulfillment of the goals of the state. In the course of political process public policies are set, scarce resources are allocated and enforceable standards of conduct for citizens and authorities are defined. In a democracy, the political process of decision making is the rule. The constitution sets exceptions to this rule. Most often, the realization of such values as economic progress, the common good, individual and social needs, equality, and social justice is left to the democratic political process that takes place in society and culminates in parliaments. It is a matter of political decision whether, say, a society chooses to live with higher inflation or more unemployment. It is a matter of political decision whether a society wants to have higher taxes and more public spending or lower taxes and more self-reliance and nongovernmental charity. It is a matter of political decision whether a society wants to have a state-controlled medical system or a merely state-regulated system of private health insurance. Democratic politics reflect the hierarchy of social needs.

However, the experience of democratic states has provided good reason to believe that not all decisions can be left to the political process. It appears wiser and more productive to put some of them above such a process and thus introduce limits to political democracy. Three types of decisions warrant such treatment. The first concerns the political process as such. What should it be? What are the rules for making laws? What constitutes the input and how do we arrive at the output? How is power divided and how does the machinery of the government operate? If framers leave such decisions to the political process, then politics will resemble a football field filled with players playing the game at the same time that they are arguing over the rules of the game. It is assumed that it is better to give players rules and let them focus on playing the game. Thus, the "rules" are put above the process and beyond the authority of the players. Of course, it is impossible to fully protect the rules from attempts to manipulate them. However, framers can at least try to insulate to some degree the rules from the politics.

The second group of exceptions comprises minority and individual rights that can be threatened by a majority under the sway of interest or passion. Framers put them above the political process by entrenching them in a constitution. Unlike statutory rights and benefits, constitutional rights form exceptions from the political process and cannot be curtailed by democratic legislators.

The third type of exception protects these very limitations. Here, there are three or four provisions that regulate the mode of constitutional amendments, the possibility to suspend the constitution during emergency, and the power and scope of admissible limitations to constitutional rights introduced by a statute.

When we look at a constitution as a set of exceptions from the political process and something that is above politics and sets the stage for the play of emotions, passions, and interests that politics usually is, even in democracy, we can see more clearly the inherent conflict between democracy and constitutionalism.

The Logic of Democracy and the Logic of Rights

This conflict reflects the different principles governing political process and legal adjudication. Society sets its priorities via democratic process. For example, when there is a simultaneous need to build schools, roads, and bridges in conditions of inadequate resources – all three at the same time – priorities must be set. A public debate ensues, in which some people (usually parents, teachers, and others with a stake in education) suggest that schools be built first. Others (usually the car industry and car owners, particularly those who do not have school-age children) press for the roads and bridges to be built first – in part, they argue, so that children can be taken to schools by way of these new roads and bridges. Of course, despite what these examples may suggest, such a debate is not restricted to self-interests, involving more general principles and an examination of alternate visions of the future (e.g., the benefits of an educated society vs. the benefits of mobility for economy and personal freedom). The rights to assembly and to form political parties, the freedoms of expression and association, and political rights are in place to protect the debate; to assure everyone an opportunity to participate and to secure that both the debate itself and its results are fair.

The debate may lead to one group prevailing over the other or, more often, to a compromise, with the law stating that some schools and some roads be built simultaneously. But a compromise is not written in stone. Laws can be changed, particularly after elections; budgets change every year. Thus, by trial, error, and subsequent approximations, a compromise emerges that best reflects the attitudes and desires of the majority. Every debate is ongoing, though with a legislative decision the burden of proof gets transferred; from now on, no other actions except for those adopted by the legislators are permitted. Proponents of an alternative course need to argue for it with the aim to persuade legislators to change their decisions or – in the next election – to replace the legislators with others more favorably disposed to the proposals in question.

To give another example, a society decides to protect, by statute, the rights of the fetus. Opponents of such a solution may still try to abolish this law, but their actions will be limited; they have to comply with the law in their actions but are still able to challenge it with words and other forms of expression. They can say that the law is too restrictive and causes more harm than good. They can use the issue in the next electoral campaign and, if they win the support of a new majority, reverse the law with a new statute. The new law may be passed and, after some time, it too may be criticized, this time for being too liberal; then the issue will reemerge in the public debate. Eventually, a compromise may be reached that best satisfies both the need to protect the rights of the unborn and a mother's freedom of choice and her right to privacy. This way, by setting new standards and changing laws – thanks to bold moves forward under courageous leadership and cautious steps backward when experience casts doubt – acceptable compromises are reached that reflect the society's collective best possible vision of public good.

In cases of choice between public policy goals and of the allocation of resources, a compromise between interests and goals is set for one year only. This compromise takes the form of a state budget, which cannot look too far ahead for many reasons, including uncertainty about future availability of resources and changing perceptions of public needs.

But constitutions are not written for one year. Once adopted, their provisions are not subject to debate and compromise. If I claim that I have a constitutional right to something, I go to court. The judge decides whether I have this right and if this right can be applied in the given situation. There are no compromises in constitutional courts – either I win or I lose. Right-holders do not need to listen to the arguments of their adversaries and they do not have to agree to a compromise; when they prove their rights, they win, and as winner they take all.

Judicial protection of constitutional rights in a democracy is extremely important when a majority – or any agency acting in the name of the majority – threatens the life and the safety of an individual or when it aims to put aside the very principle of democracy, as was the case in Germany in the 1930s. But the judicial route is not the best one to take when a society is to decide on public choices. For when rights are treated seriously, applying them to the selection of public policy goals necessarily means supplying each person with veto power over the public good.

When we put something into a constitution, we limit the legislators' choice; they cannot violate the constitution. This essentially means that the more principles, values, rights, and goals we include in the constitution, the less room is left for democratic political process and the fewer resources are available to be freely allocated or redistributed by legislators. In a constitutional democracy that treats its constitution seriously, at the beginning of the budgetary process, the government first puts aside the resources needed to meet the constitutional obligations of the state. And constitutional organs tend to bear costs. So does the protection of citizen security from external and internal dangers, which is usually a constitutional task. Then there are the costs of courts, of access to justice, of public defense, and of various related expenditures.[19] Next are the costs related to the rights of people and

---

[19] See Holmes and Sunstein (1999, 233–6) for a presentation of the costs of protection for selected rights in the United States.

the duties of the state. Only after it has put aside the money for all these expenditures can a government begin the political process of bargaining and arguing about the allocation of whatever is left. In this way, every constitutional right takes away resources that could otherwise be available for democratic debate and compromise.

Here, we have what appears to be a paradox of modern constitutionalism: the more there is in the constitution, the less room there remains for democracy and for compromises within society and, consequently, the less power for parliament and more power for those courts in which constitutional claims are settled. For this reason, Mary Ann Glendon blames precisely the revolution of rights for the atrophy of democratic politics, particularly in the United States.[20] Glendon claims that the essential element of democracy is not mere voting but the publicly open process of setting goals, making choices between values and interests, and assigning resources to the implementation of such goals. Constitutions protect entry into public debate, as well as its openness, but they should not preclude the outcome of such debate. In the case of constitutional rights, however, there is nothing to debate: the outcome is pre-determined by a constitution and the executive and legislative branches of government are obliged to set aside the resources needed to fulfill a bevy of rights-based obligations. Moreover, with constitutionalization of social policies, power gets transferred from parliaments to the courts in which constitutional claims are settled.[21]

A slightly different perspective is that a constitutional right can be compared to a veto power. A right-holder is entitled to say to the majority: "No, you cannot go trampling over my right." In most cases, this is justified by the basic character of rights: they protect the values and resources necessary for the security and dignity of an individual. However, when constitutional rights go beyond these limits to protect the whims of individuals or group interests, they can disrupt the political community by providing too many people with too broad a veto power. Consequently, citizens and pressure groups can end up disrupting necessary cooperation in pursuit of their own selfish interests.

Excessive constitutionalization of rights also affects the character and content of political debate. Political conflicts are, after all, necessary to offer voters a choice. People would not know for whom to vote if everyone agreed with all other contenders. Ever since the birth of modern democracies in late nineteenth century, the main area of conflict has been the role of the state in the redistribution of national

---

[20] "The rights revolution has contributed in its own way to the atrophy of vital local governments and political parties, and to the disdain for politics that is now so prevalent on the American scene. (...) To many activists, it seemed more efficient, as well as more rewarding, to devote one's time and efforts to litigation that could yield total victory, than to put in long hours at political organizing, where the most one can hope to gain is, typically, a compromise" (Glendon 1991, 5 and 6).

[21] One argument against the constitutionalization of social and economic rights is that when such rights are in a constitution, the decisions about budgetary expenditures shift from the government and the legislature to courts, which lack competence in budgetary matters.

income. Politicians have been arguing about taxes and expenditures, duties and subsidies, minimum wage, state purchases, and other incentives to the economy. But with constitutional entrenchment of social and economic rights, many of these conflicts are now being preconcluded.[22] As a result, political conflicts have been gradually shifting away from the economy and into symbolic values, issues of national and religious identity, historical controversies, and the sphere of emotions.[23] These themes are, after all, at the basis of the conflicts that pose the greatest threat to the rights of minorities.

The complex interplay between rights and democracy suggests caution in defining what ought to belong to a constitution and what should be left for democratic public policy. Some matters should simply be set and adjusted in the political process and not be framed as constitutional rights. Similarly, the interests of particular social groups, even those of the most powerful or numerous (be they workers, peasants, capitalists or politicians), should be left out of the constitution to be deliberated in a democratic political process. Constitutions should be limited to necessary institutions, procedural rules, and the very basic rights, without getting into matters of public policy that benefit from being left to open debate and political solutions. All this is because the inflation of constitutional rights can weaken democracy. That deserves to be the guiding principle during the process of constitution making.

The Challenges of Democratic Constitution Making

The pressure to entrench in the constitution not only the rights but also the interests of society's various groups has been particularly strong – and often irresistible – during constitution making in the transition countries. As a rule, any simultaneous systemic shift to both constitutionalism and democracy seems to obey the following principle: the more democratic the framing process, the more rights are inserted into a constitution, and, consequently, the less room for future democracy is left in the new constitution.[24]

This problem is further exacerbated by the dynamics of transition itself. Usually, during authoritarian rule, demands for change are formulated in terms of rights. People living under a dictatorship believe that every right put into the constitution will further limit the dictator's discretionary power, so strengthening the society.

---

[22] In the European Union, the scope of national politics is further limited by the decisions of the European Commission and Parliament.

[23] Another reason for this is globalization. Most national governments are unable to counteract economic decisions made by global powers that affect the value of national currency, wages that would be competitive on global markets, prices of imports and exports, and so on.

[24] Osiatyński (2000a, 154).

Human rights seem especially attractive to the excluded, because those who are excluded generally do not hope for access to decision making. When such access is, in fact, possible, people tend to put their hopes in democracy instead. "When we are finally permitted to freely elect *our* government, it will be a *good* government and it will take care of our needs" – so goes the common hope at the beginning of any democratization process. Such expectations, however, almost inevitably end up as frustrations for a number of good reasons. The most common is the lack of adequate resources to meet all needs and expectations fast enough. Conflicting interests, contests among new elites, corruption, and other factors magnify the frustration. What follows are new attempts at social mobilization on the one hand and the return of human rights claims on the other.

Recent transitions from authoritarian rule reveal a pattern of progression from demands being formulated in terms of human rights to calls for democracy and, finally, back to the acknowledgment of the need for rights. What changes, however, is the character of the rights being demanded, as they come to reflect precisely those needs that have not been met and thus caused the frustration. Although political oppression gives rise to calls for civil and political rights, social exclusion favors the redefinition of rights in the social and economic (or developmental) sense. Participation, inclusion, social rights, and the right to development are called for once democratic hopes and expectations have led to frustration.

ILLIBERAL AND POPULIST DEMOCRACIES

Conflicts between rights and democracy have resurfaced with many recent transitions to democracy. A single crucial element of the so-called promotion of democracy by the United Stated and its allies is the requirement that states hold popular elections, seen as a precondition for international recognition of a regime as well as for any foreign aid. According to democratic theory, free elections provide the necessary legitimacy to elected authorities. In fact, however, in many countries lacking democratic traditions or prior social and institutional structures conducive to democracy, the choice provided by elections has often been illusory. And even in more mature democracies, elections have often done little to help voters exercise control over elected officials.[25] An analysis of a number of European countries undergoing the transition to democracy following the 1989 demise of communism[26] has revealed that populist governments have risen to power, even despite the accession of these

---

[25] This suggests that the promotion of democracy should reach far beyond mere elections and toward creating durable institutions that could preserve open political competition, limit the government, and protect human rights.

[26] Butora et al. (2007).

states to the European Union. In the recent decades we have witnessed the rise of what Fareed Zakaria has named "illiberal democracies."[27]

A common characteristic of these illiberal and populist "democracies" is a conviction shared by their leaders that electoral victory gives them unlimited power. Many of them have attempted to weaken the separation of powers and have sought to control all independent institutions, including the judiciary. Usually, populist leaders use all accessible means to spread fear among citizens, precisely so that they will be seen as the ones who are able to save the voters from real or imaginary threats. Fear is crucial for both dictatorships and populist democracies. The difference is that a dictator's message is "fear *me* or I will harm you." A populist, instead, says "fear *them* and I will save you." In practice, both illiberal and populist "democracies" justify violations of human rights by quoting the alleged interest "of the people." Populist leaders say that they respond to opinions and preferences of a majority of citizens.[28] With time, however, they almost inevitably depart from democracy itself. The examples of Iran under Khomeini, Venezuela under Chavez, Belarus under Lukashenka, and Russia under Putin should be convincing. Poland under the rule of the Kaczyński twins came dangerously close to this line, too.

The last example proves that even membership in the European Union (EU) does not guarantee protection from populism. Interestingly, the EU has been the most important agent of change in favor of human rights in Central Europe, upholding rights among the preaccession criteria. As a result, all accession countries have had to adjust their legislation and institutions to human rights standards. After accession, however, it has become obvious that the EU does not have the effective mechanisms for monitoring and enforcing continued adherence to standards.[29] As a result, the European Union is unable to counteract populist threats to human rights emerging in member states both old and new.

It can be said that populist politics essentially replace rational arguments with appeals to fear and other emotions. However, a similar shift away from rational discourse is also present in most well-established democracies.[30]

---

[27] Zakaria (2003, 89–118).

[28] This claim contradicts the essential character of what Sunstein calls a *deliberative democracy*. "Deliberative democracies do not respond mechanically to what a majority currently thinks. They do not take snapshots of public opinion. A deliberative democracy requires the exercise of governmental power, and the distribution of remedies and burdens, to be justified not by the fact that a majority is in favor of it but on the basis of reasons that can be seen, by all or almost all citizens, as public-regarding." Sunstein (2001, 239).

[29] On the initiative of this author and with the support of hundreds of NGOs active in the region, a special fund to support human rights monitoring and watchdog organizations in the new EU member countries was created in 2005.

[30] According to Sunstein a growing tendency to replace deliberation with polarization is visible in public institutions, in the media, and in the Internet. See Sunstein (2001, 36–47 and 240).

Electronic Democracy

At the core of democratic theory is the conviction that open, rational, public debate brings about the best possible social outcomes. For decades political discourse in democracies has been concerned with the issue of allocation and redistribution of resources. Politicians argued about a state's proper goals and tried to assure the resources necessary for the fulfillment of these goals. Public debate concerned needs and the strategies for meeting them, the choice of proper public policy, the degree of state intervention in the economy, and decisions regarding taxes and expenditures. Such debating usually followed the principles of logic and rational argument. Of course, at times leaders would appeal to emotions and symbols, but logical arguments and hard numbers were the meat of political campaigns. The freedoms of speech and association and the right to assembly have always assured open entry into such debates. Civil liberties and political rights were always there precisely to prevent those in power from monopolizing and manipulating the debate. Opponents were encouraged to utilize media, political parties, citizens' organizations, or assemblies to voice their opinions and offer alternatives, which would be submitted to the leaders competing for the support of voters.[31] But the language of politics has changed everywhere, and the most important reasons for this are constitutionalism, globalization, and modern electronic media.

The impact of excessive constitutionalization has already been analyzed. When too many decisions are already made and too many resources precommitted, politicians cannot argue about them. Analogously, in the European Union, national politics cannot debate decisions taken at the supranational level. This tendency is further exacerbated with globalization, which has been causing most national states to lose power over their economies as decisions are made by multinational corporations and money managers. Where once these "capitalists" invested in mines and factories, now they profit from the electronic transfer of billions of dollars or, increasingly, the euro and other currencies from one country to another, often destabilizing local economies in the process. And whereas physical investments required long-term stability and rule of law, monetary speculators do not need to bother with the political systems of the countries they affect. National governments are powerless over these developments. Often, major economic decisions are taken by offshore funds that evade control of any state. With the exception of the United States (and, recently, China), governments are unable to control decisions affecting their economies.[32]

---

[31] This is the essence of deliberative democracy. "Constitutional institutions, such as a system of checks and balances, are best understood not as a way of reducing accountability to the public but as a guarantee of deliberation," writes Sunstein (2001, 239).

[32] Richard Falk (2002, 72) observes that globalization has a "dual tendency to evade state controls by penetrating them at will or by situating key activities beyond territorial control." Falk also suggests that

Thus, one of the most important subjects of public debate is being removed from politics, except when opposition parties accuse governments for their failure to control what has became uncontrollable.[33]

As a result of this and many other factors, the political discourse has been moving away from politics and into symbols and emotions. Some of these changes are valuable. For example, the political discourse in the West has become more sensitive to the rights and needs – including identity-based needs – of women, minorities and vulnerable groups than it has ever been before. However, nationalism and ethnic pride, crime and fear, and personal politics and private accusations that once were the domain of yellow press and societal gossip found its way to the public debate, politics, and parliaments. It is significant that political debate in the biggest democracy in the world focused for over a year on the president's affair with his intern.

Politicians find emotional conflicts attractive. Their predecessors could be held accountable when they promised more housing or more welfare spending. But how can one's performance be assessed on a promise of, say, increased national pride or respect for transcendental values? Emotional politics is also attractive for the electronic media. It is widely assumed (perhaps incorrectly) that a television viewer cannot focus his attention for more than a few seconds and hence is unable to follow a rational debate. Thus, the media thrive on sensationalism, crime, and blame. To secure airtime or print space in the media – and thereby access to potential voters – politicians are prompted to participate in the manipulation of symbols and emotions. But the resulting derationalized public discourse does not need rights and freedoms; rather, it thrives on spreading fear. Leaders of modern democracies often threaten voters with dangers that they then promise to counteract. This can be fear of crime, fear of terror, or fear of "the others." So has the growth of populism in a number of democracies also been shifting public debate further away from rational arguments and pushing it instead toward symbols, fears, and threats. In the United States, the abuse of vocabulary of war during the G. W. Bush administration neither nourished rational debate nor did it promote human rights – anywhere.

It may even be that human rights are, in fact, worse off in democracies than in dictatorships. After all, under arbitrary rule of an authoritarian government, many people are oppressed and no one can predict whether she will become a victim of

the challenge of globalization "can only be successfully met by a radical extension of democracy that goes well beyond state/society electoral relationships and brings democratic procedures and values to global areas of authority" (ibid., 63). Among global institutions that should be democratized are the World Bank, WTO, and IMF; the fact that they are being attacked by antiglobalist movements reflects the actual role of these institutions as more important centers of global power than the United Nations.

[33] However, the banking crisis of late 2008 restored the consciousness of the need for greater role of states in the economy. This doesn't change the reality that in a globalized economy effective measures need to be adopted on a supranational level.

police abuse or other violations by government officials. Therefore, human rights have popular support. In a democracy, however, pretty much everyone can plan a strategy for successful living without fear of government. Human rights, in effect, end up important only to those who want to participate in public life and oppose the government. The majority, however, does not fear surveillance, police abuse, or torture – because they do not get involved in activities that would pose such risks. And they are indifferent to the violations of rights of those people whom they consider a threat to their own security, which is why increased fear further affects people's attitude toward human rights negatively. Fear of crime causes the public's indifference to the widespread abuse of pretrial detention and violations of fair trial rights, as people begin to prefer to have potential predators in jails instead of bothering with the presumption of innocence. Fear of terror leads to popular support for emergency measures, abuses of the rights of suspects, and even of the curtailment of civil liberties for everyone. Mass media do little to counteract this tendency; in fact, they often fuel it.

Populist leaders often employ national sentiments and references to the fear of "the others." This tendency threatens the rights of minorities, particularly because in the twentieth century, those who are considered minorities – both those who were victims of the Holocaust and those being targeted today – significantly differ from those who were considered minorities by the early theories of democracy. In eighteenth-century political philosophy, minorities have been perceived as those parts of the common body of citizens who had been outvoted in elections. The essential element of democracy as majority rule is the belief that any (temporary) minority can use civil liberties and political rights to influence voters and, possibly, become a new majority.[34] In fact, civil liberties and political rights arose in part to assure that the ruling majority does not prevent a minority from acting toward this goal.

This concept of democracy – commonly accepted in the nineteenth-century world of national states – did not take into account that there can exist, within a single state, durable minorities based on identities that differ from those of the majority of citizens, differences that will preclude these minorities from becoming majorities.[35] Such durable minorities – ethnic, national, and religious – first became widespread in the postcolonial world.[36] Their exclusion from decision making has

---

[34] A good example of this type of analysis of the relationship between the majority and a minority is *The Federalist*, written by James Madison, Alexander Hamilton, and John Jay during the campaign for the ratification of the U.S. federal Constitution.

[35] John Stuart Mill was firmly convinced that "free institutions are next to impossible in a country made up of different nationalities." (See Beetham 1998, 97.)

[36] The issues of minorities first emerged at the crisis of the Turkish empire and gained momentum after World War I with the disintegration of the Russian and Austro-Hungarian empires into multiple independent states. In every new state, the nationals of the former master-state became

been at the root of secessions, acts of terrorism, and civil wars.[37] The concept of rights seemed to be of limited use for the leaders of such groups.

INDIVIDUAL AND GROUP RIGHTS

This leads us to the issue of group rights. Even though many human rights – perhaps a majority of them – were intended to protect collective interests,[38] they are granted to individuals and not to groups. Moreover, they are enforced by individualized court action. A single *person* can join an association, marry, form a family, join a church or labor union, or sign up for a political party. The classical theory of rights assume that no such group is directly protected by human rights, nor can a group claim human rights for the benefit of the group as such.[39] According to this theory, group interests are better served by the instruments of public policy than by rights asserted in courts.[40] The essence of public policy is to seek compromises between the interests of various social groups. The rights of individuals and minorities were to set limits to such compromises and policies.

The rights of minorities are closest to group rights. The attitudes toward the protection of minorities have changed a number of times following historical developments. As discussed above, after World War I, at the Paris Peace Conference, special minority treaties were imposed on the newly independent states of Central and Eastern Europe. But the Versailles system failed – minorities were not protected, anti-Semitism and xenophobia were rampant, tensions between nations and states grew, and numerous treaties were recalled. Moreover, Hitler used the alleged protection of German minorities in Czechoslovakia and Poland as justification for annexation and invasion. This was one of a number of reasons why the founders of

minorities. Moreover, in the centers of the former empires, those who had migrated from the provinces that had gained independence also became minorities. The same pattern has been observed since the 1960s, after the grant of independence to the colonial nations of Asia and Africa and, once again, in the 1990s, after the collapse of the Soviet Union and Yugoslavia.

37   A major reason for postelectoral violence and civil wars in sub-Saharan Africa has been the formation of political parties along ethnic lines. A recent example was the January 2008 bloodshed after the elections in Kenya.

38   See Raz (1986, 251–4).

39   This does not mean that social groups cannot have rights; perhaps they can even have natural rights – but groups, according to Henkin (Henkin et al. 1999, 6), cannot have human rights. Waśkiewicz (1977, 24) warns that such group rights should not be confused with human rights "because there exists a danger that natural rights of natural social groups will devour human rights of the individuals."

40   For the opposite view, see Freeman, who argues that "some collective rights have the same nature and justification as well-established individual rights" (1995, 28). Stavenhagen claims that without collective rights, individual rights of ethnic minorities and indigenous people cannot be achieved. Therefore, "group or collective rights should be considered human rights to the extent that their recognition and exercise promotes the individual rights of their members," states Stavenhagen (1996, 152).

the new world order after 1945 were skeptical about the rights of minorities.[41] They hoped that members of vulnerable groups could be sufficiently protected by assuring every person fundamental human rights combined with bans on discrimination on the grounds of national origin, race, religion, or sex.[42]

However, with the collapse of colonial empires, with new ethnic tensions and conflicts, and with the evident insufficiency of liberal-democratic institutions to deal with such conflicts, the issue of minority rights returned. Accompanying this process was a wave of interest in cultural identity and the growing self-worth of indigenous groups and other minorities. Rather than attempt to assimilate into the majority, these groups now derived their self-esteem from their own cultural peculiarities. This attitude shift has been reflected in many of the international instruments adopted since 1990 that aim to protect minorities.[43] On a national level, various institutional mechanisms ranging from autonomy to protected quotas for minorities and power sharing have been introduced. At the same time, in a number of constitutions the formation of political parties on the basis of ethnicity, nationality, or religion is prohibited. Some authors have also suggested that there exists differentiation of citizenship rights along cultural criteria. Will Kymlicka suggests that "in culturally plural societies, differential citizenship rights may be needed to protect a cultural community from unwanted disintegration."[44]

Simultaneously, the individualism inherent to the liberal concept of rights has been challenged by communitarian philosophers who argue that no individual exists in a vacuum, independent of a community and culture. In fact, it is the community that provides the individual with the categories of perception and the instruments of communication. The community affords its members their symbols, values, identity, and sense of meaning. Taking into account this crucial role of community for an individual, we should treat cultural communities on the basis of their position, strength, and capacities in the given cultural and national context. When necessary, members of communities that are threatened within the larger national state should

---

[41] See above, Chapter 1. However, the atrocious persecution of such minority groups as the Jews, Roma, Sinti, and homosexuals by the Nazi regime did not go unnoticed. The Convention on the Prevention and Punishment of the Crime of Genocide was adopted in December 1948 to prevent the destruction of "national, ethnic, racial, or religious groups."

[42] During the drafting of the UDHR, "it was even said that the very concept of 'minorities' is inconsistent with the principle of absolute equality enshrined in the Charter of the United Nations and in many national constitutions, as the term 'national minority' signifies 'a category of citizens whose political, economic, and social status was inferior to that of the citizens belonging to the majority,'" writes Henkin (Henkin et al. 1999, 427).

[43] Examples include the UN Declaration on the Rights of Persons Belonging to National or Ethnic, Religious and Linguistic Minorities (1992), the European Framework Convention on the Protection of National Minorities (1994), the European Charter for Regional and Minority Language (1992), and, more recently, the UN Declaration on the Rights of Indigenous People (2007).

[44] Quoted in Beetham (1998, 91).

be treated differently from other citizens.[45] For example, indigenous people and linguistic and religious minorities should be offered special protection by the state.[46] Such protection may include electoral quota or other mechanisms to assure the participation of indigenous populations in democratic decision making.[47] It is up for debate, however, if such protection of cultural minorities is to take the form of rights or if such rights would belong to individual members of a minority or to the minority as such.[48] The United Nations Declaration on the Rights of Indigenous People (adopted on September 13, 2007) speaks about "indigenous people and individuals."[49]

Another category of rights that resembles group rights consists of some of the so-called third-generation rights, including but not limited to the rights to peace, development, cultural heritage, and a clean environment.[50] Such "solidarity rights"

---

[45] Will Kymlicka (2001, 458–60) distinguished between indigenous communities and immigrant groups that also have a distinct cultural identity. The latter can be compelled to respect liberal principles, "so long as immigrants know this in advance, and nonetheless choose to come" (459). By contrast, indigenous people were not asked if they want to belong to a larger community imposed on them by the conquerors. On this basis, Kymlicka supports the claim of Pueblo Indians to be exempt from the decisions of the U.S. Supreme Court.

[46] David Beetham (1998, 90) summarizes the communitarian argument as follows: "From this socially rooted conception of the person, and of individuality itself, it follows that states cannot be neutral about the well-being of different cultures within their territory; and they can justifiably take measures to ensure their survival when under threat, even if this means treating their members differently in certain respects from other citizens."

[47] The rules for the April 2008 elections to the Constitutional Assembly in Nepal included such a mechanism. A preset percentage of names on every party list was to be assigned to candidates from indigenous groups. Furthermore, 26 of the 601 seats of the Constitutional Assembly were not to be allotted on the basis of election but were instead to be distributed by the future Council of Ministers to those delegates from among the fifty-nine groups belonging to the Federation of Indigenous Nationalities that did not obtain representation as a result of election. (In fact, among the elected CA members 33.39 percent were candidates from indigenous groups, elected from party lists. See napalnews.com archive May 8, 2008.)

[48] "The concept of minority protection can become fully operational only by transcending the still dominant framework of individual rights, and adopting the concept of collective rights," claims Jovanović (2005, 638). Similarly, Varady (1997, 39) suggests that the widespread Eastern European "denial of bilingual road signs, place names, and minority schools can hardly be conceived as anything but an attitude and a gesture towards a group; it would be quite difficult to structure opposition against such denial on the basis of individual rights" (quoted in Jovanović, 635).

[49] A great majority of rights in the Declaration is assigned to "indigenous people." Rights to a nationality (Article 6) and to life, physical and mental integrity, liberty and the security of person (Article 7.1) are assigned to "indigenous individuals." In one case, the Declaration uses the notion of collective rights, stating that "indigenous peoples have the collective right to live in freedom, peace and security as distinct peoples and shall not be subjected to any act of genocide or any other act of violence, including forcibly removing children of the group to another group" (Article 7.2). For a detailed description of the process of adoption of the Declaration, see Tauli-Corpuz (2007).

[50] Stavenhagen (1996, 153) claims that "the right to the environment is simultaneously a collective and an individual right. As an individual right it can be protected only in collective form, so it must also be considered a collective human right."

imply cooperation between the individual and the state rather than conflict and opposition.[51] Nevertheless, the status of third-generation rights as human rights is a matter of controversy.[52] Western democracies do not recognize third-generation rights as human rights.[53] Moreover, some collective rights may be used as an excuse for placing limitations on individual rights.[54]

The relationship between the protection of the individual and the protection of social groups is at the core of the conflict between two different visions of democracy and rights in constitutional and legal order. Although liberals tend to protect the rights of individuals, conservative authors often emphasize that rights protect natural subgroups of society from intrusion by the state, postulating a ban on state actions aimed at the protection of individuals who can be oppressed within such groups as the family or the church. In a liberal response, Will Kymlicka distinguishes between "good" and "bad" group rights.[55] Some liberals would extend the state's intervention to the protection of the rights of individuals violated within groups, especially if the structure, organization, and traditional customs governing a group allow for some degree of coercion.[56] For this very reason, David Beetham postulates that minority rights proposed by the communitarians should be counterbalanced by the protection of members of a community against abusive cultural practices: "If states should not be neutral about the well-being of cultural communities within their borders, neither should they be neutral about practices which violate basic human rights standards,

[51] Many such rights make sense only when understood as granting every individual a right to initiate action aiming at the protection of collective goods. In this framework, we can talk about "the right to a clean environment" in the following terms: The environment can be protected by instruments of individual rights when every person has the right of access to information concerning the environment, including information about the environmental effects of a given activity, collective or private, as well as the right to demand from the state an action that would stop environmentally harmful activity. It is a similar situation with the right to peace: "It is plausible to insist that if a state launches war, courts war, or engages in policies likely to lead to war, any one of its inhabitants might claim a violation of one or more established human rights," writes Henkin (Henkin et al. 1999, 479).

[52] Meron (2006, 447) has observed that the focus on procedural rights is merely one of a number of ways in which human rights and environmental protection have been interrelated. Others include "the formulation and recognition of an individual substantive right to a satisfactory, decent, healthy environment. Another approach has been to consider the conservation and improvement of environmental quality as a way to satisfy human rights." (For analysis of human rights-based adjudication on environmental protection, see ibid., 446–61.)

[53] The "third-generation" rights were included into the African Charter on Human and People's Rights (1982).

[54] "Collective rights often turn out to be society's counter-claims to individual rights and may therefore have an anti-individual-right consequence" (Shestack 1989, 37).

[55] "In many cases, group rights supplement and strengthen human rights, by responding to potential injustices that traditional rights doctrine cannot address. These are the 'good' group rights. There are cases, to be sure, where illiberal groups seek the right to restrict the basic liberties of their members. These are the 'bad' group rights" (Kymlicka 1996, 446).

[56] The conflict between these two visions was a dominant controversy during the last stage of constitution making in Poland in 1997. (See Osiatyński 1997b, 37–44.)

such as preventing individuals from leaving the community; discriminating against women; campaigning for the denial of rights to members of other communities, or advocating supremacy over them, and so on."[57] Will Kymlicka allows outside intervention in such cases: "In some cases, these illiberal practices are not only bad, but intolerable, and the larger society has a right to intervene to stop them."[58]

With political conflicts shifting from the economy into the realms of symbols, emotions, and identities, the danger of oppression within natural groups is as serious as the threat to various minorities. Even in democratic societies, individual and groups require stronger protection than ever before. However, formal democratic institutions may prove insufficient for such protection. Democratization may, in fact, fuel ethnic conflicts, particularly when political leaders seek to use it for electoral purposes. This often occurs when a particular ethnic group has played an important economic role before democratization and the first free elections.[59]

Exclusion

Minorities are among those groups that feel excluded from democratic participation. In Western democracies, majorities have become increasingly indifferent to social and political exclusion. They have come to believe that there should be no exclusion, with political rights assuring participation in the political process, social rights offering a minimum of security and the rise of the welfare state resulting in everyone sharing the benefits of growth. But the introduction of neoliberal economics and politics on a global scale in the 1980s has resulted in a significant increase of the gap between the rich and the poor, leading to the growing exclusion of many people from the well-being of societies, even in wealthy countries. Affected groups include refugees, national minorities, and the structurally unemployed. For many of them, in addition to any sense of economic or social security, their physical security is lost, particularly in countries where war and violence have become the means of providing for many people's basic needs. In addition, poor and disadvantaged populations

---

[57] For Beetham (1998, 90), both special protection of communities and the possibility of intrusion into a community's practices have the same justification in the interests of individuals: "If the justification for the protection of cultural communities derives from their value to the individuals who comprise them, then the interests of individuals also set limits to the range of cultural practices that such protection can be allowed to validate" (ibid.).

[58] Kymlicka (1996, 446).

[59] This was the case of the Jews in Central Europe after World War I, and today it is the case of the Chinese in Southeast Asia and Indians in East Africa (see Chua 2003). Neier adds two circumstances that can be exploited by political leaders: One is when a particular ethnic group has been favored before democratization (e.g., the Tamils in British Ceylon and the Tutsi in Rwanda). The second, exemplified by Kenya, occurs when "members of different ethnic groups are opponents in an election and one side is believed to have fraudulently claimed victory" (quoted in Neier's presentation for the Africa Forum in Dakar, February 1, 2008).

worldwide are also excluded from legal protection.[60] Despite claims to equality and fairness, law often perpetuates exclusion. Those who have knowledge and control resources use law for their own benefit.[61]

It is evident that the beneficiaries of growth are not themselves eager to share their profits with poorer and weaker people, even when the latter contribute to the advantage of the former or suffer a disproportional share of the environmental and social costs for other people's prosperity. Nevertheless, calls for inclusion can hardly be cast in the language of rights, particularly its Western version, because it is so focused on civil and political rights. Although these rights can protect the autonomy and ownership of those who already possess property, they seem inadequate for protecting the basic life interests of powerless people who have little to lose and even less to protect. So the underprivileged look to governments for the provision of minimal social services and for the creation of new mechanisms for inclusion, but this requires both an active role of the states and new global regulations. However, there exists no system of global governance that would be sensitive to the needs of the poor.

Mechanisms for inclusion should aim at both basic security and participation.[62] Rights can be granted without much discussion about which rights warrant protection or what should constitute public priorities. This paternalistic origin of rights is pretty common in the contemporary world, especially when rights are borrowed into national constitutions from the international law of human rights rather than from internal dialog about the needs of the people in a given country.

Not surprisingly, political activists in postcolonial societies and developing countries are concerned primarily with the empowerment of disadvantaged populations and with real participation in the process of defining rights, particularly during the constitution-making process. They hope that broad participation will ensure the legitimacy of a constitution and, at the same time, provide the most adequate

---

[60] "More than half the world's population lives outside recognized and enforceable laws, without effective legal means to protect their families, homes or other possessions," writes Mary Robinson, former UN Commissioner for Human Rights (quoted in Commission on Legal Empowerment of the Poor 2008, volume 1, 29). The Commission claims that "around four billion people, the majority of the world's population, are excluded from the rule of law" (ibid., 19).

[61] "When people can use the law when it benefits them and ignore it when it does not, typically preexisting inequalities will be reinforced and frequently exacerbated," write de Langen and Barendrecht (2009, 7). This reality led Sunstein (2001, 155–82) to formulate an anticaste principle in which he suggests that democratic constitutions should forbid "a situation in which laws turn a morally irrelevant characteristic, especially if that characteristic is highly visible, into a systematic basis for second-class citizenship" (ibid., 242).

[62] Carol C. Gould (1988, 191) suggests that "in addition to the right to democracy, which is most often included among the protected political rights, there is yet another fundamental human right, namely, the right to participate in the making of decisions concerning social, economic, and cultural activities outside the political sphere."

content for rights.[63] Such was the guiding principle of the electoral law for the
Constitutional Assembly in Nepal.[64] The April 2008 elections amounted to a double
revolution. Political victory went to the radical Maoist Party that had launched a violent rebellion lasting from 1996 to 2006.[65] The social revolution, in turn, manifests
in a radical change of the political elite, with the former elites (the "others," in the
language of electoral law) holding just over 33 percent of the seats in the Assembly,
while two-thirds have gone to representatives of formerly marginalized or excluded
social groups.[66]

It remains open whether such democratic participation and political inclusion
can truly assure social inclusion, particularly in conditions of scarce resources. Even
if the definition of rights is limited to basic human needs, their implementation
requires political will and adequate resources. National constitutions may promise
security, but they will not increase the amount of resources to be shared, nor can they
instill much willingness to transfer wealth from rich to poor. Similarly, international
human rights documents are of limited use without effective international mechanisms for worldwide redistribution of resources. Such redistribution, however, as
well as other forms of international aid, cannot be treated as an absolute right of
leaders of underdeveloped countries to claim help and then to refuse to demonstrate
how the aid is used. In today's world both inclusion and accountability should be
global concerns.

---

[63] The paramount importance of participation in constitution making was the dominant thesis of the
presentation by African participants in a conference on comparative constitutionalism in Eastern
Europe and Africa held in Warsaw in May 2001 (see Rosen 2003).

[64] Distributed by election were 575 seats in the Constitutional Assembly. (As noted, 26 seats were to be
allocated after the elections to those indigenous groups that would have obtained no representatives
as a result of the elections.) Two hundred forty seats were contested in first past the post system and
335 in proportional electoral rules. For proportional elections, every contending party was obliged
to meet a preassigned quota for various social groups and minorities. The quota for women was
50 percent of the candidates for proportional representation and at least 33 percent of all candidates
to the Constitutional Assembly. Of the candidates (male and female), 31.2 percent were to be the
Madhesi (i.e., people of southern Nepal, generally descendants of migrants from India close to people
of Bihar and Uttar Pradesh); 13 percent were to be Dalits (i.e., the so-called untouchables or outcasts,
belonging to the lowest cast); 37.8 percent were to be Janajatis (i.e., members of oppressed groups,
including indigenous populations); 4 percent were inhabitants of backward regions (primarily in the
mountains), and 30.2 percent were "others." The latter category includes the Hindu Brahmins and
the Chetris, who had dominated Nepali politics and society prior to the 2008 elections.

[65] The Maoists have 220 (or 36.60 percent) of seats, the National Congress (a traditional ruling party) 110
seats (18.30 percent), and the United Marxists-Leninists 103 seats (17.14 percent). The remaining seats
are shared by 22 smaller parties. Sixty-seven of the 92 parties that participated in the elections did not
meet the threshold. (For the rise of the Maoists in Nepal, see Thapa 2003.)

[66] The Constitutional Assembly has a 33.22 percent representation of women, 34.09 percent Madhesis,
8.17 percent Dalits, 33.39 percent Janajatis, and 3.83 percent candidates from backward regions. Other
groups (comprising the former elites) have 33.91 percent representation.

One reason for this is that in poor countries democratization may prevent development and necessary reforms. In a democracy, a majority makes the decisions. When this majority is poor or excluded, it may use its voting power to elect leaders who make empty promises. What is worse is that this majority might elect leaders who find scapegoats and point to "others" as guilty of the people's misery. The majority may also use its votes to press for increased consumption rather than economic reforms that would make the economy more efficient in the long run. Every transition country has experienced such difficulties with leadership during reforms. People vote the reformers out of power. Effective in mitigating this type of democratic pressure are the constitutional independence of central banks and limits on budget deficit.

But even with such safeguards democratic politics in many countries is under constant pressure from the poor. Some observers fear that political mechanisms will prove unable to resist the redistributory pressures of majorities. In such a context, further radical reconceptualization of political theory may be suggested. One hypothetical example could be to link the power of electoral votes to tax returns. Those who pay little tax could have the power of one vote. People with higher stakes in society and economics, who pay, say, ten times more in taxes, would have the power of two votes; the super-taxed citizens would have three. This aggregated majority would have more at stake and could be more responsible economically. But for all the sense it makes, such a scheme resembles nineteenth-century censuses too closely to be easily accepted – unless a completely new social contract is implied. To prevent the rich from dominating the system even further to the detriment of the poor, basic economic security would have to be assured to everyone as a matter of an enforceable right. Then, the majority could accept the deal without worrying about any loss of dignity resulting from having these "less valid" participatory rights. In that way, social rights would become constitutional.

Such hypothetical suggestion contradicts so deeply basic democratic premise of equality that it should be rejected outright. But does it really differ from "compacts" implied in formally democratic elections taking place in Zakaria's "illiberal democracies," where people trade their right to influence the government for a mere promise of economic security? Here, at least, that promise would be enforceable.

The challenge for every advocate of democracy and human rights lies in restoring a sense of inclusion, dignity and self-respect to the millions of people who are considered "useless" today.

Citizenship and Welfare

An important assumption of the democratic welfare state is that every citizen should be able to benefit from a social welfare network organized by the state. But this conviction, until recently widely accepted in the European Union, has been weakened by new waves of immigrants, particularly from non-European cultures, who chose to reject much of what makes up the assimilation to new countries. Moreover, many states have changed their immigration and nationality policies, either by making the process of acquiring citizenship rights more difficult or by depriving entire segments of their population of citizenship rights – or both.[67] With the threat of terrorism virtually everywhere, a growing gap has been dividing the treatment of citizens and nonnationals. In recent years, the problem of citizenship has become one of the most sensitive human rights issues worldwide. It affects Arab and Muslim immigrants in France, former British subjects in Great Britain, people of Russian descent in the Baltic Republics and the "erased people" in Slovenia, among many others. It involves the much broader issue of the application of human rights to noncitizens.

The French Declaration of 1789 granted rights and freedoms "to all men," with the exception of political rights[68] and rights related to taxation and public spending.[69] (Surprisingly, the Declaration limited the freedom "to speak, write and publish freely" to citizens, even though it also stated that "the free communication of thoughts and opinions is one of the most precious rights of man."[70])

In the majority of contemporary constitutions, political rights and social benefits are restricted to citizens. After all, such rights involve expenditures and arise from the social and political relations within a society.[71] However, it makes equal sense that noncitizens who participate in such relations should not be deprived of relevant rights. In the EU, noncitizens who are permanent residents have the right to vote in elections to local self-governments. In some countries, social rights are also extended to those noncitizens who are permanent residents and pay taxes, because such rights are perceived as based on the principle of social cooperation. According to William N. Nelson, "obligations corresponding to any one person's rights would be possessed only by those other members of his society who benefit from cooperative social relations."[72] In a majority of contemporary constitutions, civil liberties are granted to all persons under the jurisdiction of a state.

---

[67] See Open Society Justice Initiative (2004, 10–19).

[68] Article VI restricted to citizens the rights "to concur personally, or by their representatives in the formation of law" and to be "equally eligible to all honors, offices and public employment."

[69] Article XIV granted only citizens the right "to determine the necessity of the public contribution, either in person or by their representatives, to consent freely thereto, to watch over its use, and to determine the amount, base, collection and duration thereof." This right corresponded to the duty of said citizens to contribute "in accordance with their abilities" to state expenses imposed also only on citizens by Article XIII.

[70] Article XI; this suggests that the framers of the French Declaration considered the freedom "to speak, write and publish freely" as merely a political right and not a civil liberty.

[71] "Some basic rights, including rights based on principles of distributive justice, may best be construed as special rights arising out of social or political relations and held only by members of a given society against other members of the same society" (Nelson 1981, 294).

[72] Ibid., 287.

The problem of striking the proper balance between the rights of man and the rights of citizens has become more important with globalization. Symptomatic of this process are, after all, the increased movement of people beyond state borders and the growing number of individuals living abroad without formal citizenship in the new country. Many of them are refugees and asylum seekers. Although international conventions grant some rights to refugees and people who have already been granted asylum, those individuals who still intend to apply for refugee status and asylum seekers are left with little protection.

In recent years, many states, particularly in Africa, have adopted legal steps leading to the exclusion of ethnic or religious minorities from citizenship.[73] According to an estimate endorsed by both the United Nations High Commissioner for Refugees (UNHCR) and Refugees International, more than eleven million stateless individuals are living in the world today. "Critically, discrimination is both a cause and consequence of statelessness," proclaims a report dealing with statelessness and citizenship. "States routinely marginalize unpopular racial and ethnic groups by denying them access to or stripping them of citizenship. Stateless persons are vulnerable to myriad human rights violations and have no recourse to legal protection."[74] In short, a stateless person is unable to claim and enforce his or her rights.

One of the reasons for making citizenship law more restrictive is the desire to control minorities. The economic factor is also important: with the growth of the state's positive obligations toward citizens, citizenship bears costs. Many governments want to reduce these costs. Counteracting such measures is difficult because, although there exists a comprehensive and detailed international legal framework on racial discrimination, the normative framework governing state discretion in restricting access to citizenship is less developed. Thus, "citizenship-based distinctions commonly serve as a pretext for racial discrimination."[75] An important step would be to adopt a new international treaty that affirms the right to citizenship and prohibits statelessness.[76] But unless such principles are internationally accepted and enforced,

---

[73] For example, in Cote d'Ivoire, a quarter of the population, which totals 16–18 million people, lives without a proof of citizenship. In the Dominican Republic, hundreds of thousands of ethnic Haitians who were born in the Dominican Republic are denied recognition of citizenship. In Pakistan and Bangladesh, many Urdu-speaking people are deprived of citizenship. In Dubai, only 17 percent of residents are citizens. (See Open Society Justice Initiative 2007b. For analysis of the discrimination related to citizenship in Africa see Open Society Justice Initiative 2004a.)

[74] See Open Society Justice Initiative (2006a). See also Goldston (2004.)

[75] Open Society Justice Initiative (2004, 2). For analysis of examples of racial discrimination in access to citizenship (the cases of Rohingya in Burma, Dominicans of Haitian descent, the Bidun of Kuwait, the hill tribes in Thailand, the Maskhetians in Russia, and Kenyan Nubians), as well as the deprivation of citizenship (the cases of the Bhutanese of Nepali origins, Banyamulenge in the Democratic Republic of Congo, and ethnic Serbs in Croatia) see ibid., 10–19.

[76] Preliminary steps toward the development of a new set of standards on citizenship and nationality have been taken within the UN framework. In 2005, the Human Rights Commission adopted a resolution to undertake a study on the right to nationality and the arbitrary deprivation of nationality.

a growing number of people will not be able to benefit from the rights of citizens – even despite the existing provisions on nationality and citizenship in international human rights law.[77]

The benefits of social citizenship are becoming problematic not merely for excluded minorities. One cause of this tendency is demographic change. After World War II, welfare policies in Western Europe were developed in a period of constant economic growth. This meant that the majority of people were employed and relatively secure economically. The aim of welfare was to provide relief for the minority below the poverty level and for those who had become unable to care for themselves for reasons such as loss of one's job or one's physical health. Although this group of recipients was a small minority, many people were actually uncertain whether they would not one day find themselves in this minority and in need of help. Therefore, such policies had broad popular support. The precondition for this Western model of welfare was that markets produce the surplus necessary to finance welfare.

The situation is vastly different in societies beginning the transition to market economy. In former communist states, social benefits were granted before markets were developed. Today, people use their democratic rights to vote and elect governments to assure social benefits before the market has produced the surplus necessary for any profits to be shared. And in a majority of underdeveloped countries the needy make up an overwhelming majority of the population.

What follows is a need to look differently at the welfare policies in the developed countries of the West and those in former communist states and in the South. In Africa, for example, a great number of people cannot find any significant role for themselves in their nations' economies and are considered not needed or even useless. In the West, the indicator of economic activity that measures the percentage of working-age people who actually work ranges from 74 percent in Western Europe to 83 percent in the United States; in Poland and other transitory countries, it hovers around 50 percent; in the global South, it is far below that.[78] Finding significant

---

[77] There exist a number of international documents on nationality, citizenship, and statelessness. Article 15 of the Universal Declaration of Human Rights provides: "Everyone has a right to nationality" and "no one shall be arbitrarily deprived of his nationality nor denied the right to change his nationality." Article 1 of the 1961 Convention on the Reduction of Statelessness mandates that a "Contracting State shall grant its nationality to a person born on its territory who would otherwise be stateless." The right to nationality is also affirmed by the Inter-American Convention of Human Rights (Article 20), as well as by the 1997 European Convention on Nationality. The latter document states that the "rules on nationality of each State Party shall be based on the following principles: (a) everyone has the right to a nationality; (b) statelessness shall be avoided; (c) no one shall be arbitrarily deprived of his or her nationality" (Article 4). However, the right to citizenship is not assured in the International Covenant on Civil and Political Rights. The problem with the existing conventions and documents is that none of them require a particular state to confer its nationality under the defined circumstances.

[78] For update of these numbers, see http://unstats.un.org/unsd/cdb/cdb_series_xrxx.asp?series_code=4270.

social roles for the remainder of the working-age population seems more difficult than assuring minimum economic security for them.

The low level of economic activity results in a growing burden on public social expenditures. Fewer people who are economically active have to produce goods and services for those who are inactive. Moreover, in the developed countries the basic economic calculations underlying the systems of social security and healthcare have changed dramatically in recent times. When modern welfare systems were being designed, the average life span was much shorter than that of today. It was assumed that people would live on pensions for about 5 years after retiring from work. But unprecedented, unforeseeable progress in the automation of tasks, nutrition, and healthcare, coupled with changes in lifestyle, have resulted in significant extension of life. In economic terms, this means that pensions, healthcare expenditures, and other benefits cost the state far more than originally expected. But democratic societies do not want to decrease the level of benefits voluntarily and hence the inability to reform the social welfare systems of France, Germany, and other countries. The majority of the population wants to keep the existing benefits, even if this hampers economic growth and undermines prospects for the future. The common sense of entitlement to social rights makes this issue even more difficult. Thus, the legal character of social rights and their mechanisms of enforcement have become of crucial importance. We will return to the issue in the next chapter.

IS DEMOCRACY ENOUGH?

There exists a common assumption that democracy will protect people against abuses of power. When constitutional rights are neglected or abused in a democracy, it holds, one can use the democratic process and vote out those in power. In a system of limited government based on a coalition of a number of parties, minorities can effectively support or oppose governments to ensure that their interests are accommodated in a political process.

This is a rather naive belief. Although it may reflect the bargaining power of well-organized minorities, it hardly applies to individual victims of abuse or to weak minorities and vulnerable groups with little social support. Without traditions of limited government and strong institutions enforcing such limitations, democratic mechanisms, on their own, are insufficient to protect individual rights against encroachment by the majority or by state officials. In a modern society, an individual or a weak minority is simply unable to mobilize voters to change – or influence – abusive authorities. Without institutional guarantees of limited government such a process would be too long and too costly and, even if it were to be successful, in the absence of institutional guarantees of limited government it would most probably lead to the replacement of one elite by another, as insensitive to individual rights and public interest as the previous one. Of course, it is better to have two or more elites competing for power than just one, but this does not assure effective protection of individual rights.

Constitutional democracy calls for institutions limiting the government and for the entrenchment of a set of individually available remedies for the protection of the rights of individuals and minorities against violations by the government and self-governments. The dearth of efficient remedies is one of the most troubling shortfalls of democratic transitions and may result from long-held illusions that a "real democracy" cannot abuse rights and a "real self-government" cannot turn against the people. Countries undergoing transition have been learning by experience that even in a democracy, there are conflicting interests, and rights can easily be violated in the adjudication between these interests. Rights can also be threatened by popularly elected authorities, as has been proven with the emergence of populist governments.

It is also important to address the widespread instrumentalization of democracy. Illiberal and populist governments are more interested in legitimization than in democracy. Often, formal elections are merely mechanisms employed to legitimize authoritarian regimes. Therefore, the methods for scrutinizing fair conduct in elections – including transparency of financial contributions and spending, equal access of all candidates to the media, and the ban on the use of administrative resources by incumbent parties – are indispensable. Equally important are checks and balances on the use of power by officials after they have been elected. Such mechanisms should permit public scrutiny into government spending. Accountability and transparency are the most indispensable elements of democracy.[79] A prerequisite for accountability, in turn, is the enforceable right of access to information pertaining to every detail of a government's activity.[80]

In addition to voting rights and the right to information, there should exist mechanisms enabling people to actually participate in governance and to influence the government's agenda. The freedoms of expression and association are of crucial importance. So are legal mechanisms for the protection of rights. A democratic state should support individuals in seeking remedies against that state. In totalitarian systems, dissidents facing a monolithic state addressed the moral consciousness of the people and sought support of the international community. In a constitutional

---

[79] Collier (2007, 135–56) suggests that the transparency of natural resources and public finance should be enforced internationally by a set of laws and charters.

[80] Laws on access to information exist in 65 countries (28 Freedom of Information acts have been passed since 2000). The quality and effectiveness of such laws vary significantly. The Open Society Justice Initiative has developed an Access to Information Monitoring Tool, which has been used to compare the freedom of information in fourteen countries (Argentina, Armenia, Bulgaria, Chile, France, Ghana, Kenya, Macedonia, Mexico, Nigeria, Peru, Romania, Spain, and South Africa). On the basis of this review, Ten Justice Initiative Principles on the Right to Know have been formulated (see Open Society Justice Initiative 2006b, 27–9).

democracy, in turn, the individual should be able to take one part of the state along in his struggle against another part of that state. "Under constitutional law, rights bring the power of one branch of the government to bear upon wrongdoers from other government agencies."[81] Usually, that branch is a "normal" judiciary available to citizens against the executive. Alternatively – constitutional courts are available against the legislative. That is why the protection of individual rights can hardly exist without the separation of powers and an independent judiciary.[82]

But even an independent judiciary is not sufficient for the protection of constitutional rights. Individuals need to be supported in their efforts to bring cases to regular and constitutional courts, especially as the legal process is long, costly, and requires specialized legal knowledge. One instrument of access to state mechanisms for the protection of rights is the institution of the ombudsman whose task is to help individuals and groups in the protection of their rights.[83] An ombudsman is particularly effective in countries where powerless individuals and social groups face reprisals from state officials and powerful interest groups to whom these corrupted officials are linked. In such cases, which are common in Africa and many rural communities in other regions, simply bringing an individual complaint can cause retribution from the local elite.

An ombudsman can also play an important role in educating people about their rights and the remedies accessible to them. This is particularly important in countries undergoing the transition to constitutional democracy. However, an ombudsman alone is unable to fill the gap between the people and the protective institutions of the state. This task should belong to the organizations of civil society, with the state facilitating this process.

Charles Epp has demonstrated that it was only when nongovernmental organizations and law firms acting in the public interest emerged and were supported by the state that the "rights revolution" took off in the United States and in Canada.[84] Strategic litigation enhanced the rights of vulnerable populations and helped to change society in the United States and other countries.[85]

---

[81] Holmes and Sunstein (1999, 55).

[82] The need for state assistance for the protection of rights is implied in the very definition of rights proposed by H. C. Black (1990, 1324): "But leaving the abstract moral sphere, and giving the term a juristic content, a 'right' is well defined as a 'capacity residing in one man of controlling, *with the assent and assistance of the state*, the actions of others" (emphasis added).

[83] For a comparison of offices of the ombudsman in Denmark, Finland, New Zealand, Norway, and Sweden with mechanisms to deal with citizens' complaints in Yugoslavia, Poland, the Soviet Union, and Japan, see Gellhorn (1966). Since then, ombudsman offices have been created in Yugoslavia, Poland, Russia, and other transition countries.

[84] Epp (1998, 44–70, 171–96, passim).

[85] Strategic litigation, however, cannot solve all social problems or protect the rights of all vulnerable populations. Aryeh Neier (1982 and 2003) analyzed when litigation brought about desired results and

A number of institutions can facilitate access to the "protective arm" of the state. One example is free legal service offered in cases of abuse of rights. Another is special legislation for public interests firms and NGOs that assist people whose rights have been violated. The state can support such organizations either through direct donations or by granting them tax privileges. Any institution that facilitates access to justice helps make rights enforceable. A special role is played by NGOs that not only help to make use of rights but also support government and international organizations in monitoring whether states are conforming to their constitutions and to international human rights standards.[86]

LEGAL EMPOWERMENT

The need for agencies capable of making use of rights is particularly acute in developing countries. In many of them, "laws benefiting the poor exist on paper but not in practice unless the poor or their allies push for the laws' enforcement," writes Stephen Golub, an advocate of legal empowerment of the poor and disadvantaged people.[87] In most developing countries, courts are hardly accessible and are often corrupt, ineffective, and discriminatory.[88] The promotion of the rule of law in developing countries through top-down strategies that focus on reforming the judiciary seldom addresses barriers to access and inequality in the application of law. Carothers suggests that the promotion of the rule of law with its focus on formal legal systems with the objective of genuine judicial independence fails to address mechanisms of legal exclusion.[89] In reality, attempts to promote the rule of law often lead to

---

when it turned out to be ineffective. The latter was the case mainly with the large social problems, such as ending poverty or challenging war.

[86] It is important to note, however, that such monitoring and watchdog organizations should not depend to a significant degree on public funding for this would undermine their independence. Moreover, this type of NGO should be prohibited from having "positive" programs, such as providing social services or other activities. They should also not be able to influence political decisions, for this raises the issue of an NGO's legitimacy. "Many of these groups have surprisingly weak ties to the citizenry. They are self-appointed representatives of an assumed public interest, following the rather particularist agenda of a circumscribed set of activists (and often their foreign funders)," writes Carothers (2006b, 10).

[87] Golub (2003, 3, 6, and 25).

[88] de Langen and Barendrecht (2009) described six barriers to justice (geographical, financial, and language barriers, complexity, cultural norms, and delay) as well as two most common mechanisms of exclusion (gatekeepers and uncertainty about the law). The authors demonstrated that such barriers and mechanisms are not neutral and affect poor people much more severely than rich ones.

[89] See Carothers (2006a). In an earlier analysis of the USAID's rule of law assistance, Carothers pointed to the inability to change the "enduring realities of limited access to justice, vested interests devoted to the *status quo*, corruption, clientelist appointments, etc." See Carothers (2003, 170; quoted in Golub 2003, 13. For a detailed analysis of the shortcomings of the "rule of law orthodoxy" as applied to developing countries, see Golub, ibid. 8–25).

the "rule of lawyers."[90] "Everything is known by the lawyer, nothing is known by the client," said Carlos P. Medina, Jr. of the Ateneo Human Rights Center in the Philippines.[91] Bukovská claims that even the human rights field, "dominated by close networks of elites and professionals and excluding those who are directly concerned, hardly encourages the independent initiative of victims."[92] As a result, "far from being a badge of honour, human rights activism is, in some places . . . increasingly a certificate of privilege," writes Chidi Odinkalu.[93]

Recently, a new approach has been postulated to complement the top-down measures focused on the rule of law. It is known as legal empowerment. It is based on rights and driven by a community. It involves specific mechanisms – that include not only courts – aiming at the alleviation of poverty, protection of rights of vulnerable people, and assuring for them access to justice. In short, "legal empowerment is the use of legal services and related development activities to increase disadvantaged populations' control over their lives."[94]

Major elements of legal empowerment include setting priorities together with disadvantaged people rather than for them; emphasis on civil society and community-based groups; the supportive rather than leading role of lawyers; and the use of mediation and other court mechanisms for conflict resolution that can be easily accessed by the poor. An important task is training and ongoing development of paralegals, particularly from among vulnerable populations.[95] Without formal legal education, paralegals are able to give advice and access lawyers or other legal resources when needed. Clinical legal education that encourages law students to help people in need as well as so-called street law are other mechanisms of legal empowerment.[96]

An international nongovernmental Commission for The Legal Empowerment of the Poor, chaired by Madeleine K. Albright, former U.S. Secretary of State, and Hernando de Soto, president of the Institute for Liberty and Democracy in Peru,

---

[90] " . . . attorneys are sometimes part of the problem rather than part of the solution. Bar associations in some societies are self-serving guilds that effectively limit access to justice, or that work against social and economic equity. These associations may well advocate political freedoms and judicial independence, but be much less sensitive to the needs and priorities of the poor, particularly where those priorities challenge the interests of prosperous clients or the attorneys themselves," writes Golub (ibid., 22).

[91] Closing remarks at the Regional Conference on Lawyering for Social Justice and Human Rights. Makati City, Philippines, March 26–28, 2008. (Author's notes from the conference.)

[92] Bukovská (2008, 15).

[93] Quoted in ibid., 14.

[94] Golub (2003, 25). For differences between legal empowerment and the rule of law efforts, see ibid., 4.

[95] See Open Society Justice Initiative (2006c) and Maru (2006).

[96] de Langen and Barendrecht place these methods within the concept of "microjustice" based on the idea that "justice should be provided by local labor, abundantly available within the communities where the poor live" (2009, 12). For details, see also www.microjustice.org.

sees a broader role for legal empowerment. It suggests massive international and national efforts to ensure that all people – including the poorest, disadvantaged, and most vulnerable – are entitled to legal status as citizens, asset-holders, workers, and business people. It considers access to justice, property rights[97], labor rights, and business rights as four pillars of legal empowerment, each of them facilitating the fulfillment of one of four goals of that empowerment: access to justice, access to assets, access to decent work, and access to markets. Overall, such empowerment would lead to protection of rights of the poor and to their increased opportunities.[98]

De Langen and Barendrecht summarize legal empowerment as follows:

> Where traditional access to justice programs often focus on training judges, build-ing more courts, raising legal awareness and revising legislation to implement international human rights treaties, legal empowerment programs are more likely to focus on helping people obtain a legal identity, a recognized street address, and an enforceable and protected title to land, increasing the accessibility of business registration, mending dysfunctional permit systems, protecting street vendors and improving access to financing.[99]

The common goal of these instruments is to reduce the exclusion.[100]

Even though legal empowerment is a new idea, there have already been many practical experiences with its implementation – from the Philippines to South Africa, Bangladesh, and many other countries.[101] The accumulated experience helps to fine-tune legal empowerment programs[102] and to focus them on mechanisms that will help excluded and vulnerable people to benefit from promises offered in constitu-tions and international human rights documents.

CONCLUSIONS: TOWARD A NEW CONCEPT OF DEMOCRACY

The indispensability of institutions that facilitate access to justice and make use of human rights possible suggests the need for a change in the political theory of

---

[97] According to the Commission, property rights could be democratized by the recognition of land and other resources used by the poor without formal legal titles and by the ability to use movable property as collaterals for (micro-)credits.

[98] See Commission on Legal Empowerment of the Poor (2008). For a detailed list of reform options see ibid.,Volume 1, 60.

[99] de Langen and Barendrecht (2009, 10).

[100] For an analysis of how legal empowerment addresses barriers to justice and mechanisms of exclusion see ibid., 13.

[101] See Golub (2003) and Commission on Legal Empowerment of the Poor (2008, volume 2.) for examples. See also the UNDP Web site (www.undp.org) for details of implementation.

[102] It seems that two problems will have to be watched carefully. One concerns preventing paralegals from becoming the new "gatekeepers" who would use their knowledge and skills to increase their own power; community-based paralegals seem to be less prone to this danger. A more difficult problem is how to address the issue of discriminatory cultural norms and unjust local power relations that may permeate community-based programs.

constitutional democracy. In the nineteenth century, democratic theory accepted party systems as a necessary mediating institution between individual voters and their representation in government. Similarly, constitutional democracy should acknowledge the need for institutions without which individual rights are of limited use to anyone who is not rich and powerful.

The use of courts requires specialized legal knowledge and resources beyond the reach of most citizens. But when these resources are not available, individual rights will remain no more than a lofty idea. Just as democracy implies access to the state, rights necessitate access to justice and courts. This means that the democratic process of distribution of public resources must acknowledge the need for supporting the NGOs acting in the public interest. Government and legislators ought to set aside budgetary resources necessary for helping people protect their rights against that very majority government.

Public interest NGOs should be elevated to similar status in the theory and practice of constitutional democracy as political parties. Moreover, any scheme of international aid to poor countries should make provisions – and earmark resources – necessary to establish a set of effective remedies available to the citizens and residents of recipient countries. Without public scrutiny or access to remedies, democracy and human rights will continue to clash.

Another theoretical innovation concerns the concept of limited government. It has been accepted that the government should be limited by rights; thus, constitutional rights should set limits to democracy. Actually, the opposite may also be true: the need for a viable democracy should set limits to constitutional rights. Rights should protect fundamental values and those goods without which people's security and dignity are threatened. But they should not go beyond this and encroach on spheres best left to democratic deliberation and compromise.[103] In short, in a democracy, constitutional rights should not impoverish political debate.

Human rights are not synonymous with democracy; in fact, they limit the scope of democratic decisions and may be, at times, in conflict with democracy. Similarly, human rights may be in conflict with other important social values. Although they encourage, in the long run, economic progress and well-being, human rights may sometimes slow down economic growth by earmarking parts of budgets for "nonproductive" initiatives, by limiting the freedom of contracts, or by putting environmental limitations on producers. Although they form the basis for the rule of law, human rights are not identical with legality, and, sometimes, they clash with duly promulgated laws that may violate them. Although there are human rights to welfare benefits, human rights are not synonymous with social equality; the ultimate value

---

[103] This does not mean that there are no human rights without constitutional status. As noted, there exist many human rights that have statutory protection. Only the most basic rights should be in a constitution.

protected by them is basic economic security rather than equality and redistribution is just one of the means toward that end. Although human rights protect important human needs (primarily, security-related ones), rights are not identical to needs. A great majority of needs cannot be claimed as rights; they are fulfilled by mechanisms other than human rights. Some needs are fulfilled as a result of exchange, others via charity, and still others by the political, not judicial, allocation of public resources.

The relationship between rights and needs, particularly from the perspective of the so-called social and economic rights, is one of the most important ongoing debates concerning human rights.

3

Rights and Needs

It is at the juncture of rights and needs that the dual character of the very concept of human rights is revealed. On the one hand, they constitute the moral standards and aspirations for humankind; human rights were declared as such by the United Nations in 1948. On the other hand, they are also increasingly understood as the norms of behavior enforced by international human rights law, as well as by national constitutions and statutes. One of the main goals for human rights movements has been precisely to translate moral standards and aspirations into enforceable legal rights.

The main difference between moral rights and legal rights relates to the methods for their enforcement. Moral rights usually provide a justified claim to something. They do not, however, provide an effective enforcement mechanism. If one's moral rights have been violated, one can appeal to the conscience of the perpetrator, to universal moral standards, to the voice of public opinion, or to the judgment of history. And even though such appeals are often convincing, overall, they do not constitute a formalized way to seek and receive relief or compensation for the underlying moral transgressions. In fact, in cases of most malevolent perpetration by the state, these methods are easily repressed. Legal rights, in contrast, may lack moral appeal, but they do provide efficient protection.[1] One need not justify legal rights; one proves them. Thus, it is no wonder that human rights activists strive to codify human rights legally to grant them better protection. Such attempts have often proven successful.[2]

---

[1] For example, Communist dignitaries and their families enjoyed the legal right to higher pensions and other privileges. Although such rights were perceived as immoral by the people, they were nevertheless enforced by the regime.

[2] Human rights "are not claims upon love, grace, brotherhood or charity: one does not have to earn or deserve them. They are not merely aspirations or moral assertions but, increasingly, legal claims under some applicable law," writes Henkin (Henkin et al. 1999, 3).

Not all human rights, however, can or even should be binding norms. Moreover, even when moral human rights are translated into enforceable norms, not all of them should have identical protection. As we have already seen, the constitutionalization of rights gives them very strong protection against all branches of government. Statutory rights, in turn, limit only the executive branch and the judiciary. Some human rights have, at best, political protection while others are (and will most likely always remain) moral postulates.[3]

The differentiation of enforcement is particularly relevant with respect to the relationship between rights and needs. There is hardly a doubt that rights serve the realization of human needs. This does not mean, however, that all needs should be met by claiming rights. In fact, most needs are realized by individual, interpersonal, or collective efforts without any grounds or reasons for claiming them.

Some needs, however, seem to be so important that we do not hesitate to agree that they warrant being met as a matter of rights. Most often, such needs are related to the dignity, identity, autonomy, and security of a person. But even in the case of such needs, the protection offered for their satisfaction varies. This can be better explained when we look at the categories of rights that correspond to their functions.

CATEGORIES OF HUMAN RIGHTS

The most common classification of rights distinguishes among three groups: (1) civil rights and liberties; (2) political rights; and (3) social, economic, and cultural rights.[4] This distinction follows the historical development of rights and freedoms and is reflected in their differentiated instruments for protection.[5]

Civil rights and freedoms (also called civil liberties or personal rights and freedoms) safeguard an individual, in particular, his or her liberty and autonomy against

---

[3] An example is the right of a child to be loved. From the point of view of human dignity, security, and the development of human potential this is one of the most important rights. No one, however, can force adults to love children. (Indeed, one can protect children from abuse, but avoiding abuse is not the same thing as being loved.) Thus, the right of a child to be loved will always be no more than a moral right. Another important right, to live in peace, can have, at best, limited protection via international politics and security measures.

[4] Other classifications distinguish among (1) generations of rights; (2) negative freedoms and positive rights; and (3) natural, civil, political, and personal rights. (The last categorization is authored by H. C. Black 1990, 1324–5.) The three categories of rights differ from the three generations of rights, with the first generation consisting of those civil liberties and political rights (here, categories 1 and 2) that emerged in the eighteenth century. The second generation denotes the social and economic rights of the nineteenth century (here, the third category of rights). The third generations are the so-called solidarity rights of the twentieth century, which include such group rights as right to self-determination, the right to development, the right to a clean environment, etc. (For analysis of third-generation rights, see Henkin 1990, 475–88.) The status of some of these rights is discussed when appropriate.

[5] Being a product of history, the above-mentioned categorization of rights is not fully logical. As we will see, there are many questions as to why certain rights are included in one category and not another.

intrusion. They also protect personal private space and important life choices that he or she may make. Therefore, civil rights and freedoms set limits to the powers of the state.

Freedoms and civil rights can be subdivided on the basis of the specific spheres they protect. Basic civil liberties include the right to have rights, which is the recognition of a person as a person before the law, as well as the right to equal protection under law. The equality of rights without privileges or discrimination is ensured by several provisions contained in international human rights covenants and by special conventions. Discrimination on racial and religious grounds is excluded even before actual discriminatory acts take place by virtue of the ban on the advocacy of racial and religious hate.

In a world order based on the principle of the sovereignty of national states, the right of nations to self-determination aims to guarantee protection from enslavement, bondage, and any violation of rights by foreign governments. Rights of minorities protect minorities and minority cultures within the boundaries of a sovereign national state.

Life and bodily integrity are protected by the right to life, the ban on torture, prohibition against cruel and inhuman punishment, the obligation to treat detainees and prisoners humanely, and strict limitations on medical experimentation.

Personal freedom is protected by the bans on slavery and arbitrary deprivation of freedom. It is served by limitations on arrests and by a requirement that detention be ordered by independent courts and not by the police or prosecution. It is also guarded by limitations on the length of pretrial detention and the right to compensation in cases of unsubstantiated deprivation of liberty. For a lawful limitation of personal freedom, due process of law is required. The right of access to courts protects an individual from the arbitrary use of coercive power by the executive branch of government. Other procedural rights limit the judiciary by setting rules according to which an individual's guilt must be proven and the sentence administered; they include the presumption of innocence, the ban on retroactivity, a person's right to a defense and legal counsel, and other principles of criminal procedure. The protection of personal liberty against persecution is also assured by the right to asylum and by limitations on the arbitrary expulsion of aliens.

Personal liberty extends to freedom to own property and to undertake activities of one's own choosing, otherwise known as freedom of enterprise.[6] Choices are also guaranteed by the freedom of movement, which includes the right to reside in one's own country and the freedom to return to it.

---

[6] Historically, the right to property was closely connected with personal liberty, which was understood as the right to property of one's own body. "... the right to property was, in the early struggles for citizenship in Europe, as much the right to 'property in oneself' as it was about ownership and control over resources," writes Kabeer (2005, 5–6).

Personal autonomy is protected by privacy, defined as a ban on intrusion into one's personal sphere, including personal choices and family matters. More specific institutions serving this freedom are the inviolability of one's house and the freedoms of correspondence and communication. Autonomy is also protected by limitations on the power of the state to gather information about individuals. Freedom of conscience and freedom of thought are also important elements of personal autonomy.

Freedom of expression serves personal self-realization by making it possible to communicate one's beliefs and ideas to others. It implies the right to information and the ban on censorship. Freedom of religion permits a person to exercise one's religion in community with others of similar belief. Finally, the freedoms to assemble and to associate permit individuals to be heard by others and pursue common goals in cooperation with other people.

Civil rights and liberties are protecting individuals and communities against the state. Because the state can impose its will on people and enforce its decisions broadly through coercive power, the individual is in an unequal position vis-à-vis his or her state. Figuratively speaking, the state holds a sword over people's heads – and hence the people's need for a shield that protects them from the unjustified use of this sword. Human rights are such a shield, providing individuals a sense of security as they face the state. But values underlying civil liberties should also be protected against other perpetrators than the state. In fact, it is the state that should protect individuals against violations of autonomy by private parties. The main vehicles for this are criminal and civil law. In the absence of appropriate legislation, the so-called horizontal application of rights is suggested.

The individual has a choice whether to exercise personal freedoms. The state, in turn, should remain passive and not infringe on civil liberties. At the same time, the state must play an active role in creating and sustaining institutions that safeguard these freedoms.[7] For the fulfillment of state obligations to secure personal liberty, procedural rights – including a special right of access to legal remedies in cases of an encroachment on freedoms – are indispensable. This enforcement of rights is always claimed against the state and requires action on the part of the state.

Political rights have already been discussed in the preceding chapter. Note that they grant an individual access to public decision making and are at the core of people's sovereignty and political democracy; for this reason, they are often referred to as participatory rights.[8] The rights to vote in elections and to run for office, as

---

[7] Necessary for the protection of personal freedom and property are armies, police, and courts. (For a detailed analysis of the state's obligations regarding personal freedoms, see Holmes and Sunstein 1999.)

[8] In some countries, use of the instruments of direct democracy is assured as a matter of constitutional rights to participate in referenda and in citizens' legislative initiatives.

well as the right of access to public service are necessary but insufficient to assure representation and participation. Equally important are the ability to affect the public agenda and have one's voice heard in the public forum, protected under the right to assembly and freedom of association. It is worth noting that assembly for political purposes is not a mere freedom but also a right because it implies the duty of the state to provide public space and to protect political gatherings, manifestations, and demonstrations. In turn, freedom of association as a political right translates into the right to form and belong to political parties. The state is obligated to facilitate the existence of various parties and to provide public space for their activities. In some countries, the state grants resources needed for a party's activities – particularly for electoral campaigns – because it believes that the absence of such support results in political corruption.

Political rights are contingent on the pre-existence of civil liberties. To participate in public decision making, individuals and associations need to have a right to petition; this implies a primary need for freedom of expression. Participation in public decision making and setting the public agenda requires freedom of information and, more specifically, the right to demand information about the activities of the state and its agencies, including limitations on the arbitrary definition of state secrets by the authorities. The right to information, in turn, cannot exist without freedom of the press and other media. Sometimes, the right to education is also treated as a political right, for it is assumed that uneducated and uninformed citizens cannot make conscious choices in elections and are unable to make proper use of democracy.

Although freedoms protect a person's choice over his or her own unconstrained actions within protected spheres, rights imply claims against the state to act in a given way and thus impose duties on the state. Procedural rights limit arbitrariness. Such rights impose on the state a duty to create and sustain a system of institutions necessary for the implementation of procedures, as well as to use those procedures in dealings with citizens. All political rights presuppose an active role of the state in creating and sustaining democratic institutions. To make use of one's political rights, an individual needs to perform such activities as voting, running for office, and taking part in public debate – but he or she has no duty to do so.[9] With few exceptions, political rights put obligations on the state and create opportunities for citizens.

Although both freedoms and political rights are claimed against the state, freedoms suggest the passive role of the state. In the case of rights, the state is obligated to act to help individuals claim said rights. In the case of so-called entitlement-rights, claims against the state are not limited to the instruments for the protection of rights

---

[9] Except for countries where there exists a duty to take part in parliamentary elections (e.g., Belgium, Australia, and a number of Latin American states, including Brazil).

but involve a material substance of rights: what is claimed is not protection nor participation in decision making but rather specific goods or services.

Such is the case with the rights to healthcare, social security, and education and many other social, economic, and cultural rights. One cluster of such rights protect the economic security of a person. Here we find the right to social security, which usually includes unemployment compensation, entitlement to pensions for the elderly, disability allowance, and basic healthcare. Essential security also includes the right to food, clothing, and housing. In some constitutions there are separate provisions about the rights of the handicapped and the rights of tenants.

Family rights consist of protection of family, sometimes protection of the marriage, and special protection of children.

Labor relations are regulated by the right to work, which includes the right to a choice of work (and an implied ban on compulsory work in a place or occupation chosen by the state) and the right to unemployment compensation in case of a person's inability to obtain employment without one's fault. The right to work also includes the right to decent conditions at work; the right to rest and leisure, including vacations with pay; and the right to form and join free trade unions (to be able to protect other social rights).

Sociocultural rights include the right to education, which consists of free education up to a specified level, as well as the choice of education and educational institutions. Another right in this category is that to participation in cultural life. In some constitutions, the freedoms of creativity and scientific pursuit as well as the autonomy of institutions of higher learning are also included among the rights in this section.

In the moral sense, claims based on social and economic rights are directed against society. It is the society that "owes" the dependent and helpless individual a degree of economic security. Society, however, as such, is unable to act in an organized way – so it fulfills its obligation via the instruments of the state,[10] which, by acknowledging entitlement rights, undertakes the obligation to provide the specified goods and services and redistribute resources appropriately. Although the claims for these rights are also addressed to the state, their character is not of rights *against* the state but rather of rights *through* the state.

Looking at the list of social and economic rights we see that this category of rights is unclear and somewhat confused. The right to own property and freedom

---

[10] "Human rights, I stress, are rights against society as represented by government and its officials. (. . .) At bottom, the rights claimed are against the state (. . .); today they also include what society is deemed obligated to do for the individual" (Henkin 1978, 2). Similarly, the definition of human rights in the *Encyclopedia of Public International Law* refers to "those liberties, immunities, and benefits which, by accepted contemporary values, all human beings should be able to claim 'as of right' of the society in which they live" (1985, 268).

of enterprise are, in fact, basic freedoms rather than social rights: they empower an individual and limit intrusion by the state rather than call for benefits or governmental regulation.[11] Other social and economic rights also resemble personal freedoms or political rights.[12] It seems as if the chief feature shared by the rights included in the category of social and economic rights consists in the lack of agreement on the immediate judicial enforcement of these rights.

However, even when we deal with social rights in a more narrow sense, we discover that they assume a broad range of roles for the state. The free choice of employment and protection against unemployment included in the Universal Declaration[13] imply the protective role of the state. Many other social rights call for the regulatory role of the state.[14] Very few social rights demand the direct provision of goods and services by the state.[15] Finally, some social and economic rights deal with values and directives that can at best be a goal for social policy but are to be implemented by nonstate actors or through international measures.[16] There is much less confusion surrounding the other categories of rights. Civil liberties

[11] For John Locke, the right to own property was the foundation of all other liberties. Similarly, in contemporary liberal theories, property is perceived as the most basic right and the indispensable foundation of other civil liberties and political rights. An example of such an argument is provided by Cranston (1973, 49–50): "The significance of confiscation is not simply that it deprives men of their property but that it deprives them of their liberty as well. It may well be that man's natural right to property can, if taken in isolation, be justified only to the extent that that right is an earned right; but it must not be forgotten that the right to property is one member of the family of rights, intimately related to the right to freedom; and it is hard to conceive how men can possibly be free if they have no right to possessions, and are wholly dependent on the necessities and comfort of their lives on the grace of some lord or master or communistic government. Property in this sense is inseparable from liberty."

[12] For example, the right to form unions (UDHR, Article 23.4) is a form of freedom of association applied to industrial relations. Other "social and economic freedoms" include the equality before law for all children (UDHR, Article 25.2); the rights of parents to chose children's education (UDHR, Article 26.3); and the right to free participation in cultural life (UDHR, Article 27.1). The right to intellectual property (UDHR, Article 27.2) resembles the property right, whereas creative and academic freedoms (mentioned in Article 15.3 of the International Covenant on Economic, Social and Cultural Rights) are very close to the freedom of expression. Finally, the right to education (especially in the context of UDHR, Article 26.2) resembles a political right.

[13] Article 23.1.

[14] For example, the just and favorable conditions of work (UDHR, Article 23.1); equal pay for equal work (UDHR, Article 23.2); just and favorable remuneration (UDHR, Article 23.3); and the right to rest and leisure (UDHR, Article 24).

[15] Social security in the event of unemployment, sickness, disability, widowhood, old age, or any other lack of livelihood beyond one's control (see second part of UDHR, Article 25). Even here, the provision of benefits in cases of sickness and old age implies regulatory duties of the state and is implemented through medical insurances and pension funds.

[16] For example, social security (UDHR, Article 22); remuneration ensuring existence worthy of human dignity (UDHR, Article 23.3); adequate standards of living (first part of UDHR 25); protection of motherhood and childhood (UDHR, Article 25.2); and the participation and sharing in culture, arts, and scientific advancement (UDHR, Article 27.1).

simply protect individuals and civil society from undue intrusion by the state. A number of political rights essentially assume the direct action of the state to ensure citizen participation in government. Very rarely do civil and political rights directly regulate the behavior of nonstate actors who are providing benefits to others. In what follows, the focus is primarily on social rights in the narrow sense, that is, on those related to the needs of individuals related to their social security.

SOCIAL AND ECONOMIC RIGHTS AS HUMAN RIGHTS

The status of social rights as human rights is a subject of controversy. Maurice Cranston has dismissed this concept as a "lofty idea" and presented a number of arguments against social rights. His main thesis is that economic and social rights cannot be transformed easily into positive rights and secured by legislation. In addition, many of them concern only one particular group of people (e.g., employees). Therefore, they do not meet the criteria for being counted among universal moral rights. Moreover, universal moral rights have to be of significant moral importance – this can hardly be said about the right to holidays with pay. "It is a paramount duty to relieve great distress," writes Cranston, but "it is not a paramount duty to give pleasure."[17] Finally, economic and social rights – in contrast to other categories of rights – do not impose any universal duty.[18] Other critics point to the difficulty of assigning anyone the responsibility of meeting – or failing to meet – positive rights, as well as to the indeterminacy of social rights, which may mean different things for different people in different situations.[19]

Some arguments against social rights are related to doubts about the effectiveness of direct provision of services by a state, to implied arbitrariness and possible corruption, and to the purported incentive for state welfare agencies to perpetuate the problem rather than solve it. Richard Epstein has emphasized the economic arguments, claiming that welfare decreases the level of production, which could then be redistributed. "Robin Hood was a bad man with good motives. By analogy, government welfare programs are bad institutions with good motives."[20]

Still other controversies focus on the moral aspects of social rights, particularly in relation to individual incentive and responsibility for one's own life. Although the opponents of social rights emphasize their demoralizing effects, the defense of social rights focuses on dignity that cannot exist without basic social security. Without security, people are also unable to protect and claim their civil liberties and participate freely in political life.

[17] Cranston (1973, 67).
[18] Ibid. (65–71).
[19] For a short review of liberal individualistic objections to welfare rights, see Barry (1990, 79–82).
[20] Epstein (1987, 34).

Louis Henkin argues that social and economic rights are fundamental, even if they are not constitutional, as is the case in the United States. Henkin's moral argument is that all society benefits from all members, even if they can be said to be "useless" (e.g., the economy, market, and competition can all "benefit" from unemployment, thus rendering the unemployed "useful" to those who have jobs). Henkin's historical argument is that the "social contract is a continuing conception" that develops with time to embrace the needs of the people. Therefore, some rights that were not acknowledged at the end of the eighteenth century are becoming essential 200 years later.[21]

Even when social and economic rights are recognized as human rights, there is no doubt about their character as that of aspirations distinct from the clear and present enforceability of civil and political rights. Therefore, the Covenant on Social, Economic and Cultural Rights originally provided for different enforcement mechanisms than those contained in the Covenant on Civil and Political Rights.[22] Despite this, international human rights theory recognizes the indivisibility and interdependence of human rights. The synthetic concept of human rights was first formally endorsed during the Second World Conference on Human Rights in Vienna in June 1993. The Declaration and Programme of Action adopted at the Conference stated that "all human rights are universal, indivisible, interdependent and interrelated" and called on all nations, "regardless of their political, economic and cultural systems, to promote and protect all human rights and fundamental freedoms."[23] One of the many justifications for this position consists in the fact that all rights are indispensable to protect and enhance those same basic values that human rights serve.[24]

Despite the arguments behind the Vienna Declaration, however, the status of social and economic rights has been, in recent decades, at the center of one of the most important controversies surrounding human rights. Although some authors claim that social rights do not belong at all to human rights, others make a convincing case for considering them as human rights. We have seen that it has been the enforceability of social and economic rights that has separated the various concepts

---

[21] Henkin (1981, 230).

[22] In fact, it was the discussion of the issue of justiciablity rather than different importance of various rights that led to the creation of two separate covenants. (See Whelan and Donnelly 2007 and Donnelly 2007.)

[23] Sec. I, para. 5.

[24] Jack Donnelly (2007, 52) presents this indivisibility from the perspective of social and economic rights: "The centrality of economic, social, and cultural rights to international human rights norms reflects the fact that core human rights values such as dignity, autonomy, security, and equality have essential economic, social, and cultural – as well as civil and political – dimensions. The interdependence and indivisibility of human rights is an expression of the multidimensional nature of a life of dignity worthy of a human being."

of human rights: this was the crucial dividing line between the liberal concept of rights on the one hand and the socialist concept of rights on the other.

Some authors have attempted to transcend the differences between the liberal and socialist concepts.[25] The argument for interconnectedness finds a particularly elaborate dignity-based justification in the Catholic concept of rights. According to David Hollenbach, the fundamental value that underlies the Catholic concept of rights is

> neither simply the liberty of the individual person stressed in the liberal democracies nor simply the social participation and economic well-being stressed in various ways by Marxism and socialism. Rather the theory maintains that respect for freedom, the meeting of basic needs and participation in community and social relationships are all essential aspects of the human dignity which is the foundation of all rights. (. . .) Any political, economic or social system which is to be morally legitimate must provide respect for these spheres of freedom, need, and relationship.[26]

Today, the attachment to social and economic rights is at the basis of one of the main differences between the North and the South.[27]

Do Social Rights Differ from Civil and Political Rights?

An ongoing controversy concerns the differences between social rights and two other categories of rights, namely, civil liberties and political rights. One set of arguments holds that social and economic rights are realized through the state, whereas civil and political rights protect people against the state. Civil and political rights have been described as "rights from" and social and economic rights have been described as "rights to."[28] An additional argument along these lines is that social rights, in contrast to civil liberties, cost money.

All these arguments are misleading and fail scrutiny. The only valid distinction along these lines is between rights and freedoms. All rights are positive and require action on the part of the state. This includes political rights, which place obligations on the state to organize elections and make available other mechanisms for citizen

---

[25] "Freedom from fear is inextricably linked to freedom from want. Liberty and citizenship are rooted in opportunity and security," says Sunstein (2004, 234).

[26] Hollenbach (1982, 17).

[27] Adamantia Pollis (2000, 19–20) sees this difference as follows: "In both traditional and Western societies there is a concept of equality, but its meaning is substantively different. In traditional societies entitlements in terms of power, authority, and privileges are differential, dependent on one's status in the communal group, but economic and social rights are equal entitlements for all members. Conversely, in Western liberal societies individual civil and political rights are equal entitlements, but economic and social rights are differential."

[28] Isaiah Berlin (1970) has made an elaborate distinction between the negative and positive concepts of freedom.

participation in the political process. As noted, all rights cost money, including the right to participate in elections and the right of access to court, to name just two. And although freedoms imply the inaction of the state, and thus seemingly do not cost money, they are of limited value without a mechanism for their protection – which necessarily does bear costs. Freedoms need to be enforced and individuals should have a right to remedy. Even the seemingly most inactive freedom – that of contract – makes no sense in the absence of a state-run mechanism for the enforcement of contracts between individual persons. Again, we are talking about positive rights that imply action by the state and cost money.[29]

Another suggested difference between the second and the first generations of rights is that civil liberties and political rights limit the state, whereas social and economic rights increase its power. Indeed, most civil liberties directly limit the government's ability to intrude on spheres restricted for individuals and an independent civil society. Social and economic rights, on the other hand, place on the state numerous obligations that justify its intrusion into civil society and control over individuals. It is true that social rights and social welfare have often been used by authoritarian regimes as justification for violations of civil liberties and political rights.[30] However, the protection of civil liberties, the defense of internal peace, the fight against crime, and, more recently, the "war on terror" have all been used to justify limitations of other civil liberties and an increase in the use of the coercive powers of states. Even without authoritarian abuse, police and other security powers, both indispensable for the protection of civil liberties, also empower the state.

One of the elements of the empowerment of a state is an increase in its regulatory powers. It is often said that, although civil liberties and political rights apply to the relations between an individual and the state, social and economic rights call for extensive regulation of the relations between individuals. Trade relations, work conditions, insurance systems, and pension schemes are examples of such regulations. Although true at first glance, this thesis becomes more problematic when we take into consideration the protection of the values underlying particular rights. We then see that values that are protected against the state by civil liberties – such as life, personal inviolability, privacy, property, freedom of religion, and others – are also protected from intrusion or violation by other individuals. This protection is offered by the penal and civil codes, as well as other laws issued and enforced by the state. Thus, the state actively regulates interpersonal relations also in the sphere of civil liberties.

A more profound difference concerns the providing vs. regulatory functions of the state. Every state provides goods and services to its citizens. In the case of civil and

---

[29] For an extensive discussion of the costs of rights and freedoms, see Holmes and Sunstein (1999).

[30] "It should be noted that authoritarian regimes, whether Marxist or not, invariably defend the priority of socioeconomic rights," writes F. Tesón (2001, 394).

political rights, the provision of services by far outnumbers the delivery of goods (or of money that can be used to buy goods). The courts, police, and the criminal justice system do not provide goods, they render services.[31] In the case of the protection of civil liberties and the implementation of political rights, the state has a monopoly on the provision of the necessary services and goods. Social rights, by contrast, entail the state supplying some people with the very same goods and services that others, often the majority, earn on their own and buy on the market. Most people earn a living, purchase or contribute to health insurance, save part of their earnings for future pensions, and insure themselves against other risks. But some people are unable to do this. When that inability is not their own fault, these people are entitled to claim such services or goods as a matter of rights. The state plays a subsidiary role, making up for the shortcomings of markets or for individual handicaps. No one buys court services or voting rights on the market; whenever someone tries, it is punished as corruption. This difference often justifies the skepticism toward social rights from people who earn or buy their welfare, particularly those who are not eligible for social services because they just barely cross the dividing line separating those eligible for benefits from those who must take responsibility for the quality of their own lives.[32]

In conclusion, the differences between social rights and other categories of rights are not as clear-cut as is usually assumed. Undoubtedly, in the case of social rights, the state's regulatory and providing roles are more important than its merely protective functions. This means that the implementation of social and economic rights directly depends on and influences the public policy of a state. Although the limitations of the state should be clearly defined in a constitution, both the implementation of a state's positive tasks and the setting of public policy goals and priorities belong primarily to the political process. As suggested in the preceding chapter, statutes rather than constitutions are what should reflect such choices and decisions.

THE LEGAL STATUS OF SOCIAL RIGHTS

The previous argument leads us to the controversy surrounding the legal status of social rights. The most significant difference between the first two categories of rights and the third one is related to different enforcement mechanisms: civil

---

[31] The notable exceptions are goods provided directly to inmates within the prison system and to military personnel, as well as disaster relief, which are considered by Holmes and Sunstein (1999, 234–6) as a form of protection of property rights.

[32] This difference, however, preassumes the existence of both markets and health and pension insurance systems. It has been less relevant in subsistence economies, conditions of slavery and servitude, feudal villages and communist – and, to great degree, also post-communist – economies. As noted by Pollis (2000, 19–20), "in traditional societies (. . .) economic and social rights are equal entitlements for all members."

liberties and political rights are to be implemented "here and now," social, economic, and cultural rights are perceived as standards to be implemented gradually through state policies rather than via judicial enforcement. In fact, it is the enforcement of rights that defines the understanding of the entire concept. If we assume that all rights should have equal enforcement, we will tend to embrace a narrow definition of rights. However, when we acknowledge that various human rights can be enforced by different mechanisms, we may accept a much broader concept of rights.

International documents do not provide for effective international enforcement of social and economic standards. Yet the Universal Declaration of Human Rights acknowledges the rights of everyone to a vast number of social benefits, including the right to social security and to the realization by each person of "the economic, social and cultural rights indispensable for his dignity and the free development of his personality."[33]

Social Rights in International Human Rights Law

It is useful to look at the reasons for which social and economic rights found such an important place in the Declaration. Despite the prevailing "myth of the Western opposition,"[34] social and economic rights have always been high on the agenda of Western leaders. Sunstein has proven just how important these rights were for the architects of the New Deal and for President Franklin D. Roosevelt personally.[35] The inclusion of "freedom from want" among the four basic freedoms (along the freedom of speech and expression, freedom to worship God, and freedom from fear) in the State of the Union address on January 6, 1941, crowned the New Deal philosophy. Social and economic legislation was also high on the agenda for the British government.[36] Despite the doubts raised by White House advisors, in the Four Freedoms speech Roosevelt insisted on talking about freedom from want "everywhere in the world."[37] Not surprisingly, then, the Atlantic Charter promised "collaboration between all nations in the economic field with the object of securing, for all, improved labor standards, economic advancement and social security."[38]

---

[33] UDHR, 22–8. The Universal Declaration of Human Rights included all categories of rights, without distinguishing between them. "But it was recognized from the beginning that rights might be seen as falling into one or the other of these categories, that the two categories of rights may have different theoretical justification, and that each may require different normative elaboration and different articulation of the obligation to respect such rights, and different remedies for their violation," writes Henkin (Henkin et al. 1999, 321).

[34] This concept was introduced by Whelan and Donnelly (2007).

[35] Sunstein (2004, 61–95).

[36] See Whelan and Donnelly (2007, 922–4).

[37] Sunstein (2004, 83).

[38] Atlantic Charter Point 5.

This commitment of Western governments to social and economic rights was genuine and persistent, even when toward the end of the war leaders wanted to dilute the idea of human rights. At the Dumbarton Oaks conference, the great powers agreed on allowing human rights provisions in the UN Charter only in the area of "international cooperation in social and economic matters."[39] This, in fact, increased the weight attached to social and economic rights in the preparatory works. Consequently, the Commission on Human Rights was formed within the Economic and Social Council, which by its nature dealt with economic and social matters. Not without importance was the fact that the single effective element of the system of international cooperation after World War I was the International Labor Organization, created in 1919 by the Treaty of Versailles to deal with issues of social justice and working conditions and, thus, to prevent revolution. In the interwar period the International Labour Organization (ILO) adopted close to 100 international conventions, dealing with issues of working conditions, social security, and trade unions, among others.[40] ILO conventions also addressed the freedoms of association and equal treatment.[41] In 1941, the ILO was the first international body to endorse human rights ideas mentioned in the Atlantic Charter.[42] In 1946, ILO became a specialized agency of the United Nations. With time, its positive experience would influence the framers of the Universal Declaration of Human Rights (UDHR).

After World War II, poor countries also embraced social and economic rights, hoping that the wealthy West might share the resources needed for the fulfillment of social promises. According to Eleanor Roosevelt, social and economic provisions had become

> ... a symbol of [the] aspirations and needs of these countries. They did not understand or attach the same importance to civil and political rights as does the United States or some of the more developed countries (...) they look to [economic, social and cultural rights] as a lever which may help to raise them out of their present depressed conditions.[43]

The American Declaration of Rights, adopted in May 1948 in Bogota, Columbia, strongly emphasized social and economic rights. In fact, representatives of Latin American states were vocal advocates of including these rights in the Universal

---

[39] Lauren (1998, 169).
[40] Scott Davidson (1993, 9) claims that the ILO "may be seen as the precursor of the system of the protection of economic, social, and cultural rights."
[41] Whelan and Donnelly (2007, 940).
[42] Lauren (1998, 143).
[43] Quoted in Whelan and Donnelly (2007, 930–1).

Declaration. Coming from poor countries – often governed by authoritarian regimes – they did not emphasize civil and political rights but rather the rights to social security, healthcare, pensions, financial relief, and other social benefits. They were backed, in part, by P. C. Chang of China, who emphasized that "economic and social justice, far from being an entirely modern notion, was a 2500-year-old Confucian idea."[44] Another supporter of including the provisions on economic and social justice and full employment was Australian foreign minister Herbert V. Evatt.

Many Western European intellectuals, still shaken by the Great Depression of the 1930s that had paved the way for fascism, also craved guarantees for social rights. For them, democracy meant primarily social democracy, meaning workers' rights, social security rights, and the rights to healthcare, education, and broad participation in culture. Labor leaders and American New Dealers, Christian philosophers, social democrats, socialists, communists, and representatives of non-Western nations all agreed on the paramount importance of these rights.

As a result, "the inclusion of social and economic rights was an uncontroversial decision."[45] However, in the ruin and poverty that followed the war and persisted among the colonized nations, no government could afford to commit itself to grant enforceability to these rights. Moreover, the universal agreement was that social rights should be treated as goals for the state rather than justiciable rights enforceable by courts.[46] Consequently, the Declaration treats all rights that it proclaims "as a common standard of achievement for all peoples and all nations," without imposing on the states any obligation to enforce these rights in constitutions or statutes.[47] In fact, the Declaration has an exhortatory character and does not provide for mechanisms of enforcement other that the approval or disapproval of the international community. It simply calls on the national governments of party states to implement such rights.[48]

The 1966 International Covenant on Economic, Social and Cultural Rights (ICSECR) obligates its signatories to take steps toward the gradual realization of

---

[44] See Glendon (2001, 185).

[45] Samnoy, quoted in Donnelly (2007, 39).

[46] "No state, Western or non-Western, seriously proposed – in the sense of being willing to adopt as a matter of enforceable national law – treating economic, social, and cultural rights as matters of immediate rather than progressive realization," writes Donnelly (2007, 42).

[47] In her speech to the General Assembly on December 9, 1948, Eleanor Roosevelt said that the U.S. government gave its "wholehearted support" to the articles on social and economic rights, but did not consider them to "imply an obligation on governments to assure the enjoyment of these rights by direct governmental action" (quoted in Glendon 2001, 186).

[48] The Preamble stated that "human rights should be protected by the rule of law," whereas Article 8 called for "the rights to an effective remedy by a competent national tribunal" but only "for acts violating fundamental rights granted by the constitution or by law."

rights. Acknowledging the limitations caused by scarce resources, the Covenant encourages legislative measures rather than constitutional guarantees of economic, social, and cultural rights.[49] Part IV of the ICSECR provides for rather weak reporting procedure.[50] On December 10, 2008, precisely on the 60th anniversary of the adoption of the UDHR, the UN General Assembly adopted by consensus the Optional Protocol to the International Covenant on Economic, Social and Cultural Rights. It grants individuals and groups a right to submit complaints (called "communications") whenever they claim to be "victims of violation of any economic, social and cultural rights set forth in the Covenant."[51] The Committee on Economic, Social and Cultural Rights gathers information, analyzes a complaint, and makes recommendations to a party involved. The Protocol also creates an inquiry mechanism, independent from individual complaints. At the signature of the Optional Protocol, party states may also permit the Committee to investigate, report on, and make recommendations on "grave or systematic violations" of rights included in the Covenant (Article 11). With the entry of the Optional Protocol into force,[52] the situation of economic, social, and cultural rights within the UN system will be identical to the civil and political rights – in accordance with the Vienna Declaration and Programme of Action adopted in 1993.

The European Convention on Human Rights did not include social and economic rights. In 1961, the European Social Charter was adopted. It treats a broad array of social rights as "a declaration of aims" that each contracting party "will pursue by all appropriate means."[53] The implementation of the Charter is ensured by a monitoring system based on reports submitted by the states. The Charter does

---

[49] Article 2.1 of the Covenant proclaims: "Each State party to the present Covenant undertakes to take steps, individually and through international assistance and cooperation, especially economic and technical, to the maximum of its available resources, with a view of achieving progressively the full realization of the rights recognized in the present Covenant by all appropriate means, including particularly the adoption of legislative measures."

[50] Under Articles 16–19 of the Covenant, the signatory states are obligated to submit periodic reports subsequently reviewed by an expert committee, which presents the concluding observations in a report to the United Nations General Assembly. On the basis of multiple state reports, General Comments are formulated, consisting of a discussion of the more general problems and ways of implementing the Covenant's provisions. These documents, however, are not legally binding to the states.

[51] Article 2 of the Optional Protocol to the International Covenant on Economic, Social and Cultural Rights. The communications – signed by name – will be considered within a year after "all available domestic remedies have been exhausted" (Article 3).

[52] Three months after the ratification of or accession to the protocol by ten states (Article 18).

[53] Elaborate provisions of Part III of the Charter (as revised in 1996) require every contracting state to accept thirty-one rights and principles "as a declaration of the aims which it will pursue by all appropriate means" and, additionally, to be bound by at least six of nine core rights of central importance listed in Part II of the Charter and at least sixteen out of thirty-one articles or sixty-three out of ninety-eight numbered paragraphs of the Charter.

not require the contracting states to incorporate rights selected by the party states to their constitutions.

Constitutional Solutions

Nevertheless, numerous constitutions include detailed chapters on social and economic rights. One reason for the attempts to put social rights into constitutions is historical. At the end of the nineteenth century and at the start of the twentieth century, the U.S. Supreme Court consistently invalidated welfare regulations by the states as violations of both constitutional property rights and freedom of contracts. Statutes regulating labor relations were declared unconstitutional by the Supreme Court.[54] This practice of American courts was widely criticized in Europe, particularly in France, where a claim for equality has always been justified as a claim to liberty.[55] The policy of the U.S. Supreme Court has raised skepticism among European lawyers and politicians toward the very principle of constitutionalism. It has also raised the conviction among many Europeans that in the absence of social and economic rights in a constitution the interpretation of a constitution may make the statutory implementation of social policies impossible. Therefore, social reformers in Europe sought to enshrine social rights in constitutions or, at least, to insert into the constitution a general provision that would counterbalance property rights on the constitutional level.

Another reason for the constitutionalization of social rights has a political character. The poor, those discriminated against, and the most needy usually lack sufficient say about laws and budgets – even when they constitute the numeric majority. So the people who do care about the interests and needs of this social class want to formulate social rights as constitutional rights to put such rights above political process.

There exists a broad range of constitutional solutions regarding social and economic rights in Western democracies. The Constitution of the United States, for example, does not mention social and economic rights; it is assumed today that the state can undertake social and cultural programs on the basis of statute.[56] The

---

[54] The landmark Supreme Court decision prohibiting government action for public welfare was *Lochner v. New York* (198 US 45, 1905); it was overruled during the New Deal.

[55] Another reason for French hostility to judicial review was the commitment to the idea of popular sovereignty embodied in the Parliament. The 1791 Constitution declared that "the courts may not interfere with the exercise of the legislative power, suspend the execution of laws" (Title III, Chapter V, Article 3).

[56] In the 1930s, U.S. courts accepted regulatory activities of the legislature as constitutional; in the 1950s and 1960s, a number of social programs was undertaken on the basis of laws and not invalidated by the courts. "By the late 1960s, the Court seemed to be moving toward recognition of a robust set of social and economic rights" (Sunstein 2004, 162). In the mid-1970s, however, this tendency was reversed by the Burger Court (ibid., 162–8).

citizens, however, have no constitutional right to claim social and economic rights, except where constitutional principles of equal protection or nondiscrimination are involved in the access to social benefits.[57]

The Basic Law of the Federal Republic of Germany, established in 1949, includes a general clause in Article 20.1 that states that the "Federal Republic of Germany is a democratic and social federal state." It is on the basis of this clause that the German government was able to implement social programs when economic growth permitted it. At the same time, the federal Constitutional Court has stated in a number of individual cases that individual rights, enforceable in courts, can be inferred from the "social state" principle.[58]

The 1958 Constitution of the French Fifth Republic does not include a catalog of individual rights. They are alluded to in the first sentence of the Preamble,[59] which reads: "The French people solemnly proclaim their attachment to the rights of man and to the principles of national sovereignty such as are defined by the Declaration of 1789, confirmed and completed by the Preamble to the 1946 Constitution."[60]

For many years, the preambles to the 1946 and 1958 French constitutions were interpreted as having no binding legal force and creating no enforceable rights. This changed in 1971 with the landmark decision of the Constitutional Council, according to which the fundamental principles of human rights included in the preambles to both constitutions and in the 1789 Declaration of the Rights of Man and the Citizen did, in fact, give rise to obligations on the part of the state and claims on the part of citizens.[61] Since then, specific enforceable rights have been successively "discovered" by the Constitutional Council and given constitutional status; these include a number of civil liberties and political rights, such as the principle of legal equality.[62] So far, the Council has stopped short of conferring on social and economic rights, except on the matter of the right to strike.[63] Generally, it can be

---

[57] For a description of the limited constitutional protection of social and economic rights in the United States, see Henkin (1981).

[58] See Currie (1994, 20–4). It is also worth noting that the authors of the Basic Law consciously rejected the idea of including a special chapter on social and economic rights into the Constitution. Such a catalog of rights had been included in the Constitution of the Weimar Republic of 1919. It can be claimed that constitutional status of social rights that could not be implemented in a country ridden by economic crises, unemployment, and poverty, added to a lack of respect toward the constitution itself and undermined the very concept of the rule of law. Hence the cautious opening of a possibility of action in the formulation of Article 20.1 of the Basic Laws of 1949.

[59] Similarly, Sweden mentions social goals of the state in the Preamble to its Constitution (ratified in 1809 and amended in 1971). In addition, Article 2.17 of the Swedish Instrument of Government provides for the right to strike.

[60] The Preamble to the 1946 Constitution had included a broad catalog of social and economic rights.

[61] Decision no. 71–44 DC of July 16, 1971, *Associations Law*. For full text see Bell (1992, 272–3).

[62] Ibid. (199–226).

[63] Decisions no. 79–105 DC of July 25, 1979, *Strikes on Radio and Television*; no. 82–144 DC of October 22, 1982, *Trade Union Immunity*; no. 87–230 DC of July 28, 1987, *Public Service Strikes*. See ibid. (322–7).

said that the French constitutional order provides for a large degree of parliamentary discretion in defining and protecting social, economic, and cultural rights. Regardless of the constitutional status of individual rights, large-scale social programs have been enacted in France through statutes and government regulations.[64]

The 1947 Constitution of the Republic of Italy includes a broad catalog of social rights in Articles 29–47, along with subchapters on civil liberties in Articles 13–28 and political rights in Articles 48–54. All these rights have identical declaratory status and are not given special protection. The Constitution does not contain provisions about direct application, nor does it guarantee a court claim in a case of violation of constitutional rights. All rights are thus given such protection as is provided for in statutes enacted on the basis of the particular articles of the Constitution.

The status of social rights posed a difficult problem during the preparation of the constitutions of Portugal and Spain, two countries in transition from dictatorship to democracy in the 1970s. At this time, constitutions were already being treated seriously in the Western world. The revolutions, directed against right-wing dictatorships, were both won by left-wing parties. Because social rights were essential for leftist identity, there was a demand to put them into constitutions. But framers in both countries realized that these rights would not be enforced and, consequently, all constitutional norms, including civil liberties, could be devalued. Therefore, the framers in both Spain and Portugal turned to precedents in the constitutions of Ireland and India.

The 1937 Constitution of Ireland made a distinction between fundamental rights and the directive principles of state policy.[65] The 1949 Constitution of India contained in Part III a catalog of judicially enforceable "fundamental rights." Part IV of the Constitution was entitled "Directive Principles of State Policy" and included a set of socioeconomic principles that could not be enforced in courts. "The provisions contained in this Part shall not be enforceable by any court but the principles therein laid down are nevertheless fundamental in the governance of the country and it shall be the duty of the State to apply these principles in making laws."[66] The Irish and Indian models were also adopted by a number of constitutions in the newly independent states of Africa.[67]

---

[64] It is worth noting that an upsurge in the French welfare state took place in the 1980s, under conservative government and on the basis of statutes without the need to amend the Constitution. See Ambler (1991).

[65] The idea of of a separate mechanism for the enforcement of social and economic rights was elaborated on by British jurist Hersch Lauterpacht (1945, and 1950, 284–6, 355, and 357).

[66] Article 37 of the Constitution of India. In the 1980s, the Supreme Court of India extended the idea of directive principles beyond the original concept.

[67] For example, Tanzania, 1977; Nigeria, 1979; Namibia, 1990; Uganda, 1995. (See Shivji 2003, 83–4.) The Constitution of Nigeria, Chapter II, "Fundamental Objectives and Directive Principles of State Policy," includes fundamental objectives of the government, economic objectives, foreign policy objectives, social objectives, environmental objectives, political objectives, and educational objectives.

In the case of Spain and Portugal, the dividing line between justiciable rights and directive principles did not separate civil liberties and political rights from social and economic principles. Rather, the division was moved into social rights and divided the subject matter of social and economic rights into two categories. Some basic security-related rights are included among enforceable constitutional rights (along with civil liberties and political rights). Other rights, described in a separate chapter and dealing with the social, economic, and cultural tasks of the state, lie within the competency of legislatures. The constitutions of Spain and Portugal did not consider these rights enforceable and open to claims by individual citizens but suggested instead that state tasks be realized through political process.

The 1976 Constitution of the Republic of Portugal distinguishes between two kinds of individual rights: the "rights, freedoms and safeguards" and "economic, social and cultural rights and duties." Constitutional provisions on rights, freedoms, and safeguards are directly applicable and binding not only on public bodies but also on private persons and institutions.[68] Such protection is not extended to economic, social, and cultural rights. These are formulated not as individual rights but as obligations of the state to undertake activities that will achieve certain tasks and goals.[69]

A similar distinction was introduced into the 1978 Constitution of Spain. The first part of the Constitution, entitled "Fundamental Public Rights and Freedoms" includes separate chapters on "rights and freedoms" and "guiding principles of economic and social policy."[70] The latter includes provisions on the protection of family, the obligation of the state to promote social and economic development and a more egalitarian distribution of incomes, and the state's duty to organize and sustain the system of social welfare. Additionally included in that chapter are the

---

The same chapter contains sections on the obligation of mass media, the government and the people, national ethics, directive on Nigeria Cultures, and duties of the citizen. Article 13 of the Constitution provides: "It shall be the duty and responsibility of all organs of government, and of all authorities and persons, exercising legislative, executive or judicial powers, to conform to, observe and apply the provisions of this Chapter of this Constitution." Chapter IV, "Fundamental rights," includes 11 civil liberties. Article 46 (1) states: "Any person who alleges that any of the provisions of this Chapter has been, is being or is likely to be contravened in any State in relation to him may apply to a High Court in that State for redress." In Asia, social issues were included into principles of state policy – as distinct from fundamental rights – in the 2008 Constitution of the Kingdom of Bhutan (Article 9).

[68] Article 18.1 of the Constitution of the Republic of Portugal.

[69] Among the rights which were given a direct constitutional protection are many rights of employees, including the security of employment, the rights to create workers' councils and labor unions, the rights to collective bargaining, and the right to strike. Among the economic, social, and cultural rights which were not given a direct constitutional protection are the right to work, rights to safe working conditions, and the right to private property. Moreover, the same distinction of rights was upheld after the 1989 amendments that otherwise significantly liberalized the socialist undertones of the 1976 Constitution.

[70] Chapter II, Articles 14–38; Chapter III, Articles 39–52, respectively.

rights to healthcare and access to culture, a clean environment, and decent housing. The development of science, the duty to care for aged and disabled persons, and the protection of consumers are all considered to be the state's obligations.[71]

The Constitution of Spain includes different kinds of protection for social and economic provisions. Fundamental public rights and freedoms bind all public authorities directly, and every citizen can claim them before both regular courts and the Constitutional Court.[72] The guiding principles of economic and social policy are supposed to "provide direction to legislation, court practice and the activities of public authorities." They are not protected by courts, except when such protection is granted to them by statute.[73] Social policy, in turn, and the scope of social and economic rights are left for the legislature.

The constitution makers of Eastern Europe faced a similar problem as Portugal and Spain, even though their revolutions were directed against left-wing governments. They still had to balance popular expectations for social security with an economic reality that could not sustain these expectations – and with the need for people and institutions to treat constitutions seriously.[74]

Czechoslovakia found an original solution to this problem. In the Charter of Rights, enacted in 1990, all rights were included. A special provision in Article 41.1 stated, however, that certain enumerated social and economic rights "can be claimed only within the limits of the law as set out in these provisions."[75] Poland, in turn, first opted for the Spanish–Portuguese solution. The 1992 draft Bill of Rights and Freedoms included some enforceable rights to basic security, with all other social obligations of the state present in a separate chapter on the Social and Economic Tasks of the State. After the draft Bill of Rights fell through, however, the Constitution of 1997 adopted the Czechoslovak solution.

South Africa included specific social rights in the 1996 Constitution, but it was a series of important decisions by the Constitutional Court that actually gave life to these provisions. Perhaps most significant was the Grootboom Case concerning the right to housing, in which the Constitutional Court demanded that the state develop a housing policy. The Court resolved that it could not dictate policy to the state but

---

[71] It is worth noting that such traditional social and economic rights as the right to work, the right to free choice of occupation and to a decent compensation are included – along with the right to private property and freedom of enterprise – among "fundamental public rights and freedoms."

[72] Article 53.1–2.

[73] Article 53.3.

[74] The problems of the East European transition, however, were even more difficult than those of Spain of Portugal in the 1970s, with East European countries facing a much more acute economic crisis and unable to count on such immense Western help as the nascent democracies of the 1970s. Moreover, Eastern Europe essentially had to undergo a double transition – to constitutional democracy and to the free market – simultaneously. For the influence of dual transition on the formulation of rights, see Osiatyński 1997, 69–70.

[75] See Osiatyński (1994, 140–2) for details.

that it could demand and assess policy proposed by the state. When the government provided its policy, the Court declared it unconstitutional because it did not take proper care of the needs of the most vulnerable groups within the population. The Parliament had to make a new policy, subsequently accepted by the Court. This example testifies to both the far-reaching power of the Constitutional Court and the limits to this power, with the Court neither taking over the government's tasks nor imposing the policy itself.[76]

Similarly, the Supreme Court in India provided enforceability to social and economic rights on the basis of a constitutional concept of dignity and the right to life.[77] Even in the United States, the Supreme Court made a number of decisions in the 1960s and 1970s in which it came very close to giving constitutional status to social and economic rights. This trend was later reversed.[78] Nevertheless, the judiciaries in a number of countries have been relying on the general principles or formulations of state goals as included in constitutions to impose the choice of priorities on governments.[79]

RIGHTS OR NEEDS

This brief overview of the constitutional status of social and economic rights in a number of Western democracies leads to some important conclusions:

- Social and economic rights are usually given different protection from that granted to civil liberties and political rights, even when they are included in the constitution. The exceptions are the declaratory constitutions, which do not provide for the direct enforcement of any constitutional rights.
- In constitutions that do not distinguish between social and economic rights and other rights and liberties, the rule is relatively simple: the more social and economic rights in the constitution, the fewer enforcement mechanisms in the entire chapter on rights.

---

[76] See Sunstein (2004, 219–29) and Sachs (2006).

[77] "Using the flavour of Directive Principles to enrich the content of the right to life, it carved out an array of social and economic rights including the right to live with dignity, right to a livelihood, right to free legal aid, freedom from pollution and right to a clean environment, right to education, right to health and medical care, right to shelter and right to food," writes Sripati (2007, 51).

[78] Sunstein (2004, 149–71).

[79] This development suggests that the common interpretation of justiciability as the distinction between civil and political vs. social and economic rights may be false. Social and economic provision, once the principles of the UDHR and general provisions of the ICESCR are implemented in the law of a given state, became justiciable rights although this justiciability has a statutory rather than constitutional character (i.e., it can be reversed or changed by the future legislation). Claims related to such rights are heard in the courts.

- The constitutionalization of economic, social, and cultural rights does not determine, by itself, the level of social welfare. In fact, the best developed social programs have been created in countries whose constitutions declare as a general goal the implementation of social policy by the state (Sweden, Federal Republic of Germany, France).
- Western democracies have implemented social and economic rights gradually; the main instruments of implementation have been legislation and decisions of constitutional courts.
- It seems more than plausible that the economic well-being of a society is a more important factor in the implementation of social and economic rights than any constitutional provisions. Constitutions, however, are extremely important, for they help justify the inclusion of social policies in legislation and form the basis for the decisions of constitutional courts.

This diversified picture of social rights and their adjustment by courts can guide the process in newly emerging democracies, but it will not answer all theoretical and empirical questions. Some of them relate to the separation of powers and court interference with the allocation of resources and formulation of state budgets; these issues are usually restricted for the executive and legislature. The differences between the legal protection of rights and political process, discussed in Chapter 2, are particularly relevant here. Other questions are related to the effectiveness of the direct provision of services by a state and focus on the allegedly demoralizing moral aspect of social and economic rights, which are said to decrease the motivation of recipients for their own effort. After all, other people earn or purchase benefits equivalent to those provided by social rights. They may feel uncomfortable when some people receive the same goods and services without effort or contribution to society.

Finally, there is the problem of the applicability of the very concept of rights and the mechanisms for their enforcement to aspirations that are to be "achieved progressively" by each state "to the maximum of its available resources."[80] The purely legalistic language of rights may turn out inadequate to meet a number of public goals. It seems impossible to enforce the following rights proposed the ICSECR[81] by legal rights means alone: the right to work,[82] the "continuous improvement of living

---

[80] See Article 2.1 of the ICESCR. Robertson (1994) makes an attempt to give a more precise meaning to the notion of "maximum available resources" by suggesting specifically which resources should be made available for the implementation of the ICESCR and how compliance with the Covenant should be measured.

[81] Articles 6, 11, and 12 of the ICESCR, respectively.

[82] Phillip Harvey has challenged, however, the conventional wisdom of today according to which the right to work is only declaratory and means primarily the choice to work or compensation in the case of unemployment. Harvey shows how right to work is subordinated to other policy choices, primarily

conditions," the right to "the highest attainable standard of physical and mental health," or the right "to enjoy the benefits of scientific progress and its applications." However, it seems possible to assure the right to form trade unions and the right to social security.[83]

The traditional approach to social and economic rights is unable to provide answers to these questions and dispel the confusion. It seems that more clarity and far better prospects for implementation could result from shifting the emphasis from social and economic rights to social needs and treating rights as one of a number of instruments that can help to satisfy such needs.

When thinking about social and economic rights, we tend to treat as a matter of rights everything that is involved in a particular realm of social interaction. For example, when we talk about the right to health, we may think that every aspect of healthcare should be covered as a matter of rights. When we think about the right to education, we often end up reasoning that every type and level of education should be a matter of right. This tendency changes as soon as we switch to thinking in terms of needs. There can be no doubt that every person has health-related needs. This does not, however, mean that every aspect of these needs should be granted to every person as a matter of entitlement. A great majority of health-related needs are and will always remain the responsibility of a person. Our lifestyle, diet, use of substances, and exercise regime define our health to a greater extent than health services. Many health-related needs are covered by private contracts, insurances, and other instruments that do not necessarily imply universal rights that impose obligations on the state. Only some health-related needs should be fulfilled as a matter of rights. Every society should define these needs, and such a definition will be dependent on a society's situation, available resources, customs, and mode of health services.

In short, the needs-based approach to social and economic rights assumes that all people have valid social and economic needs that should not be dismissed. However, there is a very broad range of instruments to fulfill such needs. Human rights and rights-related claims are just one of a number of instruments, and subsidiary at that. This means that we should have recourse to rights when – and only when – a given need of a paramount character cannot be satisfied in any other way.

What Are Social Rights About?

All this leads us to a discussion about the essential content of social rights. After all, they are a historical construct that has evolved in time, along with people's needs,

---

to the need to counter inflation. He claims that "the right to work is entitled to far more deference that it normally receives" (Harvey 2002, 469) and argues that a functional equivalent of full employment can be achieved by the direct creation of jobs by the government.

[83] Articles 8 and 9 of ICESCR.

dominant standards, the availability of resources, and the advances of technology. Many practical problems with social rights result from the fact that they originated in a period dominated by a factory-based market economy, with the structures, technologies, and organization of work in a factory influencing the character and shape of many social rights. One example, ridiculed by Cranston and other opponents of social rights, pertains to holidays with pay.[84] But in the early stage of a factory-based economy, holidays without pay were equal to unemployment and starvation, essentially guaranteeing no possibility of rest. In an agricultural subsistence economy, this right made no sense; similarly, it makes little sense in the self-employed sectors more common today. Another example is that of work provided by women, because housework for the benefit of one's own family is usually not recognized as a type of work that earns one future rights, for example, to a pension, to healthcare, or to social security. Many other socially useful efforts are not considered economically valuable – and as such they are neither compensated nor considered grounds for rights, nor do they provide a person with self-esteem. Such a scenario requires constant readjustment.[85]

With all these changes, social rights have always served similar values. Undoubtedly, they serve human dignity. "The dignity principle requires that people not be denied the means to satisfy their basic needs."[86] Dignity, however, is a rather vague concept; its openness was one of the main reasons for its selection as the common ground on which the various philosophies of rights could be reconciled.[87] To look for the content of social rights we need to go beyond dignity itself.

Social rights are often linked with equality and social justice.[88] Although all rights assume equality in the treatment of individuals and reject discrimination, social rights, in this definition, are to lead toward economic equality. Economic equality, however, cannot be a matter of rights. It depends on social choices and can become a guiding principle for social policy, but no one can claim an equality of living conditions that disregards one's own effort. The American concept of equal opportunity, closer to the idea of liberty, is served sufficiently by civil liberties and

---

[84] Cranston (1973, 66).

[85] Of course, civil liberties are also influenced by social and technological change – such as that which has permitted the current wave of terrorism. But technological change does not call, at least so far, for the readjustment of the very core of civil liberties or the revision in our understanding of political rights.

[86] Christiansen (1982, 260).

[87] "(. . .) the notion of human dignity is nearly empty of meaning. Unless it is further specified, the notion of human dignity lacks all references to particular freedom, needs, and relationships. It is for this reason that most ideological systems can appeal to human dignity for moral legitimacy. Therefore, unless the relationship between the transcendental worth of persons and particular human freedoms, needs and relationships can be specified, the notion of dignity will become an empty notion" (Hollenbach 1982, 18).

[88] In the socialist concept of rights, social rights were clearly to serve equality. Social justice served the role of ideological justification for the communist revolution. See Wieruszewski (1988).

political rights. Social rights, in turn, are sometimes identified with well-being or welfare. But this is also misleading, because well-being should primarily be a result of personal efforts rather than a claim protected by rights.[89] Finally, social rights are also not identical with justice – even in the absence of the adjective *social*.[90]

It seems to this author that the closest and the most convincing links exist between social rights and basic needs. As mentioned, social rights do not and cannot serve all needs. They serve only some needs. Needs served by human rights are related to the security of a person. Here again, the distinction between categories of rights becomes elusive. Civil liberties, after all, protect the need for security whenever such security may be threatened by the state or by other people. Social rights protect physical security when a person's very survival is threatened, regardless of the cause of such a threat. This can be excessive exploitation by the others, state oppression, or politically or economically induced hunger. It might also be an amendable shortage of resources or a threat posed by the elements. In such cases, the concept of social rights may indeed justifiably apply.

The content of social human rights usually goes beyond mere physical security, which can be assured by 800 calories and rudimentary shelter, as proven in prison conditions. Very few people would claim that this is enough to ensure life with dignity. For life to be truly dignified, "basic needs" must also be satisfied – and so the concept of basic needs becomes crucial for understanding social and economic rights, as well as for the very capacity to make use of all other rights: "Opportunity for education, for religious observance, for companionship and for political participation, any or all of these can be effectively denied by manipulation of vital services. For when we are forced to a choice between these genuine goods and basic needs, we will usually choose the needs as more urgent."[91]

Basic Needs

Defining basic needs is not an easy task. Physical survival is a necessary but insufficient condition for having one's basic needs met. The physical survival of a slave or serf is assured, but the dignity of each is violated in that neither can give his or her life

---

[89] Here again, social policy can be oriented toward assuring everyone a relatively high level of well-being (provided there are available resources), as has been the case in Sweden and other welfare states. Of course, welfare policies, when legislated, create rights. Such rights, however, cannot be considered absolute, in the sense that they can be limited if resources are no longer adequate or social priorities change.

[90] There are many conceptions of justice that emphasize various bases for what we consider just. Merit or desert-based conceptions of justice cannot be reconciled with claiming social benefits or services. For a more in-depth discussion of the relationship between principles of justice, need, equality, and desert, see Christiansen (1982, 266–79).

[91] Ibid. (262).

meaning or value and neither can act as an autonomous person. For Christiansen, the satisfaction of basic needs results from dignity understood as one of "two corollary principles which seem to be entailed in a notion of a moral minimum. (...) The kind of dignity envisioned in the moral minimum pertains to an individual's control over goods vital to him and entails respect on the part of the authorities for that prerogative." These authorities should, accordingly, protect people from actions that exploit "an individual's basic vulnerabilities." But dignity, for Christiansen, "is not linked simply to independent control of resources, but to choice of activities and the potential to enjoy other values."[92]

Thus, basic needs connect to the concept of autonomy that is crucial for individual dignity and freedom. David Copp claims that "in order to be fully autonomous people must have the ability to meet their basic needs." This is because in the absence of the fulfillment of basic needs a person cannot set goals or make choices about one's own life.[93]

Copp suggests a list of goods and services that are "either basic needs or forms of provision for a basic need," which includes

> the need for nutritious food and clean water, the need to excrete, the need otherwise to preserve the body intact, the need for periodic rest and relaxation (which [is presumed] to include periodic sleep and some form of recreation), the need for companionship, the need for education, the need for social acceptance and recognition, the need for self-respect and self-esteem, the need to be free from harassment.[94]

This is a high order of needs. Providing everyone with entitlement to such goods and services as a matter of right would require vast resources. Copp realizes that and qualifies the right to an adequate standard of living, which is based on his concept of basic needs. "It is the right of every person to an adequate standard of living *if* his society is wealthy enough to provide an adequate standard to every member."[95]

The right to an adequate standard of living, combined with the concept of basic needs, would then serve as a guideline for a state's economic and social policy. Whenever a society has sufficient resources, assuring basic needs for everyone should

---

[92] Ibid. (260–1, 286). The other principle is decency that "requires that no one be forced to endure degrading living conditions because of a correctable mal-distribution of resources."

[93] Copp (1992, 234 and 254).

[94] See Copp (ibid., 252). In 1952, A. C. Pigou proposed a less inclusive list of needs. His minimum included "some defined quantity and quality of house accommodation, of medical care, of education, of food, of leisure, of apparatus of sanitary convenience and safety where work is carried, and so on" (quoted in Copp 1992, 249). As we can see, Copp added the needs for relationships, recognition, and self-worth that did not exist in Pigou's earlier formulation.

[95] Ibid. (236).

take priority over an increase in general welfare, economic growth, or other considerations. This is because "the goal of respecting the autonomy of the citizen ought to
have priority over the goal of promoting general welfare or economic efficiency."[96]

Even though Copp writes about "The Right," by which he means the right to an
adequate standard of living, many of the things on his list of basic needs cannot be
met through the application of the instruments of rights. Rights and corresponding
duties cannot create and sustain companionship, nor can they assure acceptance,
recognition, or self-respect. These are values that an individual needs to take care
of by his or her own efforts. No state action can be a substitute for one's individual
responsibility for the fulfillment of such needs.

The same is true for other basic needs. Even when the goods or services necessary
for their fulfillment can be provided by outside persons, primary responsibility rests
with an individual. As mentioned, social rights consist of the provision to some people
of such goods and services that others earn through their own effort or exchange
on the market for their labor. Therefore, others should not carry the burden of an
individual's irresponsibility or a person's culpable neglect of his or her own needs.
Even the proponents of welfare rights agree that such rights should not be granted
automatically.[97] One of them is Alan Gewirth, who nevertheless suggests that no
one can "rationally demand of other persons that they help him to have basic well-
being unless his own efforts to have it are unavailing."[98] Christiansen dismisses
the assumption "that a need-based conception of justice [excludes] the duty of
self help (. . .) it is mistaken to view a basic needs policy as abetting indolence,
because self-reliance is an intrinsic part of the dignity which needs policies try to
promote."[99]

Copp discusses the example of a person who has consciously gambled away the
resources provided for his family's well-being. Such a person can make pledges based
on egalitarian arguments or ask for charity, but he does not have a claim for extra
resources.[100] In fact, individual responsibility is at the very essence of Copp's right
to an adequate standard of living, for according to him this right does not entitle a
person to have their needs secured or satisfied. It is the right "to be *enabled* to meet

---

[96] Ibid. (258). Similarly, Christiansen (1982, 246–50) shows the failure of the economic growth strategy
to meet the basic needs of the poor worldwide, claiming that development strategies should focus on
the betterment of conditions for the poor rather than general economic growth.

[97] For a discussion of the relationship between positive action and personal responsibility, see Barry
(1990, 80–1).

[98] Quoted in Barry (1990, 81).

[99] Christiansen (1982, 279).

[100] Moreover, "(. . .) he could hardly justifiably complain of being treated unjustly simply on the ground
that the situation resulting from his gambling is one in which he cannot achieve an adequate standard
of living" (Copp 1992, 242).

their basic needs; I am not proposing a right to be *provided* with what one needs."[101] Gewirth seems to share this attitude in stating that we "have duties to help persons to fulfill their generic rights of agency when they cannot do so by their own efforts."[102]

Other proponents of welfare rights are more generous than Copp. Henry Shue believes that there are duties not just to enable everyone to meet their basic needs, but "to provide for the subsistence of those unable to provide for their own."[103] A great majority of advocates of the constitutionalization of social rights believe in something more than just "enabling" people to meet their basic needs. Similarly, many welfare programs provide goods and services that directly satisfy the needs of destitute people. Such goods and services are often considered a matter of rights.

Such rights, however, differ from civil liberties and political rights in two respects. First, a claim is contingent on some attempts on the part of a person to fulfill her need through her own efforts. We demand that those on unemployment benefits actively seek employment. We do not, by contrast, make police protection of one's personal integrity contingent on a person's ability to practice self-defense against assault. We do not expect a person exercising the right to court to try to solve the dispute on his own. Second, this author proposes that we may, in fact, render the provision of needs contingent on a recipient's contribution to society.

The Conditionality of Social Rights

This is a controversial point. Civil liberties and political rights are absolute. They are not contingent on the performance of duties to one's state or society. In fact, the most elaborate constitutional provisions in the sphere of civil liberties concern the protection of people who have violated or potentially violated their duties toward other persons and the community: convicted criminals in prisons and those under investigation or on trial for crime. The reason is that they are exposed to the naked coercive power of the state and need special protection. Why should we treat social rights differently?

Two separate differences between the two generations of rights may be of key importance here. First, already discussed, is the fact that social rights provide some people with goods and services that others must earn through their own effort. In fact, those who do earn their own way must also contribute an extra effort – collected through taxes and other mechanisms – to cover the costs of meeting the needs of the recipients. Entitlement to benefits without some form of "countercontribution" to others may violate people's sense of fairness and justice.

[101] Copp (1992, 252).
[102] Gewirth (1996, 61).
[103] Shue (1980, 53).

The second difference is of historical character. Civil liberties and political rights emerged as rights and obligations on the part of state followed. English nobles demanded freedoms, so the king – when he needed service from the nobility – granted them the Magna Carta, thus assuming an obligation not to violate the liberties acknowledged. The nobles, in fact, believed that they had had these freedoms before the year 1215. So did colonists in America – before the Declaration of Independence. In the nineteenth century, democrats claimed that people have a right to participate in government, so the authorities were made to comply. Obligations of governments and limitations imposed on them followed.

In the case of social rights, the sequence of events differed.[104] These rights emerged from preceding obligations. Initially, these consisted of obligations between individuals within a society. A member of a rural community was not to pass a needy person without offering mercy and charity. The needy also had obligations – to help the more needy or to do something for the community. These obligations were strongly emphasized by religion (as in the parable of the good Samaritan), by other moral authorities in society, and by parents and teachers in the upbringing of children. They were enforced by parish rules, the threat of damnation, and the customs of society.[105] In the medieval city, caring for the needy was a task for the patricians and municipal authorities; hence the original meaning of "*hospedale*" (from which we now have the words *hospital* and *hospice*): a place of care for all people in need and not merely the sick ones. Inhabitants and clients of a *hospedale* had certain obligations to work, provided they were able to do so. During the period of absolutism, these social obligations within society were taken over – along with society's other institutions – by absolutist kings and states.[106] With the language of rights becoming more potent, the original obligations were transformed into rights.[107] But

---

[104] The very distinction between ciivil liberties and political rights on the one hand and social and economic rights on the other hand has historical character. Even though charity was known in Medieval Europe, civil liberties emerged long before the concept of social rights was formulated. Martin P. Golding (1978, 50) points to a theoretical difference between option-rights discussed by William Ockham in the fourteenth century and the claim rights formulated, according to Golding, by Rudolf von Ihering in the second half of the nineteenth century.

[105] One example is the *denunciatio evangelica* mentioned above.

[106] "The history of the welfare state goes back to the eighteenth century and the enlightened monarchs. It is indeed both in the governmental initiatives and the theoretical works of that age, particularly in German lands, that we find the belief that the state ought to care for the material, cultural and moral well-being of the people, from the cradle to the grave. The enlightened king, the 'first servant of the state', was responsible for that policy. He knew what was best for his subjects, because his position and education gave him a wider and correcter understanding of the needs of society. He had to look for the welfare of the citizens who were in no position to decide for themselves: 'everything for the people, nothing by the people!'" (Caenegem 1995, 22–3).

[107] The revolutionaries of the nineteenth century did not use the language of rights, perhaps because they did not have access to courts or other mechanisms for the enforcement of social rights. Thus, they had no choice but to use the language of revolution.

the underlying bonds of mutual obligation were lost in the process. Nevertheless, even during and after the Great Depression, the needy were helped within a broad – and extremely successful – program of public works. Today, however, the sense of unconditional entitlement and the absence of any remaining link between help and obligations have had detrimental effects on all parties to the social assistance equation.[108]

In fact, this author postulates that the right to an adequate standard of living or to having one's basic needs met should not be unconditional. Instead, it ought to be made contingent on a proven effort to have one's own needs met and on an obligation to contribute in some way to society.[109] Guaranteed income is morally acceptable only if it is a payment for some type of service – and not a handout. The requirement of contribution also addresses the issue of dignity and self-worth, thus far neglected by the institution of benefits without contribution to others.[110] The organization of ways in which such contribution could take place without risk of coercion should be one of main tasks for public authorities, particularly on the local level.[111]

SOCIAL RIGHTS IN A LIMITED STATE

The needs-based approach to social rights calls for a limited and diversified role of the state in enabling an individual to meet his or her needs. Most often, the social and economic needs of individuals are met by personal and community efforts. People satisfy them directly within the family or earn the means required to buy necessary

---

[108] Many of the highways and dams that have been constructed in the United States and Germany since the 1930s were built by the unemployed on relief. Plenty of these highways are still in use. In Poland, in the late 1990s, an unemployment level of nearly 20 percent coexisted with the absence of a viable national highway system – and an utter lack of people willing to perform simple, menial labor with pay just slightly above unemployment benefits.

[109] Such contribution would not have to resemble a formal full-time job. Various forms of part-time work, including serving the community in times of emergency, constitute acceptable solutions. The decisive factors should be the needs of the community and the abilities of the recipient. For example, Jencks suggests that for the single mothers of young children half-time work would be a "far more reasonable goal that full-time work," provided that "all school districts offered year-round half-day pre-kindergarten programs" (Jencks 2005, 86).

[110] Such a solution would require a new way of thinking about what kinds of activities merit respect and self-worth. I believe that there are vast possibilities for unemployed and needy people in the realm of personal services and the betterment of people's quality of life. The problem is that, typically, such services as reading to children or to the elderly are not considered "work."

[111] In 1996, before the replacement of the Aid to Families with Dependent Children program with the Temporary Assistance for Needy Families bill, President Clinton's welfare team unsuccessfully "had hoped to guarantee jobs for able-bodied welfare recipients who could not find work and child care for those who could. Republicans wanted to save money so they rejected these guarantees" (Jencks 2005, 76).

goods and services on the market. Many social, economic, and cultural needs are satisfied collectively, within extended family, local community, or professional and other associations. The role of the state should be subsidiary – although, at times, it can become crucial. The state can play a number of distinct functions to satisfy society's needs, and many of these functions require neither the existence nor the enforcement of rights.

The Regulatory Function

The proper fulfillment of social and economic needs may call for state regulation of markets, conditions of work and environmental protection measures, as well as for the criminalization of certain behaviors threatening the social, economic, and cultural needs of others. Redistribution schemes and taxation needed for social programs also constitute forms of regulation.

Market relations based on private contracts create rights between the persons involved. Such contracts are enforced by the state in the same way as all other contracts. There exist, however, contracts that are forced and guaranteed by the state. This is the case with social security insurance, health insurance, and pension plans, where the contracts among employer, employee, and the insuring agency have been made compulsory by the state. The state also often assumes responsibility in a form of insuring the agency in case of its insolvency; if this happens, an insured person has a secondary claim against the state for the fulfillment of the contract.

The state can also support or enhance charity – through tax deductions, by providing private charitable lotteries with public space and state resources for this purpose, and through other incentives. Such activities do not create formal obligations on the part of the donor nor rights on the part of the beneficiary, except for the issue of fairness whenever there is a risk of corruption or favoritism.

One of the state's regulatory functions consists of protecting the weaker party in private contracts. Labor laws and consumer regulations are good examples. In such cases, the state creates rights that can by used by private persons against other private persons and that are enforced in state courts. The concept of basic needs leads some authors to conclusions that may increase this protective function of the state.[112] Others recognize society's obligations toward individuals – even if such obligations are merely of moral nature and do not necessarily create rights.[113] It

---

[112] For example, Shue suggests that the right to subsistence creates a duty of the state "to protect people against deprivation of the only available means of subsistence by other peoples" (Shue 1980, 53).

[113] Copp (1992, 244) claims that a poor society has a duty "to strive for the capacity of providing something as close as possible to an adequate standard of living for all it members as soon as it can." It also "ought to enable as many as it can to come as close as possible to an adequate standard of living while treating each of its members fairly." Copp does not explain, however, how a society can fulfill this duty.

seems that these long-term goals can be fulfilled, for and in the name of society, by the state.[114] This leads us to the second function of the state in the fulfillment of economic needs.

Setting Public Policy Goals

The state can introduce policies aiming at maximizing employment, facilitating housing, protecting the environment, and promoting public health, for example. The implementation of such public policy goals requires the allocation of resources in the state budget. In a majority of modern democracies, there exists an unwritten consensus that public policy should also take into consideration the needs of the poorest and most helpless and vulnerable groups. This is particularly important for the basic needs concept because many basic needs cannot be served without proper public policy. In fact, some needs can be better served by public policy than they can through the instruments of rights.

Many needs that have a collective character can be met only by public action, as in the case of water supply, sanitation, and schooling. Even though people generally build and purchase homes individually, housing for the needy usually requires public policy. The fulfillment of basic needs also calls for specific government programs and policies to stimulate employment or to assist in the case of unemployment (e.g., through subsidy of basic commodities or public employment).[115] Copp has suggested that, even though the state does not have a duty to feed every person, it "must ensure the availability of food supply sufficient to enable everyone to have a nutritious diet."[116] This definitely requires the adoption of public policy.

One example of the increased sensitivity by authors of public policies to the diversified needs of citizens is the concept of "gross national happiness" that could replace a one-sided indicator in the form of gross national product.[117] There is a

[114] "States parties are obligated, regardless of the level of economic development, to ensure respect for minimum subsistence rights for all" declared the Limburg Principles on the Implementation of the ICESCR, adopted by the UN Commission on Human Rights in 1987 to provide better definition of the Covenant (quoted in Robertson 1994, 702).

[115] Christiansen (1982, 263) claims that "employment is rightly conceived as the primary goal of needs policy, not only because it is the surest way to make men and women self-supporting, but also because it is an important element in upholding self-esteem and a sense of purpose in people's lives."

[116] Copp (1992, 242).

[117] The idea of gross national happiness was first postulated by the king of Bhutan, Jigme Singye Wangchuck soon after his enthronement in 1972. He claimed that the concept of the GDP did not deal with actual redistribution and use of the national product; it left out many aspects of life that could not be measured by simple addition of the market value of goods and service. Consequently, even countries with high GNP had widespread poverty and many important human needs are not met. Since then, the Commission for National Happiness (that replaced the Planning Commission) in Bhutan has developed a number of indicators and measurements of national happiness related to socioeconomic development, conservation of the environment, preservation and promotion of culture,

growing interest in using various measurements of growth as the guidelines for developmental policies. The idea of capabilities,[118] as well as the concept of legal empowerment (already discussed in Chapter 2),[119] and other new ideas are postulated to guide public policy, and not only in the developing world.[120]

Beyond mere public policy, the state should design institutions that help people meet their basic social and psychological needs. This is particularly relevant to basic needs that cannot be satisfied by the state such as self-respect or social acceptance. Copp gives an example of a national health insurance scheme "that would provide a person with an entitlement to psychological counseling."[121] Gewirth suggests that the state should introduce "appropriate and justified macroeconomic policies and institutions" by virtue of which "even the poorest can gradually surmount their economic and related afflictions and move closer to equality."[122]

Generally, policies resulting from the concept of basic needs should serve the most underprivileged segments of population. Redistributive policies are included here, although basic needs are not identical with equality.[123] In fact, the satisfaction of basic needs actually creates clear-cut limits to redistributive policies. Such policies cannot worsen the situation of those better off to make them, in turn, unable to meet their basic needs. They should also provide for the termination of support once

and good governance. The indicators, which include social relations and other security-based needs as well as physiological and spiritual well-being, are measured and mechanisms are being developed to introduce these factors into public policies. See Thinley (2007). There has been a growing interest in this concept outside Bhutan. (See *Rethinking Development*, 2007, for the proceedings of the Second International Conference on Gross National Happiness held in 2005 in Antigonish, Nova Scotia, Canada.)

[118] The concept of capabilities was first proposed by Amartya Sen in *Commodities and Capabilities* (1982). It was further developed by Sen (1999, 74–110) and by Martha C. Nussbaum, according to whom, capabilities approach is not limited to formal rights but is interested in what a right-holder is "actually able to do and to be." " . . . it is concerned with what is actually going on in the life in question: not how many resources are sitting around, but how they are actually going to work in enabling people to function in a fully human way" (Nussbaum 2001, 222). Nussbaum expanded the list of capabilities to include the ability "to express justified anger" and of having "opportunities for sexual satisfaction." Both Sen and Nussbaum agree that the development of capabilities should be the goal of public policy. It seems that this approach offers a new perspective on the fulfillment of basic needs.

[119] "In its broadest sense, empowerment is the expansion of freedom of choice and action. The distinguishing feature of legal empowerment is that it involves the use of any of a diverse array of legal services for the poor to help advance those freedoms," writes Golub (2003, 25).

[120] A number of such ideas is included in Human Development Reports published by the United Nations Development Program since 1990.

[121] "But a state clearly could not ensure that people are able to meet needs of these kinds" (ibid., 252).

[122] Gewirth (1996, 99).

[123] Feinberg (1973, 111) considers the principle of need "not an independent principle at all, but only a way of mediating the application of the principle of equality." Miller claims that the concepts of needs and equality are almost identical. Runciman considers need a subordinate norm to equality, which for him is the key principle of justice. For a discussion of their ideas, see Christiansen (1982, 268–9), who disagrees with them and treats needs and equality as separate principles.

the formerly needy individual has reached the opportunity to enjoy an adequate standard of living.[124]

Does public policy create rights? There is no simple answer to this question. Some specific rights are postulated within the basic needs concept. One of them is the right to subsistence, which implies state duties that should be fulfilled through appropriate policies and services. Shue claims that the right to subsistence implies the duty of the state "to provide for the subsistence of those unable to provide for their own."[125] A derivative of this right is the state's duty to avoid depriving a person of his or her only available means of subsistence. If Shue's ideas are accepted, the duty and correlative right he proposes in fact enlarge the very concept of personal liberty. That would mean that the state could not intrude – through otherwise legitimate taxation or justifiable confiscation resulting from liability or punishment – into those properties that are necessary for one's subsistence. Inviolability protected by personal freedom would extend into the means necessary for subsistence. Understandably, such a postulate has radical consequences.

The Enforcement of Public Policy Goals

In practice, the most difficult problem with social rights is the enforcement of public policy goals. Such goals are usually implemented by political means. However, there exists a danger that the democratic political process may neglect the needs of the most vulnerable and needy groups of citizens.[126] Therefore, some special mechanisms supporting needs-based policies can be designed. Such mechanisms can grant social policies special position as compared to other political choices. This can be accomplished either through constitutional provisions on social policies (or social rights) or by decisions of constitutional courts. In both cases, a general norm in a constitution is indispensable, though such a norm does not necessarily make a particular social right directly enforceable by the courts.[127]

---

[124] See Copp (1992, 247). Elsewhere, he claims that "the better off have a duty to pay their share *until* the point is reached that the worst off are enabled to meet their basic needs" (ibid., 260).

[125] Shue (1980, 53).

[126] "It is understandable that welfare philosophers should demand the constitutional protection of welfare rights, since it is almost certainly the lax political rules of majoritarian democracies, and the discretion granted to officials, that have caused the failure of postwar welfare policies aimed at both equality and the relief of deprivation: coalitions of group interests have submerged the widespread desire for some form of welfare for the needy that exists in a community" (Barry 1990, 80).

[127] Of course, social rights in a constitution play the same role of assuring priority to certain goals in political decision making about the allocation of resources. It seems that protection of the weakest is an important motivating force behind Phillip Harvey's defense of the right to work. According to him, it deserves a place in economic policy debates "precisely because they are likely to conflict with public preferences. In political democracies, majoritarian interests tend to be self-enforcing, but minority interests often need the special protection that rights-based claims provide." Harvey argues

One example of giving special treatment to the state's social tasks was Poland's draft Bill of Rights and Freedoms, proposed in 1992 and later aborted. It contained a section on the goals of the state in social, economic, and cultural matters. As noted, these goals did not create directly enforceable rights but instead obligated the state to take care of the enumerated goals in its policies (and, accordingly, in its budgets). To give constitutional tasks more weight in political process, the draft suggested that the government would be obligated to submit a detailed report of its own actions in the realm of social and economic goals (with a yearly absolutorium for approval of government spending). Such a report was to include not only state expenditures but also independent assessments of the effectiveness of the steps taken by the government. Another type of reinforcement of a needs-based political process – not included, however, in the draft Bill of Rights – could be the requirement of a supermajority in the voting on the motion for the absolutorium. Although all other parts of the budget could require a simple majority of votes for approval, the report on the social and economic tasks of a state might need a two-thirds majority. Without such support, the government would face the same consequences as with the rejection of the absolutorium – namely dismissal.[128]

Experience proves that vulnerable populations and the weakest groups of a society cannot always rely on political process, even if their needs and social goals are included in a constitution. In such cases, courts can intervene by using constitutional provisions to demand from legislature and the executive the development of public policy in the sphere of social welfare. They can also make the judgment as to whether a given public policy protects constitutional values and principles, as was the case with the government's housing policy in South Africa, discussed above. To respect the principle of separation of powers, courts should refrain from issuing executive orders designing specific welfare policies. This task should be left to the executive and legislative and may be reviewed, if necessary, by a constitutional court.

In general, public policy by itself does not create enforceable rights. It seems implausible that employment policies create an automatic right to get a job or that a housing policy would translate into an enforceable right to a house. However, when a given public policy is implemented and used to introduce a mechanism for the provision of goods or services, those eligible acquire a right to receive benefits.

that "unemployed workers constitute just such a minority in need of special protection, particularly in periods of relative prosperity, when their interests are likely to conflict with the policy preferences of a majority of the population" (Harvey 2002, 470).

[128] Another solution was suggested by David Trubeck at the very beginning of the post-Communist transition in Poland. While discussing the lack of available resources for welfare in bankrupt economies, Trubeck noted that by the time resources will be generated a new power structure will emerge capable of opposing increased welfare spending. Trubeck proposed that a constitution precommits a certain percentage of future GDP growth to social expenditures. (Trubeck made this suggestion at a discussion on new constitutions in post-Communist countries, held in Kazimierz, Poland, in 1990.)

Such rights usually have statutory character and can be terminated when the policy changes.

Constitutional Social Rights

Public authorities may also directly provide goods or services to members of vulnerable groups who cannot provide for themselves, lack the sufficient means to buy needed goods and services on the market, or are victims of past discrimination.

As noted, the state may be necessary to provide the poor with such basic services as water supply, health clinics, schools, and, when needed, the distribution of food. Some goods and services can be provided as a matter of rights. These include the provision of goods and services necessary for the satisfaction of the basic needs of all people kept under coercive power of the state, including prisoners and people committed by courts to mental institutions as well as all others temporarily deprived of freedom. Such rights should have constitutional protection.

Social and economic rights may be made contingent on a recipient's prior effort and her contribution to the welfare of the society. However, constitutional rights should be granted unconditionally to vulnerable populations, including the disabled, whose potential for contributing to society is usually neglected by today's market and politics.

Constitutional rights should not exceed the minimum necessary for enabling an individual to meet her basic needs. Rights in excess of this threshold can be granted by a statute and limited later if a democratic society decides to change its priorities. Such rights could also be enforced, on the basis of individual claims, by the court but only within the limits set in a statute.

Every individual should have a constitutionally guaranteed access to courts in the case of discrimination in the enjoyment of rights, regardless of their constitutional or statutory character. However, such a claim would need to be based primarily on the general antidiscrimination clause in the constitution rather than on provisions regarding particular rights.

CONCLUSIONS

Social rights have always been a matter of choice between the protection of rights and setting public policy goals in a constitutional democracy. In the context of public policy it seems more useful to talk about social and economic needs than rights. It is useful to differentiate between needs that should be protected by constitutional rights, needs that should be protected by statutory rights, and needs that should merely be a subject of public policy. The balance between these three types of protection should be a matter of ongoing public debate. In this debate, it would be helpful to remember that rights are not goals in and of themselves but rather means for assuring other goals. In the case of social rights, these goals are the dignity and economic security of a person. Social rights should be applied whenever other instruments to achieve and protect dignity and security are ineffective or insufficient.

It seems that the needs-based approach may be helpful to limit some confusion implied by the very notion of social and economic rights as rights. The needs basis clarifies the distinction between social policies and rights and helps to understand the difference between the various remedies attached to particular rights. The main postulates of the needs-based approach to social and economic rights can be summarized in five key points:

1. The state should play a subsidiary role in the fulfillment of people's social and economic needs. In some cases, however, this role is crucial for a person's very possibility of living a dignified life.

2. The most important mechanism of state intervention into social spheres consist of the regulation, adoption, and implementation of general policies; creation of mechanisms and institutions that enable the satisfaction of collective needs; and, exceptionally, direct provision of goods and services to the needy. For these roles, statutory regulations and statute-based policies and rights are a norm. Social policies imply the redistribution of resources and choices to be made between competing values; such choices belong to the political process rather than to judicial competence.

3. Constitutional principles should assure that the needs of vulnerable populations and those most underprivileged are not neglected by political process. Constitutional courts may demand the formulation of proper public policy and review its constitutionality.

4. Constitutional rights should guarantee basic needs, particularly for vulnerable populations along the principles discussed above.

5. All remaining social and economic needs can be left to the social policy of the state as defined by statutes and state budgets. The statutory character of social and economic rights would also render them less "absolute" and facilitate making the exercise of such rights contingent on the two conditions discussed above – the recipient's prior effort to satisfy her own need and the requirement of her contribution to society.

It is important to always keep in mind that state-enforceable rights and state action in general cannot replace individual and social responsibility for the majority of basic human needs.

Many social and economic needs cannot be satisfied even with the use of rights. Making social rights constitutional does not necessarily help the situation of the right holders. Rights are not easily translated into the improvement of social conditions nor do they easily increase an individual's control over her life. To change the conditions and give people a dose of control over their lives, the access of vulnerable populations to vital resources needs to be increased.

One can expect that the demands for social rights will continue to be made – in step with attempts to resist such demands. But the future of social rights will not be determined solely by such demands nor by the will of parliaments and constitution makers. These rights are vestiges of the industrial age, when they were a response to the breakdown of the traditional community and of family-based model of social security. Similarly, the character of these rights can – and should – change with new societal developments and technological innovations that are occurring today and will occur in the future.

4

Rights and Cultures

Another important debate concerns the universality of rights. Actually, when applied to human rights, the term *universality* is almost tautological. Universality is implied in the very word *human*, which means that rights belong to every human being at all times and in all situations.[1] Such a statement, however, clearly defies observable reality. Most people throughout history have not enjoyed their human rights. Therefore, we talk about the universality of standards. Every human being should have her human rights recognized and observed, and every community should attempt to reach such a standard. This universality of standards is justified by the fact that it is what protects the dignity of every person and makes human cooperation possible.

The concept of human rights provides universal legitimacy to all those who oppose tyrannies, oppression, and the violation of human rights, anywhere in the world. Despite the widespread (one could say "universal") problems with their violation, human rights are universal in the "normative" sense of global adherence to human rights norms and treaties. Almost all governments have signed the UDHR and ratified various human rights treaties. Far less universal are the actual observance of these treaties, fulfillment of the resulting obligations, and adherence to formally accepted standards.

Debates about human rights initially concerned mainly the justification for such failures and violations. Because human rights consist of a number of norms and serve various values that can be in conflict with one another, justification has been sought through the prioritization of rights, with many attempts made to place certain rights before others. Recently, however, the very idea of human rights has been challenged. Debates about the content and hierarchy of rights have been augmented by questions about the applicability of these standards to all societies. New questions have also

---

[1] H. J. M. Milne has observed that if the idea of human rights and particularly the notion "human" are to be taken seriously, then "the idea of human rights must be the idea that there are certain rights which, whether or not they are recognized, belong to all human beings at all times and in all places" (Milne 1986, 2).

been raised: Who defines the standards? Whose interests do human rights really represent and protect?

This chapter reviews these debates.[2] Central to its main thesis is the need to distinguish between the *normative* universality of human rights as standards and the *philosophical* universality of beliefs, values, and worldviews. People who reject the philosophy of human rights nonetheless can be expected to observe human rights norms, similarly to the way all people are expected to observe the norms of criminal law, regardless of their adherence to the underlying philosophy. Once we acknowledge the differences between norms and values – between rules and principles – we may insist that human rights norms should be universal, even if the philosophy of human rights is not.

UNIVERSAL ORIGINS OF HUMAN RIGHTS

Universality is precisely what distinguished the twentieth-century idea of human rights from the eighteenth-century idea of individual rights. In contrast to its antecedents, the Universal Declaration of Human Rights (UDHR) extended protection to all human beings regardless of their sex, race, nationality, religion, wealth, and so on. It was accompanied by hope that all signatory states will adopt the Declaration's provisions into their internal laws and be concerned with abuse of rights occurring anywhere, beyond the boundaries of states. Finally, implicit in the Declaration's content was the belief that the basic values and principles underlying it, as well as the very concept of human rights, are of a universal nature.

As discussed, these values and principles include the idea of individual liberty; the belief in democracy and political rights that enable everyone to participate in government; the acknowledgement of social and economic rights, extended into the private sphere of labor relations and work conditions; and the protection of the family. The Declaration presupposed an active state having positive obligations toward its citizens. The state was to help individuals in the fulfillment of their potential; moreover, such fulfillment was included among the basic rights. Furthermore, the entire concept of human rights was justified by their contribution to world peace, which was considered a dominant value of the Declaration and the supreme goal for the United Nations.

A formulation accurately reflecting such diverse values and principles was necessarily the result of a broad compromise. As we have seen, the compromise was not limited to the two philosophies of freedom that had developed in the West – the liberal, Anglo-American tradition of civil and political rights and the European

---

[2] This review is limited to the main arguments used in the debate about the universality of rights. For a comprehensive presentation of views held by specific cultures, see Brems (2001); Donnelly (1989); Sajo (ed., 2004).

tradition combining freedom with equality and rights with duties. This compromise included also important ideas from Christian social thought (e.g., the concept of dignity; the simultaneously Christian and Marxist concept of freedom as fulfillment of one's potential) and from socialism (most importantly the importance of social and economic rights). Emphasis on the rights of the family and the connection between rights and duties were also attractive to European conservatives, who had been rather skeptical of the language of rights prior to the 1940s.

A broad compromise of ideas, the Universal Declaration was also acceptable to leaders of non-European countries. In fact, they placed great hopes in the idea it represented, perceiving the Declaration as a step toward the self-determination and national independence of the hitherto colonial states. The independent non-Western states saw in the Declaration a promise that the rich West would share both its resources and the promise of better life with the rest of the world.

The active participation of many non-European leaders and philosophers in the preparatory works reflected a broad cross-cultural consensus about the universal value of the Declaration and its underlying principles.[3] This was confirmed in a General Assembly vote held on December 10, 1948, with all member states voting in favor and only eight abstaining. Of these, six were motivated by political opposition (the USSR and five allies), one by its own fundamental rejection of political and legal equality (South Africa, which had established apartheid just eight months earlier), and one by cultural differences (Saudi Arabia, whose representatives claimed that the freedom to marry according to one's individual choice and the right to change one's religion are based on Western ideas and should not be applied universally).[4]

It is important to remember that the original consensus on human rights was limited to their content and did not extend to the enforcement of rights. The 1948 Declaration remained a set of ideas and moral standards for guiding the behavior of governments. But when the Declaration was to be translated into enforceable pacts, it became clear that the rights included in it could not all be granted identical protection. As a result, two separate Covenants were adopted in the 1960s.[5] In the meantime, Western European nations had reached procedural consensus in the European Convention of 1950.

In December of 1948, the Declaration's framers believed that human rights were a universal idea, capable of overcoming the historical, cultural, religious, and political

---

[3] For analysis of the impact of Arab and Muslim states on the UDHR and subsequent UN human rights covenants, see Waltz (2004) and (Mayer 2007, 13–25). "Muslims made important contributions to the genesis of international human rights law and have been increasingly outspoken in their demands to enjoy the protections that it affords," writes Mayer (ibid., xv).

[4] Articles 16 and 18 of the UDHR, respectively. Other countries with a Muslim majority did not share Saudi's concerns.

[5] Though adopted in the 1960s, these covenants did not go into force until the mid-1970s.

differences separating the world's people and nations. At that time, to them, human rights were merely ideas, aspirations, and hopes to be fulfilled. The optimism subsided, however, with the first attempts at the implementation of the principles of human rights. As soon as those lofty hopes attached to human rights became frustrated, the entire idea was challenged. Of key importance here has been the temptation to use the idea of human rights as a tool of international politics, particularly during the Cold War, or, more recently, to put them aside during the war against terrorism. Overall, since the late 1970s, human rights have become a subject rife with controversy.

It is worthwhile to distinguish between the challenges to human rights as such and challenges to the thesis that human rights are universal. In what follows, we will focus primarily on controversies surrounding the universality of human rights.

CHALLENGES TO UNIVERSALITY

The first controversy is of a merely theoretical or "scientific" character and dates back to the very inception of the human rights idea, when on June 24, 1947, the Executive Board of the American Anthropological Association issued a statement addressed to the United Nations' Committee on Human Rights. This statement warned against the perils of universalism and called for the acknowledgment of the differences dividing separate cultures. "Standards and values are relative to the culture from which they derive so that any attempt to formulate postulates that grow out of the beliefs or moral codes of one culture must to that extent detract from the applicability of any Declaration of Human Rights to mankind as a whole," argued the American anthropologists.[6] This position was counterbalanced with a report prepared by a group of philosophers for the United Nations Educational, Scientific and Cultural Organization (UNESCO), who concluded on consultation with Confucian, Hindu, Muslim, and European thinkers that some fundamental principles are widely shared by various cultures and religions, including ones that do not know the concept of rights.[7] The UNESCO philosophers stated that "basic human rights rest on 'common convictions,'" even though those convictions "are stated in terms of different philosophic principles and on the background of divergent political and economic systems." They also agreed that "even people who seem to be

---

[6] Quoted in Winston (ed., 1989, 119). Continuing: "What is held to be a human right in one society may be regarded as anti-social by another people, or by the same people in a different period of their history." This statement was authored primarily by Melville Herskovits (see Engle 2002, 345).

[7] Interestingly, UNESCO did not publish the AAA's statement in the 1949 volume that contained answers to the questionnaire on universal validity of human rights that had been sent to world philosophers and leaders. Engle (2002, 360) posits that, "although it has plagued anthropologists for the past fifty years, the AAA's Statement seems to have little or no impact on either UNESCO or the Commission on Human Rights."

far apart in theory can agree that certain things are so terrible in practice that no one will publicly approve them and certain things are so good in practice that no one will publicly oppose them."[8] Of course, the American Anthropological Association's (AAA) statement had also acknowledged a universal desire for rights and freedoms,[9] but its stance was that "a statement of the rights of men to live in terms of their own traditions" should be incorporated into the text of the Declaration.[10] The AAA eventually came to consider its 1947 statement an "embarrassment" and significantly muted its former position against the universality of human rights. "The AAA clearly has moved from being skeptical of human rights law and discourse to embracing them," writes Karen Engle.[11] However, the AAA's original argument continues to crop up even today, continually raising the question of whether human rights and their content are limited only to the West, after all.[12]

The next major controversy came in the late 1970s, when human rights had already become one of the tools of international politics. The monitoring conducted by Western governments and nongovernmental organizations soon revealed that human rights were being violated in many postcolonial countries, often on a massive scale. A new theory was soon postulated to defend – or simply explain – these violations, one in some respects similar to the socialist concept of rights developed after the adoption of the human rights covenants and the Helsinki Agreement.

Authoritarian Development

One of the most important theses underlying the socialist concept of rights was the conviction that a state can waive or trump individual rights in the pursuit of its economic and social objectives. This has become a core element of one new

[8] Glendon (2001, 222).

[9] "The worldwide acclaim accorded the Atlantic Charter (. . .) is evidence of the fact that freedom is understood and sought after by peoples having the most diverse cultures," declared the AAA's original statement (Winston 1989, 120).

[10] Also suggested is that the "rights and duties of human groups as regards each other" be the next step in declaring human rights (ibid., 120). On the AAA's position on the need to include collective or group rights along with individual rights, see Engle (2002, 347).

[11] Ibid., 360. In 1999, the AAA issued a "Declaration on Anthropology and Human Rights," which was considered by the newly organized AAA Committee for Human Rights to be a reversal of the 1947 position. Engle (ibid.), however, demonstrates substantial continuity in the AAA's approach. See also Kabasakal Arat (2006, 419).

[12] H. J. M. Milne noted that many provisions of the 1948 Declaration reflect the values, needs and institutions of modern liberal-democratic industrial nations. Most of the world, however, is not an industrial liberal democracy; therefore, it is impossible to talk about universal standards. "West may be best for Westerners; but to assume that it must be so for humanity is largely unwarranted. This objection casts doubt upon any idea of human rights which presents it as a universal ideal standard. Such an ideal, with its constitutive values and institutions, must, if it is to be coherent, be drawn from a particular tradition of culture and civilization. Those who belong to a different tradition have no reason to accept it" (Milne 1986, 4). According to Milne, the concept of human rights as an ideal universal standard ignores cultural diversity as well as the social basis of personal identity.

challenge to the universality of rights that has survived the socialist concept. In 1979, Pollis and Schwab published a book entitled *Human Rights: A Western Construct with Limited Applicability*. The authors emphasized modernization, economic development, and the building of national states as the main goals of governments in newly independent non-Western countries. In pursuit of these goals, governments may need to put aside certain individual rights, should these be in conflict with economic development. In a more recent formulation, it has been claimed that the idea of human rights does not contribute to solving the most important problems plaguing non-Western societies today. The formulation's radical version even claims that the idea of human rights is in conflict with important developmental goals of non-Western nations and can be sacrificed for the benefit of such goals.

That sacrifice was said to be insignificant because of the absence of individualism in traditional cultures, whose members purportedly derive identity and status from their allegiance to a social group rather than on the basis of their own accomplishments.[13] With decolonization, this allegiance to one's group was transferred from traditional communities to the state.[14] As a result, "whatever rights an individual possesses are given to him by the state, and this state retains the right and the ability to curtail individual rights and freedoms for the greater good of the group."[15] In keeping with the socialist concept of rights, Pollis and Schwab gave priority to social and economic rights over civil liberties in the Third World context.[16] Pollis and Schwab concluded,

> In summary then, it is evident that in most states in the world, human rights as defined in the West are rejected or, more accurately, are meaningless. Most states do not have a cultural heritage of individualism, and the doctrines of inalienable human rights have been neither disseminated nor assimilated. More significantly the state – as a substitute for the traditional communal group – has become the embodiment of the people, and the individual has no rights or freedoms that are natural and outside the purview of the state.[17]

[13] "Traditional cultures did not view the individual as autonomous and possessed of rights above and prior to society" because an individual has always been "conceived as an integral part of a greater whole, of a 'group' within which one had a defined role and status" (Pollis and Schwab 1979, 8).

[14] "With independence, a multiplicity of new 'sovereign' nation-states were established and, at least in theory, these new entities defined group membership. The notion of the primacy of the group and the submission of the individual to the group persisted, although the confines and boundaries of the group have changed to become coterminous with the state" (ibid., 9).

[15] Ibid., 9.

[16] According to the authors, the experience of colonial exploitation "gave credence to the notion of human dignity as consisting of economic rights rather than civil or political rights. Freedom from starvation, the right for all to enjoy the material benefits of a developed economy, and freedom from exploitation by colonial powers became the articulated goals of many Third World countries." In pursuit of these goals, "the state was to replace traditional group identities but was to retain the same supremacy as traditional groups" (ibid., 9).

[17] Ibid., 13.

The authors' final point resembled the Communist conception of rights: "It is not individuals who have rights but states."[18] We see that Pollis and Schwab combined economic, political, and cultural arguments to argue against the universality of human rights. Not surprisingly, their arguments were attractive to many authoritarian leaders of non-Western countries.

Cultural Relativism

Perhaps the most comprehensive formulation of cultural relativism as grounds for the rejection of universalism occurs in the concept of the so-called Asian values formulated by the philosophers and politicians of Southeast Asian countries (most notably by the leaders Lee Kwan Yew of Singapore and Mahathir bin Mohamad of Malaysia). In 1993, before the World Conference on Human Rights in Vienna, a group of Asian countries adopted the Bangkok Declaration, which stated: "while human rights are universal in nature, bear in mind the significance of national and regional particularities and various cultural and religious backgrounds."[19] Foreign minister of Singapore Won Kang Sen stated at the Vienna Conference that "universal recognition of the ideal of human rights can be harmful if universalism is used to deny or mask the reality of diversity."[20] Chinese delegate Liu Huaqiu added to the record the proposition that "individuals must put state rights before their own."[21] Eventually, the Conference agreed on the following compromise: "While the significance of national and regional particularities and various historical, cultural and religious backgrounds must be borne in mind, it is the duty of States, regardless of their political, economic and cultural systems, to promote and protect all human rights and fundamental freedoms."[22] The Bangkok and Vienna declarations reflect rather well the difference between the particularist and the universalist understanding of human rights.

The idea of "Asian values" holds that the value system predominant in Asia is less concerned with freedom and more so with order and discipline than that in the West. Consequently, human rights, and particularly civil and political rights, are less relevant in Asia than in the Western world. The "Asian values" in question include – in addition to order and discipline – duties rather than rights; hierarchy, social stability, and harmony rather than conflict; the subordination of an individual to family and to the local community; loyalty to a workplace; and obedience to the state. Those values are served by such institutions as a quasiauthoritarian government

---

[18] Ibid., 14.
[19] Quoted in Brems (2001, 58).
[20] Ibid. (60).
[21] Quoted in Sen (1997, 9).
[22] Quoted in Brems (2001, 67–8).

and capitalism combined with the major role of the state. The proponents of "Asian values" firmly believed that authoritarian governments were to credit with having fostered development in Asia and they supported this claim by citing the rapid economic growth that took place in the 1970s and 1980s.

In a more elaborate theory presented by Prime Minister Lee Kwan Yew of Singapore, excessive claims of rights encourage people to be self-regarding and lead to an atrophy of the sense of belonging. The philosophy of rights enhances individuals to focus on what they can claim from society and others rather than on their responsibilities and what they owe to the community and its members; it also produces a higher degree of social conflict. "Asian values," or, more specifically for Lee, "Chinese values," offer order and harmony instead of liberty and equality, selflessness and cooperation instead of individual independence, and conformity to orthodox truth instead of freedom of individual conscience.[23]

One version of these "Asian values" underpins the contemporary Chinese approach to human rights. According to Andrew Nathan and Randle Edwards, in China rights are perceived as a creation of the state; "rights provisions will generally be worded in the positive, as an express grant," welfare rights are more emphasized and political rights are restricted, rights are contingent on the performance of duties, the state's interest is in limiting rights rather than the opposite, and rights can be restricted by a statute.[24] We see that Chinese cultural specificity is clearly submerged in the socialist concept of rights discussed above.[25]

Cultural relativism has become widespread among many African politicians and scholars, as well. Often, the focus of arguments adapts to African societies the concept of Asian values. "Some Africans have argued that they have a complex structure of communal entitlements and obligations grouped around what one might call four 'r's': not 'rights' but respect, restraint, responsibility, and reciprocity."[26] Some Islamic spokesmen have been attacking the concept of universal human rights, relying on a number of arguments against universality used by cultural relativists.[27] The most common are that the idea of human rights sanctifies an individual over the community and that human rights by default stress rights over duties and responsibilities. In non-Western cultures both propositions are held as questionable or simply alien.

---

[23] This interpretation of Lee Kwan's views was formulated by Taylor (1999, 130).

[24] Davis (2000, 11). See also Edwards et al. (1986).

[25] Interestingly, this "cultural specificity" seems limited to today's mainland China and does not apply to older cultural traditions in China, including Confucianism.

[26] Tharoor (1999/2000, 1; html version).

[27] In 1984, Iran's UN representative, Said Raja'i-Khorasani stated: "The Universal Declration of Human Rights, which represents secular understanding of the Judeo-Christian tradition, could not be implemented by Muslims and did not accord with the system of values recognized by the Islamic Republic of Iran; his country would therefore not hesitate to violate its provisions" (quoted in Mayer 2007, 9).

An essential element of cultural relativism is the belief that

fundamental values are culturally specific and that the communal group – whatever that might be (tribe, village, or kinship), and not the individual – is the basic social unit. A person's identity is prescriptive, dependent on membership in a group, and the person's status and role in this community. The language of rights, a modern Western construction, is nonexistent in most cases. Interpersonal relations are governed by a mutuality of unequal rights and obligations, which are diverse, as are their underlying values and behavioral expectations. However, what is common is that notions such as the autonomous individual, individualism, freedom of choice, or legal equality are alien, often meaningless concepts. The person is submerged within the communal group whose well-being and welfare has primacy, albeit the particulars of what constitutes the community good varies.[28]

Anthropological studies confirm that the basic ideas of the language of rights may be alien to a majority of non-Western cultures. Even though the notion of human dignity is almost universal, it has usually been protected by the set of duties rather than by rights. Donnelly has observed that many non-Western societies "recognize that certain social guarantees are essential for realizing human dignity, and they have elaborate systems of human duties designed to protect human dignity."[29] Even when a culture – as in the case of China – imposes on the ruler an obligation to take care of the subjects, such duties do not translate into the rights of the ruled.[30] Donnelly claims that a doctrine that focuses solely on the duties of a ruler is not merely a "different approach to human rights" but an altogether alternative approach to human dignity – one that simply does not involve human rights.

The New Crusade of the West

Advocates of relativism use two kinds of historical arguments against the universality of rights. The first concerns the origins of the concept of rights and the institutions for their protection. Most of the rights included in the Universal Declaration first appeared in European and North American bills, constitutions, and other documents.

The second historical argument for relativism suggests that the Universal Declaration was imposed by the West upon non-Western countries – first in 1948, and later by the Western-controlled UN system and other means of global domination,

---

[28] Pollis (2000, 11–12).

[29] Donnelly (1989, 50).

[30] "Although elaborate duties were imposed on rulers, obligation is only one side of rights-based relationship. Obligation does not in itself even suggest, let alone establish, the existence of rights on the part of those in whose interests one is obliged to act" (ibid., 54).

including force. In a less drastic formulation, the argument reduces to the use of force by the West to impose human rights. In a more radical version, the West is accused of using force to impose the philosophy of human rights.

Makau Mutua believes that the philosophy of human rights is "an alien ideology" for non-Western societies and that the human rights movement has become a "civilizing" crusade aimed primarily at the Third World.[31] This claim belongs to an array of political rather than cultural arguments against universalism. Rights were defined as an instrument of global domination and neocolonialism by a number of participants of the international conference entitled "Politics and Political Uses of Human Rights Discourse."[32] More recently, human rights have been accused of being a weapon of American imperialism, especially because justification for the war in Iraq shifted from the country's alleged possession of weapons of mass destruction to the defense, by the United States and their allies, of freedom and human rights in Iraq. Arguments that human rights are an instrument for the protection of the global interests of the United States give as an example the U.S. State Department's insistence that free trade is one of the most basic human rights.[33]

Accounts of inmate abuse in the Abu Ghraib prison in Iraq and in Guantanamo have heavily compromised the U.S. human rights rhetoric, giving rise to accusations of double standards in the enforcement of rights. Double standards also accompanied human rights politics during the Cold War, when the West criticized abuses in the Eastern bloc but turned a blind eye to similar atrocities in allied countries.[34] With the collapse of Communism, it seemed that standards could finally be applied universally. However, the war in Chechnya proved that even gross violations of rights remain unchecked when perpetrated by one of great powers. More recently, the antiterrorist coalition that rallied a number of atrocious regimes, including Pakistan and Uzbekistan, to the side of the United States has reinforced the practice of double standards. Unequal enforcement of human rights has always undermined the claim of universality; instead of guaranteeing a universal standard of behavior, rights have been seen as no more than a privilege for the rich and powerful.

---

[31] "The relentless efforts to universalize an essentially European corpus of human rights through Western crusades cannot succeed" writes Mutua (2004, 58); or: "Like earlier crusades, the human rights movement . . . " (ibid., 62). Mutua also sees human rights "as part of the colonial project" (ibid., 63).

[32] See presentations by Makau Mutua, Talal Asad, and Partha Chattterjee given at the November 9, 2001, Conference at Columbia University. Elsewhere Mutua has pointed out that international human rights NGOs that reflect ideologically domestic NGOs in the United States "have set the agenda and scope of the worldwide human rights movement" (quoted after Crenshaw 2000, 62).

[33] See Neier (2005, 141).

[34] Examples of double standards in the U.S. Middle East policy are given by Mayer (2007, 6–7). In addition to the ongoing support to Saudi Arabia, the United States helped Zia's regime in Pakistan (1977–1988) and General Nimeiri's rule in Sudan (1983–1985), both of whom realized the brutal policy of Islamization.

ARGUMENTS AGAINST CULTURAL RELATIVISM

The list of arguments against the universality of human rights continues, and many of the claims cannot be disputed. It is an observable fact that human rights have never been universally respected, adhered to, or even accepted. It is a fact that many cultures know other instruments for protecting dignity (and sometimes even for limiting the power of their authorities). Facts such as these constitute support for critics of the universality of rights. Interestingly, these relativist critics do not necessarily reject the very concept of rights. After thorough examination of critical arguments, Eva Brems concludes that one important motivation for the critics

> is the fact that international human rights, both in theory and in practice, are strongly oriented toward the needs, concerns and values of the West, because of their historical development as well as because of the distribution of power in international relations. As a result, the needs, concerns and values of Non-Western countries that differ from those of the West, are underrepresented in human rights, which undermines the claim of human rights to universality.[35]

Brems observes that "Westerners confronted with these particular critiques have too easily qualified them as 'cultural relativism,' a label that refers to a school of thought in Western social sciences that rejects the possibility of universal norms and values, and hence opposes the idea of universal human rights."[36] Brems believes that many non-Western critics, in fact, accept human rights, but want the concept to be enlarged so it reflects their values and thus becomes truly universal.

Regardless of the validity of the motives of relativists, many of their arguments have been disputed by those who believe in the universal validity of human rights. The following is a discussion of their reasoning.

The "Asian values" thesis was challenged by Nobel Prize laureate Amartya Sen, who proceeded to examine both Asian and Western traditions. In Asia – and it is a typical European exaggeration and inaccuracy to consider the existence of some single, unified "Asian" value system – Sen found many components of freedom and tolerance present in Hindu, Muslim, and Chinese traditions. Admitting that there exist at the same time many perspectives opposed to freedom in Asia, Sen points to the traditional elements of intolerance and authoritarianism historically present in European cultures.[37] He then dissects the modern concept of human rights into two parts – one is the acknowledgment of the value of freedom and tolerance; the other is

---

[35] Brems (2001, 509).

[36] Ibid. (510). For example, Jerome Shestack (1998, 228) writes that cultural relativism "has scant claim to moral validity."

[37] "There is nothing remotely Western about religious freedom and tolerance," writes Franck (2001, 199), recalling examples of religious persecution in Europe.

the acknowledgment of the equality of freedom and tolerance. For most of Western history freedom and tolerance have been accepted, but they were granted to the few. Only relatively recently were they extended to include every person. Today, the rest of the world is simply where Europe once was. Sen concludes that the "Asian values" so often invoked to justify authoritarianism are not especially Asian at all because they have also been present in the West and the contrast between the West and the rest of the world is exaggerated. "Notions like 'Western civilization,' 'Asian values,' 'African cultures,' etc., are not only intellectually shallow, they also add to the divisiveness of the world in which we live."[38]

Freedom and Development

Sen also challenges the argument that authoritarianism enhances economic development, a thesis that was extremely popular in the 1960s and 1970s.[39] "There is, in fact, little evidence that authoritarian governance and the suppression of political and civil rights are really beneficial in encouraging economic development."[40] Sen mentions a number of policies that foster economic growth, such as openness to competition; the use of international markets; high rates of literacy and education; and economic incentives for investments, exports, and industrialization. "There is nothing whatsoever to indicate that any of those policies is inconsistent with greater democracy and has to be sustained by the elements of authoritarianism," writes Sen.[41] He also demonstrates that civil and political rights are effective instruments in preventing major disasters, including famine. "No substantial famine has ever occurred in any independent and democratic country with a relatively free press," writes Sen.[42]

As noted, one of the first authors to justify violations of rights for the benefit of economic development was Adamantia Pollis. Hopes for authoritarian development that seemed to be substantiated by the fast rise of the "Asian tigers" fell after excessive involvement by the states in the economy led to the financial and economic crisis of the late 1990s. Then, in a courageous reversal of her original position, Pollis observed: "Interestingly, little has been heard of 'Asian values' since the 1998 financial crisis in the region, an understandable political retreat given that a principal rationale for

---

[38] Sen (1997, 31).

[39] "In the 1960s, the necessity of temporarily sacrificing both civil and political rights was the reigning orthodoxy. In the 1970s, authoritarian repression was still widely viewed as useful or even essential for development" (Donnelly 1989, 163). See ibid. (163–202) for a critical discussion of the "development-rights trade-offs" thesis.

[40] Sen (1997, 11).

[41] Ibid. (12).

[42] Ibid. (12).

repression – for maintaining 'social order' and the denial of individual liberties – was the East Asian countries' success in bringing about development and prosperity."[43]

The relation between rights and development has never been simple.[44] The need for the right to development has been strongly emphasized by the countries of the global South. The Declaration on the Right to Development, adopted on December 4, 1986, by the UN General Assembly, suggested that UN human rights programs focus on social and economic rights, most notably on the right to development.[45] Some governments had treated this right as a basis for the demand to transfer resources, capital, and technology from the rich North to poor South. Even if such a claim could be justified in humanitarian and historical terms as relief to the most destitute and as a compensation for colonial devastation, the claims justified in the name of the right to development are often discouraging, even to those otherwise guided by humanitarian motives. This happens in particular when state leaders invoke the right to development to attain international aid and then use the principle of state sovereignty – strongly emphasized, for example, in the Charter of the Organization for African Unity[46] – to keep those who have contributed this aid from checking on how it is used or distributed. Finally, the same leaders justify violations of their citizens' civil liberties and political rights by citing developmental needs and use cultural relativism as a shield protecting them against international surveillance.

The 1993 Vienna Declaration took such abuses seriously. While it reaffirmed the right to development "as a universal and inalienable right and an integral part of fundamental human rights," it also positively linked the human rights movement

[43] Pollis (2000, 27–8). Shashi Tharoor expressed criticism of the authoritarian development thesis more simply: "If religion can be fairly used to sanction oppression, it should be equally obvious that authoritarianism promotes repression, not development. Development is about change, but repression prevents change" (1999/2000, page 4 of the html version).

[44] For more on the right to development in general, see Baxi (1998). Just for the sake of discussion, I suggest that any unit undergoing transition (nation, country, multinational organism) underwent the first stage of modernization (the so-called extensive phase of industrialization, during which the supply and processing of raw materials, energy, and communication infrastructure for further development is created) with massive suppression of rights. Even when such suppression was executed by market forces and private capitalists, it would not have been possible without support from the state in various forms (e.g., the protection of property and contracts, even when they were unjust, the use of police and army to fight unions and put down strikes, military support for colonialism, and so on). Such methods would become ineffective only when modernization evolved to the "intensive" phase, when coercive regimes opened up, usually under pressure from the advancing social strata of businessmen, professionals, the intelligentsia, and students. The coercive character of Western modernization was observed by Rhoda E. Howard-Hassmann (2007, 2): "No international law obliged the West to protect human rights during its own era of economic expansion. Thus, the West could practice slavery, repel surplus populations and colonize other parts of the world. Genocide and ethnic cleansing were not prohibited."

[45] The very concept of the right to development, particularly as a human right, was contested by a number of scholars. See Baxi (1998, 109–14).

[46] Article 3.

itself with development, declaring in Operating Principle 6 that "the efforts of the United Nations in the field of human rights contribute to stability and to social and economic development."[47] The crucial elements of the new right were the combination of individual and national development, the emphasis on the need for the participatory character of developmental decisions and reconfirmation of traditional civil liberties like freedom of speech and freedom of expression as a precondition for development. Both the 1986 UN Declaration on the Right to Development and the Vienna Declaration stated expressly that development should serve human rights and not limit them.[48]

The framers of the Vienna Declaration were aware that the right to development might be used as bait to capture cultural relativism and use it to justify oppression. Interestingly, one of the first critics to analyze this phenomenon was Pollis, who had coauthored the original thesis about the limited applicability of human rights outside the West. In a 1996 article, Pollis admitted that cultural relativism had been captured by the regimes to justify oppression and terror. In 2000, she warned: "Unfortunately, this doctrine has been exploited in recent years, most forcefully by East Asian states, to justify their repressive regimes."[49] Most recently, however, the right to development has been creatively used to prevent pillage of natural resources in Africa and to persecute those responsible for illegally appropriating natural resources.[50]

The justification of oppression as the main motive behind the rejection of universality by authoritarian and dictatorial regimes was suggested by a number of authors. Commenting on the Iranian claim that the UDHR embodies a Judeo–Christian understanding of rights "unacceptable to Muslims" and the policies of Lee in Singapore, Glendon observed: "When leaders of authoritarian governments claim that the Declaration is aimed at imposing 'foreign' values, their concern is often domestic: the pressure for freedom building among their own citizens."[51] Sen noticed that the theory of "Asian values" is often combined with the need to resist Western domination to suppress the rights of citizens.[52] Ann Elizabeth Mayer claims that

---

[47] Quoted in Brems (2001, 68).

[48] "While development facilitates the enjoyment of all human rights, the lack of development may not be invoked to justify the abridgement of internationally recognized human rights," states Operating Principle number 10 of the Vienna Declaration. Such provision existed also in Article 9 (2) of the 1986 UN Declaration on the Right to Development.

[49] Pollis (2000, 12).

[50] In November, 2007, the African Commission on Human and Peoples' Rights granted seizure on the basis of an OSI Justice Initiative claim that Equatorial Guinea's corrupt system of acquiring important State assets and diverting State revenues from public coffers violates the African Charter's (Article 21) provision concerning the right to development.

[51] Glendon (2001, 224).

[52] "The linking of the two issues (. . .) uses the political force of anticolonialism to buttress the assault on basic political and civil rights in postcolonial Asia" (Sen 1997, 28).

theories of Islam's incompatibility with human rights "should be seen as part of a broader phenomenon of attempts by elites – the beneficiaries of undemocratic and hierarchical systems – to legitimize their opposition to human rights by appealing to supposedly distinctive cultural traditions."[53]

Similarly, the notions of "Asian values" and cultural relativism are most often professed by members of the ruling elites in Asia,[54] with the notable exception of Japan.[55] By contrast, most of the representatives of nongovernmental organizations in Asia, Africa, and the Middle East[56] emphasize the universality of human rights. Similarly, we have not yet heard about a victim of torture who would justify the abuse of her rights with the notion of cultural relativism.

It seems logical to view cultural relativism from a historical perspective. With independence, new elites emerged that adopted the colonial state and legal systems to suit their needs. But the high hopes brought out at the onset of independence soon turned into disillusionment. Elites became more selfish and oppressive and began to need justification for their oppression. Anti-imperialism and cultural relativism provided the necessary justification.[57] In their pursuit of power and economic enrichment, postcolonial elites, often together with business corporations owned by former colonizers, first disrupted local communities and then used the traditional allegiance of individuals to their community to justify the claim that full subordination is now due to the state – however oppressive and disruptive to local communities that state might have been. At stake here are not really cross-cultural differences at all but the fact that in each culture there are oppressors and the oppressed; violators of rights and those whose rights are violated; and, finally, those who justify such violations that, in reality, are beneficial to economic, religious, or patriarchal elites.[58]

---

[53] Mayer (2007, 203).

[54] At the 1993 Bangkok regional meeting, Asian countries accepted the principle of "non-use of human rights as an instrument of political pressure" (Operational Principle 5), which meant that developmental help could not be made contingent on the observance of human rights standards.

[55] At the 1993 Vienna Conference, Japanese delegate Nobuo Matsunaga supported the link between development assistance and human rights and generally distanced Japan from the thesis of "Asian values" (see Brems 2001, 66).

[56] The Beirut Declaration in the Regional Protection of Human Rights in the Arab World issued in 2003 by the representatives of 36 Arab NGOs and a number of international NGOs and intergovernmental organizations as well as legal, academic and media experts "affirmed human rights universally and included as Principle 3 an unqualified rejection of the use of 'culture' or 'Islam' to restrict human rights," writes Mayer (2007, 19). The Declaration also confirmed the universality of rights: "Civilization or religious particularities should not be used as a pretext to cast doubts and to question the universality of human rights" (ibid.).

[57] "The idea of cultural relativism is nothing but an excuse to violate human rights," writes Shirin Ebadi, an Iranian lawyer who received, in 2003, the Nobel Peace Prize for her defense of human rights. In 2004, the Doha Declaration for Democracy and Reforms, signed by over 100 Arab intellectuals "dismissed the pretexts that regimes have used to defer democratic reforms" (Mayer 2007, 200).

[58] See Pollis (1996, 2000).

In addition to having been abused for political reasons, cultural relativism also has theoretical shortcomings.[59] According to Pollis, relativists tend to mistake the lack of a language of rights in traditional societies with the lack of rights and often ignore spheres of personal autonomy and choice that exist in communal societies. They also "reify" traditional cultures, viewing them as static and unchanging. Most relativists also (erroneously) presume total subordination of women to men in all non-Western societies.[60]

ARGUMENTS FOR UNIVERSALISM

The weaknesses and faults of cultural relativism do not, by themselves, prove universalism right. Universalism, too, can be abused and exploited for partisan purposes. Some critics suggest that the allegedly universal principle of free trade serves the interests of the stronger actors on international markets.[61] Universal protection of intellectual property and the free flow of cultural products likewise tends to undermine the cultural identity of weaker players. It has also abetted the worldwide distribution of some of the most violent, primitive, and abuse-centric entertainment productions in existence. Often, human rights have been used to cover up political interests – even aggression, as has been the case, for example, with the human rights–based justification of the invasion of Iraq. Although the two largest global human rights nongovernmental organizations (NGOs), Amnesty International and Human Rights Watch, refuse to accept any government money, many human rights nongovernmental organizations are financed by Western governments and wealthy foundations. Critics view these NGOs as merely another mechanism for imposing the Western cultural and political agenda and needlessly universalizing the Western conception of human rights.[62]

[59] As noted, one argument says that human rights do not contribute to solving the problems of non-Western societies. Human rights, however, were not meant to solve societal problems (this is the task of politics and society) but to safeguard people from being the victims of such political solutions to problems. (I am indebted to Lea Simokovic, a student of the *Individual and Human Rights* course I offered in fall 2008 at the Central European University in Budapest for making this argument.)

[60] Pollis claims that the picture is more complex. While subordinated in some roles, African and Asian women play dominant roles in other spheres (e.g., "market women" in Africa). Generally, for arguments summarized here, see Pollis (2000, 17ff). Waltz (2004) and Mayer (2007, 16) show the role of Islamic women in the formulation of the human rights covenants.

[61] A. Neier notices that in the U.S. National Security Strategy of September 2002 "free trade is referred to as 'moral principle'. This is immensely damaging," writes Neier. "Many people in Latin America tend to see the free trade policies, or the manner in which the United States espouses free trade policies and labels them as fundamental rights, as part of the problem with democracy. This has caused a popular disenchantment with democracy and human rights in Latin America" (Neier 2005, 141).

[62] Even Glendon, a fierce defender of the universality of human rights, warns against "the danger of human rights imperialism" (2001, 229). For a comprehensive review of human rights NGOs, see Forsythe (2006, 188–217).

Despite the reservations, there exists a number of strong arguments in favor of universalism and they fall into several categories. One concerns the universal existence of certain elements of the language and practice of rights, and it has been exemplified above with accounts cited from Sen and Pollis. All cultures can be said to respect human dignity, even if the ways in which dignity is protected are culture specific. All cultures know the concepts of justice, integrity, and mutual respect. Social harmony, humanity, and brotherhood (or sisterhood) are also universal, despite hierarchies allowed by various cultures that are so often encouraged or championed by governments and dominant churches. Finally, some form of personal autonomy is also perhaps universal, even though the degree of autonomy allowed varies from culture to culture.

In fact, in scholarly literature proof has been mounting that non-Western philosophies, religions, and political ideas not only include components of human rights but are altogether consistent with the philosophy of rights.[63]

Modernization and Rights

Another set of arguments relates to the universal need for human rights. People everywhere have similar basic needs for social, public, and economic security, and suffering is similar everywhere. In 1993, Daniel Lev observed that the

> argument of cultural specificity cannot override the reality that we all share the most basic attributes in common. We are all capable, in exactly the same ways, of feeling pain, hunger and a hundred kinds of deprivation. Consequently, people nowhere routinely concede that those with enough power to do so ought to be able at will to kill, torture, imprison, and generally abuse others. There may be no choice in the matter, given realities of power, but submission is different from moral approval.[64]

The need for universality in setting human rights standards and enforcing them has become even more pressing with modern advances in technology and globalization.[65] Technology creates new threats to human life and to people's security, privacy, and other basic rights; it also makes an individual more susceptible

---

[63] In one interesting example of such research, Azizah al-Hibri (1997) exposes the differences between the teachings of the Koran and Islamic jurisprudence regarding women's rights: the former can, in fact, be interpreted in support of women's equality; it is the interpretation of Islamic law by male clerics that is patriarchal. (See also Mayer 2007, 99–146.) More generally, on the relationship between various religions and the idea of human rights, see Bloom et al. (1996).

[64] Quoted in Glendon (2001, 233).

[65] "What brought about the transformation to personal autonomy in religion, speech, and unemployment as well as equal legal rights for the races and sexes?" asks Thomas M. Franck. "Although these recent developments occurred first in the West, they were caused not by some inherent cultural factor but by changes occurring, at different rates, everywhere: universal education, industrialization, urbanization, the rise of a middle class, advances in transportation and communications, and the spread of new information technology. These changes were driven by scientific developments capable of affecting

to abuses of power, not only by one's own state but also by other actors, including multinational corporations, private persons, and terrorist networks. Other threats to rights include those related to the degradation of the natural environment. All of these threats are active beyond state boundaries and many are global – and that calls for an acknowledgment of the need for universal rights to be protected by all states and international institutions.

The universal need for human rights only increases with modernization and the growing domination of the modern state. Donnelly claims that in a changing society human rights are the best instruments with which to protect human dignity, realize development goals, respect social justice, and assure stability:

> Westernization, modernization, development and underdevelopment (. . .) have in most places significantly separated the individual from the small, supportive traditional community. (. . .) Furthermore, in most places these communities have been penetrated and often radically transformed or disrupted by the modern state. (. . .) Society which once protected a person's dignity and provided a place in the world, now appears, in the form of a modern state, the modern economy, and the modern city, as an oppressive, alien power that assaults people's dignity and that of their families. (. . .) In such circumstances, human rights appear to be a 'natural' response to changing conditions, a logical and necessary evolution of the means to realize human dignity. The individual needs individual rights.[66]

Donnelly's concept has a strong evolutionary flavor. He claims that non-Western countries today are facing similar social and political problems as Western Europe encountered 300 years ago, at the beginning of the era of individual rights. Buddhist philosopher Robert Thurman uses the following metaphor: inhabitants of Africa or Asia did not have cars and therefore did not need seat belts, which had been invented in Europe. When cars entered the Third World and drivers began to cause accidents, however, the need for seat belts appeared. Similarly, modern markets and the modern state invaded people in non-Western countries, causing disruptions that call for a response in the form of human rights. Donnelly writes: "Human rights are the best – I would suggest the only effective – political device yet devised by human ingenuity to protect individual dignity against the standard threats of modern society."[67]

Evolutionary Arguments

Evolutionary arguments form an important component of universalist theories. Evolutionism permeates the theories of Sen, who demonstrates how the Western world

---

equally any society." . . . Human rights "are the consequence of modernizing forces that are not culturally specific," concludes Franck (2001, 200 and 202).

[66] Donnelly (1989, 59–60).

[67] Ibid. (65).

evolved from the acceptance of freedom and equality for some privileged elites to the conviction that there should be equal freedom for all. Present in Pollis's argument is the observation that, before the industrial revolution, "Western Europe was itself a communitarian society."[68] Similarly, Charles Taylor has emphasized that only by looking into abuses of rights in Europe's own history can we come to cross-cultural consensus on human rights.[69]

Evolutionary arguments claim that human rights are universal as a mechanism for constraining the "animal" parts of human (and social) nature. The evolution of humankind has led to such norms as a ban on killing the sick or children born with defects, leaving the elderly to die and killing in general. It has led to the prohibition of looting and raping as reward for participation in armed conflicts. Adoption of such standards of civilization (in other words, of constraints on savageness) is not a submission to Western imperialism. It is rising to human dignity. Within this argumentation, we can think about human rights as standards at which all cultures may at some point arrive. After all, the "human rights shortcomings" of other cultures (often described in the context of cultural relativism) simply resemble the practices predominant in Western cultures in previous epochs. Certain specific characteristics of non-Western cultures – for example, the role of religion, paternalism, the dominant role of a ruler, and his obligation to care for the people's well-being, and so on – are similar to those that existed in the West during the period of absolutism. This way of thinking has been summarized, in 1948, by Charles Malik in these words: "Men, cultures and nations must first mature inwardly."[70]

Evolutionary arguments are convincing. They point to the universal need for human rights. They show historical similarities, such as the existence of communitarianism and authoritarianism in the West and components of freedom existing in non-Western cultures. The shortcoming of evolutionary theories is their relative silence about the ways in which the original seeds of freedom in the West led to the emergence, acceptance, and implementation of human rights. What were the social conditions that favored the emergence of a theory of freedom? To say that modern society disrupts traditional communities is just the beginning of the story. Much more interesting would be to learn how and why some societies have managed to deal effectively with this disruption while others have failed. How and when has an effective transition been possible from the elements of freedom to the full-fledged theory and practice of freedom and rights? The relative absence of convincing historical research on the conditions necessary for the emergence of individual and

---

[68] Pollis (2000, 15).

[69] "Contrary to what many people think, world convergence will not come through a loss or denial of traditions all around, but rather by creative re-immersions of different groups, each in their own spiritual heritage, traveling different routes to the same goal," writes Taylor (1999, 144).

[70] Quoted in Glendon (2001, 239).

human rights conducive to their implementation in Western countries is possibly the weakest part of the entire theory of human rights.[71] It is not precluded that such research would automatically support evolutionary arguments. Research should not aim to tell non-Western people what they should do to follow the West in its evolution to human rights and freedoms. A much-needed "soft" universalism, postulated by this author, would not impose Western standards and mechanisms on the rest of the world. There are many dimensions of individual and social life in which just sharing one's experience is more effective than imposing one's ways. A record of what has happened in the West should simply become better known – and made available to others.

POINTS OF DEBATE

Even though the debate between universalism and cultural relativism has been abused for political reasons and abounds in misunderstandings, there are profound elements to be found in it. Any serious attempt to defend universalism demands critical discussion of certain arguments used to challenge the universality of human rights.

Imposition by the West

Recently, criticism of universalism was presented most bluntly by Makau Mutua in the following words: "It is now accepted fact that the West was able to impose its philosophy of human rights on the rest of the world because it dominated the United Nations in 1948."[72] A similar idea has been expressed much earlier, albeit in less radical form, by Pollis and Schwab, who claimed that the acceptance of rights was a condition for independence.[73]

Significant for this argument is the fact that many countries, particularly in sub-Saharan Africa, were not yet independent and, thus, not represented in the UN in 1948. But, as we have seen, Third World representation was, in fact, significant and

---

[71] Positive exceptions are recent book by Lynn Hunt (2007) and Marcello Flores (2008). However, any history focused just on the elements of freedom in various historical epochs would be basically ahistorical and misleading.

[72] From Mutua's speech at the Conference on the Universality of Human Rights held at Columbia University in October, 2001; repeated by Mutua at a similar conference at the Central European University in Budapest in June, 2002. (See Mutua 2004, 61.)

[73] "For British colonies, the Westminster model, including its provisions for individual rights, became practically the sine qua non for independence" (Pollis and Schwab 1978, 7). In 2000, Pollis did not uphold the thesis of the imposition; instead, she pointed out that the ratification of human rights documents was merely "an assertion of membership in the world community and not a commitment to the implementation of these rights or to their legitimacy" (Pollis 2000, 15).

it influenced to a large degree both the content of the UDHR and its process of adoption. The Third Committee, which discussed the final draft in 1948, included representatives from the predominantly Islamic Afghanistan, Egypt, Iran, Iraq, Pakistan, Saudi Arabia, Syria, Turkey, and Yemen, as well as from the largely Muslim India; also involved were officials from the largely Buddhist China, Burma, and Siam. Africa was represented by Egypt, South Africa, Ethiopia, and Liberia. Proponents of the imposition thesis claim that these "representatives" of non-Western cultures were, in fact, representing their countries' Westernized elites.[74] Glendon believes, however, that

> their performance in the Commission on Human Rights suggests something rather different. Not only did each contribute significant insights from his own culture, but each possessed an exceptional ability to understand other cultures and to 'translate' concepts from one frame of reference to another. Those skills, indispensable for effective cross-cultural collaboration, were key to the successful adoption of the Declaration without a single dissenting vote.[75]

Similarly, in debates on human rights covenants that took place in the UN Third Committee in the early 1950s, "Third World diplomats were among the strongest defenders of universality."[76] It is true that during these debates cultural relativism was used as an argument against the universality of human rights, but remarkably only by the delegates from Great Britain, Belgium, and France. At the time, delegates from the Third World spoke against cultural relativism, as exemplified by Egyptian representative Azmi Bey's proclamation that cultural relativism "was only too reminiscent of the Hitlerian concept which divided mankind into groups of varying worth."[77]

In the first decades after World War II, human rights did not seem incompatible with non-Western cultures. When asked by UNESCO to reflect on human rights, non-Western philosophers attempted to find in their cultures values supportive of

---

[74] "Although non-Westerners, both Malik and Chang were educated in the United States and were firmly rooted in the European intellectual tradition of the day. The contributions of these two prominent non-Westerners were not steeped in the philosophies or the intellectual and cultural traditions from which they hailed," claims Mutua (2004, 61).

[75] Glendon (2001, 225–6).

[76] Burke (2006, 963). As noted, the same attitude was present by leaders of Asian and African countries at the Bandung Conference in 1955. Burke convincingly challenges Glendon's opinion that the Bandung conference "signaled trouble ahead" for human rights (see Glendon 2001, 223–4). "Far from being opposed to the rights discourse as a neo-colonial imposition, the sort of nationalism embraced by many African and Asian independence leaders had important affinities with human rights," writes Burke (2006, 962). Similarly, in 1972, the Charter of the Organization of the Islamic Conference, an organization to which all Muslim countries belong, reaffirmed the "commitment to the UN Charter and fundamental human rights." (For a different view on the Bandung Conference, see Afshari 2007, 55–8.)

[77] Burke (2006, 963).

human rights, despite the notion of rights itself being absent.[78] Generally, they concluded that "a few basic practical concepts of human rights are so widely shared that they 'may be viewed as implicit in man's nature as a member of society.'"[79] Similarly, Wellington Koo, China's delegate in Dumbarton Oaks, did not justify the right of all people to equality and nondiscrimination in Western terms but "went on to speak out about the influence of Confucius, Mo Zi and Sun Yat-sen, explaining that 'the thought of universal brotherhood had been deeply rooted in the minds of the Chinese for more than two thousand years.'"[80]

If the philosophers present at the Commission on Human Rights or questioned by UNESCO could be accused of "internationalism," a similar claim could not be held against the representatives of governments bound on the principle of state sovereignty and responsive to local elites and hierarchical institutions on the basis of tradition in their own countries. Nevertheless, during the final voting in the General Assembly only eight countries abstained. Saudi Arabia, the sole non-Western state among them, claimed that the Declaration contains provisions incompatible with the nation's culture.[81] However, no other Arab and Islamic country supported Saudi Arabia in these objections.

This does not mean that representatives of the Islamic world did not share the Saudis' concerns. Ann Elizabeth Mayer quotes Fereydoun Hoveida, advisor to the Iranian delegate to the Third Committee, who said that "in Muslim countries, religious leaders disapproved of the Declaration." According to Hoveida, reports Mayer, in private conversations "delegates and journalists from the Third World did criticize the project, those on the left seeing in it a colonialist instrument of Western domination and those on the right seeing it as destructive of local traditions that bound people together." Apparently, the main reason for the official silence was fear of offending the United States. According to Mayer, "Third World reactions to U.S. power were central to the emergence of a consensus – in reality somewhat artificial, strained consensus – on the universality of human rights."[82] Achieving compliance

---

[78] The results of the UNESCO inquiry were collected in *Human Rights: Comments and Interpretations* published by UNESCO in 1949.

[79] Glendon (2001, 226).

[80] Lauren (1998, 167).

[81] However, Jamil Baroody, Saudi delegate, "did not invoke Islam as the reason for his opposition," writes Mayer (2007, 13). In Article 18 Baroody suggested that "in a provision affording freedom of religion, the language concerning the freedom to *change* religion was superfluous" (ibid.). Baroody also noted that some elements of Article 16 were in conflict with Islamic law in force in some Muslim countries and proposed that women would be entitled to "the full rights as defined in marriage laws of their country." Interestingly Baroody (a Syrian Christian rather than a Muslim himself) was most fiercely criticized by a Pakistani (Muslim) delegate who said that Baroody's formulation "would enable countries with laws discriminating against women to continue to apply them." (Both quotations after ibid., 14.)

[82] Ibid. (2004, 354).

was relatively easy because very few people believed that the "exalted principles" of the Universal Declaration would be treated seriously by the signatory states.

Hoveida's opinion also helps to understand the breakdown of the consensus on human rights that took place in the late 1970s, precisely at the moment when the Declaration's principles were beginning to be treated seriously. International Covenants of Human Rights had been signed and ratified. The United States and the West had elevated human rights to a major principle of their foreign policy, which had become a tool in the Cold War confrontation with the Soviet bloc as well as a standard for assessing the behavior of other countries. Third World leaders were now expected to apply to themselves the same norms that they originally wanted to direct against the West. As we have seen, they had never internalized that aspect of human rights that limited governments' behavior vis-à-vis their own citizens and they perceived international human rights primarily as a vehicle for self-determination and anticolonial struggle. In many postcolonial states, governments were responsible for massive abuses, including cannibalism in Uganda under general Amin. Some countries have become the battlefield for ethnic conflicts, massacres, and genocide, as in cases of the Democratic Republic of Congo, Biafra, Rwanda, Darfur, Indonesia, and Cambodia.

When leaders of the developing countries in Asia and Africa were criticized for violations of human rights at home, some of them "made a complete reversal of formal positions toward universal human rights."[83] They decided to reject the whole concept altogether. One useful strategy was to demonstrate the incompatibility of the human rights idea with cultural traditions and developmental needs.

This incompatibility was, in fact, much greater in the 1970s that in 1948. First, in many postcolonial countries early attempts to build a multiparty democracy failed and one-party authoritarian systems of government became dominant. The way these regimes exercised power was very different from the principles of the Declaration. The second factor had to do with the shift in the dominant ideologies of postcolonial elites.

A Change of Ideology

At the dawn of their independence, the elites of newly established countries tended to be secular and development oriented. With the weakness of local capital and a failing industrial class, the nations' leaders believed in the developmental role of the

---

[83] Afshari(2007, 63). The same author observed: "To the degree that the 'Third World consciousness' sensitized the world to the injustices of colonialism and racism, it contributed to the evolution of human rights; to the degree that it neglected and even denigrated the civil and political rights provisions of the UDHR, it became antithetical to the evolution of human rights" (ibid., 66).

state. Statism was an important ideology to be augmented, and at times replaced, by a Third World version of socialism, launched first in the 1950s by the president of Egypt, Gamal Abdel Nasser. These developmental ideologies were compatible with the broad human rights consensus reached in 1948. The Declaration made room for a strong, active state; it equaled collective forms of ownership with private property; and it provided benefits that were to be distributed by the state. Presumably, the only country that did not share such a developmental dream was Saudi Arabia, whose representatives abstained from voting on the Declaration. So the Saudis stuck to their premodern cultural and religious principles. These principles, however, were presumably obsolescent, or not sufficiently important, for the modernizing elites in other countries. For them, giving up certain values that were not at the top of their own list of priorities was a small concession when compared with the hope that the West would assist the Third World on its path to self-determination, development, and modernization.[84]

By the late 1970s, it had become evident that development in the postcolonial world was proving much more difficult than what had been hoped for in the 1940s. On the one hand, modernization had threatened the position of traditional elites, including the chiefs and the clerics. On the other hand, when fast change proved impossible and the social role of former elites increased once more, they became more militant in opposing further change. "Thus, some of what appears to be an Islamic reaction against human rights, perceived as an artifact of secular Western culture antithetical to Islam, may actually be part of a broader pattern of resistance to Western hegemony and to the unsettling transformations that Muslim societies are undergoing."[85]

Ayatollah Khomeini was the first leader to realize that the developmental utopia realized by the Shah of Iran with the help of the ruthless security police was hopeless. So Khomeini replaced it with values that were in abundance – Islam, Allah, religion, and tradition. In some other countries fundamentalist movements began to challenge the secular, developmentally oriented elites. In contrast to developmental ideologies, fundamentalism could not be reconciled with the idea of human rights.

The rejection of human rights can thus be perceived as a part of a broader conflict accompanying modernization in general. Everywhere, old elites – social, political, religious, cultural – were skeptical to developmental processes that unsettled

---

[84] One example of these tendencies was a significant role of women in the delegations of the Islamic states (Iraq, Libya, Morocco, and Pakistan) to the UN bodies that worked on human rights covenants. An Iraqi delegate, Bedia Afnan, influenced strong provisions on women's equality in Article 3 of both conventions while a female delegate from Libya advocated equal rights for both spouses in marriage. (See Mayer 2007, 15–16.)

[85] Mayer (2007, 75).

them and limited their influence.[86] This universal reaction took, at time, radical forms:

> Autocratic elites have learned to fight historical inevitability by destroying the engines of social progress. The cultural Luddities of the Taliban, by disempowering women and dismantling their society's educational and health infrastructure, hoped to delay their eventual overthrow. Idi Amin had that in mind when he demolished Uganda's Indian mercantile community in the 1970s. Pol Pot almost succeeded with a similar project in Cambodia. And George Speight recently pursued the same goal in Fiji. Each sought to catapult society back to a premodern age when race or class purification justified everything.[87]

As a result of this process, the modernizers, a great majority of whom had became dictatorial well before the 1970s, clashed with authoritarian conservatives, both pushing human rights out of the political spectrum and drastically changing the position of the developing countries in the United Nations. Neither those in power nor their opponents were upholding human rights as an idea. Moreover, the counteroffensive of authoritarian (when in opposition) and dictatorial (when in power) conservatives resulted in the increase of violations of rights by traditional cultural customs. To defend their popular support in the face of a conservative counteroffensive, the modernizers significantly decreased measures that aimed to change such customs and accepted many cultural demands of the conservatives. As a result, human rights were pushed still further away from the public sphere.

A Change in Content

There was one more reason for the breakdown of consensus. As noted, the concept of human rights that came to prominence in the 1970s differed from the idea agreed on in 1948. This difference mattered most for the non-Western countries. The UDHR was a broad compromise that included elements of various ideologies and contained all three categories of rights: civil liberties; political rights; and social, economic, and cultural rights. In the 1970s, however, the idea of human rights was narrowed to the first two categories. Such was the natural outcome of the way in which the notion of human rights had reappeared after 30 years of "hibernation."

The change went unnoticed in most of the West. After all, Western tradition dictates that individuals have equal protection of civil and political rights and it is

---

[86] One of many Western examples can be seen in the opposition of the great part of the Catholic Church as well as right-wing politicians and their supporters to market reforms, democratization, and the enforcement of human rights in Poland, after 1989.

[87] Franck (2001, 203).

economic and social status that can be differentiated. In traditional non-Western cultures, however, the community is supposed to provide the needy with a minimum of food and shelter and other necessities of life. This obligation assumed by the community itself had created rights of a sort – ones much like the right to welfare. Consequently, the entire non-Western understanding of rights focused primarily on the individual's entitlements to social and economic benefits.[88]

With modernization, emergence of markets, and the disintegration of traditional communities the situation changed and the difference between Western and non-Western countries deepened. In the modernized West, traditional mechanisms of social protection within a community were taken over by the market and the state. These were state-enforced contracts between employers and their employees to secure fair treatment, pensions, healthcare, and insurance from other risks. Whenever the market failed, civil society would play an auxiliary role, providing assistance through various forms of charity. Where social pressure was strong enough and economic efficiency permitted new expenditures, welfare benefits were introduced as a matter of public policy. Social rights differed from other kinds of rights in one fundamental aspect: the recipients of benefits are a minority in a society. The majority bought their necessary goods and services on the market. And the minority that could not afford to do so was entitled to them as a matter of statutory rights created by welfare policies. This contrasted with civil liberties and political rights, in the case of which the state has a relative monopoly on the provision of services for everyone.

In the non-Western world, markets ended up ineffective in the provision of social services. With social protection remaining a task for the community, the disruption of local communities rendered an overwhelming majority – not just a minority – of non-Western populations in need of social services. For many people, social benefits were not merely a way to claim one's share under the traditional understanding of entitlement; instead, they had become a matter of survival. As powerless individuals, these members of the majority began to demand such benefits as a matter of rights.[89] However, the absence of these rights from international human rights policies – and

---

[88] Pollis (2000, 19–20) presents a profound explanation of this difference. "As noted, the language of rights, a Western construct, has been nonexistent in traditional societies. For cultural relativists this is conflated with an absence of rights, a position reinforced by most ethnographic studies. Yet a closer look reveals that in many traditional societies what in a rights vocabulary are labeled as socioeconomic rights are obligations of the community toward all its members. Obligations are the reverse side of rights. Thus, if the community must ensure food, shelter, and care for the aged, the disabled, and in fact all its members, in essence all group members possess equal rights to entitlements. Such a concept of obligations and/or rights differs radically from the Western notion of legal rights."

[89] Susan Waltz has demonstrated that, during the formulation of the international human rights covenants, diplomats from the Islamic world "actively opposed the isolation of socioeconomic rights into a separate covenant" (2004, 799).

to a great extent also from the international human rights movement – in the 1970s provoked a reaction from the only forum that represented non-Western states: the United Nations. Not surprisingly, it was as if the international human rights movement and the UN had begun to speak different languages. The growing disparity only further substantiated claims that the Western concept of human rights, truncated in comparison to the broad compromise of the UDHR, was not a fair reflection of the values and needs of non-Western countries and that it was being imposed on them by the West.

The Individual and the Community

An important element of the debate between universalism and cultural relativism concerns the relations between the individual and her community. It is argued that in most traditional societies "group rights have always taken precedence over individual rights, and political decisions have been made through group consensus, not through individual assertion of rights."[90] Relativists claim that the philosophy of human rights alienates members of non-Western cultures because it puts the individual above the group to which she belongs. Such an idea is clearly in conflict with traditional cultures, in which the individual is subordinate to a group that provides its members with a sense of identity, security, and well-being.[91] This argument is serious and worthy of reflection.

It is true that human rights are claimed not only against the state but also, at times, through the state against a community. It is also true that a claim of rights can limit the pursuit of a particular interest of a majority or of the entire community. It is true that rights are often overused – or abused – to justify selfish goals and particular interests. But such abuse does not mean that the conflict between rights and the values of community is inevitable.

In fact, human rights have had strong communal aspects from the very beginning. Many rights were originally designed to protect groups and group interests from intrusion by the state. But when individual rights began to be identified with philosophical, moral, and legal individualism, these origins of individual rights were forgotten. Joseph Raz suggests that "many rights were advocated and fought for in the name of individual freedom. But this was done against the background that secured

---

[90] Tharoor (1999/2000, 1; html version).

[91] "Since the group, not the individual, is of primary importance, the social order proceeds not on the basis of individual rights but, rather, on the basis of obligations. Obligations themselves are not so sharply distinguished between legal and moral as in the West. Justice consists not in enforcing rights, but in bringing about harmonious settlement between the disputants, so that group cohesion is assured," writes Sinha with regard to African and, more generally, non-Western cultures (quoted in Lindholt 1997).

collective goods without which those individual rights would not have served their avowed purpose."[92]

Religious freedom would not be needed if its essence were to permit an individual to pray to the gods of her choosing in the privacy of her home. Rather, it is needed to permit people to gather in public spaces with others of the same faith and profess that faith free of intrusion by the government or by people who do not share their beliefs. Conscientious objection was justified by the values of a group to which one belonged. Freedom of contract and economic activity "presupposes and depends for its value on the existence of at least one collective good: the free market." Freedoms of speech and of the press preserve "the character of the community as an open society."[93] They would be meaningless without the recipients of speech. Participatory rights empower people to participate in the decisions of the group. Rights against discrimination serve the collective good related to individual and group identity.

> Discrimination on grounds of religion, nationality or race affects its victim in a more fundamental way. It distorts their ability to feel pride in membership in groups identification with which is an important element in their life. (. . .) The important point is that the right is meant to foster a public culture which enables people to take pride in their identity as members of such groups.[94]

Thus, many individual rights enable an individual to participate freely in a social group of one's choice and they protect such groups and their members from intrusion by the state. Instead of outright conflict, there is an entire scope of relationships between individual interests and collective goods protected by rights.[95] The same is true in cases of violations of rights. Most often, the human rights of individuals are violated precisely because these individuals are members of a certain group. This is the case for women, people of various races, victims of ethnic cleansing, indigenous people, and numerous other discriminated groups. The enforcement of rights serves such groups as a whole, as well as their individual members.

When we acknowledge this communal aspect, we see that the philosophy of human rights neither puts the individual above the group nor subordinates group interests to the individual. Even the most radical philosophy of rights agrees that

---

[92] Raz (1986, 251).

[93] Ibid. (251–3).

[94] Ibid. (254). The right to jury trial, at least in the version established by the Magna Carta of 1215, could be added to Raz's list – trial by jury protected the nobility as a group from being tried arbitrarily by the king at his court.

[95] "We find that fundamental moral rights cannot be conceived as essentially in competition with collective goods. On examination either they are found to be an element of the protection of certain collective goods, or their value is found to depend on the existence of certain collective goods" (ibid., 254).

groups, communities, and states are empowered to make decisions about their own priorities and directions for growth. Human rights philosophy is closely linked with the theory of democracy and the democratic political process. The shared assumption is that individuals are subordinated to the group and should follow legitimate group decisions. Such decisions are not made "through individual assertion of rights" but through legitimate political process. The only thing human rights do is they set limits on the coercive powers of the group over individuals by enumerating, as exceptions, the things that cannot be done to the individual by the group or its leaders – in the name of group interests. In such cases, and only in such cases, the individual has a veto power of a sort over the decisions of a group. The group is in power, but this power is limited; a group cannot act arbitrarily against the paramount interests of its members. In reality, human rights often are invoked to limit the discriminatory character of customary norms or unjust relations of power and domination on local levels.[96] Protecting a victim from injustice within her community is not the same as putting an individual above community. Certainly, it does not mean that an individual endowed with rights can impose her will on a group in matters other than her enforceable rights.

The balance between the needs of a group coupled with the obligations of group members on the one hand and individual rights that protect against the excessive power of a group over an individual on the other needs to be set in each culture in a way that enhances two important values: identity, which is something one usually derives from a group, and individual dignity. The emphasis on the individual versus the social rationale distinguishes two major traditions of rights in the West: the "individualist" of England and the United States and the "dignitarian" of continental Europe. The continental tradition puts more emphasis on family, communities, and citizens' duties. Although the first tradition has found limited support in Asia and Africa, the second one was more compatible with the traditions of non-Western countries. According to Glendon, the Universal Declaration embodies the spirit of the second tradition.[97] A crucial

---

[96] de Langen and Barendrecht (2009, 7) noted an important aspect of local norms, i.e., the coexistence of discrimination and protection offered by a group. "The group grants protection and informally regulates access to essential goods and services among group members. The individual sees some of his interests and rights protected, and has to submit to the norms and wishes of the group in other matters. The wellbeing of the collective may thus become relatively more important than that of the individual." One of the possible outcomes "is that local, customary norms become unjust, at least as seen through the lens of Western human rights lawyers. Because these norms are more or less a trade-off between protection and other interests, they often discriminate against those disadvantaged by these relationships: women, subsistence farmers, or the poor more generally. Unjust norms at the local level may even migrate upward into the formal legal system."

[97] See Glendon (2001, 226–8). "In the spirit of the latter vision, the Declaration's 'Everyone' is an individual who is constituted, in important ways, by and through relationships with others. 'Everyone' is envisioned as uniquely valuable in himself (there are three separate references to the free development

concept of this "dignitarian" tradition – dignity itself – constitutes the very foundation of human rights.

Perceived as limits on the application of coercive power, human rights can be reconciled with many non-Western philosophies in which limits on arbitrary power are imposed by various instruments – for example, the duties of a ruler. On the other hand, in every culture it is important to temper the excesses of individualism and limit selfishness. Undoubtedly, a lot can be done today to make better use of the communal aspect of rights and to use rights to strengthen civil societies and give individuals a sense of belonging rather than separate them from others and from the community. As we will see, rights also imply a sense of self-restraint.

All of this, however, does not change the fact that the argument about the alleged subordination of a group to the whim of an individual wrongly suggests the imposing rather than protective nature of right.

CAN A CROSS-CULTURAL CONSENSUS ON HUMAN RIGHTS BE RESTORED?

We now see that the consensus on human rights accepted in 1948 ended up relatively shallow and short-lived. There is growing doubt whether such consensus can be restored at all. The reasons why this may be so difficult have already been discussed. Basically, powerful leadership groups in many parts of the world are just not interested in human rights. The rational ideas of the 1940s have been replaced by a more emotional, symbolic set of ideas essential for various fundamentalisms. Such is the case in not only Islamic countries. Furthermore, because the idea of human rights has been in use as an instrument of foreign policy, it has been rejected by those who believe that the policy of the West, particularly as represented by the United States, is aimed against them or against their interests.

Even among those who respect human rights, rifts have appeared. Western Europe, for instance, disagrees more and more strongly with the methods of promoting democracy and human rights adopted by the United States. In addition, the European Union's policy on human rights is extremely ineffective.[98] Recently, also the international human rights movement has been torn by divisions and conflicts.

---

of one's personality), but 'Everyone' is expected to act toward others 'in a spirit of brotherhood.' 'Everyone' is depicted as situated in a variety of specifically named, real-life relationships of mutual dependency: families, communities, religious groups, workplaces, associations, societies, cultures, nations, and an emerging international order. Though its main body is devoted to basic individual freedoms, the Declaration begins with an exhortation to act in 'a spirit of brotherhood' and ends with community, order, and society" (ibid., 227).

[98] The EU lost the ability to form a majority behind its proposals in the UN Human Rights Council that replaced, in 2006, the Committee on Human Rights (where the EU had such a majority). See Gowan and Brantner (2008).

Differences divide donor-driven human rights organizations, which usually adopt the agenda of the donors, and membership-based local NGOs that pursue their own priorities, most often with scarce resources.[99] Barbora Bukovská described how monitoring and advocacy by international human rights NGOs can "reduce victims to passive objects" and use them for their own purposes rather than helping them or protecting against the "potential backlash that they might face because of reports."[100] Most big international human rights organizations continue to focus almost exclusively on civil and political rights. Meanwhile, local human rights NGOs are more sensitive to the set of rights related to exclusion from society, among them many social and economic rights.[101] Among major Western foundations, the shift toward embracing the needs of indigenous people has been relatively slow.[102] When the U.S. government began to cite the protection of human rights and freedoms as its new justification for the war in Iraq, some local NGOs in Arab and Islamic countries rejected the Western human rights agenda altogether. In other countries, governments turned against human rights organizations, calling them instruments of Western imperialism or espionage. Well-known examples here include Belarus under Lukashenka and Russia under Putin.

In short, human rights organizations today pursue many different goals and represent a number of diversified interests; not surprisingly, they also adopt different strategies. They have to compete for decreasing resources from the West and for limited resources in societies in which they are active. The resulting differentiation has led to diminished hopes for the human rights movement ever reunifying successfully again. It is difficult to define a common set of ideas and values to which a majority of human rights organizations could subscribe.

---

[99] "With few exceptions, most international human rights NGOs purporting to speak for the masses are clearly not representatives of larger constituencies of human rights victims: their constituencies are their donors, their employees, other international organizations and governments," writes Barbora Bukovská (2008, 14). For the difference between donor-driven and membership-driven human rights NGOs, see also Crenshaw (2000, 62). On the role of fundraising for building local constituency in the Arab world, see *International Aspects* . . . (2000, 57–63).

[100] Bukovská (2008, 6 and 9). She claims than "unaccountable to anyone other than themselves or their donors, international human rights NGOs often can lose touch with the powerless and voiceless whom they claim to represent" (ibid. 14).

[101] For a description of the different agendas of international donors and local human rights organizations, see El Din Hassan (1999). For the differences and conflicts between international human rights organizations and indigenous NGOs in the Caribbean, see Martinez (2000). Martinez claims that "whole categories of victims and types of abuses have been excluded from human rights reports and advocacy."

[102] Most recently, the Ford Foundation has become interested in social rights. In 2001, the Open Society Foundation formed the OSI Justice Initiative, whose foci include issues of equality, citizenship, and inclusion, as well as legal aid for poor indigenous defendants. In 2008, a number of international NGOs offered support for alternative law groups that defend the rights of the excluded groups and indigenous populations in Southern and South East Asia.

The very language of human rights has become a source of debate and confrontation rather than consensus. The different categories of human rights have always been in conflict with each other. Social and economic rights dictate a limitation on freedom of property and freedom of contracts. Respect for privacy limits the freedom of expression. Protection of physical security can be in conflict with the freedom of movement and with other liberties. Today, these differences are at the core of the different concepts of rights. Conservatives emphasize freedom of religion, protection of family, and power of the original groups in society over the individual freedoms of members of such groups. Solidarity rights are viewed as opposed to liberal freedoms.

With too many different things being expected from rights it is difficult to hope for universal adherence to the philosophy of rights. A single agreed-on philosophy of rights has been replaced by various disparate philosophies, and the very idea of human rights has been abused by double standards and selective enforcement. When a once-universal language of the oppressed becomes adopted as the language of power, consensus breaks down. Powers, after all, have their self-serving goals and interests, ones that cannot be easily reconciled with the needs of those who are most vulnerable.

Human Rights and the Philosophy of Human Rights

It is possible that the consensus on the philosophy of rights has been damaged beyond repair. Fortunately, human rights can still be observed without restoring that consensus. The distinction between the universality of human rights and the universality of the philosophy of human rights may be helpful. The philosophy of human rights dictates an entire set of assumptions about the nature of a society and a state, about the relationships between the individual and the state, and so on. Human rights, by contrast, imply a set of rules for behavior. Rules that should be observed even when someone does not share – or does not know – the underlying philosophy. This is similar to the norms and rules included in a penal code that have to be observed by each individual, regardless of whether she shares (or even knows) the philosophical assumptions underlying the code.

In fact, such has been the idea behind human rights since their very inception. In 1948, it was already much easier to reach consensus on rules than on the underlying principles. For the framers, universalism in the context of rights primarily meant uniform rules and standards of behavior rather than the philosophical justifications of norms and values included in the Universal Declaration. This difference between rules and principles has been stressed by Jacques Maritain in an address to the second International UNESCO Conference, held in Mexico City in November 1947: "Since the aim of UNESCO is a practical aim, agreement among its members can be spontaneously achieved, not on common speculative notions, but on common practical notions, not on the affirmation of the same conception of the world, man and knowledge, but on the affirmation of the same set of convictions concerning action."[103]

Similarly, today the universality of human rights need not mean that the entire world should subject itself to the Western philosophy of rights or to the Western cultural model. It means only that there are certain fundamental rights that no government in the world may violate. It is the selection and definition of such a catalog of human rights that should be the subject of debate. However, no debate can justify the grave abuses perpetrated in the name of cultural differences. Regardless of philosophical and cultural differences, there are some things that every society rules out. According to Milne, "all societies impose restraints on the use of force and violence by their members. (. . .) No culture or ideological system, for example, condones arbitrary and indiscriminate destruction of life, or incarceration."[104] Charles Taylor believes that it is possible to reach an "overlapping consensus" on certain norms of conduct because all cultures condemn "genocide, murder, tortures, slavery, as well as, say, 'disappearances' and the shooting of innocent demonstrators."[105] Adamantia Pollis writes that "no philosophic/cultural system sanctions arbitrary killings, disappearances or torture."[106]

Such universal norms, restraints, and prohibitions form a basis for the list of specific norms that can be accepted by all cultures. For Pollis, what justifies this list is the universality of the notion of human dignity. Onuma Yasuaki avoids using the term *dignity* because of its Western origin. Instead, he suggests the phrase "spiritual and material well-being of humanity" to denote the ultimate and universal value that human rights should serve.[107] Steven Lukes, in turn, defines universal human rights as the indispensable mechanism for limiting the intrusion of a political system into the life of an individual.[108]

The cross-cultural consensus on human rights should, then, focus on very specific rights and not on theoretical or philosophical considerations. Moreover, a list of universal rights should be minimal to avoid both the inflation of rights and disputes about specific norms that could be challenged by individual cultures. Such a minimal list of rights would include those rights that are deemed indispensable in every state – regardless of the dominant culture, religion, or tradition. Each state could go beyond this minimal list and be offered support from other states in the protection or fulfillment of any added obligations. But failure to protect such "additional"

---

[103] Maritain (1951a, 77).
[104] Milne (1986, 15).
[105] Taylor (1999, 125).
[106] Pollis (2000, 23).
[107] Yasuaki (1999, 123).
[108] Lukes (1993, 436).

rights would not create grounds for international criticism or intervention. Only the agreed-on minimum would be enforced internationally.

Attempts have been made to formulate such a minimal list of rights. Most authors agree that the following basic rights and freedoms are indispensable[109]:

- The right to life
- The right to recognition as a human being
- The right to legal personhood (including the right to citizenship)
- Basic autonomy in personal matters
- The right to physical integrity, including a ban on torture and the prohibition of cruel, unusual, and arbitrary punishment and executions; a ban on forced disappearance
- Freedom from involuntary human experimentation
- Freedom from slavery, the slave trade, and servitude
- Freedom from arbitrary detention
- Specific rights of people under custody and detention
- The right to a fair trial and due process
- Freedom from imprisonment for debt
- Freedom from retroactive application of criminal punishment
- Freedom of thought, conscience, religion, and expression
- Equality before the law and freedom from discrimination
- Participation in government

The list focuses both on the protection of individuals from the coercive power of the state and on the basic guarantees of a person's very ability to possess rights. Some rights on the list can be debated and their content may be culturally defined. For example, the degree of protected personal autonomy or the specific forms of participation in the political process can vary. In some cultures, Henkin's assumption about equality as a universal value would, unfortunately, be limited to males alone.

One striking characteristic of the above list is the absence of the rights to association and assembly – the very rights that form the basis for both political participation and the survival of independent civil society. There are strong reasons for insisting that

---

[109] The original list was suggested by Myres McDougal, Harold Lasswell, and Lung-Chu Chen (1969, 237; as quoted by Pollis 2000, 3). Louis Henkin's core list of human rights includes "the right to the physical and psychic integrity of the person (ban on torture; ban on cruel, unusual and arbitrary executions, ban on disappearance), basic autonomy, freedom from slavery, freedom from arbitrary detention, autonomy in personal matters and equality before the law." These rights "are as dear to Eastern as to Western man" (Henkin 1990, 187). Steven Lukes also includes on his minimal list social rights: "I think it follows that the list of human rights should be kept both reasonably short and reasonably abstract. It should include the basic civil and political rights, the rule of law, freedom of expression and association, equality of opportunity and the right to some basic level of material well-being, but probably no more" (1993, 436).

these rights be included. A minimal list of human rights should also include basic economic security, even if such a right cannot be made enforceable by courts.

The above list includes rights that primarily aim to assure certain end goals of the political process, limit arbitrariness in public decisions, and guarantee the right to appeal from such decisions. The list contains what governments cannot do and what they should do rather than how they are to do it. The decision on how to reach these goals, in turn, is left open and can be culturally determined.[110] A universally accepted list of rights would still leave up to each culture matters of consistency between these norms and the culture's philosophy, religion, and traditions. One example is Japan, where individualism has been rejected and replaced with the individual's subordination to the community and the nation. Yet Japan has managed to establish a relatively good record of observing human rights norms and reconciling them with the country's culture.

This approach actually questions the universality of some basic assumptions of the Western conception of human rights. The lack of the rights to association and assembly has already been mentioned (however, note that this author considers it a mistake). The focus on outcomes rather than the process renders Western political institutions (e.g., parties, traditional elections, and perhaps even the paramount role of the judiciary) less universal in solving all kinds of disputes.[111] Vast evidence suggests that parliamentary democracy fosters respect for human rights. However, the number of "illiberal democracies," where elections and even freely elected parliaments are not sufficient to protect freedom, has been growing.[112] Should there exist a universal standard for decision-making processes and the organization of the government? That is an issue worthy of a thorough debate.

A comparison of minimal lists of rights reveals that there exist two crucial philosophical assumptions that should be upheld universally: the principle of freedom (i.e., the principle of limitations of a government's invasion on individual freedom) and the principle of equality (i.e., freedom construed as belonging to everyone without discrimination). There are also at least two principles attached to the Western

---

[110] Milne claims that his list being "a universal minimum moral standard, because it only sets minimum moral requirements, would still be compatible with considerable cultural diversity" (1986, 8–9). Jacques Maritain has said about the UDHR that "many different kinds of music could be played on the document's thirty strings" (quoted after Glendon 2001, 230).

[111] One example involves paralegals stepping in for lawyers in countries where the latter are in limited supply. With the help of the Open Society Justice Initiative and the World Bank, the Sierra Leone NGO Timap for Justice trains paralegals who provide counsel in the country. (See Maru 2006; Open Society Justice Initiative, 2006c). An important element of this approach is helping people use traditional mechanisms of conflict resolution whenever they can be reconciled with the protection of human rights. However, when rights are violated, the appeal to national legal institutions or international mechanisms is needed.

[112] See Zakaria (2003, 117).

philosophy of human rights that do not seem universal. One such difference concerns the connection between rights and individualism, specifically, the belief that an individual is the center of the universe. Individual rights emerged before individualism and protected important group interests. Adherence to the philosophy of human rights is possible without the idolatry of excessive individualism. The second assumption concerns the thesis that rights are not dependent on the fulfillment of duties by a right-holder. True, most rights are granted to individuals not only when they fulfill their societal obligations, but even when they violate the rights of other people. If rights protect dignity and if dignity is inalienable and manifests in the undeprivable element of being human, then no one should be deprived of rights. It seems, however, that at least some rights can be made contingent on the fulfillment of obligations to society and to other people. In particular, this seems justifiable in the case of positive rights. As already suggested, recipients of social benefits can have the obligation to contribute to society in a way they are fit to do so. Such revisions of Western theory could make the concept of rights more acceptable in communitarian cultures.

All this leads to the issue of the universality of social and economic rights. These have been discussed in depth in a separate chapter, so here we are concerned with only the different approaches to their universality. It has been widely accepted that social rights primarily belong to the realm of a state's public policy and do not need constitutional protection. And because policy itself can differ from one state to the next, it would be difficult to defend a thesis about the universality of social rights – and more difficult still were we to undertake the task of pruning the tree of rights and limiting our list to the basics. However, some minimal economic and social security seems indispensable for the enjoyment of other rights.[113] Thus, select rights warrant universal validity, with the remaining social and economic rights best left to a state's public policy. It is important to note that an international agreement that universalizes basic social rights would require the existence of an efficient mechanism for the international redistribution of resources.

Two Types of Violations

Agreeing on a short list of basic universal rights necessitates an answer to the question of how the international community can help to implement such rights in those states and cultures that reject the very concept of rights. In considering the answer, it is useful to distinguish between two types of violations. One consists of violations

---

[113] As noted, the authors of minimal lists of rights differ in this respect. Whereas Milne (1986) excludes social rights from the list of rights required by a universal minimum moral standard, Lukes (1993, 436) includes on his list not only liberal freedoms but also basic rights needed for survival.

perpetrated by dictators and oppressive regimes. The other – of violations of human rights standards by indigenous cultures. Each type requires different mechanisms of enforcement and different strategies for prevention.

The abuse of rights by oppressive regimes has at best superficial legitimacy. Even where a local population is complacent with oppression, people usually do not rush to defend a tyranny when it is being abolished. True, many arguments have been raised in defense of abuses of rights. Tyrants talk about protecting people against the enemy. Their spokesmen talk about the need for development and threats to progress. Scholars write, often in the best faith, about the conflict between individualism and modernization. Intellectuals and professors write elaborate essays about cultural relativism and the limited applicability of rights in non-Western cultures.[114] But all these arguments are pretty superficial. As far as the violations of rights by dictators and authoritarian governments (as distinct from violations motivated by traditional cultures) are concerned, such arguments tend to represent the position of the abusers rather than the victims.[115] The real test of cultural relativism would occur in a situation when a victim of a gross violation of rights, such as a group rape by soldiers, a lone survivor of a family killed by militia, or a victim of torture by security forces, were to be removed from the country of oppression and freed from any fear of retribution. If this victim were to say that he or she does not mind the suffering inflicted because her culture differs from Western standards and permits such behavior, only then would we have proof of cultural relativism.[116] Usually, however, when freed from fear, victims express their pain, anger, and sense of injustice. And others, in non-Western cultures, when free to do so, console the victims of abuses and not the deposed tyrants.[117]

Violation of rights by traditional cultures, however, are less clear-cut and a much more difficult issue to resolve.[118] Such violations have their legitimacy, and at times

---

[114] "Today, culture has became a language of rulers, particularly in the ex-colonial world," observes Mamdani (2000, 2).

[115] "Lee Kwan Yew and Mahathir bin Mohamad, all their cant about Asian values notwithstanding, consciously adopted the authoritarian platitudes (and institutions) of the British empire-builders," observes Ian Buruma (2005).

[116] Glendon (2001, 232) presents a telling account of a 1998 symposium at Harvard University, during which Chinese dissident Xiao Quiang turned to Makau Mutua who had just rejected human rights as a Western idea, saying "if you were to voice dissent from the prevailing view in China, you would end up in jail, and there you would soon be asking for your rights, without worrying about whether they were 'American' or 'Chinese.'"

[117] According to Shestack, "any observer of state practice can cite example after example where repression that one authoritarian government excuses as cultural identity, turns out *not* to be a cultural tradition at all when a democratic government replaces the authoritarian one" (1998, 231).

[118] In some cases, it is even difficult to speak about "violations." Members of many cultures accept hierarchy as something normal. Others do not care about voting and other political rights. From the human rights perspective, they are deprived of rights but they do not perceive it as a violation.

this legitimacy is quite high.[119] Muslim women usually do not complain of sex discrimination and do not claim sexual equality. Victims of female genital cutting (or mutilation)[120] and victims of other violations, including exclusion on the basis of sex or sexual preference, tend to consider their suffering as something normal; often, they have no sense of victimization. In fact, they usually blame themselves for this suffering. Even if in their hearts they object against the violations, they may still feel guilt. Local communities view external defenders of rights as abusers and invaders, and their efforts are often undermined by the victims themselves. Abolishing a tyrant does not by itself change cultural practices. Military intervention and economic sanctions by outsiders are of limited use. Changing laws, however, has brought effects.[121] What seems to work best is convincing local authorities and cultural elites about the harm caused by some practices and helping them undertake appropriate efforts.[122] For example, the government of Nigeria has outlawed stoning for adultery and authorities in Ghana, Senegal, and several other African states (including Egypt in 2007) have designated female genital mutilation a crime.[123] Other effective methods for fighting the violation of rights by traditional cultures include aid for

---

[119] Kabasakal Arat claims that "traditional cultural norms and practices include numerous discriminatory stipulations. (. . .) Violations often occur as a result of fulfilling some cultural requirements" (2006, 425). The author perceives international human rights instruments as an attempt "to change local cultures and replace them, at least partially, with one that upholds equality and human dignity" (ibid., 418).

[120] The term *mutilation* was first adopted in 1990 at the Third Conference of the Inter-African Committee on Traditional Practices Affecting the Health of Women and Children in Addis Abbaba. In 1991, the WHO suggested that the term be used by the United Nations in its documents. In 1999, the UN Special Rapporteur on Traditional Practices called for tact and patience, and, to avoid demonizing the practice, he suggested the word *cutting* be used instead of *mutilation*. Today, the UN refers to Female Genital Mutilation, with the exception of the UN Population Fund, which uses the term Female Genital Cutting (see http://en.wikipedia.org/wiki/Female_genital_mutilation). Mutua (2004, 62) suggests that the very use of the word *mutilation* aims at stigmatizing cultures that accept this practice and "decontextualizes the cultural foundation of the practice. (. . .) It is a view that is racist," concludes Mutua. Mutua's opinion is in conflict with a number of African authorities that have, in fact, outlawed this practice. For more general anthropological arguments in defense of the genital cutting debate, see Shweder (2002 and 2004).

[121] For example, in 1821, General Governor of Bengal Lord William Bentinck outlawed *Sati*, the traditional custom of widow immolation among upper-class Hindus. The law outlawed both forced and voluntary *Sati* (see Narasimhan 1992). Similarly, it was the British administration that opposed the practice of female genital mutilation in Kenya and other African colonies.

[122] In the case of *Sati*, the call for the abolishment of this practice came from a male Bengali intellectual and reformer named Raja Rammohan Roy (1772–1833), who claimed that *Sati* had no basis in Brahmanic scripture. Nevertheless, hundreds of priests opposed the abolition of *Sati*, arguing that an official policy should follow the priestly interpretation of Brahmin traditions. See Narasimhan (1992, 61–73) and Mani (1990, 107).

[123] However, in April 2008, the parliament of Yemen upheld the legality of FGC. The practice is most popular in Guinea with 98.6 percent of girls operated, Eritrea (90 to 95 percent), and Sudan and Djibouti (91 percent). It is the least prevalent in Ghana (9–15 percent), Senegal (5–20 percent), and Tanzania (17.6 percent) (see http://en.wikipedia.org/wiki/Female_genital_mutilation).

victims[124] and empowering former victims (and perpetrators[125]) of abuse to organize themselves into movements for change and education.[126]

One important factor to consider in the case of traditional practices is the degree of harm and its reversibility. From this perspective, it is less justified to fight against the veils worn by Muslim women and much more justified to oppose genital mutilation. The former does not cause irreversible harm and does not prevent a person from exercising her freedom of choice, should she decide to remove that veil. The latter is performed on young girls, long before they can define their own priorities. It is also irreversible. Neither cultural relativism nor multicultural tolerance, however, can ever be used to justify the "honor killings" of women by their fathers and brothers.[127]

Even though traditional practices that conflict with human rights and freedoms are harmful, prevalent, and difficult to eradicate – they usually do not lead to genocide or other gross violations of human rights. The latter are the result of tyrannies and armed conflicts between tyrants or warlords. Therefore, it is the enforcement of rights against dictators and others who abuse the power of arms that should be the priority. Despite near-universal adherence to human rights, at least formally, the situation in many countries demands a decisive condemnation of the gross abuses of rights being perpetrated by rulers. Cuba and Belarus, Burma and North Korea, Iran and Uzbekistan, Sudan and Zimbabwe – these are merely a few examples.

CONCLUSIONS: "HARD" AND "SOFT" UNIVERSALISM

Clearly, the universality of human rights poses a growing number of questions. Confusion abounds about the very idea, its origins, and its practical application in

---

[124] One example is Senegal, where native women work with an international nongovernmental organization on the Tostan Project. In 1997, Demba Diawara, a local imam of Malicounda Bambara, began to walk from village to village to raise awareness about the dangers of FGC. Since then, 1271 villages (600,000 people, or 12% of the tradition-abiding population in Senegal) have voluntarily given up FGC and are also working to end early and forced marriage.

[125] The example of Ms. Isnino Shuriye in Kenya is telling. One of the most successful cutters, she was reluctant to listen to the members of Womenkind Kenya, a grass-root organization opposing the practice. She was open, however, to arguments presented by local imams, who denounced the practice as violating the Koran. The imams ruled that Ms. Shuriye should compensate each girl she had maimed with 80 camels or, at the very least, seek her forgiveness. Since 2002, Ms. Shuriye has been traveling from village to village explaining her conversion and asking forgiveness. With her help, Womenkind Kenya have persuaded a number of other cutters to denounce the FGC practice. See Lacey (2004).

[126] This strategy has a long tradition. For example, at the beginning of the twentieth century, campaigns by Chinese and Western missionaries helped to eradicate the 1000-year-old practice of foot binding in China.

[127] "Over 5000 women and girls are killed every year by family members in so-called 'honour killings,' according to the UN. These crimes occur where cultures believe that a woman's unsanctioned sexual behaviour brings such shame on the family that any female accused or suspected must be murdered. Reasons for these murders can be as trivial as talking to a man, or as innocent as suffering rape." *Stop! Honour Killings* (2007).

today's world. This chapter's main thesis holds that to restore meaning to human rights we should disconnect two ideas – namely, the notion of the universality of human rights and the concept of the universality of the philosophy of human rights. The former can be universal. The latter is not, and any claim to the universality of the philosophy of human rights creates more problems than solutions. Though 60 years ago it may have been the language of cross-cultural dialogue and a basis for compromise, the philosophy of human rights has become a language of discord that exacerbates tensions between cultures. But can universal human rights be "rescued" or protected without the underlying consensus on the philosophy of human rights? There are, it seems, two possibilities.

One was proposed recently by Leszek Kołakowski, who suggested that human rights be replaced with another pact, resembling a "penal code for governments," which would state what governments are prohibited to do against people.[128] Kołakowski's proposal goes one step further than simply dissociating human rights norms from the philosophy of human rights. He suggests to discard the philosophy of human rights altogether – and to replace human rights norms with penal law. Such an idea seems convincing, particularly in relation to certain controversial rights. Shifting emphasis from rights to the limitation of harmful behavior by others could actually be helpful in protecting the vital interests of vulnerable groups (e.g., children). It could also help to enforce a ban on cruelty toward animals, thus rendering useless the controversial concept of animal rights.

However, penal protection of important values neglects the main cause of the international success of human rights: namely, the limited usefulness of penal law to control the unlawful behavior of state organs in charge of issuing, applying, and enforcing laws. Even if Kołakowski's proposal were to be accepted, it would pose all the problems of enforcement that now apply to human rights, as well as the new problem of creating momentum for the adoption of the new "international penal code."[129] If, however, the institution of human rights is maintained, we already have the standards of behavior that were adopted in times far more favorable to the concept of human rights than the present.

---

[128] Kołakowski (2003). It seems that there should, in fact, be two codes; the second one would include all services (and perhaps some goods) that governments are obligated to provide for the people. The access to courts is just one example. In personal conversation (2004), Kołakowski agreed with the need for a second code.

[129] Such a "code" of a sort is being developed by the adjudication of international criminal tribunals. (See Meron 2008b.) It also seems that the concept of the "Responsibility to Protect" that provides criteria for intervention could be further developed to fulfill the role suggested by Kołakowski. It combines prohibitions on certain behavior with obligations to provide specific goods (particularly within the "Responsibility to Prevent" and "Responsibility to Rebuild" phases). Even though the notion of "Responsibility to Protect" has been criticized as embodying a form of "Western imperialism," its most enthusiastic supporters at the United Nations include representatives of Ghana, Mali, and Rwanda (along with Canada, Argentina, Sweden, Switzerland, and the United Kingdom).

Important reasons warrant keeping the concept of human rights alive, particularly with the rise in populism and the growing number of "illiberal democracies" in today's world. First, even the most democratic and liberal countries need a mechanism by which newly emerging moral standards can be transformed into law. Second, even in the best of worlds, cases of rights violations and abuses of power will occur. Human rights provide the victims of such violations with much needed moral justification for their calls for dignified treatment. Third, the temptation for resorting to authoritarian rule, corruption, and abuse of power will always exist. Whenever this threat appears, the need arises to impose limits on abusive leaders from abroad. Human rights provide the necessary criteria for such limitations.

Therefore, instead of disposing with the idea of rights, it seems more prudent to retain the notion of human rights, to prune its content, to detach human rights from the philosophy of human rights, and to develop new, effective mechanisms of enforcement for this new content of human rights. Such rights, narrowed to what is truly common to human nature and shared by most cultures, stand to reclaim their universality. But before either of these routes can be selected, it seems useful to distinguish between the two varieties of universalism already mentioned.

"Hard" universalism holds that the philosophy of human rights is, or ought to be, universal, as well as that it is compatible with all other social philosophies and various cultures. Furthermore, those cultures that do not embrace it are said to be at lower stages of development and should change. "Soft" universalism, in turn, suggests that human rights should be at the core of those common values, without which human coexistence is difficult. It permits, however, that such values be expressed in different ways according to forms defined by different cultures. It also examines criticism against human rights and is open to incorporating select needs, values, and concerns raised by critics as necessary elements of the concept of human rights.[130] "Soft" universalism also concerns itself with helping and empowering members of marginalized or neglected groups that are, at present, outside the allegedly universal concept of human rights.[131]

---

[130] In this respect, "soft" universalism resembles the "inclusive universality" postulated by Brems in conclusion of her seminal book on the subject. Instead of treating non-Western criticism as a call "for exclusion of certain parts of the world from international human rights," one can assume that the critics "ask for improved universality of human rights in the sense of true inclusion of the people, the needs, the concerns and the values of all of the world's societies on all levels of international human rights protection" (Brems 2001, 510). Brems understands criticism as a call for "improved universality of human rights, which at present is unsatisfactory." Her theory proposes "to reconcile international human rights and the diversity of human societies" by making all societies "more receptive to human rights" and by making "international human rights more receptive to a diversity of contexts" (ibid., 511).

[131] One such group is women, despite the high number of women's rights groups and various women's movements. In fact, the status of women may be one of the most difficult cultural differences to reconcile. Hussaina J. Abdullah's comparison of women's groups in Nigeria with the contribution to

"Hard" universalists take a militant stance. They aim at the universalization of values, practices, and institutions. Not only should the ends of political activities be universal but so should the instruments toward these ends. They believe in the evolution of the human species and of cultural practices; thus, they require those who are behind to evolve along the same path taken by the leaders. They are eager to use force – or allow the use of it by others – to impose changes in norms and institutions. At times, "hard" universalists resemble the tyrants themselves, in that their ideas mask and justify ulterior purposes, whether they be world supremacy, greed for resources, or the benefits of free trade.

"Soft" universalists focus on the universality of values and standards and leave room for differentiated cultural practices and institutions, provided these do not increase the violations of rights. They think about protections against potential abuse of political power rather than about the goals and objectives of exercising of power. Though they share the belief in the evolution of societies and standards, they do not impose any evolutionary road. They merely try to share their own road with others. "Look, we have been where you are today, and the following is what helped us to get where we are today. That is how we changed and here are the costs we incurred for it. Perhaps you want to take something from our experience. Here it is." That is the "soft" universalist's message to other cultures. She does not require that others follow her exact path. She does not impose her philosophy of rights on others. She is not certain that individualism is the core of rights and she recognizes the importance of natural communities and other social groups. The "soft" universalist is very cautious about defining the rights that should be universally protected. She distinguishes violations of rights perpetrated by dictators from the ones inflicted by cultures and takes into consideration the specific harms that result from particular violations. She looks for positive mechanisms to limit or stop violations of rights before they assume genocidal proportions and seeks consensus before intervention in other people's affairs. She focuses on helping victims of abuse as much as on punishing the perpetrators.

There are, however, commonalities. Neither "hard" nor "soft" universalism should tolerate genocide, torture, tyrannies, honor killings, genital mutilation, or any kind of public or private oppression, even if it is being justified on political, religious, or cultural grounds. Some acts should be ruled out no matter what their motivations and despite all justifications used to explain them. Human rights must always set the limits on inhuman behavior.

the women's cause by international and local human rights NGOs has led to the conclusion that "in order for the international human rights system to be able to incorporate women's rights issues into a radical transformatory project a reconceptualization of the human rights concept is needed. (. . .) What is needed is a more inclusive and holistic concept of human rights that will embrace the needs and aspirations of all minority and historically marginalized groups, including women" (2000, 119–20).

The "soft" universalist treats human rights primarily as a moral instrument of self-limitation; that is to say, a soft universalist feels obliged to respects the human rights of all people – including those who do not respect such rights between themselves and even if they, most probably, would not respect this universalist's rights. This is why the idea of human rights is incompatible with double standards in international politics, colonialism, or any other expression of superiority. It does for the individual what constitutions do for states. Jon Elster's[132] theory of constitutional precommitment suggests the following analogy: human rights bind the individual to the mast so that this individual is not lured by the sirens "within" destructive emotions such as fear and anger or prejudice against other human beings.

[132] Elster (2002).

5

Human Rights and Other Values

In the past several decades, the language of rights has become extremely popular, with rights at last being recognized as inherent attributes of every human being. Previously, the ability to claim had been a privilege rather than a right. The universality of rights was, at best, a postulate, with their inherent character justifying the proposition that the rights of every person deserve to be respected. But throughout history and across diverse regions of the contemporary world, the majority of people have been deprived of their most basic rights. To claim anything, one had to have power – either sheer physical power (such as that power exercised by a male head of a family over his wife or wives and children); political power (ultimately upheld by the physical power of the sword or another means of coercion); economic power (which elicits favorable responses to demands by an employer or an owner among dependent people); market power (including the use of advertisement or propaganda to influence people's choices); or, finally, power over symbols and emotions, including fears (which renders the rhetoric of gods, national interest, and other cherished values irresistible). For most of history, people who have wielded these types of power have constituted a small fraction of any population. Those who have had the power to make claims on their inferiors have simultaneously had to respond to claims made on them by their own superiors. Most people, however, as slaves or serfs or otherwise dependent persons, could claim nothing. Only relatively recently have the concepts of liberty and rights promised freedom from servitude and prospects for a better life for a larger number of people.

In the 1970s, the rights revolution brought human rights into parliaments, courts, and the new, growing world of nongovernmental organizations (NGOs). The language of rights quickly became the lingua franca of the entire world, providing justification for demands of equality and well-being to non-White people, women, the handicapped, and other excluded groups. People who heretofore could only petition for benevolence or ask for mercy embraced the language of rights, recognizing in it their own ability to claim and their own power to make such claims enforced. Not surprisingly, rights and claims became widespread in politics, society, and personal relations.

Equally unsurprising is the fact that the language of rights has been overused. In international politics, for instance, it is constantly being abused, such as when the double standard and selective enforcement are applied to violations of rights by friendly governments (say, during the Cold War or the "war on terror"), while similar abuses by governments in the opposite camp are met with disapproval or outrage. Actually, such abuses were implied at the very introduction of international human rights, as these restricted the standing to claim violations against the individual to foreign states rather than to the victim of abuse.

A more benign abuse of the rhetoric of rights occurs in those spheres where rights do not belong or when this rhetoric is overapplied where rights may belong with some limitations. There is no surprise that when we have a particularly useful tool we want to believe that it will solve all our problems. So as science searches for that one universal all-encompassing principle of the universe, we attempt to find the key that opens every door to what we perceive as happiness or well-being.

Human rights are often considered such a key. But their success has led to an inflation of rights. For a quarter of a century, almost all needs – not only those related to security and dignity but also the desires for a better life – were formulated and justified within the context of human rights. Thus, human rights have lost their focus, having been watered down to encompass such categories as international relief, the redistribution of resources, and the naive promises of equality and prosperity for all. Many have placed excessive expectations on human rights, only to fault the concept as soon as it turned out that exclusion, wars, violence, and other vices persist. The language of rights, by encouraging people to claim, has fostered the spirit of entitlement. But such an attitude can often lead to conservative reactions that demand replacing the language of rights with one of duties.

The over-application or misapplication of the language of rights may have negative consequences for democratic politics, a viable society, interpersonal relationships, the individual's sense of responsibility, and the collective and personal search for meaning in life. In fact, the inflation of the rhetoric of rights may eventually weaken the idea of rights to such a degree that it leads to its disappearance. History abounds in evidence of great ideas that almost disappeared primarily because of their abuse.[1] Let us, therefore, look more carefully into the spheres where rights should be applied and where they do not belong.

---

[1] Laws of society, social contract, social Darwinism, progress, and the very notion of civilization are just a few examples.

RIGHTS AND DIGNITY

The protection of human dignity is one of the most important functions of all rights.[2] The very act of claiming asserts independence and implies freedom. This is an empirical, observable fact: a serf or a slave begs, while the free individual claims – and does so with dignity.[3] Though claiming expresses dignity in the case of all types of rights, human rights are distinguished by the fact that they were designed specifically for the protection of dignity. The Preamble to the Universal Declaration of Human Rights ranks "inherent dignity" on par with "equal and inalienable rights" as "the foundation of freedom, justice and peace in the world." The reason why the notion of dignity was singled out from other philosophical justifications was largely that the framers of the Declaration could agree on it despite the otherwise insurmountable ideological differences dividing them.[4] "Inherent dignity," as mentioned in the Universal Declaration of Human Rights (UDHR), differs from the concept of "empirical dignity" described and postulated by Feinberg. According to Gewirth, "*Inherent dignity* signifies a kind of intrinsic worth that belongs equally to all human beings as such, constituted by certain intrinsically valuable aspects of being human."[5]

---

[2] For Ronald Dworkin (1977, 199), dignity also justifies having and claiming rights. "It makes sense to say that a man has a fundamental right against the Government, in the strong sense, like free speech, if that right is necessary to protect his dignity, or his standing as equally entitled to concern and respect, or some other personal value of like consequence. It does not make sense otherwise."

[3] "Indeed, respect for persons (this is an intriguing idea) may simply be respect for their rights, so there cannot be the one without the other; and what is called 'human dignity' may simply be the recognizable capacity to assert claims," says Feinberg (1989, 70). Jeno Szucs (1981, 301–302) pictures how dignity was preserved "even under subjection" in a feudal contract: "In general outside Europe – but even in Russian principalities – a 'man of service' would bow to the ground, kiss the hand of his lord or even throw himself down and kiss the hem of his lord's garment. In the Western ceremony of *homagium* the vassal would go down on one knee with head erect, then place his hands into the clasped hands of his lord. The new relation was finally sealed with a mutual kiss." This sense of dignity went along the hierarchy of feudal contracts, all the way down to the peasantry: "every peasant revolt in the West was an expression of enraged human dignity at the landlord's breach of contract, and a demand for the right to 'freedom.'"

[4] Ideological and philosophical controversies preceding the formulation of the Universal Declaration of Human Rights are discussed in detail in Morsink (1999). See also Glendon (2001, 73–8 and 139–46), and Lauren (1998, 219–25).

[5] Gewirth (1992, 12). Inherent dignity has its roots in Immanuel Kant's *Fundamental Principles of the Metaphysics of Morals* (Kant 2001, 191–192), where dignity was opposed to price. Anything that has price can be substituted with or exchanged for something of equivalent value. Although empirical dignity can have a value, Gewirth argues that "inherent dignity cannot be replaced by anything else, and it is not relative to anyone's desires or opinions. It is such inherent dignity that serves as the ground of human rights" (Gewirth 1992, 13).

The connection between human rights and dignity was first examined by Jacques Maritain,[6] whose philosophy of Christian personalism introduced the concept of the equal dignity of each person[7]:

> The human person possesses rights because of the very fact that it is a person, a whole, a master of itself and of its acts, and which consequently is not merely a means to an end, but an end, an end which must be treated as such. The dignity of the human person? The expression means nothing if it does not signify that by virtue of natural law, the human person has the right to be respected, is the subject of rights, possesses rights. These are things which are owed to man because of the very fact that he is man.[8]

In Maritain's interpretation, dignity was linked with the categorical imperative formulated by Immanuel Kant that demanded that a human individual never be used by others or by oneself as the means to other ends.[9]

Human rights certainly serve dignity as understood in Kantian terms. To see this clearly, one needs to go beyond the merely abstract concepts of dignity and rights and look for specific rights that protect and serve the dignity of a person.[10] For it is precisely this connection to dignity that gives deeper meaning to the classification of rights (discussed in Chapter 3) with each category of rights serving dignity in a different manner.

---

[6] In 1947, as a French delegate to the first General Conference of UNESCO in Mexico City, Maritain stated that in conditions of philosophical, ideological, and cultural pluralism it seems impossible to reach consensus on the justification of human rights. He suggested, however, that the dignity of a human person can form a foundation for human rights that every culture can agree on. (See Sugranyes de Franch, 1984. Quoted in Mazurek 2001, 129.)

[7] Before then, dignity was connected with stratification and hierarchy; dignity was acquired with a high office as indicated by the stem of the word *dignitary*. It was this rank-based meaning of dignity, for example, that was used by Edmund Burke in his *Reflections on the Revolution in France*. Meyer (1992, 3–6) claims that, despite the fact that Kant in his moral philosophy located dignity in the nature of man and Thomas Paine called for universal recognition of the "natural dignity of man," Burke's understanding was the dominant one during the Enlightenment. This conventional understanding was contradicted by the notion of "inherent dignity," which would reappear in the UDHR. It is worth noting, however, that the Universal Declaration did not yet recognize dignity as the foundation of human rights. Dignity and rights were considered equally important foundations of "freedom, justice and peace in the world." In 1966, the International Pacts of Human Rights stated that "these rights derive from the inherent dignity of the human person."

[8] Maritain (1951, 65).

[9] In *The Metaphysics of Morals* (Part II, Chapter I, section 2, paragraph 38) Kant suggested that man "is obligated to acknowledge, in a practical way, the dignity of humanity in every other way. Hence he is subject to a duty based on the respect he must show every other man." This duty implies a correlative right. "Every man has a rightful claim to respect from his fellow man." (Kant, 1964, 132, quoted in Gewirth, 1992, 11.) "Thus it is human dignity that justifies the duty of respect and, with it, human rights," concludes Gewirth (ibid.).

[10] Brian Orend (2002, 87–89) questions dignity-based justifications for human rights precisely on the grounds of the vagueness of the abstract concept of dignity.

Civil liberties protect the autonomy of an individual and ban the state from intrusion into the realm of the individual's freedom. By limiting the arbitrariness of decisions by state officials, civil liberties grant a person the degree of security and certainty necessary for one to have rational expectations about one's life. They permit the individual to make her own decisions, to predict the consequences such decisions may have, and, thus, to be able to plan one's actions and to create one's own life rather than merely react to the arbitrary, unpredictable decisions of a superior authority. Civil liberties also provide space for the individual in which to grow. By setting boundaries around that space and granting the individual freedom of choice, civil liberties permit a person to give sense and meaning to one's own life, to be the author of one's destiny. By protecting the rights to expression and association, civil liberties also permit an individual to transcend one's own boundaries and to influence others and bond with other people. As it happens, being the autonomous owner of one's own life and having the ability to give meaning to one's own life are essential elements of dignity.

Political rights allow a person to know about matters concerning the community and to participate – whether by assembly, association, voting, being elected, or other instruments – in the decisions of a community. Here, human dignity is served by the fact that one becomes the subject rather than the object of decisions that concern both the individual and the community to which one belongs. Actually, it has often been argued that a decision made by a benevolent ruler can be better for the subjects than one arrived at by a democratic process heavily influenced by emotions, passions, and interests; often, decisions made by experts are of better quality than ones made by parliaments. Democracy, however, is not about the quality of decisions but about the quality of a community. A society in which no one is excluded from the decisions by way of which rules are instilled, public priorities are set, and resources are distributed is of far better quality than one in which some members are excluded from such decisions.[11] The individual who has a right to participate lives in his community in a more dignified way than one who finds him- or herself under even the most benevolent paternalistic order.

Finally, *economic and social rights* provide the individual with a minimum of economic security, without which one could not participate in society or claim one's

---

[11] The differentiation between goal- and value-related decisions and technical decisions is worth noting in this context. Everyone should participate in the former types of decisions, while the latter type, regarding how to best implement the goals set by the society, can be left to the experts. (For example, a society should decide if it is useful to send a mission to Mars or to allocate resources to another social goal. Once such a decision is made, however, it is experts who should decide how to get to Mars and back safely.) Technocracy's great danger is precisely that the experts, who are not impartial, often have the dominant say in setting public goals. (Examples follow: space experts deciding if the mission to Mars is to take place at all; the military deciding on the need for armaments; or law enforcement agencies deciding on drug policies.)

rights in a dignified way. Although the Universal Declaration of Human Rights does not define the relationship between human rights and dignity, treating them as the common "foundation for freedom, justice and peace," two exceptions can be noted with regard to social rights.[12] Unlike the 1966 covenants on human rights, however, the UDHR does not claim that rights have their origins in dignity but, rather, that dignity cannot exist without rights.

Jacques Maritain strongly emphasizes that social rights are a necessary element of dignity. His description of the dignity of a worker endowed with rights resembles Feinberg's description of the dignity implied by civil liberties. "Involved in a whole cluster of social and economic rights," reasons Maritain

> is first of all the dignity of work, the feeling for the rights of the human person in the worker, the rights in the name of which the worker stands before his employer in a relationship of justice and as an adult person, not as a child or as a servant. There is here an essential datum which far surpasses every problem of merely economic and social technique, for it is a *moral* datum, affecting man in his spiritual depths.[13]

Maritain was not alone. An entire generation of framers of future economic, legal, and political world orders considered full employment an essential goal for the future. Wheelan and Donnelly write, "Beyond the economic and material reasons for seeking a revival of economic activity, and thus employment, Western planners and leaders, haunted by the memory of sustained mass unemployment during the 1930s, stressed the sense of dignity, autonomy, and full and equal participation in society that a job provided."[14]

Deprived of minimal nutrition, shelter and means to face the risks posed by life, one can rarely defy the temptation to use oneself as the means to other people's ends or to stop others from using one as such means. In conditions of deprivation, dignity is always threatened.[15] Social rights that alleviate human plight pave the way

---

[12] "Everyone (. . .) is entitled to realization (. . .) of the economic, social and cultural rights indispensable for his dignity and the free development of his personality" (Article 22). "Everyone who works has the right to just and favorable remuneration insuring for himself and his family an existence worthy of human dignity" (Article 23.3).

[13] Maritain (1951, 104–5).

[14] Whelan and Donnelly (2007, 937).

[15] Leandro Despouy, the United Nations special rapporteur for the study of *Human Rights and Extreme Poverty* submitted to the UN Commission on Human Rights in 1997 made a direct link between poverty, the absence of rights, and the deprivation of dignity. In a section devoted to the principle of "equal dignity of all human beings," Despouy wrote: "'It is not right that we are treated like this – we are human beings, after all,' very poor people often say. 'We feel as though we are dogs. But the dog kennels in the center of town have water and electricity, and we do not. This is really an injustice.' These affronts to dignity follow people living in extreme poverty to the very end of their lives" (quoted in de Vos van Steenwijk 1999, 416.)

toward dignity and facilitate conditions for personal growth made possible by civil liberties.[16]

This complex set of relationships between human rights and dignity provides an argument for the interconnectedness and indivisibility of all categories of human rights – simply because in the absence of any of them, human dignity is threatened. The concept that encompasses all three categories of rights is citizenship.[17] It implies the ability to use legal remedies for the protection of civil liberties, social inclusion, and participation in politics. However, the relationship between rights and politics is mutually reinforcing and limiting. It requires self-limitations on the part of the political actors and on the part of the advocates of rights.

RIGHTS IN THE PUBLIC SPHERE

Rights between the Individual and the State

Essential to the relationship between the individual and the state is the latter's ability to resort to coercion. It is in this sphere that human rights and constitutional rights apply most directly. Human rights have become an attractive instrument to pursue in the public arena – especially as the constant growth of the regulatory function of states and their intrusion into new spheres of social and private lives calls for a countervailing mechanism. Rights provide just such a mechanism, protecting individuals from intrusions, or at least making these intrusions less arbitrary and less painful.[18]

Rights can be construed as a shield that is supposed to protect an individual from abuse by a coercive power or from the state's intrusion into any realm restricted for personal choices. Claim rights assure each individual access to the state, including access to justice that is paramount for one's sense of personal security. This same need for security may also justify some degree of access to state-controlled resources.

---

[16] It is important to be reminded, in this context, that social and economic rights related to dignity are limited to basic economic security rather than equality or other human needs. Moreover, social entitlements, when extended too far and granted unconditionally and irrevocably regardless of one's effort, may be counterproductive to individual responsibility for one's life, actually threatening both the agency and the dignity of an individual.

[17] Dignity is often mentioned in connection with citizenship. For example, in a 2001–2002 study of the attitudes toward citizenship in low-income families in Rio de Janeiro, Joann S. Wheeler found that 75 percent of the participants identified dignity as the most important characteristic of citizenship. "For the participants in this study, it was not their poverty or lack of rights that meant that they had no dignity. Rather, it was the aggregation of everyday interactions and experiences, conflicts and triumphs that meant the difference between dignity and exclusion," writes Wheeler (2005, 109).

[18] See Donnelly (1989, 64).

Somewhat more complex is the role of rights in the public decision-making process. It is assumed that a democratic society makes most of its decisions (which concern either the establishment of universally binding rules of conduct or the redistribution of scarce resources) by way of political process. One essential element of such process is the interplay of interests, principles, and visions of common good. And it is significant that debate about these issues need be ongoing because interests, available resources, visions of common good, and even standards of behavior evolve with time and space. Still, some values are of such fundamental character that they should be designated beyond the reach of political process and insulated from control by a majority. The rights of individuals and minorities are such viable, necessary exceptions from political process. In a well-designed society they are granted constitutional protection.

When treated as trumps, however, rights enter into conflict with democracy, encroaching on the livelihood of the latter and limiting public discussion about values and resources. Overuse of rights limits debate and makes compromise more difficult. Glendon blames the revolution of rights for the atrophy of democratic politics: "Gradually, the courts removed a variety of issues from legislative and local control and accorded broad new scope to many constitutional rights related to personal liberty."[19] Glendon does not propose to dispose of the notion of rights; she agrees that rights "have given minorities a way to articulate claims that majorities often respect, and have assisted the weakest members of society in making their voices heard." She suggests, however, that "one must ask whether an undifferentiated language of rights is really the best way to address the astonishing variety of injustices and forms of suffering that exist in the world."[20]

Glendon can be considered a conservative and critical supporter of rights.[21] But even the most liberal advocates of human rights need to consider very seriously the complex, and often contradictory, relationship between rights and the political process, particularly in a democracy.

In the search for political solutions to social problems, rights may be less effective than debate and compromise. At times, the language of rights even seems misleading. One example concerns the rhetoric of rights often applied to environmentalism. Glendon, for instance, points out that "conservationists are coming to recognize that, where environmental issues are concerned, the biblical language of stewardship may be more appropriate than endowing trees with rights, and more conducive to

---

[19] Glendon (1991, 5–6).
[20] Ibid. (15–16).
[21] Following *The Rights Talk*, Glendon wrote an enthusiastic account of the preparation and implementation of the Universal Declaration of Human Rights. See Glendon (2001).

responsible use of resources than vague promise that everyone has a 'right' to healthy environment."[22]

Understandably, controversy surrounds the role of principles in a constitutional order. Traditionally, most constitutions have included the fundamental principles of a society – most often in the preambles and sometimes also in specific constitutional provisions. Indeed, when a traditional national state concerned itself exclusively with what its citizens had in common, formulating such principles was a relatively straightforward exercise. But in the modern pluralist multicultural society, principles often divide people, giving rise to exclusion. Therefore, some arguments hold that constitutional norms should not include the ultimate principles but, rather, focus on the rules enabling people to coexist, cooperate, and make reasonable expectations of one another – regardless of the differences in principles to which they may adhere.[23]

Rights and Society

It is possible to imagine a constitutional order that need not explicitly state any basic principles. But the society itself cannot exist without them. A society consists of individuals, clustered into such natural groups as family, churches, and neighborhoods, as well as of an extensive network of markets, organizations, and associations whose members join forces to defend their interests and pursue their shared goals. In a pluralist society, there may well be ongoing, open dialog about competing principles and their respective importance. But without principles, be they established or in flux, societies perish. Thus, although a state has just one basic normative order, consisting of the constitution and laws enforced by the state, in a society there coexist multiple sets of principles, as promoted by churches, moral authorities, spokesmen for traditions, and representatives of various types of social groups.

In addition to principles, society needs rights – for a number of reasons. First, rights protect the natural groups within a society from capture, intrusion, or excessive control by the state. Second, rights and freedoms are necessary for safeguarding the conditions conducive to debate within a society. Freedom of speech, freedom of the press, freedom of association, the right to assembly, and other rights and freedoms protect a society not only from threats posed by the state, but also from the danger that the more powerful groups of a society seize control over the less powerful ones and limit the ongoing debate. Furthermore, members of a society have the right to

---

[22] Glendon (1991, 176).

[23] Advocates of the conservative and liberal visions of constitutional order have debated this issue at length. Much of the controversy surrounding the Constitution of the European Union (particularly the values mentioned in its Preamble) is also relevant here. On more about the difference between rules and principles, see Sunstein (1996, 21–34).

be protected from oppression by any other nonstate actors. Such protection usually takes the form of statutes and their enforcement by the state. In the absence of such statutes, international human rights can be applied horizontally.[24]

Thus, rights are indispensable for the existence of a free society. However, rights alone are inadequate for such a society to flourish. In other words, rights provide a necessary but insufficient condition for good society. As mentioned, rights separate individuals from one another, limit dialog and cooperation, make compromises more difficult, enhance competitiveness and conflict, and weaken natural groups. They may also put individual interests above the common good. Conservatives claim that rights weaken the natural groups of society, such as family and church. Communitarian critics suggest that rights weaken local communities and lead to certain interests being placed above the common good – or, in fact, the placing of the individual above the group. This argument should not be taken lightly. Even though, as we have already seen, rights put limits on the coercion that a group can exercise over an individual rather than make the group subordinate to that individual, there exists a danger that individuals may abuse rights and turn them against legitimate interests of a community. Whenever rights turn into excessive claiming and into overwhelming sense of entitlements or selfishness, they may be perceived as undermining a sense of mutual obligations and the moral fabric of the community.

Another communitarian argument against rights holds that "too exclusive a focus on rights (. . .) neglects the crucial importance of political trust" upon which "free societies vitally depend."[25] Because that trust is weakened by the fact that over-litigation of societal discourse limits room for cooperation and compromise, the argument goes, rights wind up separating citizens from one another. This argument also should be taken seriously. It is true that rights may be used to promote selfishness to the neglect of communal values and turn inimical to traditional institutions and cultural norms that serve to limit excessive individualism. Such may be the unintended costs of rights and conscious attempts should be made to limit them.

We now see that rights by themselves are not enough to form and keep society alive. Society needs to be based not just on rights but also on bonds, mutual responsibilities, and the duties undertaken by its members. Although in a constitutional order citizens have just one basic duty – namely to obey the law – in a society, there exists a much richer network of duties, imposed by religion and morals, tradition and customs,

---

[24] The horizontal application of rights seems particularly relevant when one party in a durable relationship can use coercion in any form (physical force, psychological manipulation, or economic control) over another and controls the exit from the relationship.

[25] Taylor (1999, 130).

common standards, and individual expectations.[26] In fact, society's very growth is based on mutual obligations and the people's shared responsibility for the common good. A healthy society is one that manages to turn such a sense of responsibility into an internalized value for most of its members.

Although no society is – or ever should be – free from competition and conflict, there exists more room for compromise in a society that in the state. In fact, in a society many different lifestyles, ideologies, values, and principles can easily co-exist, without any need for compromise. And wherever compromises are needed, society has at its disposal far more abundant resources than any state. After all, the state deals primarily with limited resources, so the appropriation of budgetary reserves to one goal diminishes the amount left for other purposes. A society, by contrast, has at its disposal various unlimited resources; unlimited because their use by one person does not diminish how much is left over for others. Friendship, mutual help, compassion, and love are examples of such resources. If anything, their quantity tends to increase with use. Although by definition neglected in politics, these "human" resources are extremely important for a person's social and individual sense of well-being.[27] In April 2005, the power of love-as-a-resource could be seen in the widespread reaction to the death of Pope John Paul II.

Rights are practically irrelevant to the use and proliferation of these kinds of resources. As noted, the right of every child to be loved unconditionally can be considered the most basic human right. But such a right can never be enforced. Unlike the case of protection from abuse, we cannot actually force adults to love children. Here the language of duties and obligations imposed by a society's moral authorities may be more adequate, even with such moral norms not being enforceable by the courts.

HUMAN RIGHTS IN THE PRIVATE SPHERE

An even larger pool of unlimited resources is available in those private relations between individuals that permit diversified degrees of intimacy. However, in such relationships there exists a great potential for abuse and violence. Immoral laws and practices are not necessarily limited to the relations between the individual and the state. They may also put a person in the intolerable position of subservience, slavery,

[26] It is worth noting, however, that a network of voluntarily accepted duties and obligations can exist only in conditions of freedom. A slave or serf can be under immense pressure from legal and customary duties but is very unlikely to perceive them as constituting obligations toward the community. This may be one reason why in the posttotalitarian state claims and demands based on entitlements are seldom accompanied by an expression of responsibility toward one's community.

[27] This may be a major reason why in most public opinion polls people rank the general economic situation and economic prospects (related to limited resources) as worse off than their personal sense of well-being and happiness.

or victimization vis-à-vis another person. Many abuses take place in private relations that do not involve the state. Moreover, it is often private persons who pose the much more serious threat to the rights of other people than state authorities. Criminals threaten personal security; corrupt entrepreneurs and dishonest employers violate the civil liberties and other rights of employees. It is also increasingly difficult to protect one's rightful interests against abuses by mega-corporations, monopolies, and utility companies. New methods of surveillance; special lenses; Web access to personal data such as credit card information; and numerous other emerging technologies being used by corporations, media, and criminals pose unprecedented threats to privacy and other rights. The question arises: Can human rights be applied between individuals who do not exercise state power? Do they protect individuals against private abuse?

The Horizontal Application of Rights

This problem is known as the "horizontal" application of human rights and it is a subject of much debate.[28] Although in principle the Anglo-American liberal doctrine rejects the application of human rights in the private sphere, in German constitutional theory such an application, called *Drittwirkung*, is considered possible because of the fundamental character of human rights.[29] A comprehensive study on the European Convention on Human Rights contains the following arguments: "Precisely on the account of the fundamental character of these rights it is difficult to appreciate why they should deserve protection in relation to public authorities, but not in relation to private individuals."[30] Furthermore, it has been suggested that the European Convention neither mandates nor prohibits the "horizontal" application of rights, even though among its remedies it does not recognize complaints related to violations of rights by private persons.

It seems logical that rights and freedoms should be protected against all kinds of violations, irrespective of who is the perpetrator. It is law, however, and not human rights that should protect freedoms in private relations. In statutes, codes, and other laws, legislators set limits to people's behavior that affects others. It is a state's duty to protect the rights of everyone within its borders from abuse by other individuals; first, by the criminalization of certain actions and, second, by prosecution of those who break the law. For example, the violation of privacy – say, opening my correspondence without my consent – by a private person is a crime that should be prosecuted in the course of a "normal" application of the penal code.

---

[28] See Sajo and Uitz (2005) for a comprehensive discussion of horizontality.

[29] An additional argument is the concept of a comprehensive scope of the constitution according to which the entirety of social life is subject to the basic principles of the constitution. (See Preuss 2005).

[30] Van Dijk and van Hoof (1990, 17).

The state enforces such laws and gives the individual the power to decide when she wants the state to act in her defense. Civil law protects rights that originate in contracts and torts. Criminal law protects people's freedom and integrity against violations by private persons. Labor law protects an employee from violations of rights by the employer. In cases of private abuse an individual justifies her claims in terms of the law rather than in terms of rights.[31] This strategy is usually simpler and more effective than claiming human rights.

Furthermore – such a strategy is also safer. The horizontal application of human rights involves risks, particularly when it leads to the incorporation of private duties into human rights law. Knox claims that there is no room in human rights law for duties to the society that would be enforced by government acting on behalf of the society. Such duties "have the potential to undermine human rights because the government may rely on them to offset the duties it owes to the individual under human rights law."[32] Within the human rights paradigm, it is the state that has the duty to the individual rather than the individual owing a duty to the state. Human rights enforce such duties of the state and limit the possibility of the state's abuse of its power.[33]

Individual and human rights emerged precisely because it was difficult for an individual to apply "normal" laws when her rights were violated by the state or state officials.[34] Human rights can also be invoked when some rights and freedoms are not protected in the legal order. In such cases, citizens can demand that the state issues laws that will protect their rights and freedoms from "private" violations or apply human rights horizontally using the subsidiarity principle.[35] If the state fails to comply, a citizen can hold this state responsible for harm caused by the neglect.[36] The European Court of Human Rights has stated that the rights included

---

[31] The difference between law and rights is often confused, particularly in languages which use the same core word in both cases (e.g., the Slavic root *pravo*). A relatively simple way to describe the difference is that law regulates the behavior of everyone, including an individual (by mandating or prohibiting certain behaviors), whereas rights regulate the behavior of other persons only.

[32] Knox (2008, 2).

[33] We can also talk about the "horizontality of human rights violations," which takes place when a government knows that it may be held responsible for the abuse of police power. To avoid responsibility, governments often subcontract violence to various formations of private militia. (Such was the case during the January 2008 unrest in Kenya.)

[34] In France, for example, Article 75 of the 1797 Constitution protected state officials against court claims, even when they abused power.

[35] This concept of subsidiarity was applied to horizontality by G. Durig, according to whom "when the good of an individual implied in his citizens' rights is not sufficiently protected by private law, a horizontal application of rights can be used" (quoted in Kedzia 1980, 285).

[36] Van Dijk and van Hoof (1990, 16) suggest that on the grounds of the European Convention such claims are legitimate: "States (. . .) are obliged under the general guarantee clause of Article 1 of the Convention to protect the rights and freedoms set forth in the Convention via the national legal

in the European Convention impose on the states a duty to adopt "measures designed to secure respect for private life even in the sphere of relations of individuals between themselves."[37]

Human Rights as Guiding Principles

It is apparent that some relationships between private parties should be regulated in ways that resemble the human rights paradigm. For example, in situations of hierarchical subordination, the superior party should treat subordinate persons with respect for their autonomy and dignity. Authority needs to be defined in such a way that it limits arbitrariness and gives subordinates a sense of personal security coupled with the ability to predict consequences of actions and plan one's behavior accordingly. Any assignment of authority should also endow subordinates with the right to petition and provide them with accessible instruments to challenge (through the right to appeal) those decisions of their superiors that they consider harmful or unjust.

Human rights should also be considered as a guiding principle whenever an individual falls into relations with other persons and nonstate institutions in which any quasicoercive power can be used against this individual. Such coercion may range from economic domination to religious pressure, subordination within a sect, social disapproval, or exclusion from the group. In extreme cases, the state should be able to use its regulatory power to protect the rights of weaker parties, even when entry into the dependent relationship had been voluntary.

Some social and interpersonal relations resemble the authority of the state over an individual. This is the case whenever a relationship is a durable one and the stronger party can disregard the opinion and will of the weaker party, setting the norms and resorting to coercive measures to enforce them – and thus controlling the weaker party's capacity to exit from the relationship. On one extreme of this spectrum are children and on the other are old people with a diminished mental capacity to express their own will or their lack of physical ability to enforce it. Pupils in school; medical patients (particularly psychiatric patients); and, in many cultures and legal systems, wives and rural workers on plantations in, say, southern India; as well as multiple other groups belong to this category. Yes, the rights of many of these

system. If one starts from the principle of Drittwirkung, such states also have to secure to individuals protection against violations of their fundamental rights by other individuals by means of national provisions of penal and civil law. If the competent national authorities default in this respect or if the said provisions of national law are not enforced, responsibility arises for the State concerned, a responsibility which may be brought up via the procedure under Article 25, or Article 24, of the Convention."

[37] Quoted in Clapham (1993, 89). The case of X and Y v. The Netherlands, 1985 (see ibid., 197–201).

groups are protected by international conventions and national laws.[38] But whenever such protections turn inadequate, there are strong arguments that in relations such as these the concept of human rights deserves to be applied directly. In fact, there exist subsections of human rights theory dealing specifically with children's rights, pupils' rights, patients' rights, and the like.[39]

Customary use – and, often, abuse – of force by parents, teachers, and other authorities, combined with the inherent arbitrariness of parental authority and the inability to clearly define its limits, has prompted some framers to offer constitutional protection to children. Indeed, children lack the ability to define their rights, assess their own interests, and perceive those situations in which their rights are abused. They also lack the capacity to defend themselves. Therefore, some countries have created special constitutionally grounded offices of the ombudsman for children rights.[40] Increasingly, children are also offered an opportunity to speak their mind. The Convention of the Rights of the Child gives children the right to express their views "freely in all matters affecting the child, the views of the child being given due weight in accordance with the age and maturity of the child," as well as the right "to be heard in any judicial and administrative proceedings affecting the child."[41]

Children's rights are controversial. The main arguments in favor of such rights focus on a child's interests, autonomy, and development.[42] Martin Guggenheim,

---

[38] For example, the UN Convention on the Rights of the Child (1989), preceded by the Geneva Declaration of the Rights of the Child of 1924 and the Declaration of the Right of the Child adopted by the UN General Assembly in 1959.

[39] Another category of this kind consists of prisoners. But this does not involve the problem of horizontal application, for prisoners are under the jurisdiction of the state. Thus, human rights apply to prisoners directly, even if the state places them in private prisons. In private prisons, however, the potential for abuse grows and the ability to monitor and challenge abuse diminishes. This is one of a number of reasons why private prisons are immoral and should be banned in any state that claims to respect rule of law and human rights.

[40] For an example, see Article 72, section 4 of Poland's Constitution.

[41] Article 12 of the Convention. A similar right is provided for in Article 72, section 3 of the 1997 Constitution of Poland, where the inclusion of children rights in the Constitution caused a bitter debate before the document was ratified by popular referendum. The provisions on children's rights were perceived by the Catholic Church and conservative parties as an attack on the integrity and autonomy of the family. Ultimately, the argument prevailed that the child should have rights protecting her from gross abuse, family violence and disrespect to a child's dignity. But the proposal to extend such protection across relations within the marriage was rejected by Poland's Constitutional Assembly. A similar controversy accompanied the 1992 debate on a provision of the draft Bill of Rights banning corporal punishment. (See Chrusciak and Osiatyński 2001, 202–13.)

[42] Eekelaar combines all three arguments: "Under my ordering, the claims revolve around children's 'basic' interests (to physical, emotional and intellectual care); their 'developmental' interests (that their potential should be developed so that they enter adulthood as far as possible without disadvantage) and their 'autonomy' interests (the freedom to choose a lifestyle of their own). The first of these has preeminent status" (1992, 230–1). The developmental aspect of children's rights is emphasized in Article 29 of the UN Convention on the Rights of the Child. (See Eekelaar 1992, 231; Freeman 1992, 65; and Campbell 1992, 18.)

however, a long-time defender of children and advocate of their interests, has pointed out some negative consequences of the ascent of children's rights.[43] First, campaigns for children's rights may disrupt and negatively influence families. Often, children end up institutionalized in cases when patience and caring work to heal the family would be more beneficial. Second, an assertion of children's rights does not, in fact, grant more rights to children. They are still dependent; it is merely that the control over them moves from the family and into the hands of impersonal courts and state officials. Third, the rhetoric of children's rights is primarily aimed at families and does not protect children from the state; moreover, because children are treated in the same way as adults (who do possess constitutional rights), the United States is the only country in the world that has actually tolerated both the death penalty and life imprisonment as legitimate punishments for minors. Guggenheim suggests that the protection of children from the state would be more effective if the focus were moved from children's rights to constitutional limitations on the application of state power to any human being and to the assertion of the needs of children.[44] Finally, the campaign for children's rights has led to the emergence of a lobby of children's lawyers who have effectively become the leaders of the movement and whose campaigning has saturated family relations with legal reasoning and conflicts.[45] Often, children's rights are claimed by lawyers not in the interest of the child but in their own professional self-interest or in the interest of other adults who use children for their own aims. In actuality, the interests of children would be much better served by emphasis on children's needs and the responsibilities of adults than by the direct claiming of children's rights.[46] "If children's rights advocates could recast claims on behalf of children from rights to what is fair and just for children, perhaps we could recapture a time when adults would better accept their responsibilities toward children. However inadvertently, our current emphasis on children's rights reduces the pressure on adults to do right by children," concludes Guggenheim.[47]

This criticism is valid. An excessive rhetoric of rights can be counterproductive and harmful to interpersonal relationships. Nevertheless, in cases of abuse, violence, or drastic neglect, children should be protected even within their own family. But

---

[43] Guggenheim (2005).

[44] "At least in the United States, the strongest arguments for treating children better, in almost every context, will stress their needs and interests. It is considerably more straightforward to argue against an adultlike sentence for children based on children's interests and needs" (Guggenheim 2005, 265).

[45] Ibid. (8).

[46] Similarly, Onora O'Neill recognizes both theoretical and political reasons to focus on the obligations of adults rather than on children's rights directly: "If we care about children's lives, we will have a number of good reasons not to base our arguments on appeals to children's fundamental rights" (1992, 39).

[47] Guggenheim (2005, 266).

such protection should be assured by family law and penal law alone, without the need to invoke the concept of rights. However, when the law does not offer such protection – or when the law exists but is neglected – the assertion of rights can protect victims and compel state authorities to issue and enforce proper laws.[48]

An analogy with human rights may also apply to relations within the marriage, particularly when the principle of "husband authority" is combined with the use of violence toward wives.[49] There is no doubt that in a number of contemporary societies women are subordinated to the durable coercive power of men and do not have the power to exit from this situation of subservience.[50] A number of countries alleviate the situation by adopting laws on domestic violence,[51] but a more general issue of women's rights vis-à-vis men's domination still awaits an adequate constitutional and international solution.[52] The difficulty lies in the fact that the gravest, perhaps insurmountable, differences between disparate cultures in today's world concern precisely this issue.

Between Morality and Law

We have just seen an additional role of human rights. Rights are helpful in developing and shaping norms that can be applied between individuals. Such standard-setting roles of rights can be generalized.

As is known, not all human rights are enforced. Some rights are unenforceable because of the lack of suitable mechanisms, others because of the absence of political

---

[48] Guggenheim's probable agreement with this conclusion is implied in his belief that "modern society recognizes its responsibility to protect vulnerable children from abuse, even when that abuse is inflicted by their parents" (ibid., 2).

[49] A special category of "wives' rights" could be justifiably created. In a great number of countries in today's world, marriage in practice means that a woman gives up, in relations with her husband, those instruments of protection that defend her from strangers. For example, if a stranger beats or rapes a woman, she can seek redress. But when the perpetrator is a woman's husband, the wife, when seeking help from police, prosecutors, or ministers, usually ends up being told that she should be a better wife.

[50] In Peru, up to two million young girls from poor rural families (of a total population of twenty-four million) are kept as domestic servants in the nation's cities, often in conditions of slavery and without any legal assistance. In Africa, Central and Eastern Europe, and other regions, young women are deprived of all rights and personal freedoms and forced into prostitution. In Asia, child labor is still prevalent. Domestic violence is a worldwide problem.

[51] In December 1993, the UN General Assembly adopted the *Declaration on the Elimination of Violence Against Women*. Protection from domestic violence is granted by domestic laws in most of the states of the Unites States of America. In Latin American states, victims of violence are also protected by the Inter-American Convention on the Prevention, Punishment, and Eradication of Violence Against Women (1994). In India, the *Protection of Women against Domestic Violence Act* was adopted in 2005. These laws, important as they are, have not yet changed the actual situation of women.

[52] Until very recently, perpetrators of rape in noninternational armed conflicts were not held criminally responsible (see Meron 1993 and 2008b, 14). This has begun to change with the establishment of international criminal tribunals.

will, and others still will forever remain in the realm of ideals and moral standards because of their very nature. It would be unwise to legalize rights that cannot be implemented by force of law. For example, every person may enjoy moral and human rights to happiness, but such rights cannot be enforced. Every person has a moral and human right to live in truth, but it is impossible to enforce that no one lie to anybody else. Some human rights will remain moral human rights in the sense that they cannot be enforced by law even thought they still can be upheld by customs, traditions, churches, and other social institutions and the other tools by which moral standards are sanctioned. As noted, the right of a child to be loved will forever remain a moral right, even though such a right morally overrides many other values.

Some human rights were granted legal protection only after having first been claimed for some time as moral rights. In fact, it seems that the very concept of human rights plays an important role as a mechanism that helps to legalize changes to moral standards. Such changes usually begin with a group of people who are either dissatisfied with the normative constraints of a time or seek acceptance for new lifestyles and freedoms. Recently, many such moral claims are being justified in terms of human rights. And if a new claim reflects the concerns and needs of a majority, it may be accepted as a matter of right. Most often, however, it takes time and effort for the proponents of a new standard to convince the majority – or the judiciary – to acknowledge such standard by law.

Human rights, then, can be used as a mechanism through which new moral claims (e.g., to new dimensions of privacy) or moral claims of members of discriminated or newly identified social groups (e.g., ethnic or cultural minorities, homosexuals or HIV-positive people) can push their way into the legal order. New human rights may also emerge when societies recognize that they can afford to protect legally claims that had not been recognized as human rights in the past. In this way, some Western societies granted social rights legal protection as a result of economic growth, through statutory instruments of the welfare state. Maurice Cranston observed that "the moral claims of today are often the legal rights of tomorrow."[53]

The concept of human rights works in a negative capacity as well by helping to delete from the books of law those norms that violate human rights standards. Examples include bans on torture and degrading forms of punishment, outlawing corporal punishment, and deleting from penal codes provisions that limit a person's freedom to choose lifestyles (e.g., same-sex sexual acts).[54]

---

[53] Cranston (1973, 82).
[54] "Human rights as moral rights constitute the moral background of institutional rights (legal rights) and provide legal and moral agents with feasible criteria of moral justification and moral criticism of positive law and legal order (created by the state) or of other institutional settings (. . .) they set up universal standards of appraisal of political systems and legal orders, stimulate changes in existing

Considering this role of human rights as an instrument of transmission between morality and positive laws, the various declarations of rights in international documents and constitutions begin to appear in a new light. It is true that without mechanisms for enforcement such rights cannot be practically claimed or used in the defense of individuals and minorities. But even the declarations provide justification to the moral claims of the victims of abuse and people who struggle for their rights.[55] A declaration of rights is a political acknowledgment of a moral right, even when it is not enforced. It provides criteria for the assessment of the law itself, as well as arguments for those who want to change immoral laws.[56] They can succeed if they persistently act to change social conditions and human consciousness. But even if they fail, the very struggle for rights can give them a sense of meaning and purpose in life. Such struggle may be, in fact, more meaningful than the rights themselves.

BEYOND RIGHTS

The horizontal application of human rights renders them useful not only in the public sphere but also in private relationships. This is particularly true in the age of globalization, with many abuses being committed by private parties acting outside the territory of their own state and thus escaping control. But this is not the only reason why rights are so attractive in private relationships. Rights (any rights, not just

legal regulations and are good reasons for disobedience to inhuman laws enacted and enforced by the states" (Lang 1991, 18).

[55] As noted, until the late 1960s, the anticommunist opposition in Poland justified its claims by invoking otherwise empty provisions of the 1952 Polish Constitution. In the mid-1970s, however, with the ratification of the human rights pacts and with the Helsinki Agreement, the justification shifted to international human rights. Ultimately, the Communist Constitution was discarded altogether by the opposition.

[56] The justification of laws in moral terms has been a perennial problem for lawgivers, who have always looked for ways of sanctifying the law. Moses claimed that he received his tables directly from God. Before enacting the Laws of Twelve Tables, Hammurabi reported being enlightened by the goddess Ishtar and the god Marduk. Grzybowski (1967, 19) explains how the rulers of ancient kingdoms nationalized religion and provided gods with a new role, that of the source of justice and the laws imposed by the rulers. Similarly, also allegedly God-given were the laws promulgated in modern times by absolutist rulers (who also invoked the newly elaborated concept of state sovereignty). With the Enlightenment it seemed that the "supernatural" sanction given to laws was replaced by reason and tradition; God, however, was still present. A popular late-eighteenth-century American etching presents George Washington as a giver of God's laws to Americans (see J. P. Elven 1800; the etching was presented at the Utopia exhibition in the New York Public Library in 2000–2001. For the reproduction, see Shaer et al. 2000.) With nineteenth-century positivism, the source of laws shifted to the sovereign power of the state. With democracy – to voters. But when the dangers of majoritarian democracy were seen and experienced during World War II – human rights were conceived to limit sovereign power and to serve as justification for "just" laws. The acceptance of human rights as the criteria for assessment of positive law was their first victory over the principle of sovereignty.

human rights) truly are the most effective strategy of getting what we need or want from others.

Claiming vs. Giving

In 1970, in a famous article published in *The Journal of Value Inquiry*, the great philosophar of law, Joel Feinberg, invented an imaginary place called "Nowheresville" – essentially an unnamed but familiar "anytown" distinguished by only one thing: the absence of rights. Feinberg argued that the lack of rights would make Nowheresville "too ugly to hold too long in contemplation."[57] Without rights, people can ask, petition, or beg those who make the decisions in matters that influence their lives – but they are not able to claim. Such methods all imply the weaker position of the petitioner, encouraging servility or manipulation. Claiming, in contrast, reflects a basic equality of situations, despite the actual (and often desirable) differences in social position or the existing structure of decision making and power. "Having rights, of course, makes claiming possible; but it is claiming that gives rights their special moral significance," wrote Feinberg.[57]

In the absence of rights, there exist three ways in which a person can fulfill one's needs that cannot be satisfied by her own actions. One such strategy is taking, including the taking of the products of one's own labor. The problem with taking is that most goods have already been taken by somebody else, and now they are protected by property laws that strongly discourage any further taking by others. Once upon a time, this discouragement was by threat of the gallows; today, it is imprisonment. Furthermore, often virtually all of the fruits of one's toil are taken away by land owners, the proprietors of workshops, or the mega-corporations that do the hiring; the owners are the ones with the claim to the greatest share.

Another strategy for getting what one wants consists of asking, begging, and otherwise pledging, so that a person who controls something needed by a petitioner becomes willing to grant the request. Asking, however, reflects and reinforces an inequality of positions. When I ask, I make myself vulnerable: you can either give me what I want or you can refuse my request at will. Such arbitrariness is hard to cope with. Refusal is commonly perceived as rejection, and it can cause a sudden drop in one's self-esteem and sense of worth. Everyone who has ever faced refusal, particularly in the sphere of intimate relations, knows how painful and destructive it can be.

The third strategy consists of manipulation, and it actually aims to minimize the risk inherent to pursuing what one wants because, in manipulating, one simply does not ask directly for what he or she wants. Instead, say I create a situation in which you are supposed to guess my needs and fulfill them without my asking. If you do not, I can judge you as "merciless," "heartless," "insensitive," or "selfish." Manipulation is an

---

[57] Feinberg (in Winston 1989, 87).

extremely popular life strategy, particularly among powerless people. In fact, it seems to be the only accessible strategy to slaves, serfs, adolescent children of controlling parents, and wives dominated by their husbands. Manipulation is quite effective, but it has its price. It consists of treating other people instrumentally and prevents the manipulator from taking responsibility for her own life. In addition, because both parties either know or sense the dishonesty inherent to the manipulation, that price is the loss of trust. Nevertheless, many individuals and subcultures encourage manipulative behavior.

Most cultures support asking, pledging, and petitioning. More precisely, most cultures impose some duties and obligations on those who control power and resources to limit the potential for abuse of power and to "humanize" the use of resources. Thus, mercy and charity are duties of gods, and providing slaves and serfs with basic food and shelter are duties of a master. Though such moral obligations are sometimes confused with rights, or considered to be antecedents of rights, they do not result in the individual's ability to make claims on those who exercise power or control the resources. Finally, in cases of asking or manipulation, one cannot truly control the outcome; claiming a right, in turn, permits the individual to plan his or her own future and to be in control of his or her life.

The ability to claim implies both an equality of position and the availability of a mechanism for the enforcement of one's claim. These features characterize only privilege and, more recently, rights. Joel Feinberg has posited that it is, in fact, the ability to claim that is essential for self-respect and dignity.

> Having rights enables us to "stand up like a man," to look others in the eye, and to feel in some fundamental way the equal of anyone. To think of oneself as the holder of rights is not to be unduly but properly proud, to have that minimal self-respect that is necessary to be worthy of the love and esteem of others. (. . .) To respect a person then, or to think of him as possessed of human dignity, simply *is* to think of him as a potential maker of claims.[58]

Thus, claiming can be said to be the most attractive strategy for getting our needs and desires met.

Claiming, however, also has its costs. It may distance people or even separate them entirely from each other. Rights are designed to set boundaries and shield us from others who might abuse their power or position. In fact, it would be very difficult to build significant bonds between human beings on the basis of rights alone. In a rights-based society any stranger can be perceived as a potential adversary. Conflict and litigation, in turn, limit our tendency for cooperation and compromise, potentially even thwarting our ability to listen to the reasons, values, and motivations of another

---

[58] Ibid. (69–70). For Feinberg (1970), it is the activity of claiming that "makes for self-respect and respect for others, gives a sense to the notion of personal dignity" (ibid., 74).

person. Glendon observes that the language of rights may actually "foreclose further communication with those whose point of view differs from our own."[59] Such a tendency may impoverish human relations, which tend to grow freely only when there is room for coexisting viewpoints and ideas and only when there exists mutual respect, despite naturally occurring disagreement. Human relations also require that we employ our ability not to always be right – and to admit that one has been wrong. The strict application of rights interferes with these human needs. An excessive focus on rights essentially weakens human bonds, limits trust, and precludes intimacy.

The Right Not to Claim Rights

In Feinberg's "Nowheresville," where citizens had no ability to claim, no one could feel the rightful owner of one's life. People would react instead of acting. There would be no room for self-respect, for respecting others, or for human dignity. The place described by Feinberg looks grim.[60]

Feinberg's essay quickly became popular and it was reprinted in numerous books. One of them, *Bioethics and Human Rights*, was published just 8 years after the original. This time, however, Feinberg asked the editors to permit a two-page "Postscript."[61] In this addendum, Feinberg asks the reader to imagine Nowheresville II, "where almost everyone performs his duties to others faithfully and always insists upon his own rights against others." In such a society, "debtors are never forgiven their debts, wrongdoers pardoned, gratuitous debts conferred, or sacrifices voluntarily made, so long as it is within one's rights to refuse to do any of these things."[62]

Feinberg was saying that being truly human implies the ability to waive one's right. If we were always to enforce all our rights and could never waive them, the world would be an inhuman place, devoid of love, compassion, giving, and forgiveness. No bonds would form on the basis of trust. There would be no affection at all.

This does not mean that affection would flourish in a world without rights or that a benevolent ruler could deprive people of rights to foster affectionate bonds between them. Just the opposite; one has to have rights in the first place to be able to waive them.[63] Such choice in exercising rights is essential to our moral capacity. "To have a right, typically, is to have the discretion or 'liberty' to exercise it or not,

---

[59] Glendon (1991, 9).

[60] Grim, but not impossible. When I first read Feinberg's essay, in Poland, under Communist rule, I wrote "Nowheresville is where we live" in the margin.

[61] Feinberg (1978).

[62] Ibid. (32).

[63] "Understanding that one has rights, of course, is not *sufficient* for one to have an admirable character, for one might yet be a mean-spirited Pharisee, unwilling ever to be generous, forgiving, or sacrificing. But consciousness of one's rights is *necessary* for the superogatory virtues, for the latter cannot even be given a sense except by contrasts with the disposition always to claim one's rights" (ibid., 33).

as one chooses. This freedom is another feature of rights-ownership that helps to explain why rights are so valuable." It is only

> when a person has a discretionary right and fully understands the power that posses-sion gives him, he can if he chooses make sacrifices for the sake of others, voluntarily give up what is rightfully his own, freely make gifts that he is in no way obligated to make, and forgive others for their wrongs to him by declining to demand the compensation or vengeance he may have coming or by warmly welcoming them back into his friendship and love. Imagine what life would be like without these saving graces.[64]

To benefit fully from the concept of rights and to use them to foster the growth of our human potential then, we need to have a complete concept of rights. We need to know not only when and how to claim our rights, but also when and how "to release, waive, or surrender" them. In interpersonal relationships, we should be able not only to claim but also to risk asking other people what we want of them. As noted, the risk in asking is that our request may be refused: we feel rejected, our self-esteem receives a blow, and our self-worth declines. One way to minimize this risk is to explicitly acknowledge the other person's right to say no. It is also important to detach the request and any potential refusal from one's sense of self-worth. If you ask me for my pen and I refuse, I have not made a statement about you or your worth in my eyes; I have merely made a statement about myself and the worth of my pen for me. I need this pen or I am attached to this pen and I do not want to part with it. The same applies when one asks somebody else for help, a favor, or attention.

In an ideal world, human relationships would be based on love, compassion, friendship, and affection. In the real world, however, friendships often end, love is betrayed, compassion can be abused, and feelings wind up misguided. Therefore, we need some instruments for protection when good intentions fail. For Jeremy Waldron, rights play the role of such fall-back mechanisms precisely when inter-personal bonds based on feelings fail or when communitarian bonds turn out to be inadequate or oppressive. "Having something to fall back on if attachment fails may be a condition of being able to identify intensely with one's attachments, rather than something which derogates from that intensity."[65] When affection fails and the trust on which personal relationships are based is betrayed, rights are needed. They are also important in every type of more intimate relationship (including, of course, marriage) in which there is room for coercion or abuse, regardless of whether the victimized party accepts it.

Feinberg and Waldron's theories seem to complement each other. Although Feinberg begins with rights as the necessary condition for social relations, Waldron

---

[64] Ibid. (32).
[65] Waldron (1988, 647).

believes that rights do not – and should not – play the most important role in the social aspects of life, suggesting that liberals should "concede that the structure of rights is not constitutive of social life, but instead to be understood as a position of fall-back and security in case other constituent elements of social relations ever come apart."[66]

According to Waldron, rights are needed not only when bonds are broken. Welfare rights play a similar role of fall-back mechanisms in private contracts and on labor markets. Rights also help strangers enter into new relationships because, among strangers, there is little preexisting trust and, thus, little room for affection.

> The structure of impersonal rules and rights not only provides a background guarantee; it also furnishes a basis on which people can act to initiate new relationships with other people even from the position of alienation from the affective bonds of existing attachments in community. Impersonal rights provide basis for new beginnings and for moral initiatives which challenge existing affections, driving them in new directions or along lines that might seem uncomfortable or challenging to well-worn traditional folkways.[67]

Here we see the role of rights in human relationships. Though not basic to such relationships, they nonetheless provide the necessary conditions for a relationship to flourish. First, there can hardly be affection, compassion, or giving in the absence of rights and the ability to waive rights. Second, even when we put rights aside to benefit from the growing depth of a relationship, we do not give them away for good. We remain entitled to take our rights back if our trust is betrayed or abused.

Such is the essence of the inalienability of rights. They are not inalienable in the sense that we cannot forsake a right or that we always have to exercise and enforce what rights we have. But, even when we act on the basis of deeply felt trust, we should not be able to forfeit our rights for good. For when our trust, love, and compassion are betrayed, we should be able to retrieve our rights in the act of justified self-defense.[68] Rights are needed – even when it may be nice to forget about them. But it is certainly useful to forget about them if we want to have meaningful relationships with other people. Such relationships cannot be based on rights. Trust, friendship, and love demand commitment, affection, and, at times, sacrifice. Compassion, giving, and

---

[66] Ibid. (629).

[67] Ibid. (631).

[68] This is not too great a departure from the sense of inalienability described in John Locke's original theory, which placed inalienability in the context of the social contract in which people transferred some limited powers to the ruler (thus alienating these powers from themselves). They retained, however, all other rights (which were inalienable). Locke posited that even if people were to give these latter rights away to a ruler on the basis of contract, such a contract would be not valid. If a ruler were to fail to fulfill his obligations, or to abuse power, the people would be entitled to revoke the contract and repossess even those rights which they had transferred.

forgiveness, as discussed by Feinberg, are not enhanced by strict adherence to rights. A meaningful relationship is not possible in the absence of the freedom to choose whether one wants to stay in that relationship or leave it. Rights protecting each party from abuse are necessary, but a relationship's depth is to be discovered through the exploration of values and attitudes other than the exercise of one's rights.

RIGHTS AND THE PURSUIT OF HAPPINESS

For Thomas Jefferson and the coauthors of the Declaration of Independence, the pursuit of happiness was one of the three inalienable rights, as basic as life and liberty. But most people would say that happiness is more than just a right. Rather, happiness is a highly complex concept and its pursuit requires more than mere liberty. In fact, the notion of happiness is closer to a person's sense of meaning in life than to rights as such.

Of course, it is difficult to give purpose and meaning to one's life without rights and freedoms. Without certain rights, a person cannot be the owner of his or her own life. For it is rights and freedoms that delineate an individual's boundaries and bestow on him or her the space to be, act, grow, and live according to one's own plan and values. Without rights one does not act but merely *reacts* to the acts of others.

Rights and freedoms are necessary preconditions for our conscious actions and choices but they do not predetermine these choices. By themselves, rights do not provide our lives with meaning. Let us consider the difference between freedom and the fight for freedom in conditions of oppression. A freedom fighter exercises fewer freedoms than other members of his or her – otherwise oppressed – society. He or she does not frequent public places, avoids normal telephone communication, often goes into hiding and restricts exercise of tens of other everyday rights and freedoms that permit others to feel relatively happy. At the same time, however, the freedom fighter usually has less trouble finding meaning in his or her life than the completely free person. The freedom fighter limits his or her own freedom to give life purpose.

The same holds under less extreme conditions. A sense of meaning or purpose in life constitutes a philosophical and ethical concept rather than a legal one, and it is less about one's relations with others and more about one's relation with oneself. Often, it is also a concept closely tied to the relationship one experiences with a protecting transcendental being in whose existence and guidance one believes. The sense of purpose in life is far less likely to come from consumption and far more likely to follow self-limitation, self-restraint, and commitment. And the essential element of commitment is precisely the self-limitation over one's freedoms that must be assumed for the benefit of those other, more meaningful values. Thus, meaning and purpose can be derived from family, nation, revolution, friends, the God of one's understanding, and anything else that provides one with a mission. And it is living up to one's commitment that, quite often, gives people the deepest sense of happiness.

To be able to make a commitment, one needs to be free in the first place.[69] Even the most benevolent ruler cannot make a commitment for anybody else. A ruler cannot say: "We all know that freedom by itself doesn't give happiness. Therefore, I will restrain your freedom to give meaning to your lives and to make you happy." The people will not be happy. Sooner or later, some will begin to fight against this oppression. And when they win their freedom, they will have to find out what to do with it. They may abuse it, or lose it, or arrive at a meaningful commitment. If, indeed, what they find is commitment, they will thus leave the realm of law and rights and enter the sphere of ethics.

RIGHTS AND ETHICS

The discipline of ethics is not about rights. It is about self-restraint and self-limitations. Conversely, rights are not necessarily about ethics. Rather, rights are simply good for protecting our freedoms and possessions and for claiming what others owe us. But the rhetoric of rights has little to say about sharing and giving or love, forgiveness, and similar principles of personal ethics mentioned in the Sermon on the Mount and other sacred texts. Religion is much closer to ethics than are rights.[70]

Ethics can exist without rights and freedoms. Ethical systems can be based on duties and limits imposed on the individual, as is the case with a great majority of religious systems. Moral restraints can be built on fear of punishment and eternal damnation; hierarchical churches that upheld their norms by such beliefs usually

---

[69] In the mid-1980s, as I was developing a university course titled "Rights, responsibilities and commitments," I had trouble with finding a Polish term for "commitment." When I realized that professional translators whom I consulted had similar difficulties, it occurred to me that Polish culture, as reflected in language, might not have yet developed a sense of responsible freedom.

[70] Perry (1998, 5) claims that the very idea of human rights has "ineliminably religious character." It is so because the basic tenet of the philosophy of rights, i.e., that human rights are sacred, is religious. Perry rejects Ronald Dworkin's thesis that there can also exist a secular justification of the sanctity of life (see ibid., 25–29). Regardless of that discussion we have seen that basic values underlying human rights are also present in a majority of religions. Moreover, a great number of people who fought for rights of others or helped victims of abuse – from the abolitionists to individuals who helped the Indians in North America and the aborigines in Australia, to the people who risked their lives to save the Jews in Nazi-occupied Europe, to those who carried relief and medical help to Srebrenica and Rwanda – were motivated by religious beliefs and the spirit of brotherhood expressed in the story of a good Samaritan. Some of the most well-known applications of socially responsible economic activity sprung from religious motivation. Basic tenets of social investing were first outlined by one of the founders of Methodism, John Wesley (1703–1791). It was the Religious Society of Friends (Quakers) who first prohibited members from participation in slave trade (1758).

are hostile to the very concept of rights.[71] One can even be held responsible for one's acts without rights, as when the nonfree person, such as a slave or serf, is punished for a purported transgression. But one can rarely *feel* responsible for one's acts without rights and freedoms. Without the ability to make significant choices about one's own life, no person can truly feel responsible for it. There can exist no ethics of responsibility without freedom.[72]

It seems that rights can also play a more specific role in the ethical system. First, rights can still constitute the fall-back mechanism that reinforces the ethical system with the power of the state in those cases where ethical norms are insufficient to protect people from abuse or violations. Second, human rights can play an important role as a guide for the self-limitations postulated by ethics. When I adhere to the philosophy of human rights and treat rights seriously, I should respect, in my own behavior, the rights of all human beings, even when some of them do not observe the same human rights norms, be it among themselves or in their acts directed toward me. This latter limitation is a difficult one to accept and belongs to the highest ethical standards.

Claiming rights takes place on a lower level of the ethical system. The remainder of ethics stretches far beyond rights. Whenever we enforce our rights strictly, we act according to the law, but we tend to fall below the standards of ethics. In the words of Feinberg, again:

> Even knowing that one has rights and being prepared to act accordingly are not sufficient (but only necessary) for a fully human and morally satisfactory life. A person who never presses his claims or stands on his rights is servile, but the person who never waives a right, never releases others from their correlative obligations, or never does another a favor when he has a right to refuse to do so is a bloodless moral automaton. If such a person fully understands and appreciates what rights are and invokes that understanding in justification of his rigid conduct, he is a self-righteous pig as well. If he can also truly testify that he always conscientiously performs *his*

---

71 The relationship between organized religions and human rights is complex. On the one hand, the churches can violate rights and lead to extermination as was the case with religious wars and persecution, with the church's protection for the conquista and other forms of colonial expansion, and with the jihad. ("It takes religion to make good people to do evil" goes a popular saying.) On the other hand, many churches have provided help and relief to individual victims of abuse. Often, religious scripts can be read as providing arguments both in favor of rights and against them. This seems to be the case with Islam. "'Islam' has become the vehicle both for political protest against undemocratic regimes and for the repression meted out by such regimes, simultaneously expressing aspirations for democracy and equality and providing rationales for campaigns to crush democratic freedoms and perpetuate old patterns of discrimination," writes Mayer (2007, xiv).

72 The issue of responsibility was crucial for those Catholic philosophers, including Emmanuel Mounier, Jacques Maritain, and Karol Wojtyła, who combined ethics based on the Commandments and the Sermon on the Mount with the concept of human rights.

duties to others and respects *their* rights, he has then achieved "the righteousness of the scribes and Pharisees."[73]

CONCLUSION

In lieu of a conclusion, I include a letter that I used to send – along with graded final exams – to students who took a course on individual and human rights.

Dear Student,

Congratulations on the successful completion of a course on human rights. I hope that you will be able to claim your rights and respect and protect the rights of others. I also hope that you will be able to distinguish between those situations in which your rights should come to the foreground and those in which they should be kept in the background and used only when necessary. Below, I'm including some guidelines.

Be aware of your rights – and of the mechanisms that may help you exercise them – whenever you face a coercive arm of the state. But as a citizen and a voter, try to balance those interests and desires that should be protected by rights with those that are open to compromise in the process of setting public policy goals. Remember that your participation in such compromises, even when it involves costs on your part, makes society better. In the relations you engage in as a member of society and its various social groups, carefully balance your rights with obligations, duties and all other mechanisms that enhance mutual trust and respect between you and others.

Enter private relationships with hope, trust, and a measure of caution. Do not give up your rights too soon. But when you establish personal bonds with somebody, forget about your rights. Remember – you're not forfeiting them. Your relationships will be richer when they are based on friendship, love, compassion, giving, and forgiving. But when you are betrayed or abused, do not hesitate to take your rights back. You are a free person and not a slave to your family and friends.

In your search for meaning and pursuit of happiness, treat your rights and freedoms as the floor upon which you can act, but from which you may also need to spring up – toward a spirituality of your choice, values you cherish, and commitments to others. Without being a martyr, try to live a life of healthy self-discipline. Think about your happiness, but also about your own limits. Use the rights of others as guidance for establishing your self-limitations. Try not to violate the rights of others even if they do not recognize such rights, except when acting in justified self-defense.

---

[73] Feinberg (1978, 32).

When you consider rules, values, and principles, try to see the various instruments that can be used to achieve different goals. Do not try to use rights as a universal key that will open every door in front of you. Rights are very important for humankind. Do not take part in their abuse or abet their inflation to the point that they may fall into oblivion.

Your grateful teacher,

Wiktor Osiatyński

Bibliography

Abdullah, Hussaina J. 2000. Religious revivalism, human rights activism and the struggle for women's rights in Nigeria. In Mamdani (ed.): 96–120.

Afshari, Reza. 2007. "On Historiography of Human Rights: Reflections on Paul Gordon Lauren's *The Evolution of International Human Rights: Visions Seen.*" *Human Rights Quarterly* 29: 1–67.

Alston, Philip, Stephen Parker, and John Seymour (eds.). 1992. *Children, Rights, and the Law.* Oxford: Clarendon Press.

Al-Hibri, Azizah. 1997. "Islam, Law, and Custom: Redefining Muslim Women's Rights." *American University Journal of International Law & Policy* 12: 1.

Ambler, John S. 1991. "Ideas, Interests, and the French Welfare State." In John S. Ambler (ed.), *The French Welfare State.* New York: New York University Press: 1–31.

American Anthropological Association, Executive Board. 1947. "Statement on Human Rights." *American Anthropologist* 49: 539. (Reprinted in Winston 1989, 116–20.)

Amnesty International. 1998. *United States of America: Rights for All.*

Andropov, Yuri. 1975. "A Report of the Committee for State Security to the USSR Council of Ministers of December 29, 1975." (Translated by Svetlana Savranskaya). Dmitrij A. Volkogonov Papers. Washington, D.C.: U.S. Library of Congress, Manuscript Division (reel 18, container 28).

An-Na'im, Abdullah Ahmed (ed.) 1992. *Human Rights in Cross Cultural Perspectives: A Quest for Consensus.* Philadelphia: University of Pennsylvania Press.

Bandman, Elsie L., and Bertram Bandman. 1978. *Bioethics and Human Rights.* Boston: Little, Brown and Company.

Barak, Aharon. 2007. "Seeking Common Sense: Proportionality and Balancing." A Marek Nowicki Memorial Lecture delivered on November 30, 2007, at Warsaw University. Available at: http://www.infoengine.pl/index.php?s=pliki&id=301&lang=pl.

Barry, Norman. 1990. *Welfare.* Minneapolis: University of Minnesota Press.

Bauer, Joanne R., and Daniel A. Bell (eds.). 1999. *The East Asian Challenge for Human Rights.* Cambridge/New York: Cambridge University Press.

Baxi, Upandra. 1998. "The Development of the Right to Development." In Symonides (ed.): 99–116.

Beatty, David M. 1994. *Human Rights and Judicial Review: A Comparative Perspective.* Dodrecht/Boston/London: Martinus Nijhoff.

Beetham, David. 1998. "Democracy and Human Rights: Civil, Political, Economic, Social and Cultural." In Symonides (ed.): 71–97.

Belden Russonello and Stewart Research and Communications. 2007. *Human Rights in the United States: "The Things to Strive For."* Washington, D.C.: Author.

Bell, John. 1992. *French Constitutional Law.* Oxford: Clarendon Press.

Benes, Eduard. 1942. "The Organization of Postwar Europe." *Foreign Affairs* 20: 226–42.

Bernheim, Franz. 1933. "The Petition to the League of Nations." *The New York Times.* May 27, 1933. (ProQuest Historical Newspapers, *The New York Times* (1851–2003).

Berlin, Isaiah. 1970. *Four Essays on Liberty.* Oxford: Oxford University Press.

Betton, John. 2008. "The Global Context of Human Rights Violations: The Impact of the Alien Torts Claims Act." *Journal of Business Systems, Governance and Ethics* 3(1): 17–26.

Black, Henry Campbell. 1990. *Black's Law Dictionary: Definitions of the Terms and Phrases of American and English Jurisprudence, Ancient and Modern,* 6th edition. St. Paul, MN: West.

Bloom, Irene, J. Paul Martin, and Wayne L. Proudfoot (eds.). 1996. *Religious Diversity and Human Rights.* New York: Columbia University Press.

Brems, Eva. 2001. *Human Rights: Universality and Diversity.* The Hague: Martinus Nijhoff.

Breviarium Fidei. *Wybór doktrynalnych wypowiedzi Kościoła.* (Opracowali Stanisław Głowa, S.J. i Ignacy Bieda, S.J.). 1988. Poznań: Księgarnia Św. Wojciecha.

Brown, Richard D., and Richard Ashby Wilson (eds.). 2008. *Humanitarianism and Suffering: The Mobilization of Empathy.* New York: Cambridge University Press.

Brysk, Alison (ed.). 2002. *Globalization and Human Rights.* Berkeley/Los Angeles/London: University of California Press.

Buergenthal, Thomas. 1997. "The Normative and Institutional Evolution of International Human Rights." *Human Rights Quarterly* 19: 703–23.

Bukovskå, Barbora. 2008. "Perpetrating Good: The Unintended Consequences of International Human Rights Advocacy." PILI Papers Number 3, April 2008. New York/Budapest: Public Interest Law Institute.

Burgers, Jan Herman. 1992. "The Road to San Francisco: The Revival of the Human Rights Idea in the Twentieth Century." *Human Rights Quarterly* 14: 447–77.

Burgess, Greg. 2002. "The Human Rights Dilemma in Anti-Nazi Protest: The Bernheim Petition, Minorities Protection, and the 1933 Sessions of the League of Nations." Working Paper No. 2. Melbourne: Contemporary Europe Research Center, the University of Melbourne.

Burke, Roland. 2006. "The Compelling Dialogue of Freedom: Human Rights at the Bandung Conference." *Human Rights Quarterly* 28: 947–65.

Buruma, Ian. 2005. "The Indiscreet Charm of Tyranny." *The New York Review of Books* 36.

Butora, Martin, Olga Gyarfasova, Grigorij Meseznikov, and Thomas W. Skladony (eds). 2007. *Democracy and Populism in Central Europe: The Visegrad Elections and Their Aftermath.* Bratislava: Institute for Public Affairs.

Caenegem, R. C. van. 1995. *An Historical Introduction to Western Constitutional Law.* New York: Cambridge University Press.

Campbell, Tom D. 1992. "The Rights of the Minor: as Person, as Child, as Juvenile, as Future Adult." In Alston et al.: 1–23.

Carothers, Thomas. 2003. "Promoting the Rule of Law Abroad: The Problem of Knowledge." Carnegie Endowment Working Paper No. 34, Rule of Law Series, Democracy and Rule of Law Project. Washington, D.C.: Carnegie Endowment for International Peace.

Carothers, Thomas. 2006a. *Confronting the Weakest Link: Aiding Political Parties in New Democracies*. Washington, D.C.: Carnegie Endowment for International Peace.

Carothers, Thomas. 2006b. "The Rule of Law Revival." In Thomas Carrothers (ed.), *Promoting the Rule of Law Abroad: In Search of Knowledge*. Washington, D.C.: Carnegie Endowment for International Peace.

Carstens, Ronald W. 1992. *The Medieval Antecedents of Constitutionalism*. New York: Peter Lang.

Centre for Bhutan Studies. 2007. *Rethinking Development: Proceedings of the Second International Conference on Gross National Happiness*. Thimphu: Author.

Chalidze, Valery. 1974. *To Defend These Rights: Human Rights and the Soviet Union*. New York: Random House.

Chrusciak, Ryszard, and Wiktor Osiatynski. 2001. *Tworzenie konstytucji w Polsce w latach 1989–1997* (The Constitution-Making in Poland, 1989–1997). Warszawa: Instytut Spraw Publicznych.

Christiansen, Drew. 1982. "Basic Needs: Criterion for the Legitimacy of Development." In Hennelly and Langan (eds): 245–88.

Chua, Amy. 2003. *World on Fire: How Exporting Free Market Democracy Breeds Ethnic Hatred and Global Instability*. New York: Doubleday.

Clapham, Andrew. 1993. *Human Rights in the Private Sphere*. Oxford: Clarendon.

Clapham, Andrew. 2007. *Human Rights: A Very Short Introduction*. Oxford: Oxford University Press.

Clinton, Robert Lowry. 1997. *God and Man in the Law: The Foundations of Anglo-American Constitutionalism*. Lawrence: University Press of Kansas.

Collier, Paul. 2007. *The Bottom Billion: Why the Poorest Countries Are Failing and What Can Be Done about It?* Oxford/New York: Oxford University Press.

Commission on Legal Empowerment of the Poor. 2008. *Making the Law Work for Everyone*. (Volume I. *Report of the Commission on Legal Empowerment of the Poor* and Volume 2: *Working Groups Reports*). New York: United Nations Development Programme.

Copp, David. 1992. "The Right to an Adequate Standard of Living: Justice, Autonomy, and the Basic Needs." In Paul, Ellen Frankel, et al.: 231–61.

Cranston, Maurice. 1973. *What Are Human Rights?* New York: Taplinger.

Crenshaw, Kimberle. 2000. "Were the Critics Right about Rights? Reassessing the American Debate about Rights in the Post-Reform Era." In Mamdani (ed.): 61–74.

Currie, David P. 1994. *The Constitution of the Federal Republic of Germany*. Chicago/London: The University of Chicago Press.

Cushman, Thomas. 2005. "The Human Rights Case for the War in Iraq: A Consequentialist View." In Wilson: 78–107.

Dahrendorf, Lord, Yehuda Elkana, Aryeh Neier, William Newton Smith, and Istvan Rev (eds.). 2000. *The Paradoxes of Unintended Consequences*. Budapest: CEU Press.

Dalai Lama. (Tenzin Gyatso, The Fourteenth Dalai Lama of Tibet). 1999. *Ethics for a New Millenium: Ancient Wisdom, Modern World*. Boston: Little, Brown and Company.

Danieli, Yael, Elsa Stamatopoulou, and Clarence J. Dias. 1999. *The Universal Declaration of Human Rights: Fifty Years and Beyond*. Amityville, NY: Baywood.

Davidson, Scott. 1993. *Human Rights*. Philadelphia: Open University Press.

Davis, Michael C. 2000. "Chinese Perspectives on Human Rights." In Michael C. Davis (ed.), *Human Rights and Chinese Values: Legal, Philosophical and Political Perspectives*. Hong Kong/Oxford/New York: Oxford University Press: 3–24.

Dijk, P. van, and G. J. H. van Hoof. 1990. *Theory and Practice of the European Convention on Human Rights*. Boston: Kluwer Law and Taxation.

Dippel, Horst. 1977. *Germany and the American Revolution 1770–1800: A Sociohistorical Investigation of Late Eighteenth-Century Political Thinking*. Chapel Hill: The University of North Carolina Press.

Donnelly, Jack. 1989. *Universal Human Rights in Theory and Practice*. Ithaca/London: Cornell University Press.

Donnelly, Jack. 2002. "Genocide and Humanitarian Intervention." *Journal of Human Rights* 1(1): 93–109.

Donnelly, Jack. 2007. "The West and Economic Rights." In Hertel and Minkler (eds.): 37–55.

Drake, Paul W., and Matthew D. McCubbins (eds). 1998. *The Origins of Liberty: Political and Economic Liberalization in The Modern World*. Princeton: Princeton University Press.

Dudai, Ron. 2008. "Can You Describe This?: The Language of Human Rights Reports and What It Tells Us about the Human Rights Movement." In Brown and Wilson (eds.).

Duffy, Helen. 2005. *The "War on Terror" and the Framework of International Law*. New York: Cambridge University Press.

Dworkin, Ronald. 1977. *Taking Rights Seriously*. Cambridge, MA: Harvard University Press.

Edwards, R. Randle, Louis Henkin, and Andrew J. Nathan. 1986. *Human Rights in Contemporary China*. New York: Columbia University Press.

Eekelaar, John. 1992. "The Importance of Thinking That Children Have Rights." In Alston et al.: 221–35.

El Din Hassan, Bahey. 1999. The Credibility Crisis of International Human Rights in the Arab World. In *Human Rights Dialogue* 2.1. "Human rights for All?" URL: http://www.cceia.org/resources/publications/dialogue/2_01/articles/600.html.

Elster, Jon. 1993. "Majority Rule and Individual Rights." In Shute and Hurley, 1993: 175–216.

Elster, Jon, Claus Offe, and Ulrich K. Preuss. 1998. *Institutional Design in Post-Communist Societies: Rebuilding the Ship at Sea*. New York: Cambridge University Press.

Elster, Jon. 2002. *Ulysses Unbound: Studies in Rationality, Precommitment, and Constraints*. New York: Cambridge University Press.

Elven, J. P., after H. Singleton. ca. 1800. *Washington Giving the Laws to America* (etching and engraving). New York: New York Public Library, Miriam and Ira D. Wallach Division of Art Prints and Photographs.

Engle, Karen. 2002. "From Skepticism to Embrace: Human Rights and the American Anthropological Association from 1947 to 1999." In Shweder et al. (eds.): 344–362.

Epp, Charles R. 1998. *The Rights Revolution. Lawyers, Activists, and Supreme Courts in Comparative Perspective*. Chicago: The University of Chicago Press.

Epstein, Richard A. 1987. "The Uncertain Quest for Welfare Rights." In Gary C. Bryner and Noel B. Reynolds (eds.), *Constitutionalism and Rights*. Provo: Brigham Young University: 33–62.

Evans, Gareth, and Mohamed Sahnoun. 2002. "The Responsibility to Protect." *Foreign Affairs* 81(6).

Falk, Richard. 2002. "Interpreting the Interaction of Global Markets and Human Rights." In Brysk (ed.): 61–76.

Favoreau, Louis. 1990. "Constitutional Review in Europe." In Henkin and Rosenthal: 38–62.

Feinberg, Joel. 1970. "The Nature and Value of Rights." In *The Journal of Value Inquiry*, Vol. 4 (Winter 1970): 243–57. (Quoted after Winston 1989: 61–74. Also reprinted in Lyons 1979: 78–91.)

Feinberg, Joel. 1973. *Social Philosophy*. Englewood Cliffs: Prentice-Hall, Inc.

Feinberg, Joel. 1978. "A Postscript to the Nature and Value of Rights." In Elsie L. Bandman and Bertram Bandman (eds.), *Bioethics and Human Rights*. Boston: Little, Brown and Company: 32–4.

Flores, Marcello. 2008. *Storia dei diritti umani*. Bologna: il Mulino.

Forsythe, David P. (ed.). 2000. *The United States and Human Rights: Looking Inward and Outward*. Lincoln/London: University of Nebraska Press.

Forsythe, David P. 2006. *Human Rights in International Relations*. New York: Cambridge University Press.

Forsythe, David P. 2008. "The United States and International Humanitarian Law." *Journal of Human Rights* 7(1): 25–33.

Franck, Thomas M. 2001. "Are Human Rights Universal?" *Foreign Affairs* 80(1): 191–204.

Freeman, Michael. 1995. "Are There Collective Human Rights?" In David Beetham (ed.), *Politics and Human Rights*. Oxford: Blackwell.

Freeman, Michael. 2002. *Human Rights: An Interdisciplinary Approach*. Cambridge: Polity Press.

Freeman, Michael D.A. 1992. "Taking Children's Rights More Seriously." In Alston et al.: 52–71.

Frynas, Jedrzej George, and Scott Pegg (eds.). 2003. *Transnational Corporations and Human Rights*. Houndmills: Palgrave Macmillan.

Gellhorn, Walter. 1966. *Ombudsmen and Others: Citizens' Protectors in Nine Countries*. Cambridge, MA: Harvard University Press.

Gewirth, Alan. 1992. "Human Dignity as the Basis for Rights." In Meyer and Parent: 10–28.

Gewirth, Alan. 1966. *The Community of Rights*. Chicago/London: The University of Chicago Press.

Glendon, Mary Ann. 1991. *Rights Talk: The Impoverishment of Political Discourse*. New York: The Free Press.

Glendon, Mary Ann. 2001. *A World Made New: Eleanor Roosevelt and the Universal Declaration of Human Rights*. New York: Random House.

Golding, Martin P. 1978. "The Concept of Rights: A Historical Sketch." In Bandman and Bandman: 44–50.

Goldston, James A. 2004. *Legal Approaches to Combating Statelessness*. A contribution to the Panel Discussion on the 50th Anniversary of the Convention relating to the Status of Stateless Persons at the UNHCR Executive Committee meeting, October 6, 2004, Geneva. Avaialable at Open Society Justice Initiative Website: http://www.justiceinitiative.org/db/resource2?res_id=102227.

Goldstone, Richard. 2005. "The Tension between Combating Terrorism and Protecting Civil Liberties." In Wilson (ed.): 157–68.

Golub, Stephen. 2003. "Beyond Rule of Law Orthodoxy. The Legal Empowerment Alternative." Rule of Law Series, Democracy and Rule of Law Project, Number 41. Washington, D.C.: Carnegie Endowment for International Peace.

Gosset, Thomas F. 1963. *Race: The History of an Idea in America*. Dallas: Southern Methodist University Press.

Gould, Carol C. 1988. *Rethinking Democracy: Freedom and Social Cooperation in Politics, Economy, and Society*. Cambridge: Cambridge University Press.

Gowan, Richard, and Franziska Brantner. 2008. "A Global Force for Human Rights? An Audit of European Power at the UN. Policy Paper." London: European Council on Foreign Relations.

Grzybowski, Konstanty. 1967. *Historia Doktryn Politycznych i Prawnych. Od państwa niewolniczego do rewolucyj burżuazyjnych*. Warszawa: PWN.

Guggenheim, Martin. 2005. *What's Wrong with Children's Rights*. Cambridge, MA/London: Harvard University Press.

Hamilton, Alexander, James Madison, and John Jay. 2003 (original 1788). *The Federalist Papers*. New York: Bantam.

Harvey, Phillip. 2002. "Human Rights and Economic Policy Discourse: Taking Economic and Social Rights Seriously." *Columbia Human Rights Law Review* 33(2): 363–471.

Haughey, John C. 1982. "Individualism and Rights in Karl Marx." In Hennely and Langan (eds.): 102–41.

Hayden, Patrick (ed.) 2001. *The Philosophy of Human Rights*. St. Paul: Paragon House.

Helmholz, Richard H. 2001. Fundamental Human Rights in Medieval Law. Maurice and Muriel Fulton Lecture. Chicago: The University of Chicago.

Hennelly, Alfred, and Johan Langan, S. J. (eds.). 1982. *Human Rights in the Americas: The Struggle for Consensus*. Washington, D.C.: Georgetown University Press.

Henkin, Louis. 1978. *The Rights of Man Today*. Boulder, CO: Westview Press.

Henkin, Louis. 1990. *The Age of Rights*. New York: Columbia University Press.

Henkin, Louis. 1981. "Economic-Social Rights as 'Rights': A United States Perspective." *Human Rights Law Journal* 2(3–4).

Henkin, Louis, and Albert Rosenthal (eds.). 1990. *Constitutionalism and Rights: The Influence of the United States Constitution Abroad*. New York: Columbia University Press.

Henkin, Louis, Gerald L. Neuman, Diane F. Orentlicher, and David W. Leebron. 1999. *Human Rights*. New York: Foundation Press.

Hertel, Shareen, and Lanse Minkler (eds.). 2007. *Economic Rights: Conceptual, Measurement, and Policy Issues*. New York: Cambridge University Press.

Hicks, Neil. 2005. "The Impact of Counter Terror on the Promotion ond Protection of Human Rights: A Global Perspective." In Wilson: 209–24.

Hochschild, Adam. 1998. *King Leopold's Ghost: A Story of Greed, Terror, and Heroism in Colonial Africa*. New York: Houghton Mifflin.

Hochschild, Adam. 2005. *Bury the Chains: Prophets and Rebels in the Fight to Free an Empire's Slaves*. Boston/New York: Houghton Mifflin.

Hohfeld, Wesley. 1923. *Some Fundamental Legal Conceptions as Applied in Judicial Reasoning and Other Legal Essays*. New Haven: Yale University Press. (Originally published in 23 Yale Law Journal 16, 1913.)

Hollenbach, David. 1982. "Global Human Rights: An Interpretation of the Contemporary Catholic Understanding." In Hennelly and Langan (eds.): 9–24.

Holmes, Stephen. 1997. "What Russia Teaches Us Now: How Weak States Threaten Transition." *The American Prospect* July-August: 30–9.

Holmes, Stephen, and Cass R. Sunstein. 1999. *The Costs of Rights: Why Liberty Depends on Taxes*. New York: W.W. Norton & Company.

Holmes, Stephen. 2007. *The Matador's Cape: America's Reckless Response to Terror*. New York: Cambridge University Press.

Holzgrefe, J. L. 2003. "The Humanitarian Intervention Debate." In J. L. Holzgrefe and Robert O. Keohane (eds.), *Humanitarian Intervention: Ethical, Legal, and Political Dilemmas*. New York: Cambridge University Press: 15–52.

Howard-Hassmann, Rhoda E. 2007. "The Second Great Transformation: Human Rights Leapfrogging in the Era of Globalization." *Human Rights Quarterly* 27: 1–40.

Hunt, Lynn (ed.) 1989. *The New Cultural History*. Berkeley: University of California Press.

Hunt, Lynn. 2007. *Inventing Human Rights: A History*. New York/London: W.W. Norton & Company.

Ignatieff, Michael. 1999. "Human Rights: The Midlife Crisis." *The New York Review of Books* May 20, 46: 58–62.

Ignatieff, Michael. 2001. The Attack on Human Rights. *Foreign Affairs* 80(6): 102–16.

Ignatieff, Michael. 2003. "State Failure and Nation-Building." In Holzgrefe and Keohane: 299–321.

Ignatieff, Michael. 2004. *The Lesser Evil: Political Ethics in the Age of Terror*. Princeton/Oxford: Princeton University Press.

International Development Research Centre. 2001. *The Responsibility to Protect. Report of the International Commission on Intervention and State Sovereignty*. Ottawa, Ontario, Canada: Author.

Ishay, Micheline R. 1997. *The Human Rights Reader*. New York: Routledge.

Ishay, Micheline R. 2004. *The History of Human Rights: From Ancient Times to the Globalization Era*. Berkeley, Los Angeles, London: University of California Press.

Jelin, Elizabeth, and Eric Herschberg (eds.). 1996. *Constructing Democracy: Human Rights, Citizenship, and Society in Latin America*. Boulder, CO: Westview Press.

Jencks, Chrisopher. 2006. "What Happened to Welfare?" *The New York Review of Books* LII(20): 76–86.

Jenkins, Alan, and Larry Cox. 2005. "Bringing Human Rights Home." *The Nation*, June 27.

Johansen, Robert C. 2006. "The Impact of U.S. Policy toward the International Criminal Court on the Prevention of Genocide, War Crimes, and Crimes against Humanity." *Human Rights Quarterly* 28: 310–31.

de Jong, Jorrit, and Gowher Rizvi (eds.). 2009. *The State of Access: Success and Failure of Democracies to Create Equal Opportunities*. Washington, D.C.: Brookings Institution Press.

Jovanović, Miodrag A. 2005. "Recognizing Minority Identities Through Collective Rights." *Human Rights Quarterly* 27: 625 — 51.

Justyński, Janusz (ed.). 1991. "The Origins of Human Rights." Presented at the Nicolaus Copernicus University, May 3–5, 1991. Toruń: Wydawnictwo Adam Marszałek.

Kabasakal Arat, Zehra F. 2006. "Forging a Global Culture of Human Rights: Origins and Prospects of the International Bill of Rights." *Human Rights Quarterly* 28: 416–37.

Kabeer, Naila (ed). 2005. *Inclusive Citizenship: Meanings and Expressions*. New Delhi: Zubaan.

Kant, Immanuel. 2001 (original text 1785). "Fundamental Principles of the Metaphysics of Morals." In *Basic Writings of Kant*. Edited and with an introduction by Allen W. Wood. New York: The Modern Library.

Kant, Immanuel. 1964 (original text 1797). *The Metaphysics of Morals*. New York: Harper Torchbooks.

Kądziela, Joachim. 1977. "Chrześcijańskie ujecie praw człowieka na tle dyskusji miedzynarodowej" (The Christian concept of human rights in an international debate). *Chrześcijanin w świecie*, nr 63–4.

Keane, John (ed.) 1988. *Civil Society and the State: New European Perspectives*. London/New York: Verso.

Kędzia, Zdzisław. 1980. *Burżuazyjna koncepcja praw człowieka* (The Bourgeoisie Concept of Human Rights). Wrocław: Zakład Narodowy Ossolińskich.

Knox, John H. 2008. "Horizontal Human Rights Law." *American Journal of International Law* 102(1): 1–47.

Kołakowski, Leszek. 2003. "Po co nam prawa człowieka?" (What Do We Need Human Rights For?). *Gazeta Wyborcza*, Warsaw, October 26.

Korey, William. 1991. "Human Rights and the Policy of Leverage and Linkage: The Lesson of the Helsinki Process." In Mastny and Zielonka (eds.): 77–105.

Korey, William. 1998. *NGOs and the Universal Declaration of Human Rights: A Curious Grapevine.* New York: St. Martin's Press.

Kymlicka, Will. 1996. "The Good, the Bad, and the Intolerable: Minority Group Rights," In Hayden (ed.) 2001: 445–61.

Lacey, Mark. 2004. "Genital Cutting Shows Signs of Losing Favor in Africa," *The New York Times*, May 5.

Lang, Wiesław. 1991. "The Philosophical Foundations of Human Rights." In Justyński (ed.)

de Langen, Maaike, and Maurits Barendrecht. 2009. "Legal Empowerment of the Poor: Innovating Access to Justice." In de Jong and Rizvi. (Quoted here after prepublication manuscript provided by Maaike de Langen.)

Laqueur, Thomas W. 1989. "Bodies, Details, and the Humanitarian Narrative." In Hunt (ed.): 176–204.

Lauren, Paul Gordon. 1998. *The Evolution of International Human Rights: Visions Seen.* Philadelphia: The University of Pennsylvania Press.

Lauterpacht, Hersch. 1945. *An International Bill of the Rights of Man.* New York: Columbia University Press.

Lauterpach H. 1950. *International Law and Human Rights.* Steven and Sons. (Quoted after 1968 edition. Hamden, CT: Archon Books.)

Lemkin, Raphael. 1933. "Acts Constituting a General (Transnational) Danger Considered as Offence against the Law of Nations." Available at: http://www.preventgenocide.org/lemkin/madrid1933-english.htm.

Lijphart, Arend (ed). 1992. *Presidential versus Parliamentary Government.* Oxford: Oxford University Press.

Lindholt, Lone. 1997. *Questioning the Universality of Human Rights: The African Charter on Human and People's Rights in Botswana, Malawi and Mozambique.* Dartmouth: Ashgate.

Locke, John. 1980. (Originally published in 1690). *Second Treatise of Government.* Indianapolis, Cambridge: Hackett Publishing Company.

Lukes, Steven. 1993. "Five Fables about Human Rights." *Dissent*, Fall: 427–36.

Lyons, David (ed). 1979. *Rights.* Belmont: Wadsworth Publishing Co.

Madison, James. 1788. *The Federalist.* Number 47 and 48. In Hamilton, Madison, and Jay. 2003, 292–305.

Mamdani, Mahmood (ed.). 2000. *Beyond Rights Talk and Culture Talk: Comparative Essays on the Politics of Rights and Culture.* New York: St. Martin's Press.

Mamdani, Mahmood. 2008. "The New Humanitarian Order." *The Nation* 287(9): 17–22.

Mani, Lata. 1990. "Contentious Traditions: The Debate on Sati in Colonial India." In Sangari and Vaid (eds.): 88–126.

Maritain, Jacques. 1951a. *The Rights of Man and Natural Law.* New York: Charles Scribner's Sons.

Maritain, Jacques. 1951b. *Man and the State*. Chicago: The University of Chicago Press.

Martinez, Samuel. 2007. "The Two Worlds of Rights Advocacy: Conflict and Complimentarity between International and Domestic (Haitian-Dominican) NGOs." (Unpublished paper made available by the author).

Maru, Vivek. 2006. "Between Law and Society. Paralegals and the Provision of Justice Services in Sierra Leone and Worldwide." *Yale Journal of International Law* 31(2): 427–76. Available at: http://www.yale.edu/yjil/PDFs/vol_31/Maru.pdf.

Marx, Karl. 1843. "On the Jewish Question." In Tucker (ed.): 26–52.

Mastny, Vojtech, and Jan Zielonka (eds.). 1991. *Human Rights and Security: Europe on the Eve of a New Era*. Boulder, CO: Westview Press.

Mayer, Ann Elizabeth. 2004. "Shifting Grounds for Challenging the Authority of International Human Rights Law: Religion as a Malleable and Politicized Pretext for Governmental Noncompliance with Human Rights." In Sajo 2004: 349–74.

Mayer, Ann Elizabeth. 2007. *Islam and Human Rights. Tradition and Politics*. 4th edition. Boulder, CO: Westview.

Mazower, Mark. 2004. "The Strange Triumph of Human Rights, 1933–1950." *The Historical Journal* 47(2): 379–98.

Mazurek, Franciszek Janusz. 2001. *Godność osoby ludzkiej podstawą praw człowieka* (The Dignity of a Human Person as the Foundation for Human Rights). Lublin: Redakcja Wydawnictw Katolickiego Uniwersytetu Lubelskiego.

McDougal, Myres, Harold Lasswell, and Lung-Chu Chen. 1969. "Human Rights and World Public Order: A Framework for Policy Oriented Inquiry." *American Journal of International Law* 63: 237–69.

McFarland, Sam, and Melissa Mathews. 2005. "Do Americans Care about Human Rights?" *Journal of Human Rights* 4: 305–19.

McIlwain, Charles Howard. 1947. *Constitutionalism: Ancient and Modern*. Ithaca, NY: Cornell University Press (quoted after 1987 edition).

Merkl, Peter H. 1982. *The Origins of the West German Republic*. Westport, CT: Greenwood Press.

Meron, Theodore. 1993. "Rape as a Crime under International Humanitarian Law." *American Journal of International Law* 87: 424–8.

Meron, Theodore. 2006. *The Humanization of International Law*. Leiden/Boston: Martinus Nijhoff.

Meron, Theodore. 2008a. "A Life of Learning." Haskins Prize Lecture delivered on May 9, 2008, at the American Council of Learned Society. Available at: http://www.asil.org/pdfs.meronspeech.pdf.

Meron, Theodore. 2008b. "The Humanization of the Law of War." Marek Nowicki Memorial Lecture delivered at the Central European University in Budapest on November 27, 2008.

Meron, Theodore. 2008c. "Human Rights Law Marches into New Territory: The Enforcement of International Human Rights in International Criminal Tribunals." Marek Nowicki Memorial Lecture delivered at Warsaw University on November 29, 2008.

Mertus, Julie, and Tazreeba Sajjad. 2008. "Human Rights and Human Insecurity: The Contributions of U.S. Counterterrorism." *Journal of Human Rights* 7(1): 2–24.

Meyer, Michael J., and W. A. Parent. 1992. *The Constitution of Rights: Human Dignity and American Values*. Ithaca/London: Cornell University Press.

Mill, John Stuart. 1869. (Originally published 1859). *On Liberty*. London: Longman, Roberts & Green.

Milne, A. J. M. 1986. *Human Right and Human Diversity: An Essay in the Philosophy of Human Rights*. Albany: State University of New York Press.

Mitoma, Glenn Tatsuya. 2008. "Civil Society and International Human Rights: The Commission to Study the Organization of Peace and the Origins of the UN Human Rights Regime." *Human Rights Quarterly* 30: 607–30.

Monahan, Arthur P. 1994. *From Personal Duties toward Personal Rights: Late Medieval and Early Modern Political Thought, 1300–1600*. Montreal/Kingston: McGill-Queen's University Press.

Montesquieu, Charles-Louis de Secondat, Baron de. 1990 (original 1748). *The Spirit of the Laws*, Amherst, New York: Prometheus Books.

Moravcsik, Andrew. 2000. "The Origins of Human Rights Regimes: Democratic Delegation in Postwar Europe." *International Organization* 54: 217–72.

Morsink, Johannes. 1999. *The Universal Declaration of Human Rights: Origins, Drafting, Intent*. Philadelphia: The University of Pennsylvania Press.

Mutua, Makau. 2004. "The Complexity of Universalism in Human Rights." In Sajo (ed.): 51–64.

Narasimhan, Sakuntala. 1992. *Sati Widow Burning in India*. New York: Doubleday.

Neier, Aryeh. 1982. *Only Judgment: The Limits of Litigation in Social Change*. Middletown, CT: Wesleyan University Press.

Neier, Aryeh. 1989. "Not All Human Rights Groups Are Equal." Letter to the Editor, *The New York Times*, May 27, p. 22. (Reprinted in Steiner and Alston 1996, 459).

Neier, Aryeh. 2000. "Economic Sanctions and Human Rights." In Power and Allison (eds.): 291–308.

Neier, Aryeh. 2003. *Taking Liberties. Four Decades in the Struggle for Rights*. New York: Public Affairs.

Neier, Aryeh. 2005. "How Not to Promote Democracy and Human Rights." In Wilson (ed.): 137–42.

Nelson, William N. 1981. "Human Rights and Human Obligations." In Pennock and Chapman (eds.): 281–96.

Nordahl, Richard. 1992. "A Marxian Approach to Human Rights." In An-Na'im (ed.): 162–187.

North, Douglas C., and Barry R. Weingast. 1998a. "Limited Government and Liberal Markets: An Introduction to 'Constitutions and Commitment.'" In Drake and McCubbins (eds): 13–15.

North, Douglas C., and Barry R. Weingast. 1998b. "Constitutions and Commitment': The Evolution of Institutions Governing Public Choice in Seventeenth-Century England." In Drake and McCubbins (eds): 16–47.

Nurser, Canon John. 2003. "The 'Ecumenical Movement, Churches, 'Global Order', and Human Rights: 1938–1945." *Human Rights Quarterly* 25: 841–81.

Nussbaum, Martha C. 2001. "Capabilities and Human Rights." In Hayden: 212–40.

O'Neill, Onora. 1992. "Children's Rights and Children's Lives." In Alston et al.: 24–42.

Open Society Justice Initiative. 2004. *Racial Discrimination and the Rights of Non-Citizens*. New York. Also Available at: http://www.justiceinitiative.org/db/resource2?res_id=101639: Author.

Open Society Justice Initiative. 2004a. *The AfricaCitizenship and Discrimination Audit Preparatory Meeting*. Report of the Conference held in Dakar, Senegal on July 19–20, 2004. Available at: http://www.justiceinitiative.org/db/resource2?res_id=102081.

Open Society Justice Initiative. 2006a. "Mainstreaming a Human Rights Approach to State-lessness within the UN System." New York: Open Society Justice Initiative Equality and Citizenship Program.

Open Society Justice Initiative. 2006b. *Transparency & Silence: A Survey of Access to Infor-mation Laws and Practices in 14 Countries.* New York: Author.

Open Society Justice Initiative. 2006c. *Between Law and Society. Paralegals and the Provision of Primary Justice in Sierra Leone.* New York.

Open Society Justice Initiative. 2007a. *"I Can Stop and Search Whoever I Want": Police Stops of Ethnic Minorities in Bulgaria, Hungary and Spain.* New York.

Open Society Justice Initiative. 2007b. "Towards Clearer Principles on Citizenship?" Paper presented at the OSJI executive committee meeting, October. New York.

Open Society Justice Initiative. 2008. *Pretrial Detention.* New York.

Open Society Justice Initiative. 2009. *Ethnic Profiling in the European Union: Pervasive, Ineffective and Discriminatory.* New York.

Orend, Brian. 2002. *Human Rights: Concept and Context.* Peterborough, Ontario, Canada: Broadview Press.

Orentlicher, Diane F. 2008. *Shrinking the Space for Denial: The Impact of the ICTY in Serbia.* New York: Open Society Justice Initiative.

Osiatyński, Wiktor. 1990. "Constitutionalism and Rights in the History of Poland." In Henkin and Resenthl (eds.): 284–314.

Osiatyński, Wiktor. 1991. "Revolutions in Eastern Europe." *The University of Chicago Law Review* 58(2): 823–58.

Osiatyński, Wiktor. 1994. "Rights in New Constitutions of East Central Europe." *Columbia Human Rights Law Review* 26(1): 111–66.

Osiatyński, Wiktor. 1996. "Social and Economic Rights in a New Constitution for Poland." In Sajo (ed): 233–69.

Osiatyński, Wiktor. 1997a. "A Brief History of the Constitution." *East European Constitutional Review* 6(2–3): 66–76.

Osiatyński Wiktor. 1997b. *Twoja Konstytucja* (A Constitution for You). Warszawa: Wydawnictwo Szkolne i Pedagogiczne.

Osiatyński, Wiktor. 2000a. "Constitutionalism, Democracy, Constitutional Culture." In Wyrzykowski (ed.): 151–8.

Osiatyński, Wiktor. 2000b. "The Constitutional Honeymoon Is Over: The Paradoxes of Post-Communist Constitution-Making." In Dahrendorf et al. (eds.): 143–54.

Osiatyński, Wiktor. 2000c. "Human Rights for the 21st Century." *Saint Louis-Warsaw Transat-lantic Law Journal* 2000: 29–49.

Osiatyński, Wiktor. 2006. "Beyond Rights." In Sajo (ed.): 309–27.

Osiatyński, Wiktor. 2007. "Needs-Based Approach to Social and Economic Rights." In Hertel and Minkler (eds.): 56–75.

Papal Commission Iustitia et Pax. 1974. *The Church and Human Rights.* State of the Vatican City: Author.

Paul, Ellen Frankel, Fred D. Miller, Jr., and Jeffrey Paul. 1992. *Economic Rights.* Cambridge/ New York: Cambridge University Press.

Pennock, J. Roland, and John W. Chapman (eds.). 1981. *Human Rights.* Nomos XXIII. New York: New York University Press.

Perry, Michael J. 1998. *The Idea of Human Rights. Four Inquiries.* New York & Oxford: Oxford University Press.

Pollis, Adamantia, and Peter Schwab (eds.). 1979. *Human Rights: Cultural and Ideological Perspectives*. New York: Praeger.

Pollis, Adamantia. 1996. "Cultural Relativism Revisited: Through a State Prism." *Human Rights Quarterly* 18: 316–44.

Pollis, Adamantia. 2000. "A New Universalism." In Adamantia Pollis and Peter Schwab (eds.), *Human Rights: New Perspectives, New Realities*. Boulder and London: Lynne Rienner: 9–30.

Pope John XXIII. 1963. *Pacem in Terris: Encyclical of Pope John XXIII on Establishing Universal Peace in Truth, Justice, Charity, and Liberty*. State of the Vatican City: Author.

Pope Pius XII. 1939. *Summi Pontificatus: Encyclical of Pope Pius XII on the Unity of Human Society*. State of the Vatican City: Author.

Power, Samantha, and Graham Allison. (eds.). 2000. *Realizing Human Rights: Moving from Inspiration to Impact*. New York: St. Martin's Press.

Preuss, Ulrich. 2005. "The German Drittwirkung Doctrine and Its Socio-Political Background." In Sajo and Uitz (eds.): 23–32.

Rapaczyński, Andrzej. 1990. "Bibliographical Essay: The Influence of U.S. Constitutionalism Abroad." In Henkin and Rosenthal (eds.): 405–62.

Rapaczyński, Andrzej. 1996. Popular Sovereignty and the Concept of Representation: The Relevance of American Constitutionalism in Eastern Europe. *International Journal of Sociology* 26(4): 7–16.

Raz, Joseph. 1986. *The Morality of Freedom*. Oxford: Clarendon.

Rieff, David. 2002. "Humanitarianism in Crisis." *Foreign Affairs* 81(6).

Rieff, David. 2003. *A Bed for the Night: Humanitarianism in Crisis*. New York: Simon & Schuster.

Robertson, Robert E. 1994. "Measuring State Compliance with the Obligation to Devote the 'Maximum Available Resources' to Realizing Economic, Social, and Cultural Rights." *Human Rights Quarterly* 16: 693–714.

Rosas, Allan. 1990. "Democracy and Human Rights." In Jan Helgesen (ed.), *Human Rights in Changing East-West Perspective*. London: Pinter: 17–57.

Rosen, Michaela Serban. 2003. *Constitutionalism in Transition: Africa and Eastern Europe*. Warsaw: Helsinki Foundation for Human Rights.

Roth, Kenneth, and Joanna Weschler. 1998. "Das Versprechen muss gealten werden" ("The Promise Is There: United Nations and Human Rights"). In Gunnar Kohne (ed.), *Die Zukunft der Menchenrechte*. Hamburg: Rowohlt: 172–84.

Roth, Kenneth. 2005. "War in Iraq: Not a Humanitarian Intervention." In Wilson: 143–156.

Rudolph, B. (ed.). 1985. "Human Rights and the Individual in International Law: International Economic Relations." In *Encyclopedia of Public International Law*, Vol. 8. Oxford: Elsevier.

Ruggie, John. 2008. *Protect, Respect and Remedy: A Framework for Business and Human Rights*. New York: Human Rights Council.

Sachs, Albie. 2005. "The Judicial Enforcement of Socio-Economic Rights: The Grootboom Case." In Sajó and Uitz (eds.): 79–97.

Sajo, Andras (ed.). 1996. *Western Rights, Eastern Applications*. Dodrecht: Kluwer.

Sajo, Andras. 1999. *Limiting Government: An Introduction to Constitutionalism*. Budapest: Central European University Press.

Sajo, Andras (ed.). 2004. *Human Rights with Modesty: The Problem of Universalism*. Leiden/Boston: Martinus Nijhoff.

Sajo, Andras, and Renate Uitz (eds.). 2005. *The Constitution in Private Relations: Expanding Constitutionalism.* Utrecht: ELEVEN International.

Sajo, Andras (ed.). 2006. *Abuse: The Dark Side of Fundamental Rights.* Utrecht: ELEVEN International.

Sandholtz, Wayne. 2002. "Humanitarian Intervention. Global Enforcement of Human Rights?" In Brysk: 210–25.

Sangari, Kumkum, and Sudesh Vaid (eds.). 1990. *Recasting Women: Essays in Indian Colonial History.* New Brunswick: Rutgers University Press.

Schleunes, Karl A. 2002. "From Civil Rights to Civic Death: Dismantling Rights in Nazi Germany." In Manfred Berg and Martin H. Geyer (eds.), *Two Cultures of Rights: The Quest for Inclusion and Participation in Modern America and Germany.* Washington, D.C.: German Historical Institute (and Cambridge University Press).

Schönteich, Martin. 2008. "The Scale and Consequences of Pretrial Detention around the World." In Open Society Justice Initiative. *Pretrial Detention.* New York: 11–43.

Sen, Amartya. 1997. *Human Rights and Asian Values.* New York: Carnegie Council.

Sen, Amartya. 1999. *Development as Freedom.* New York: Anchor Books.

Shaer, Roland, Gregory Claeys, and Lyman Tower Sargent. 2000. *Utopia: The Search for the Ideal Society in the Western World.* New York: Oxford University Press.

Shattuck, John. 2003. *Freedom on Fire: Human Rights Wars and America's Responses.* Cambridge, MA: Harvard University Press.

Shestack, Jerome J. 1989. "The Jurisprudential Foundations of Human Rights." Summary of lecture at the Institut International des Droits de L'Homme (manuscript).

Shestack, Jerome J. 1998. "The Philosophic Foundations of Rights." In *Human Rights Quarterly* 20: 201–34.

Shivji, Issa G. 2003. "Three Generations of Constitutions and Constitution-Making in Africa: An Overview and Assessment in Social and Economic Context." In Rosen (ed.): 74–92.

Shue, Henry. 1980. *Basic Rights.* Princeton, NJ: Princeton University Press.

Shute, Steven, and Susan Hurley (eds.). 1993. *On Human Rights.* New York: Basic Books.

Shweder Richard A. 2002. "What about Female Genital Mutilation? And Why Understanding Culture Matters in the First Place." In Richard A. Shweder, Martha Minow, and Hazel Rose Markus (eds.), *Engaging Cultural Differences: The Multicultural Challenge in Liberal Democracies.* New York: Russell Sage Foundation: 216–51.

Shweder, Richard A. 2004. "Moral Realism without the Ethnocentrism: Is It Just a List of Empty Truisms?" In Sajo (ed.): 65–102.

Simpson, A. W. Brian. 2001. *Human Rights and the End of Empire: Britain and the Genesis of the European Convention.* Oxford: Oxford University Press.

Sinha, Surya Prakash. 1981. "Human Rights: A Non-Western Viewpoint." *Archiv fur Rechts- Und Sozialphilosophie* 19(1): 76–91.

Soros, George. 2006. *The Age of Fallability. Consequences of the War on Terror.* New York: Public Affairs.

Spar, Deborah L. 1998. "The Spotlight and the Bottom Line: How Multinationals Export Human Rights." *Foreign Affairs* 77 (March–April): 7–12.

Sripati, Vijayashri. 2007. "Constitutionalism in India and South Africa: A Comparative Study from a Human Rights Perspective." *Tulane Journal of International and Comparative Law* 16: 1–46.

Stavenhagen, Rodolfo. 1996. "Indigenous Rights." In Jelin and Herschberg (eds.): 141–160.

Steinberger, Helmut. 1990. "American Constitutionalism and German Constitutional Development." In Henkin and Rosenthal (eds.): 199–224.

Steiner, Henry J., and Philip Alston. 1996. *International Human Rights in Context: Law, Politics, Morals*. Oxford: Clarendon.

Steiner, Jurg. 1991. *European Democracies*. New York/London: Longman.

Stone, Alec. 1992. *The Birth of Judicial Politics in France: The Constitutional Council in Comparative Perspective*. New York/Oxford: Oxford University Press.

Stop! Honour Killings. 2007. International Campaign Against Honour Killings Web site: http://www.stophonourkillings.com (posted on September 5, 2007).

Sugranyes de Franch, R. 1984. "Maritain, Human Rights and the United Nations," *Notes and Documents* 9 (1984) janvier–juin, 114–23.

Sumner, L. W. 1987. *The Moral Foundations of Rights*. Oxford: Clarendon.

Sunstein, Cass R. 1996. *Legal Reasoning and Political Conflict*. Oxford: Oxford University Press.

Sunstein, Cass R. 2001. *Designing Democracy: What Constitutions Do*. Oxford/New York: Oxford University Press.

Sunstein, Cass R. 2004. *The Second Bill of Rights: FDR's Unfinished Revolution and Why We Need It More Than Ever*. New York: Basic Books.

Symonides, Janusz (ed.). 1998. *Human Rights: New Dimensions and Challenges*. Paris: UNESCO.

Szucs, Jeno. 1981. "Three Historical Regions of Europe: An Outline." In Keane (ed., 1988): 291–332.

Tauli-Corpuz, Victoria. 2007. "How the UN Declaration on the Rights of Indigenous People Got Adopted." *Tebtebba Magazine*, vol. 10: 4–23.

Taylor, Charles. 1999. "Conditions of an Unforced Consensus on Human Rights." In Bauer and Bell (eds.): 124–144.

Tesón, Fernando R. 2001. "International Human Rights and Cultural Relativism." In Hayden: 379–96.

Tesón, Fernando R. 2003. "The Liberal Case for Humanitarian Intervention." In Holzgrafe and Keohane: 930–129.

Tesón, Fernando R. 2005. "Liberal Security." In Wilson (ed.): 57–77.

Thapa, Deepak (with Bandita Sijapati). 2003. *A Kingdom under Siege: Nepal's Maoist Insurgency, 1993 to 2003*. Katmandu: Printhouse and London: Zed Books.

Tharoor, Shashi. 1999/2000. "Are Human Rights Universal?" *World Policy Journal* XVI(4). Available at: http://www.mtholyoke.edu/acad/intrel/tharoor2.html.

Thinley, Jigmi Y. 2007. "What Is Gross National Happiness?" In Centre for Bhutan Studies: 3–11.

Tierney, Brian. 1989. "Origins of Natural Rights Language: Texts and Contexts, 1150–250." *History of Political Thought* X(4): 615–646.

Toffler, Alvin. 1980. *The Third Wave*. New York: Bantam Books.

Tucker, Robert C. 1978. *The Marx-Engels Reader*. New York & London: W.W. Norton & Company.

Van Dijk, P., and G. J. H. van Hoof. 1990. *Theory and Practice of the European Convention on Human Rights*. Deventer-Boston: Kluwer Law and Taxation.

Varady, Tibor. 1997. "Minorities, Majorities, Law, and Ethnicity: Reflections of the Yugoslav Case." *Human Rights Quarterly* 19: 9.

Vijapur, Abdulrahim P. 2006. "International Protection of Minority Rights." *International Studies* 43(4): 367–94.

Villey, Michel. 1969. *Seize Essais de Philosophie du Droit*. Paris: Daloz.

de Vos van Steenwijk, Alwine A. 1999. "The Poorest Teach Us the Indivisibility of Human Rights." In Danieli et al.: 411–19.

Waldron, Jeremy. 1988. "When Justice Replaces Affection: The Need for Rights." *Harvard Journal of Law and Public Policy* 11: 625–47.

Walicki, Andrzej. 1983. "Marx and Freedom." *The New York Review of Books* November 24: 50–55.

Waltz, Susan. 2004. "Universal Human Rights: The Contribution of Muslim States." *Human Rights Quarterly* 26: 799–844.

Walzer, Michael. 2002. "The Argument about Humanitarian Intervention." *Dissent* Winter 2002: 29–37.

Walzer, Michael. 2005. *Arguing about War*. New Haven/London: Yale University Press.

Waśkiewicz, Hanna. 1977. "Prawa człowieka, pojecie, historia." (Human Rights: The Idea and Its History). In *Chrześcijanin w świecie*, 6–7.

Weingast, Barry R. 1997. "The Political Foundations of Democracy and the Rule of Law." *American Political Science Review* 91(2): 245–63.

Wells, Herbert George. 1940. *The Rights of Man, or What Are We Fighting For?* Harmondsworth: Penguin Books.

Weschler, Joanna. 1998. "Non-Governmental Human Rights Organizations." *The Polish Quarterly of International Affairs* Summer: 137–154. (Also as "Pozazrzadowe organizacje praw czlowieka." *Sprawy Miedzynarodowe*. (Lipiec-Wrzesien: 143–60).

Weschler, Joanna. 2004. "The Security Council and Human Rights." In David P. Malone (ed.), *The UN Security Council: From the Cold War to the 21st Century*. Boulder, CO: Lynne Rienner: 55–68.

Wheeler, Joann S. 2005. "Rights without Citizenship? Participation, Family and Community in Rio de Janeiro." In Kabeer (ed.): 99–113.

Whelan, Daniel J., and Jack Donnelly. 2007. "The West, Economic and Social Rights, and the Global Human Rights Regime: Setting the Record Straight." *Human Rights Quarterly* 29: 908–49.

Wieruszewski, Roman. 1988. "The Evolution of the Socialist Concept of Human Rights." *SIM Newsletter* 1: 27–37.

Wilson, Richard Ashby (ed.). 2005. *Human Rights in the "War on Terror."* New York: Cambridge University Press.

Winston, Morton E. (ed). 1989. *The Philosophy of Human Rights*. Belmont, CA Wadsworth.

Wyrzykowski, Miroslaw (ed.). 2000. *Constitutional Cultures*. Warsaw: Institute for Public Affairs.

Yasuaki, Onuma. 1999. "Toward an Intercivilizational Approach to Human Rights." In Bauer and Bell (eds.): 103–23.

Zakaria, Fareed. 2003. *The Future of Freedom: Illiberal Democracy at Home and Abroad*. New York: Norton.

Index